CAPITALISM'S WORLD DISORDER

CAPITALISM'S WORLD DISORDER

WORKING-CLASS POLITICS AT THE MILLENNIUM

by Jack Barnes

PATHFINDER

NEW YORK LONDON MONTREAL SYDNEY

Edited by Steve Clark

ISBN 0-87348-818-0 paper; ISBN 0-87348-819-9 cloth
Library of Congress Catalog Card Number 97-065978
Manufactured in the United States of America

First edition, 1999

Cover painting: Detail from Hans Hofmann, *Fiat Lux*, 1963, oil on canvas,
182.9 x 152.4 cm. The Museum of Fine Arts, Houston. Gift of Mrs. William
Stamps Farish, by exchange. Courtesy of André Emmerich Gallery, New York.
Cover design: Toni Gorton
Photo pages: Sara Lobman and Toni Gorton

Pathfinder
410 West Street, New York, NY 10014, U.S.A.
Fax: (212) 727-0150 • CompuServe: 73321,414
Internet: pathfinder@igc.apc.org

PATHFINDER DISTRIBUTORS AROUND THE WORLD:
Australia (and Asia and the Pacific):
    Pathfinder, 1st floor, 176 Redfern St., Redfern, N.S.W. 2016
    Postal address: P.O. Box K879, Haymarket, N.S.W. 1240
Canada:
    Pathfinder, 851 Bloor St. West, Toronto, ON, M6G 1M3
Iceland:
    Pathfinder, Klapparstíg 26, 2nd floor, 101 Reykjavík
    Postal address: P. Box 0233, IS 121 Reykjavík
New Zealand:
    Pathfinder, La Gonda Arcade, 203 Karangahape Road, Auckland
    Postal address: P.O. Box 8730, Auckland
Sweden:
    Pathfinder, Vikingagatan 10, S-113 42, Stockholm
United Kingdom (and Europe, Africa except South Africa, and Middle East):
    Pathfinder, 47 The Cut, London, SE1 8LL
United States (and Caribbean, Latin America, and South Africa):
    Pathfinder, 410 West Street, New York, NY 10014

CONTENTS

ABOUT THE AUTHOR

JACK BARNES is national secretary of the Socialist Workers Party. Since the mid-1970s he has led the political campaign of the Socialist Workers Party and its sister organizations internationally to act on the renewed possibilities to build parties, the overwhelming majority of whose members and leaders are in industrial trade unions, actively engaged with fellow workers to support all efforts to transform the unions into revolutionary instruments of struggle defending the interests of the membership and of other workers and farmers. The 1978–1991 record of this turn in the building of proletarian parties in the United States and elsewhere is published in *The Changing Face of U.S. Politics: Working-Class Politics and the Trade Unions*.

An organizer of the Fair Play for Cuba Committee and actions in defense of Black rights, Barnes joined the Young Socialist Alliance in 1960 and Socialist Workers Party in 1961. In 1965 he was elected national chairperson of the Young Socialist Alliance and became the director of the SWP and YSA's work in the grow-

JACK BARNES TAKES PART IN FINAL DISCUSSION SESSION AT SOCIALIST EDUCATIONAL CONFERENCE, BIRMINGHAM, ALABAMA, DECEMBER 1997. (ERIC SIMPSON/MILITANT)

ing movement against the Vietnam War. He also served on the editorial board of the *Young Socialist* magazine throughout that period.

Barnes has been a member of the National Committee of the Socialist Workers Party since 1963, a national officer of the party since 1969, and its national secretary since 1972. From 1963 on he has carried major leadership responsibilities in the world communist movement.

In addition to his responsibilities as an organizer, Barnes is a contributing editor of the Marxist magazine *New International,* for which he has written many articles that record the collective political experiences and the continuity in working-class theory of the Socialist Workers Party. These include "The Fight for a Workers and Farmers Government in the United States," "Their Trotsky and Ours: Communist Continuity Today," "The Opening Guns of World War III: Washington's Assault on Iraq," "The Politics of Economics: Che Guevara and Marxist Continuity," and "Imperialism's March toward Fascism and War."

Articles, speeches, interviews, and introductions by Barnes appear in numerous books and pamphets, including *Malcolm X Talks to Young People, The Eastern Airlines Strike,* and *FBI on Trial: The Victory in the Socialist Workers Party Suit against Government Spying.*

Preface

We are at the beginning of struggles that will bring profound changes. And because this is only the beginning, we can make the mistake of not seeing it soon enough, of not responding by radically changing the understanding and — above all — the timeliness with which we act today from our starting point within, and as part of, a militant vanguard of working people.

A Sea Change in Working-Class Politics
Jack Barnes, December 1998

"A Sea Change in Working-Class Politics," the opening chapter of *Capitalism's World Disorder*, is the real introduction to the pages that follow.

In that talk, given to the closing session of the Young Socialists convention and conference in Los Angeles, California, in December 1998, Socialist Workers Party national secretary Jack Barnes emphasized a central feature of today's reality.

"A new pattern is being woven in struggle," he noted, "as working people emerge from a period of retreat, resisting the consequences of the rulers' final blow-off boom, of 'globalization' — their grandiloquent term that displays imperial arrogance while it masks brutal assaults on human dignity the world over. The emerging pattern is taking shape, defined by the actions of a vanguard resisting indignity and isolation, whose ranks increase with every single worker or farmer who reaches out to others with the hand of solidarity and offers to fight together."

There is a new mood and growing confidence among clusters of vanguard workers and farmers from one end of the country to the other. We are surprising ourselves and each other as we look around and discover we are not alone. Everywhere we begin to see others like ourselves, working people who are thinking and acting in a similar way, resisting, refusing to be beaten, using the political space that the rulers' instability has opened up, taking what the relationship of forces allows in any skirmish, strengthening ourselves for the next opportunity, broadening our field of vision as we fight, reading and studying and discussing with each other as we look for answers to explain how the wretched world in which we live came to be, how it was imposed on us, and how we can overturn it and build something new.

Capitalism's World Disorder is a handbook for workers and farmers everywhere who increasingly recognize themselves as part of this new vanguard of working people. It is a handbook for young people who are attracted to these proletarian struggles and find their lives transformed as they become part of them. The publication of this book now is more timely than at any moment since the talks included here were first given — precisely because there are increasing opportunities to apply in practice, to use as a guide to action, the facts and ideas encountered in these pages. There are increasing opportunities to measure these analyses against our own daily conditions of life and struggle, correcting and adjusting them as necessary.

The earliest presentation contained in this volume, "Youth and the Communist Movement," is a 1992 report adopted by a fusion convention of the Communist League in the United Kingdom and three groups of Young Socialists in London, Manchester, and Sheffield. The most recent, which brings the rest of the book into focus for vanguard forces at the millennium, is the summary talk at the Young Socialists Los Angeles conference in December 1998. Reading these two presentations side by side, one is struck by the clarity with which the central challenges and opportunities of working-class politics we face today were already addressed and prepared for by the communist vanguard more than six years earlier.

Comprising the bulk of *Capitalism's World Disorder* are four talks by Jack Barnes that were given between June 1992 and New Year's weekend 1995. Together they dissect the economic, social, and political underpinnings of the vast mold-shattering changes that swept world politics between the October 1987 near-meltdown of the world's stock markets, and the so-called Mexican peso crisis that hit in December 1994, coinciding with the first government default in the United States since the Great Depression, the Orange County, California, bankruptcy filing.

During those seven years from 1987 to 1995, the world the twenty-first century inherits was born. From the fall of the Berlin Wall to the disintegration of the Stalinist apparatuses in the Soviet Union; from the defeat of the white-minority apartheid regime in South Africa to the strengthening of socialist Cuba's world vanguard role; from the brutal and destabilizing imperialist assault on Iraq to the opening of the twenty-first century Balkan Wars; from the bursting of the Japanese economy's miracle "bubble," to the sharpening economic and social indigestion suffered by the German capitalist rulers as they tried to swallow whole the east German workers state — the post–World War II pattern of the twentieth century came to a convulsive end. The outlines of the major forces whose contradictory interrelation already marks the course of the world class struggle had emerged. A historical watershed is now behind us. Today what matters is our ability to use the space that has been opened, to apply what we have come to understand, and to respond with a working-class course of action. We and all others will be judged, daily and uncompromisingly, by the needs of the struggles of the workers and farmers vanguard forming itself across the United States.

If the new millennium was born prematurely, its first wail was heard as the New York stock exchange plunged 500 points on October 19, 1987, losing 23 percent of its value in one day. The tremors rocked financial markets and capitalist confidence around the world. But when all was said and done, the October 1987 crash remained a market event that most capitalists soon recovered from. It was not yet the opening of an accelerated worldwide economic and social crisis, devastating the lives of millions, with repercussions on every level of financial, banking, trade, and production relations, as well as on the unfolding of political and military conflicts.

The 1987 crash did announce the inevitable that was coming. The opening of the "Asian crisis" ten years later — from Jakarta to Moscow — confirmed that the future had arrived and was now irreversible.

Most importantly, along with that reality has come the growing resistance of the toilers worldwide, including in the imperialist centers. A shift in mass psychology has occurred. It marks every new struggle, every anticipation of the spread and polarizing results of rightist initiatives, every gesture of solidarity, every use of political space to advance discussion and unity among workers and farmers who have gone into action.

Among proletarian militants who are engaged in scattered actions *now* a communist party is being prepared. Currents and individuals, from different *pasts,* are finding out about each other and reaching in practice *today* toward a unified *future,* a political future. They are being led toward each other by the need for mutual solidarity and broader understanding of the forces behind a seemingly chaotic, conspiratorial world. Through broadening and accelerating this process, any current claiming to be communist must stand, act, fight, and be counted. Within this multifaceted effort, for a revolutionary-minded toiler nothing is impossible; outside of it, all one can do is hide for a while — more and more denying even the knowledge that such change is occurring. In one direction lies the line of march along which a communist party will be forged. In the other is the drift of the League of the Just into self-induced oblivion.

❖

Each of the presentations collected in this volume was discussed and adopted by conventions and other leadership bodies of the Socialist Workers Party, and its co-thinkers in communist leagues around the world. The usefulness of the talks, as well as their liveliness and interest, however, stems from the fact that these are not analytical essays composed in retrospect. Each chapter is based on a report given in the midst of fast-breaking events, to groups of thinking and acting vanguard workers and youth who came together, often from different parts of the globe, to discuss and deepen their understanding of the unfolding class struggle as they were in the very process of responding to its demands. In editing them for publication the sequence of points has sometimes been rearranged, and questions and discussion that took place during meetings on the same subject in different cities have been combined, but there is nothing in these pages that a reader who attended the events at which these talks and reports were given would not have heard and even joined the issue from the floor or raised their hand to vote on. As a result, this book in fact reflects the experiences of a party, not just the views of a speaker.

Capitalism's World Disorder should be read as a companion volume not only to the second expanded edition of *The Changing Face of U.S. Politics: Working-Class Politics and the Trade Unions* by Jack Barnes, published in 1994, but also together with issue no. 11 of *New International*. The centerpiece of that issue of the magazine of Marxist politics and theory is a resolution adopted by the Socialist Workers Party in August 1990. Entitled "U.S. Imperialism Has Lost the Cold War," it lays out in thesis form the main lines of change in world politics and the working-class response to them — the same themes developed throughout the talks in the present volume.

A great deal of discussion went into selecting the title for *Capital-*

ism's World Disorder: Working-Class Politics at the Millennium. At least one young worker who saw the proposed subtitle raised with the author that he thought it was a mistake for the communist vanguard to publish a book this year with the word *millennium* in its title. It would be taken on the street for one more crank, conspiracy theory volume, he pointed out, one more recipe for evasion of reality by the toilers. Young people especially are being pounded by reactionary hype poured out by the tons as the clock ticks toward a moment of no more significance than the turning of a calendar page. It is all designed to divert the oppressed and exploited from understanding, uniting, and — above all — doing something to confront the real world of social misery and economic devastation in which we live. After considering all the arguments, it seemed that far from being a drawback, however, these were good reasons to take the "millennium" diversion head on.

Yes, the working class does have an answer to the crisis felt by hundreds of millions at the millennium; it is a course of action that is based not on mysticism and superstition but science. A course that depends not on gurus but the unification of fighters.

Capitalism's World Disorder may be the only *millennium* title on bookstore shelves today whose purpose is not to obscure but to clarify. The social devastation, financial panics, political turmoil, police brutality, and military assaults accelerating all around us are not chaos. They are the inevitable products of lawful — and understandable — forces unleashed by capitalism.

But the arrival of the future capitalism has in store for us is not inevitable. It can be averted by the timely solidarity, courageous action, and united struggle of workers and farmers conscious of their power to transform the world. The urgency with which we act on this understanding today to guide the forging of a communist leadership will be decisive. This book has been written to help bring that future closer.

Mary-Alice Waters
February 1999

1

A SEA CHANGE
IN WORKING-CLASS POLITICS

The following talk by Jack Barnes, national secretary of the Socialist Workers Party, was given December 6, 1998, in Los Angeles, California, at the closing session of a conference jointly sponsored by the Young Socialists and the SWP. The conference of some 350 participants coincided with the Third National Convention of the Young Socialists in which nearly 100 people twenty-six years old and younger took part.

One of the highlights of the weekend activities, to which Barnes refers several times, was a Saturday evening panel and discussion called "Bringing Alive 'The Changing Face of U.S. Politics.'" The panel featured six Young Socialists leaders engaged in a wide range of revolutionary work from high schools and college campuses to factories, farms, and the printshop producing Pathfinder books and pamphlets, the *Militant* newspaper, and other revolutionary materials. They were joined on the panel and in the discussion by a number of leaders of strikes, lockout conflicts, and farm struggles around the country who talked about the stakes in the battles they were in the midst of and the importance of the Young Socialists gathering. These included Gary Grant and Eddie Slaughter, president and vice-president respectively of the Black Farmers and Agriculturalists Association; David Yard, a member of United

Mine Workers of America Local 1969, on strike at that time against Freeman United Coal in Illinois; and Dean Cook, a member of Oil, Chemical and Atomic Workers Local 4-227, in Pasadena, Texas, fighting a three-year lockout battle against Crown Central Petroleum.

A sea change in working-class politics

We have just heard the report by Samantha Kern on behalf of the newly elected National Committee of the Young Socialists, outlining the decisions of their convention that concluded less than an hour ago. Samantha introduced us to the members of the YS National Committee seated here on the platform.

The committee of the Socialist Workers Party that will work the most closely with this new National Committee of the Young Socialists in the coming months is the Trade Union Committee. This is a field-based leadership committee; its members work and live in cities across the United States. For the first time since the mid-1980s, moreover, the development of the trade union work of the party has reached the point where the composition of the Trade Union Committee has been able to coincide substantially with the election and reelection of the organizers of the steering committees of every one of our national industrial trade union fractions.

So, let me introduce to you the members of the Trade Union Committee who are also seated here on the platform, and tell you who they are, what they are doing, and where they are going.

First, is Tom Alter, from Des Moines, member of the United Food and Commercial Workers Union. Tom is on his way into the printshop. Nan Bailey, from Seattle, in the International Association of Machinists. Both Nan and Tom are organizers of the steering committees of their respective national fractions. Joel Britton, from Chicago, is the organizer of the Oil, Chemical and Atomic Workers union national fraction steering committee. Doug Jenness from the Twin Cities, who's a member of the United Steelworkers. Samantha Kern, from San Francisco, member of the UFCW and YS National Committee. Tom Leonard, a member of the Oil, Chemical and Atomic Workers fraction in Houston. Sam Manuel from Washington, D.C., organizer of the steering committee of the United Transportation Union fraction. Greg McCartan from Boston, organizer of the national fraction steering committee of the Union of Needletrades, Industrial and Textile Employees (UNITE). Cecelia Moriarity, the organizer of the Coal Committee of the party, had to leave an hour and half ago to get back to Pittsburgh for work. Norton Sandler, San Francisco, member of the International Association of Machinists. Amy Euston, from Des Moines, who is currently organizer of the United Auto Workers fraction steering committee but has a start date in a UFCW-organized plant. She is also a member of the Young Socialists. And Gregory Weston from the Twin Cities, organizer of the USWA national fraction steering committee.

Sam Manuel, Doug Jenness, and Tom Alter also compose the Farm Committee of the party, which has largely grown out of the work of the Trade Union Committee.

This trade union work leadership body, which includes the organizers of the steering committees of each of our national fractions, is starting to lead what we have called the third campaign for the turn.[1]

---

1. Following a July 1998 Active Workers Conference held in Pittsburgh, Pennsylvania, the National Committee of the Socialist Workers Party launched a campaign to increase the number of party members working in meatpacking jobs organized by the United Food and Commercial Workers Union (UFCW) and garment and textile jobs organized by the Union of Needletrades, Industrial and Textile Employees (UNITE), as well as to rebuild a national union fraction of coal miners organized in the United Mine Workers (UMWA). This is known in the SWP as the "third campaign for the turn" to the industrial unions. Altogether, the party has national fractions of

These are the comrades who will work most closely with the Young Socialists National Committee on the road to the April 1–4, 1999, convention of the Socialist Workers Party and conference of our broader movement, to be held in San Francisco. Above all, their job on the way to San Francisco will be to recruit to the party every member of the Young Socialists who is not in the SWP. Together they will organize their members to set the example on bringing fellow workers with them to the convention.

Many people in this room were in Pittsburgh for an Active Workers Conference hosted by the SWP and Young Socialists in July of this year. At that conference, we referred to a *sea change* in politics that was occurring. We said we would probably never use that term again, so it wouldn't become a special term of art employed by the party and no one else. But I've just used it again, because I've been seeking a word to capture what has been described here the last three days and have found nothing better. If we listen to ourselves, listen to each other, think about what has

---

its members in seven industrial unions today. Together with the two listed above, these are the International Association of Machinists (IAM); Paper, Allied-Industrial, Chemical and Energy union (PACE — formerly the Oil, Chemical and Atomic Workers, prior to a January 1999 merger with the paperworkers union); United Auto Workers (UAW); United Steelworkers (USWA); and the United Transportation Union (UTU).

The party's turn to industry, initiated in 1978, aimed at getting the overwhelming majority of the membership and leadership of the party into industry and the industrial unions to carry out political and trade union work. This is the norm for communist organizations. But the political retreat of the working class and labor movement in the United States during most of the 1950s and 1960s had made it impossible for the SWP to maintain the organized structure of industrial union fractions it had built since the 1930s.

The second campaign for the turn, begun in 1985, focused on expanding the number of union fractions in each party branch, and thereby extending the geographic spread of the party's national industrial union fractions. The first and second campaigns for the turn are documented in the book, *The Changing Face of U.S. Politics: Working-Class Politics and the Trade Unions* by Jack Barnes, as well as the booklet *Background to "The Changing Face of U.S. Politics."* Both are published and distributed by Pathfinder.

come together here at this conference and the obligations it imposes on us, we will recognize that sea change, or at least the most important aspect of it: that a shift in mass psychology is taking place in the working class in the United States of America.

The same is probably happening in other imperialist countries. I know comrades in our movement internationally think this is true. But in this summary I'll stick to our experience here.[2]

Earlier in the conference, we talked about many aspects of the working-class retreat that — to our surprise, at the time — we faced in the early years of this decade.[3] This was not what we had expected would happen, as the opening article in *New International* no. 11, "Ours is the Epoch of World Revolution," explains. We thought the union battles at Eastern Airlines and Pittston Coal in 1989–90 were more the coming pattern. But that is not the way it turned out. We faced a pause and then a renewed retreat. Battered by the way imperialism's brutal assault on Iraq ended, without a fight, and lulled by the extension of the Reagan-

2. Participating in the conference were members and leadership delegations from communist organizations in Australia, Canada, France, Iceland, New Zealand, Sweden, and the United Kingdom, including Young Socialists from these countries who were fraternal delegates at the YS convention. In addition, there were participants from several other countries.

3. On Saturday, December 5, Barnes had spoken to the party/youth conference on "Bonapartism and Polarization: Contradictions and Instability of the Leftward Shift in Bourgeois Politics." Earlier that same day, Mary-Alice Waters, editor of the Marxist magazine *New International*, had spoken on "Cuba as Part of the World: Confronting Global Capitalism's Assault on the Toilers and Winning a New Generation to Communism." Waters, who had recently returned from a reporting trip to Cuba for the *Militant* newspaper, brought greetings to the Young Socialists convention from the Association of Combatants of the Cuban Revolution, an organization founded in 1993 that brings together fighters from several generations who participated in the revolutionary war against the U.S.-backed Batista dictatorship, battles to defend the revolution from imperialist-organized aggression, and internationalist missions in Africa, Latin America, Vietnam, the Middle East, and elsewhere.

Bush economic expansion, our class went into retreat for more than half a decade.

In a period of retreat like that, defeats weigh more heavily. Most workers' minds adjust — if only slightly — toward the increased probability of defeat. Each positive development is read as incidental — important, but incidental, not symptomatic of something beginning to change. Each struggle is seen as an effort, sometimes even a glorious effort, but not necessarily a break from a pattern of retreat. Positive news for the enemy class is anticipated as the most likely outcome; negative news for our class is foreseen as the unfortunate but anticipated fact.

Struggles themselves are surrounded by a certain attitude — not an attitude of "can't win," but more a tendency to become somewhat isolated from each other, and to accept such isolation. You face the "fact" that after the struggle you are involved in winds down — and over that eight-year period, struggles did wind down — it may be a long time before you're involved in another one.

Organized communists don't see it quite the same way because of the breadth, scope, and variety of activity and practical work they're engaged in. But we, too, are affected by this. Above all, we're part of our class, of its fighting vanguard, and we share all these experiences and their effects.

Rise in resistance since early 1997

The sea change I've spoken of had begun by the opening of last year — early 1997, at the latest. That's when it became clear that no matter what the legacy — in an industry, in a union, in a region, among any segment of working people — no matter how limited the results of previous struggles, what happens now in any struggle has less and less connection to earlier defeats. Using your peripheral vision to find the fighters in the working class and among its allies becomes more and more valuable. They are often there. It's like becoming a good point guard. Develop your peripheral vision. Teammates are there!

Farmers involved in struggles an ocean apart will reach out to each other like brothers and sisters. Militant farmers who have been part of this conference will travel to England to meet farmers who will have never in their lives met anyone from North Carolina or Georgia. Farmers in England are now going into the worst agricultural crisis since the Great Depression of the 1930s. These vanguard fighters will have a new and unanticipated identification with each other.

I was grateful to David Yard for reminding us when he spoke on the panel last evening of Donnie Thornsbury and the three other UMWA brothers who were framed up in 1987 for their intransigent union-building activity in the strike against A.T. Massey Coal, and who are now sitting in the federal pen, serving long terms. Not only framed up by the government, but thrown to the dogs by the officialdom.[4] It made me think about the history of our party, of Kelly Postal, as well as the 1939 Sioux City frame-up of Teamster militants that Farrell Dobbs describes in *Teamster Politics* and *Teamster Bureaucracy.* Of the SWP Smith Act defendants who went to the federal pen in 1943 for their opposition to U.S. imperialism's war policies.[5] You didn't know

---

4. Donnie Thornsbury, president of United Mine Workers Local 2496 in Kentucky, and three other UMWA miners were convicted in December 1987 on frame-up charges of killing a scab coal hauler during the 1984–85 strike against the A.T. Massey Coal company. He and the other three miners — Arnold Heightland, James Darryl Smith, and David Thornsbury — are serving sentences ranging from thirty-five to forty-five years at the federal prison in Ashland, Kentucky.

5. From 1934 through the opening years of the 1940s, the class-struggle leadership of Teamsters Local 574 (later Local 544) in Minneapolis led the battles that built an industrial union movement in that city, organized over-the-road truck drivers throughout the Midwest, and transformed the Teamsters union in that area into a fighting social movement. In June 1941 a mass membership meeting of Local 544 voted to disaffiliate from the Teamsters and join the Congress of Industrial Organizations (CIO). In April 1942 Kelly Postal, secretary-treasurer of the local, was tried and convicted for "embezzlement" for carrying out the membership decision to transfer union

who was moving faster to get them there — the Teamsters offi-cialdom and their like-minded brethren, or the state.

David walked us through those not-so-long-ago battles by brothers and sisters in the mines who fought in a different period and couldn't find a way to win. He reminded us of what we owe to the blood that has been shed.

He talked about many other things as well, and after he sat down something interesting occurred. We began discussing how we were not going to allow a simple line of continuity to be drawn to that earlier defeat. The outcome of the Freeman strike — and the readiness of the active core of miners' leaders to move on to other battles — will be decided in struggle.[6] A boil-

---

funds to a new bank account for the CIO affiliate; he was sentenced to one to five years in prison and was paroled in May 1944 after serving eleven months.

In October 1939 seven leaders of Teamsters Local 383 in Sioux City, Iowa, Local 90 in Des Moines, Iowa, and Local 554 in Omaha, Nebraska, were con-victed and sentenced to two years in prison on frame-up charges of having burned a truck during a hard-fought and victorious bakery truck drivers strike in Sioux City earlier that year.

On December 8, 1941, eighteen leaders of Local 544-CIO and of the Socialist Workers Party, convicted in federal court of "conspiring to advocate the over-throw of the U.S. government," were given sentences ranging from twelve to eighteen months in prison. These were the first convictions under the Smith "Gag" Act, signed into law by Democratic Party president Franklin Roosevelt in June 1940. This reactionary legislation was aimed at breaking the class-struggle vanguard of the labor movement that was leading opposition to Washington's preparations to drag workers and farmers into the imperialist slaughter of World War II.

An account of the class-struggle leadership of the Teamsters, the labor bat-tles they led, and their fight against government frame-ups can be found in the four-volume series by Farrell Dobbs: *Teamster Rebellion*, *Teamster Power*, *Teamster Politics*, and *Teamster Bureaucracy*. Dobbs was a central leader of these labor battles, and subsequently national secretary of the Socialist Workers Party.

6. On December 17, 1998, members of the three striking UMWA locals ratified a contract with Freeman United Coal Company by a vote of 202 to 154. While the pact included union concessions on health benefits, seniority in

ermaker from Alabama took the floor and talked about his memories as a kid and what it had meant when striking miners marched through his hometown. He wants to see that again. Farmers fighting for their land in Georgia and North Carolina started talking about coming to Central Illinois to walk the picket lines together with the miners.

We were putting something together that reaches beyond what was there before. The lines of continuity of any given struggle do not lie primarily in the industry we work in, nor our union, nor the region we live in — although those are realities that shape our struggles. Our continuity is found along the lines of evolution of the working class as a whole, especially the section of it that wants to fight. And a change has begun. Its beginnings are well behind us.

From the origins of the modern communist workers movement 150 years ago, we have measured the success of any struggle by working people by whether or not we emerge more united, more confident of our collective strength, and more powerfully organized to advance the interests of our class and its toiling allies. "Now and then the workers are victorious, but only for a time," wrote Karl Marx and Frederick Engels in the Communist Manifesto, the founding program of our movement. "The real fruit of their battles lies, not in the immediate result, but in the ever-expanding union of the workers. This union is helped on by the improved means of communication that are created by modern industry and that place workers of different localities in contact with one another."7

There is a hunger among working people that is greater than

---

bidding on jobs, and other aspects of the prior contract with Freeman and the UMWA's 1998 agreement with the Bituminous Coal Operators Association, the central Illinois miners and their union emerged stronger from the 98-day strike. "The strike showed the strength we have," David Yard told the *Militant* newsweekly. "We are not the same people we were 98 days ago. Many guys have gained more confidence and understanding — there's a stronger bond among us."

7. See *The Communist Manifesto* (New York: Pathfinder, 1987), pp. 31–32.

in any other section of society, a political hunger among workers and farmers — the fighting coalition that will make up the government that will carry humanity into a new world. It's a hunger for solidarity, for struggle; it's a hunger to learn from each other. A refusal to accept that the pattern of struggles today is decided by past defeats. It's like watching someone weaving something. We can't yet tell what it's going to be. We don't know the details of the pattern; it's too early. We don't know what the ups and downs will be. We can't foresee the specific defeats and victories.

But we know a new pattern is being woven in struggle as working people emerge from a period of retreat, resisting the consequences of the rulers' final blow-off boom, of "globalization" — their grandiloquent term that displays imperial arrogance while it masks brutal assaults on human dignity the world over. The emerging pattern is taking shape, defined by the actions of a vanguard resisting indignity and isolation, whose ranks increase with every single worker or farmer who reaches out to others with the hand of solidarity and offers to fight together.

This is different from what we lived through for more than half a decade. The scope, the intensity, the stick-to-it-iveness, the reach — all this is different.

We've started seeing not only that there are clumps of workers and farmers who are resisting, who are saying "No!" to the demands for sacrifice by the employing class and its government. The beginning of wisdom for us is not just recognizing this, as we did at the 1997 party convention. The key was when we began recognizing that while we've gotten to know these groups of workers and farmers in the *present*, they would not have this kind of present if they didn't also have a political and collective *past*. It's embarrassing for Marxists to have to remind ourselves of that, isn't it?

And if they have this present, and they have a political and collective past, then they have also established political and leadership relations with others and have a political *future*. They have a present and a future based on relations among people who have stayed the course together. They've worked with other people, and they assume we've done the same. They respect that.

It takes some time to get to know each other, to learn to work together. You can take two very fine units of an army, bring them together, and they'll respond differently to a tactical field situation. They'll do things slightly differently, and one's not necessarily right and the other wrong. It can be two of the several tactics that can advance the fight.

This is true of many of the workers leading the fight against the Crown lockout.[8] It's true of many of the miners leading the strike against Freeman United in Central Illinois. It makes us think more deeply about the Blue Shirts at Caterpillar in Peoria, who've continued to meet and organize ongoing resistance in the wake of the 1992 and 1994–95 strikes.[9] It makes us think about

8. Since February 1996, some 250 members of Oil, Chemical and Atomic Workers Local 4-227 at the Crown Central Petroleum refinery in Pasadena, Texas, have been fighting an employer lockout. The OCAW members had refused to accept a proposed contract imposing layoffs with no regard to seniority, hiring of nonunion temporary workers, and other union-busting demands by management. They were locked out several days after the expiration of their prior contract. Crown rationalized the lockout on the slanderous grounds that the workers were engaged in sabotage. In January 1998 management filed a civil lawsuit charging fourteen workers with 400 acts of sabotage, as well as conspiracy to commit sabotage. The locked-out Crown workers have reached out for labor solidarity across North America and around the world.

9. Some 9,000 members of the United Auto Workers union at eight Caterpillar plants in Illinois, Pennsylvania, and Colorado waged a seventeen-month strike in 1994–95 against arbitrary firings and other unfair labor practices. While voting down a management contract offer by 81 percent, strikers began returning to work in December 1995 after top UAW officials called off the walkout. Continuing their fight from the shop floor over the next two years, Caterpillar workers ratified a six-year contract in March 1998 by a vote of 54 percent of the membership — but only after management agreed to rehire all 160 UAW members who had been fired during the 1994–95 strike and the earlier 163-day strike in 1992. The previous month 58 percent of the membership had rejected a contract proposal that did not include the rehiring of those workers. Organized efforts to resist the antilabor consequences of the two-tier wage setup and other concessions in the March 1998 contract,

other experiences we've had, and to realize that this is a phenomenon involving not just hundreds but thousands of workers and farmers in the United States today, and many more around the world.

These individuals and clumps of workers are the cells of a class-struggle cadre that will grow into the millions as battles accelerate.

Working class ahead of students

We have discussed the degree to which the working class today is more radical than the student population — more radical from a class standpoint. This may not be unusual in the broad sweep of modern history, but compared to the last several decades in the United States, this is different.

It's not a denigration of students. Changes are also taking place among them. We've had substantial discussion of this, and we are taking advantage of it. But the heart of those changes depends above all on the linkage to struggles of working people in this country. It is through that link that protest activities of youth cease being simply moral witness, whether individual or collective — cease being temporary acts of rebellion that will ultimately be absorbed, transformed, and perverted by the owners of capital and wielders of power.

For a number of years starting in the late 1950s, we lived through a period during which students moved out ahead of the working-class radicalization as a whole — although even this period is often presented inaccurately. Even then a vanguard section of the working population — a section predominantly Black — was ahead of the students, and that was decisive. Most histories of the Vietnam War period and the anti–Vietnam War movement are inaccurate about this. They just have a war going on. They don't include the uprising that gained momentum over

---

as well as to build solidarity with struggles by other workers, are still being waged by many union cadres and militant new hires at Caterpillar.

a period of years, the revolutionary movement being led by the political vanguard of the Black population of the United States. What happened in those years was more complex than is usually portrayed, and the interconnections deeper.

But what is happening today is new. That's a fact. The Socialist Workers Party right now is recruiting individual young workers who we meet accidentally, who we bump into in the course of struggles, as we sell papers in neighborhoods and at plant gates, someone's boyfriend or girlfriend, who knows, who cares? We bump into them and we recruit them to a workers party. And we could be recruiting more.

This is a change. I was reminded of how much a change by the remarks of Robin Maisel, the comrade in the wheelchair who spoke during the discussion on the second day of the conference. Robin was deeply involved in the opposition campaign in the United Steelworkers union in 1975–77 — the campaign for democracy, to elect Ed Sadlowski president of the USWA. I remember how powerful and attractive that campaign became, and what it did. I remember its connection with a layer of savvy union miners who had been through the struggles of the Black Lung Association in West Virginia and of the Miners for Democracy in the late 1960s and early 1970s. It sometimes seemed as if half the cadres of the Sadlowski campaign were miners on leave, especially throughout the South. But the Steelworkers Fight Back campaign was primarily linked to a long history of struggle in the Steelworkers union itself. That struggle rose, it reached out, it didn't find a large echo, and it fell. Many people in this room were part of that experience, were changed by it, changed for the better.[10]

10. Steelworkers Fight Back was launched in 1975 under the leadership of United Steelworkers District 31 director Ed Sadlowski to oust the entrenched regime of USWA president I.W. Abel. A central issue in the campaign was the fight to extend union democracy, including the right of the membership to vote on contracts. The election was held February 8, 1977. According to the official results, Sadlowski received 43 percent of the vote. He received a

What is different now is that while the outcome of no single battle is guaranteed, neither is any battle ordained to lose. This places great weight on being serious about politics, serious about tactics. It places great weight on competence. When the greatest working-class leaders I have known and worked with — Ray Dunne[11] and Farrell Dobbs — referred to a fellow worker as *competent,* that was the highest accolade they could give. It meant those workers didn't get fighters they were responsible for unnecessarily injured or killed. It meant they maximized the gains possible out of every situation, and did so in such a way that those with the greatest imagination accomplished a little bit of the impossible. It meant they were premature Cubans. Or perhaps, old Bolsheviks. The same thing.

This change is the most important thing for us to absorb. What we've seen come together at this conference is the only possible trajectory for the Socialist Workers Party. It is the road we will march along from here to the San Francisco convention, and on to an even larger Active Workers conference in Ohio late in the summer.

Is there anything in the working-class movement to reach for other than those layers — individuals, but also now *layers* — who want to fight? To those who, in the process of fighting, desire to meet each other, go through new experiences together and, as Malcolm X said, want to broaden their scope, to read, to think. They want to discuss with people who are straight with them, who they are fighting alongside, in order to figure out answers to the broader questions posed by a social system that on a world scale seems more

---

majority of votes of workers in large mills. See *The Fight for Union Democracy in Steel* by Andy Rose (New York: Pathfinder, 1976).

11. A founding member of the Communist Party in the United States in 1919, and later of the Socialist Workers Party, Vincent R. (Ray) Dunne was part of the Minneapolis-based class-struggle leadership of the Teamsters union in the 1930s. Along with Farrell Dobbs, Dunne was one of the eighteen Teamsters and Socialist Workers Party leaders convicted in the 1941 Smith Act trial.

and more out of control, in crisis, gruesome to behold.

There is nothing idiosyncratic about what came together here at this conference. The Socialist Workers Party is a small vanguard formation. The United States is nowhere close to being on the verge of a revolutionary upheaval. The acts of the Socialist Workers Party do not carry social weight in the normal sense of the word. We don't have to take back any of the cold, objective observations along these lines that we have made. They are correct, revolutionary, materialist statements. But being wrong on this score is not our greatest danger.

The greatest danger we've faced for a while now is not recognizing the degree to which every fighting worker and workers grouping that uses its strength, imagination, commitment, integrity, and capacity — that *acts* in a *timely* fashion, with all the weight it has — *can* work in a way that brings together on a national and international scale these experiences of working people. It can affect events. It can attract other sections of the population to the liberating spirit of these battles — beginning with the youth, beginning with those who don't have a million conservatizing worries and commitments draped on them from the past.

There are many things written about youth and their attitudes, their values, and some of them are true. What is forgotten by analysts who are outside the working-class movement, however, is the attraction of youth to the alternative offered by the working class, the kind of lifelong political trajectory that is open to each individual young person, regardless of class background. Lenin, who was no romantic on these questions, insisted that youth do not have a class character per se, that their class character is derived from their connections to the political formations in the country that reflect the interests of the basic social classes. He insisted that youth go through a period in their lives when they are in fact part of no class. They are in the process politically of becoming part of a class, in the midst of making that decision in thought and in action.[12]

---

12. See V.I. Lenin *On Youth* (Moscow: Progress Publishers, 1967).

In this world of accelerating capitalist disorder, where all of us gradually absorb into muscle and bone the meaning of class polarization, the propertied rulers will offer us more executions, more imperialist military assaults, more storm troopers (like private security gangs), more brutality, more social dislocation, more attempts to deny rights to working people who become determined to fight back. That's what they offer with all the degradations their system breeds. Those who are fighting against that reality offer an opposite road to young people, the possibility to join with others who have the social power to realize a different future.

Above all, the task of the Socialist Workers Party in collaborating with the Young Socialists is to organize to go with them to the working people of this country who are engaged in struggle, simultaneously reading and discussing the history and ideas that will help them understand the social realities they are repelled by and are determined to find a way to change.

I hope every Young Socialists chapter and individual YS member who reads and studies the 1990 Socialist Workers Party resolution "U.S. Imperialism Has Lost the Cold War" does it together with an SWP unit.[13] Likewise, every SWP branch should find Young Socialists, current and future, to collaborate with in organizing those classes. Above all, I urge both the party and the youth to discuss this resolution and other basic communist literature with workers and farmers involved in politics, trade union struggles, and other forms of organizing.

Workers who want to fight effectively know they'll never win if they have to reinvent the wheel every day. They resist giving up conquered ground. They want to learn from the lessons of past battles. They know previous sacrifices cannot be allowed to have been in vain. Given the changes in politics today, the concrete working-class traditions captured in the books and pamphlets

---

13. "U.S. Imperialism Has Lost the Cold War" is featured in issue no. 11 of the Marxist magazine *New International.*

produced and circulated by the communist movement become more and more important. These tools are literally irreplaceable; they are weapons of a fighting class, not just its leading party. Many before us bled — and, yes, died — in the fights out of which these lessons were learned. That's why the stakes are so high in keeping in print the entire arsenal of books and pamphlets published and distributed by Pathfinder — from works coming out of more contemporary experience, such as *The Changing Face of U.S. Politics*, the issues of *New International* magazine, and a broad range of pamphlets on current struggles and political topics; to classics of the communist movement by Karl Marx, Frederick Engels, V.I. Lenin, Leon Trotsky, Rosa Luxemburg, James P. Cannon, Farrell Dobbs, and others.[14]

Along this course, movements of social protest of which young people are a part will begin to be marked by a different character, because the activism of communist-minded youth brings a new element into them. Young Socialists are often the bearers of the linkage to the working-class movement within these protest movements. And they will be an obstacle to those who want to lead such movements on a different class trajectory.

We are not the only ones who think youth are important. Great energy — more bounce to the ounce — is attractive to all classes and all layers, to be used for their own purposes. We should never have the illusion others aren't after this energy too. Every intelligent employer is always looking for ways to absorb this energy. The trade union bureaucracy, the Democratic Party, every political current within the working-class movement, every

14. The thirst for knowledge of previous struggles among layers of vanguard fighters has spurred Pathfinder to put back in print a number of pamphlets on labor battles and political questions from the 1970s and 1980s that have not been available for a number of years. These include pamphlets on the 111-day 1977–78 UMWA coal miners strike; the 1975–77 campaign for union democracy in the United Steelworkers union waged by Steelworkers Fight Back; the fight for affirmative action in steel and other basic industries; and others.

rightist current outside the working-class movement — all are seeking young, live forces.

Trade unions and the state

One of the great truths of our epoch will now become increasingly evident. There will be more and more state interference in the trade unions, because the employers and bureaucracy alone can't always handle well-organized, intelligent militants. The same will be true for organizations of militant farmers, debt slaves.

The state — the government, cops, courts, National Guard, bourgeois parties, including, yes, the Democratic Party — all will come to be seen as the enemies they are, the bitter, brutal enemies of labor organizing to defend itself. Fighting along these lines leads vanguard layers of workers toward a program, a pattern of activity taking broader positions defending the interests of those who are fighting together with them. This leads them to further conflicts, and the necessity to fight to create democratic formations in the unions in order to expand solidarity. Political independence from the state and employers becomes a precondition to exercising simple solidarity.

We must keep our eyes on the ranks of labor while the institutions around us shatter. This is important. Under conditions of class polarization, Bonapartism, and economic catastrophe, the institutions within the working-class movement — like other popular institutions that have evolved in ways allowing them to function under "normal" conditions — will not be stable. They will tend to shatter.

As this happens the employers will be surprised. The labor bureaucracy will be surprised. But we must not be surprised. We must not depend on any of these institutions in their current form. These organizations as they exist today are *not* what they will inevitably become. Functioning as if this is not the class truth can only lead working people to unnecessary and sometimes devastating defeats.

We often say our goal is to transform the unions into revolutionary instruments of class struggle, and we excoriate anyone who would walk away from this effort within the unions as they currently exist, no matter how difficult the obstacles. I don't believe there's a single voice of dissent about that in this room. But we should understand. When we say existing union structures will shatter, this is not simply a prediction. It is more and more a statement of fact today, and it indicates a course of struggle, a course of action, a line of march. We don't start with the unions as they exist, but with those who are or should be the members of these unions. The ranks, that's who our eyes are on.

It's becoming less uncommon to have more than one union in places where previously this was not true. There will be more AMFAs.[15] At the same time, while the officialdom does nothing to organize the growing numbers of nonunion workers in industrial workplaces, they are carrying out mergers with unions in unrelated sectors of the workforce, thereby weakening the industrial character of the union movement. Such shifts will not be a true register of what is happening in the labor movement, however. The important register will be what is happening within the *ranks* of labor as currents organize and combat experience grows.

The pace of politics is increasing, and we can't make the mistake of thinking that all working people are waiting for some-

---

15. The company-minded officialdom of the Aircraft Mechanics Fraternal Association (AMFA) has organized raiding operations to break off mechanics employed by Northwest Airlines, Alaska Airlines, and elsewhere from the International Association of Machinists (IAM), which has traditionally organized mechanics in common locals with ramp workers and other more poorly paid airline workers. Some IAM members have voted for recertification out of a desire for a *change* from the officialdom's refusal to wage a fight to defend the interests of union members. The bureaucracy of the Machinists union has sought to parry AMFA's challenge by adapting to its reactionary orientation. In their unsuccessful effort in late 1998 to repel the AMFA challenge at Northwest, for example, the IAM bureaucracy aped AMFA's craft mentality by establishing a separate district for mechanics.

thing to happen to *them* before they react. As the economic crisis becomes devastating in Indonesia, in Korea; as it becomes devastating in Russia, and throughout Africa; as crisis begins to rear its head in Latin America once more, workers in this country read and think about it. They begin to see the future coming toward them. The former attitude was: "Devastation elsewhere is horrible, but it won't happen here." That is shifting. Now workers can imagine devastation striking home. Some of them anticipate it and act on that anticipation. And that is part of the sea change we are discussing.

Yesterday we discussed the surprise election of the Bonapartist candidate Jesse Ventura to the governor's mansion in Minnesota. I made the point that I don't have a scientific way of weighing all the variables that affected how people voted, electing Ventura and catching everyone off guard — including the SWP unit in that state. But I do know one thing. It was not economic and social conditions in Minnesota itself that were decisive in that election. Different classes and sections of classes there recognize the evolution of conditions around the world, and they *anticipate* what the future holds in store, including in Minnesota. That anticipation is what was decisive to the votes cast by a number of them.[16]

Bourgeois confidence begins to shatter

If we are right about all this, another shift is occurring. The confidence of the bourgeoisie is starting to get shakier. Belief in the eternity of ever-inflating paper assets, of the great stock and bond financial bubbles, is crumbling. I don't know how fast the changes will come. But I do know the key to the world capitalist economy is in this country right here. The United States of America, led by the most rapacious ruling class in history, was supposed to be able to

16. For further discussion of the emergence of Bonapartist figures in U.S. bourgeois politics, see the talk in chapter 4 of this book on, "The Vote for Ross Perot and Patrick Buchanan's 'Culture War': What the 1992 Elections Revealed."

police the world, to dominate the world, to be the only strategic pole in the world. It was supposed to purchase the goods of the world if necessary, to take over the banks and factories of the world when possible, to straighten out other countries, including other imperialist powers. You can say that no one ever really believed it was going to be like that, but I don't think that's decisive. The U.S. rulers *did* come to act as if they believed it.

When things happened that seemed to cut across their world dominance, the U.S. ruling class read them as contradictions that could be dealt with by changing presidents, or Congresses, or adjusting policies. This was their attitude, their tactical stance. It reflected their confidence. This flexibility gave solidity to their two-party system, to their social contract, to their more and more bipartisan domestic policy. That's changing. And as the confidence and homogeneity start to disintegrate, we will see the beginning of the breakup of the two-party system. That bipartisan setup is not the same thing as the domination by the Democrats and Republicans within bourgeois politics. But the *two-party system* as we have known it for decades is now showing signs of its future decomposition. That is one of the benchmarks that Ventura's victory registers.

A comrade in Minneapolis just E-mailed me an article about a meeting two days ago of the Minnesota state AFL-CIO Executive Council that governor-elect Ventura was asked to address. They had to invite him, of course. The reporter says Ventura "gave the state's top union officials a public tongue-lashing." He told them how during the campaign he had stood up to "union goons" who tried to stop him from crossing a picket line to enter a meeting. "I walked up to the biggest one. I looked him right in the eye, and I said very quietly, 'I strongly suggest you get out of the way.' He did."

Ventura spoke to these bureaucrats in a manner they are unaccustomed to hearing from a newly elected governor of any party. He addressed them with an in-your-face aggressiveness that they deferred to — and that, most importantly, posed a danger to the entire labor movement. He told the AFL-CIO officials he disagrees with a minimum wage, that government shouldn't set "the wage floor for private businesses." He told them he disagrees with the concept of a "living wage." You take what you can bargain for.

And Ventura excoriated them for not endorsing him, for not having a "bigger vision" extending beyond the Democratic Party. He reminded them how often they had begun backing "losers." They then gave him polite applause. "We applaud you for your candor and your straight-ahead style," one of the labor bureaucrats told him. Another called Ventura "a straight shooter," ta-da-ta-da-ta-da.

When a reporter present interviewed the heads of the Minnesota AFL-CIO after Ventura spoke, their main comment was that Ventura is right about one thing: they are on a losing electoral course. "It's evident that the way we're going we haven't been very successful." We keep endorsing candidates that don't win. We're discussing pursuing another course, they told the press.

This is typical. This is how the class-collaborationism of the labor officials and other misleaders of the mass movement — like the worst misleaders of the Black movement who Gary Grant spoke of at some length during his presentation — pave the way for Bonapartism, which in turn greases the skids for fascism. It's a process that takes time. It doesn't happen without struggle and differentiation. But that is the process that occurs as a long wave of world capitalist expansion comes to an end, stability erodes, and the institutions of class rule begin to shatter.

In the years that led up to World War II, throughout Europe, we saw this same process in country after country. Disappointment and frustration with the policies of class-collaborationist misleaders opened the door to support among broad sections of the middle class and even some layers of workers for demagogic Bonapartist figures. Bonapartism then prepared the way for rising fascist movements to triumph without any serious struggle from a working class that had been demoralized and disoriented by its class-collaborationist and violently factional misleaders. We're starting to see similar things again. But they don't have to reach the same outcome.

Underestimating ourselves

When struggles break out today, we don't have any idea what is possible until we've exhausted the expansion of solidarity, exhausted the outreach, including the international character of it. There are no limits to what can be accomplished until the dialectic, the give-and-take, between the struggle and its supporters worldwide has been played out to the end.

The greatest problem we face is that working people who are fighting underestimate what we are capable of, what we are actually accomplishing. We don't recognize ourselves as the true bearers of culture and decency into the new millennium. This we will learn in struggle together.

One of the goals for the April 1999 San Francisco convention of the Socialist Workers Party and the conference that will surround it — a conference that will be the common work of the SWP and Young Socialists — must be to take the comrades who are here, our comrades-in-arms in sections of the mass movement who are not yet members of our party, and increase the number of them in attendance by five- or ten-fold. We hope more of the militants with whom they are standing shoulder to shoulder will attend, and we want to work with them to make that possible. We must bring fighters from other struggles we are involved in — Ireland, Puerto Rico, Cuba, police brutality, women's rights, immigrant battles, farmers' protests, other strikes.

That gathering must be a get-together, a regroupment of forces, an introduction of all these fighters to each other, so they can see that in combination their forces are much larger than they themselves know. We must unlock every struggle from any narrow picture of its own history — and by narrow, I mean any single chain of cause and effect — and put it in this world as it's becoming. That's the road to a whole that is truly more powerful than the sum of its parts. But that takes mutual confidence gained through common combat experience, political clarity, and organization.

Obstacles falling

Recently a unionist from Norway visited the locked-out Crown workers in Houston. He came to offer the support of his union, and I was struck by the weight, the importance that a layer of the most conscious workers resisting the lockout correctly gave to that act of solidarity.

We said almost a decade ago that the world in becoming would be marked at the new millennium by the absence of the major obstacles of the previous century, by the absence of obstacles to working people worldwide seeking to exchange their experiences in struggle. We said it would be impossible for state powers to clamp down on this, and it would be impossible for any political current to dictate who you could or who you could not work with.

That's what ended with the fall of the Stalinist monolith. It ended for all time, as we explain in detail in our 1990 resolution, "U.S. Imperialism Has Lost the Cold War." We're now seeing the first baby steps of what that means in practice. We start with the Socialist Workers Party, with the Young Socialists, with our co-thinkers around the world, and with comrades-in-arms in any just fight that's going on. We start together. There is no limit to the speed and character of how this solidarity can be organized, this convergence, this fusion of the efforts of vanguard layers who are fighting. And nothing could possibly be more important in the transformation of the Socialist Workers Party, its activity and proletarian character, and the meaning of the third campaign for the turn.

The interaction of these forces is truly what will "bring to life *The Changing Face of U.S. Politics,*" as the Young Socialists comrades so aptly named the panel they organized on the second night of this conference. This is what people in this room have worked so hard for. And now it is we who must move toward this combination of effort, of solidarity, opening ourselves up to those engaged in struggle right now.

I truly meant it when I said in my talk yesterday that we must have a perspective, over time, wherever possible of fusing our party with the small parties-in-formation that are coming out of struggles today. These small groups of vanguard fighters have a history together. They have tested themselves in combat, learned to know and trust each other, and have a great time working and fighting together. They anticipate future battles that incorporate the lessons of today, and their struggles are leading them to start talking about broader questions and to the conclusion that there's something rotten about capitalism. These are men and women who literally have already donned their shrouds and are going to continue fighting, regardless of the consequences. They're the new Cubans in this country. They are us. That's who we are, too. And we want to work together, to converge. We want to be in the same party.

We will transform our movement together. We will find ourselves in small towns as well as large cities. I was reminded by one of the veterans of the Steelworkers Local 8888 battles in Newport News present here this weekend that this is the twentieth anniversary of our movement establishing a branch in Newport News, Virginia, so we could more effectively fight shoulder to shoulder with others to advance that struggle.[17] I don't remember for sure if we still had the Richmond, Virginia, branch when we moved into Newport News and into the struggle of 8888. A number of heads are nodding yes, so I guess we did. That was fun, right? Having a branch of the Socialist Workers Party in Bobby Lee's Confederate capital, at the same time we were on our way to Newport News.

---

17. Workers at the giant Tenneco shipyard in Newport News, Virginia, struck for eighteen weeks in early 1979 to win recognition for their union, United Steelworkers Local 8888. They won recognition later that year.

There are people here who built an SWP branch in Price, Utah. In Peoria, Illinois. In Charleston and Morgantown, West Virginia. In Louisville, Kentucky, and Cincinnati, Ohio. In Seaside, California. In Austin, Minnesota. In Dallas, Austin, and San Antonio, Texas. In Omaha, Nebraska, and Albany, New York. And in other cities, small and large, too numerous to list. I'm not making a prediction. I'm not saying we should go someplace in particular. I'm saying we are open to that course, and we will follow it. We will have the courage of our convictions, and our movement's leadership will be defined by a sensitivity, a responsiveness, and a competence in moving in this direction. Political openings and responsibilities will determine organizational forms.

When we published the SWP resolution "U.S. Imperialism Has Lost the Cold War" in *New International* no. 11 a few months ago, we put it side by side with, we yoked it together with, the "Young Socialists Manifesto," a kindred proclamation issued this year by the other communist organization in this country that the Socialist Workers Party has a special relationship with. We noted that the "Young Socialists Manifesto" was the piece that brought the entire contents of the magazine into focus as a guide to revolutionary practice.

In the introductory article to that issue of *New International,* we also insisted on some other facts.[18] We began with the statement that "the opportunities for organizations of communist workers and of youth to act together along the lines presented in the pages that follow have been expanding at least since early 1997."

"Signs of renewed defensive action are all around us," we noted. "More numerous strike actions reflecting the tenacity and resistance of the embattled ranks; a noticeable growth in the confidence and determination of women in industry — " (At least in our discussions since then, we have gotten out numerous examples confirming the accuracy of this judgment about women in industry. I don't know

---

18. See "Ours Is the Epoch of World Revolution" by Jack Barnes and Mary-Alice Waters, in *New International* no. 11.

why it is so difficult, but it has been like pulling teeth to get comrades to talk about what is happening and what they are doing. Then, once we start, all the experiences we're living through, the women's committees and other experiences, begin pouring out.) " — the increased weight of Black leadership in labor battles and struggles of working farmers; an upswing in the Puerto Rican independence movement; more actions in defense of immigrants' rights." And if the reports we've heard here are correct, we should add that we are seeing a revival of some aspects of the Chicano movement as well.

If these things are true, however, if this new resistance among toilers in this country is a fact, then something else is happening as well. The relationship between the ranks and the officialdom is being altered — potentially, and in reality.

This shift means that political work among women, for example, and talk about the place of the fight for women's rights should start getting a different kind of hearing than it did four, five, six years ago. Such work takes on greater weight.

Is it true that "the weight of Black leadership in labor battles and struggles of working farmers" has increased? We wrote that phrase several months ago. Is it true, or not? It's a factual question. We must make a judgment. Don't we see it, don't we hear it? Didn't we see a manifestation of it here? If the statement is true, it means new possibilities of changing leadership in the Black community itself — a bridge from fighters with a lifetime of struggle experience (not those who at one time fought and later lost their way) to a new generation of younger fighters emerging today. And it also means a new impetus to the struggle of working farmers throughout this country against land loss and debt slavery.

Don't these things mean we should be getting a slightly different response to a revolutionary newspaper when we sell the *Militant* in the Black community? To thinking farmers? Among the ranks of workers, both men and women?

Isn't the same thing true about the Puerto Rican independence struggle? Is that not our experience?

The shift in the working class, in the mass psychology of the toilers, in the emergence of vanguard layers within the class, means the beginning of a process, the opening of a fight for leadership in the labor movement itself.

This is the question of questions. This is what the San Francisco convention of the Socialist Workers Party should be about. This is why no matter what else, we will not postpone that convention.

Yesterday I said all you had to do was drive up Highway 1 from here in Los Angeles to get to the San Francisco convention. An old California hand told me I was wrong: you can't just drive up Highway 1 this time of the year; it's washed out. I say that's not talking like a Cuban. So Highway 1 is washed out? So what? You can still get to San Francisco that way.

We must study "U.S. Imperialism Has Lost the Cold War" and retake it ourselves. We must do the same with the companion book of resolutions and reports adopted in the early 1990s by the Socialist Workers Party that Pathfinder will be publishing under the title *Capitalism's World Disorder: Working-Class Politics at the Millennium*. These are tools, instruments to guide revolutionary practice, for *every* serious militant among working people.

As this process deepens, politics will not get simpler. Political work will get more complex, because bourgeois politics is marked by fewer and fewer long-run trends. Can you name any long-term trends in bourgeois politics today that are not more quickly short-circuited, that are not contradicted by counterprocesses?

We've talked about the shift to the left in bourgeois politics, for example. There's no question that's true. It is a preemptive shift out of weakness, in anticipation of the crisis that is deepening and the resistance that is accelerating. But we're talking about left and right *within* bourgeois politics. We should remember that every major war of the twentieth century has been brought to us by those riding under the banner of bourgeois liberalism. At the same time that the percentage of Democrats in Congress grows, the bipartisan policies they carry out, such as the assault on the social wage, increase. The shift to the left in bourgeois politics is not some long-term process. And it is yoked to growing class polarization, rising Bonapartism and increased adaptation to it, and increased dangers of war.

The conflicts and instability among European powers, as well as the conflicts between Washington and shifting alliances among the European powers, all will increase. Common commitment to the euro will not always be a stabilizing factor.

Political demagogy in the leadership of the union movement, in the leadership of mass movements, will grow. We're just beginning to see this process. It puts a premium on competent tactics, on vanguard fighters learning to prevent foolish, impatient things from occurring; to avoid letting anger and not strategy be our guide; to avoid unnecessary victimization; to develop habits of discipline; to hold yourself accountable for the consequences to others of every action.

When leaders of the Socialist Workers Party went to prison at the beginning of the Second World War, they were sent up because they wouldn't subordinate the unions to the war. They wouldn't subordinate the battle for colonial freedom to the war. They wouldn't subordinate the struggle for Black rights to the war. They wouldn't support the imperialist aims of the war.

At Sandstone Federal Penitentiary in Minnesota, other inmates were trying to figure out why we were there, how we fit into the social hierarchy of the cons. A couple of fellow prisoners who were doing time for bank robbery (which was relatively high on the social scale at Sandstone) asked them, What are you in for? The SWP leaders explained by saying, Well, you see, they nabbed you for trying to take a bank at a time. Sometimes you can do that quickly, with a small group, and get away with it. But sooner or later you always end up in here, or dead. Our goal is not one bank at a time; our goal is to take the whole damn thing. And that can only be done by putting together a large group — disciplined, fighting working people who have learned patience, determination, strategy; who have worked together and had to figure out how to get there.

That's what we have to offer. We're organizing to take the

whole damn thing. Working people can do this.

The capitalist rulers offer us social disaster. They offer us depression. They offer us death from curable disease. They offer us war. They offer us fascism. They offer us an unending list of horrors. But we offer ourselves the ability to prevent those horrors from becoming the final reality, the confidence that we can transform that future.

We are at the beginning of struggles that will bring profound changes. And because this is only the beginning, we can make the mistake of not seeing it soon enough, of not responding by radically changing the understanding, and — above all — the timeliness with which we act today from our starting point within, and as part of, a militant vanguard of working people.

That, more than anything else, is what I want to put before you. That's what we have to fight for all the way to the SWP convention and beyond: to recognize that the changes that have already occurred require us to organize ourselves as the turn party we are, require us to bring the Young Socialists toward working-class struggles. Require us to recognize, as the resolution in issue no. 11 of *New International* says, that communist workers are above all a fraction of the working class — a simple mathematical fraction — and a fraction of the fighting vanguard of that class. Require us to see the communist party as the leading organized fighters of the class, that generalizes the experiences of past struggles that can lead to victory — that "point[s] out and bring[s] to the front the common interests of the entire proletariat, independently of all nationality," as the Communist Manifesto explains, and that in comparison to the majority of the working class has "the advantage of clearly understanding the line of march, the conditions, and the ultimate general results of the proletarian movement."[19]

This is possible. This is what we concentrate all our energies on. This is what the third campaign for the turn aims to accom-

19. *The Communist Manifesto*, pp. 35–36.

plish. This is why we say to groups of fighting workers who have reached a certain stage of discussion, confidence, and generalization of their experiences — Join the Socialist Workers Party. We want to work with you, with an eye to fusing with your forces so we all have a stronger organization.

Along this course we offer every Young Socialist a chance to be an absolutely unique and irreplaceable part of proletarian action. And we will attempt to recruit every one of you who is not in the Socialist Workers Party to the party, as we work to recruit every worker who is fighting to our party as well.

That is the road to San Francisco. It is up to you to decide whether the course is justified, the goal worthy of the effort. If so, we ask you to join us in making it happen.

2

SO FAR FROM GOD, SO CLOSE TO ORANGE COUNTY

THE DEFLATIONARY DRAG OF FINANCE CAPITAL

The following report is based on a talk and closing presentation to a regional socialist educational conference held in Los Angeles, California, over the 1994–95 New Year's weekend. The gathering was one of three held in U.S. cities that weekend cosponsored by the Socialist Workers Party and Young Socialists. Participants in the Los Angeles, Philadelphia, and Minneapolis-St. Paul conferences included members of Socialist Workers Party branches and industrial union fractions, supporters of the communist movement, revolutionists from Canada and several other countries, and workers, young people, and others who had learned about the events from co-workers on the job or in the course of other struggles.

The report was discussed and adopted by delegates to the SWP's 38th National Convention, held July 8–12, 1995, in Oberlin, Ohio, and by delegates from eight countries to a July 13–14 international leadership conference.

Capitalist deflation and debt crisis

On the first day of December 1994, at a solemn ceremony held in the San Lázaro Legislative Palace, seat of the Congress of the United Mexican States, outgoing president Carlos Salinas de Gortari — dreaming of an imminent appointment to head the World Trade Organization safely ensconced in Geneva, Switzerland — passed the sash of presidential authority to his successor, Ernesto Zedillo Ponce de León.

As I watched the late-night CNN rerun of the swearing-in ceremony on television, I could not help wondering what else must have been going through Salinas's head at his moment of great triumph — a moment for which his exclusive university education in the United States and years of apprenticeship in Mexican bourgeois politics had prepared him. I wrote down a list.

Perhaps Salinas was dreaming that Mexican stocks would close out the year among the best-performing shares on Wall Street itself. After all, there had been a massive influx of short-term portfolio capital during his presidency, pushing Mexican stock prices to their highest levels ever and putting the country toward the top of the list of world capitalism's "emerging markets." Telmex, the state telephone company, was Salinas's special darling. Although Telmex still provides only nine phone lines for every one hundred people, it had done much better where it counts, for the owners of capital. It had attracted hundreds of millions of dollars from investors in the United States and elsewhere, making it the favorite "foreign" stock on the U.S. market.

Or maybe Salinas was thinking about the $26 billion in foreign currency reserves the Mexican government treasury built up during his presidency. That is the largest amount of dollar reserves ever held by Mexico's rulers. It is very big for a semicolonial country, and greater than the dollar reserves held by the ruling classes in Canada and some other imperialist countries.

Or Salinas may have been thinking back on his years at Harvard. The cost of his patrician education was alone much more than the lifetime income of most peasant and many workingclass families in Mexico.

What happened to the dreams? We have all been following the news over the past several days.

The dream about Telmex came true. Just a few days ago it became the first stock in the history of North America to sell more than a billion shares on the New York Stock Exchange in a single year — something IBM, General Electric, General Motors, Lockheed, British Petroleum, or other imperialist monopolies had never done. But Telmex accomplished this feat by a massive sell-off in which its stocks lost 20 percent of their value in just a few days.

As Wall Street closed out its final transactions of 1994 yesterday, more than half of the twenty-five biggest losers for the year among all foreign stocks were issued by companies headquartered in Mexico. More than half! Mexican stocks held by U.S. owners had dropped by nearly $7 billion by the end of last week, losing one-third of their value. U.S. capitalists' holdings in pesos and Mexican bonds lost some 20 percent of their value over the same period.

All this following Zedillo's announcement December 20 of a devaluation of the Mexican peso, in response to which international currency traders unloaded the peso hand over fist, driving it down 40 percent against the dollar by the middle of last week.

What of Salinas's treasured $26 billion in dollar reserves? The government spent all but $6 billion in this single month alone buying up pesos in hopes of stemming the currency's plunge.

They will soon borrow much more than that, and at usurious interest rates, from their close friends up north.

That is the situation as Salinas, with his Ph.D. in economics from Harvard, and Zedillo, with his Ph.D. in economics from Yale, prepare to celebrate New Year's Day tomorrow. As an act of contrition to world finance capital, Zedillo has just replaced his appointee as finance minister — a brother Yalie also with a Ph.D. in economics — with another technocrat with a Ph.D. in economics from Stanford. Stanford is a bit closer to Mexico than Yale, but it is also closer to Orange County.[1]

We should remember the speech Zedillo gave as he was inaugurated a few weeks ago, freshly adorned by the coveted presidential sash. First and foremost, the new president pledged to protect Mexico's sovereignty, saying he would serve "with dedication . . . with pride . . . with an unbreakable spirit and nationalist conviction."

Second, Zedillo said he would "defend lawfully and decisively the dignity and human rights of those Mexicans living beyond our borders" — a clear reference to the immigrant-bashing Proposition 187 that had been adopted in California the previous month, and its clones being prepared elsewhere.[2] He said his "strongest commitment is to the fight against the poverty in which millions

1. Orange County, part of the Greater Los Angeles metropolitan area, filed for bankruptcy on December 6, 1994. The managers of the county's investment fund had borrowed heavily and purchased highly leveraged securities called derivatives that simply bet on a continuing drop in interest rates. The county lost almost $2 billion when the gamble failed, as short-term interest rates began rising in early 1994.

2. The anti-immigrant Proposition 187 passed with a 59 percent majority in the November 1994 elections in California. The proposition aims to deny public education, health care, and social services to immigrants without documents. It requires school, health, and welfare officials to report suspected "illegal immigrants" to state authorities. In November 1995 a federal court struck down portions of the law as unconstitutional, on grounds that only the federal government can regulate immigration.

of Mexicans live." He pledged to spur economic growth, generate new jobs, and guarantee education for all through high school. Better living conditions for every Mexican family, he said, would be achieved through the "free market."

Zedillo committed his administration to the search for "a just, honorable, and definitive peace" in Chiapas, the region in southern Mexico where the regime has used brutal military force against superexploited peasants over the past year on the pretext of combating armed guerrillas. He said he would crack down on drug trafficking and other crimes at the highest levels, and he indirectly acknowledged that many Mexicans believe the ruling Institutional Revolutionary Party (PRI) protects the interests of moneyed layers. "Fair treatment means fighting monopolistic practices, abuses, and privileges," Zedillo said. This includes the ability "to defend oneself against possible abuses on the part of authorities."

But in a matter of weeks, literally, every single one of those promises had been exposed as fantasies or lies or both. The illusion of economic progress suddenly exploded, like the ashes that began spewing from the long-dormant Popocatépetl volcano near Mexico City at about the same time. For the first time in his life, Zedillo may even have thought some working people might be better off than he was — at least those living in "Popo's" shadow could move until the volcano settled down.

Whatever Salinas and his successor Zedillo may have been dreaming of on December 1, by the end of the month the new president must have been bitterly reminded of the note he received from a rebel leader in Chiapas just a few days after the swearing-in ceremony. "Welcome to the nightmare," wrote Subcomandante Marcos.

The newspapers are now saying that Zedillo will soon announce his "plan" to deal with the crisis. But the terms of a deal have already been worked out and dictated by Wall Street and Washington, with the craven concurrence of the most powerful capitalist families in Mexico.

More of the national patrimony will be put on the auction block.

This includes many assets considered off limits to Yankee and other foreign capital since the high point of the Mexican revolution in the second decade of this century and the resurgence of anti-imperialist mobilizations in the late 1930s. The latest plans are already being floated in the press. Finance capital is pressing for bigger openings for U.S., Canadian, German, British, Spanish, and Japanese banks to operate in Mexico, including for the first time to establish outright ownership of Mexican banks. The government had nationalized all banks in 1982 at the height of Wall Street's debt squeeze on Mexico, but had begun reprivatizing them in 1991. And earlier this year Salinas permitted imperialist banks to set up shop in the country for the first time in decades.[3]

Wall Street and Washington are demanding that the Mexican government accelerate the privatization and sale of other previous "untouchables," such as the ports, public utilities, and the railroads and other transportation. Above all, the imperialists want to make inroads against Pemex, the state oil enterprise. Pemex has been regarded by Mexican working people as a symbol of national sovereignty and dignity since the country's petroleum resources were taken back from pillage by British and U.S. monopolies in 1938. Just a few years ago, Salinas had to back off

---

3. Of the eighteen banks that were privatized, one-half collapsed and were placed under government control following the peso crisis. Under new legislation, several Mexican banks were for the first time taken over by imperialist banks, including Wall Street's Citibank. An extension of that legislation in December 1998 authorized 100 percent foreign takeover even of Mexico's three largest banks, which had previously been exempted; that same new law ratified a government "bailout" of the Mexican banking system of some $60 billion — 16 percent of the country's gross domestic product.

Bourgeois propaganda to the contrary, Mexico's banks never "recovered" from the 1994–95 crisis. Their Wall Street bank ratings remain among the world's lowest (an "E" in August 1998, defined as "very weak intrinsic financial strength"). Loans granted by Mexican banks in 1997 remained at about one-tenth the level of several years earlier. And the peso itself has continued to slide, from about 3.5 pesos to the dollar prior to the December 1994 devaluation to roughly 10 pesos to the dollar in late 1998.

from an initial probe to begin privatizing petrochemical operations. But government and Pemex officials are now using the peso crisis to float a variant of the idea as a trial balloon.[4]

Far from defending the economic and human rights of Mexican working people — on either side of the border — Zedillo and his new finance minister are readying their "anti-inflation" program. Interest rates are being driven up, prices are soaring, and government officials are already predicting that inflation — which had been hovering around 7 percent this year — will reach 15 to 20 percent in 1995; it will actually be a miracle if it is held to that. So the Mexican president is now gravely reminding us that wage hikes are responsible for inflation — a reactionary falsehood — and trying to convince workers that "all of us" must sacrifice for the good of the nation.

The employing class and their government in Mexico are now demanding that the three-way pact, the "Pacto," with the trade unions be renegotiated to guarantee that wage hikes are capped at 7 percent and no more. It does not take a Yale Ph.D. to figure out what is bound to happen to real wages and take-home pay of those who work for a living. Or to know that many more of Mexico's 25 million peasants are going to be driven off the land by rising costs and interest rates.[5] Nor will there be the promised

4. In mid-1995 the Mexican government announced plans to sell off sixty-one secondary petrochemical plants, at an estimated price of $1.5 billion. In face of mounting nationalist opposition to the planned privatization, the Zedillo regime in October 1996 revised these plans, saying that only a minority stake in these operations would be put up for sale. Only in late 1998 did Mexico's Energy Ministry begin the selloff of the first of these plants.

5. In fact, the official inflation in 1995 peaked at almost 50 percent in Mexico, and still stood at nearly 19 percent at the close of 1998. Rates on mortgages, car loans, and credit cards ranged as high as 180 percent in the wake of the crisis, and short-term rates remained at nearly 35 percent in November 1998. Class polarization has deepened, as real wages have dropped each year since the 1994–95 crisis. The government-set minimum wage, in real terms, fell by a third between 1990 and the end of 1998.

While inflation soared during 1995 and the first half of 1996, Mexico sank into its worst recession since the 1930s. According to official figures, the

national crusade for universal secondary education. To the contrary, the government will try to slash budget expenditures for schools, hospitals, housing, food subsidies, pensions, and other programs that have been won by workers and peasants, and through which a tiny portion of the wealth they, and they alone, produce is restored to them. In fact, Zedillo and his advisers north and south of the Rio Bravo will undoubtedly soon announce their "discovery" that a too rapid increase in social spending was among the causes of the peso's collapse.

Those in Mexico's relatively sizable new urban middle class and professional layers are being hit hard too. The Mexican bourgeoisie has fostered enlargement of the middle class as a buffer between themselves and the much more rapidly expanding urban proletariat. But Mexico is still far from having the modern class structure that has helped maintain substantial social and political stability in most imperialist countries since the wave of capitalist expansion that began soon after World War II. Salinas's class, nonetheless, stakes a great deal on the solidity and political support of the middle class.

These petty-bourgeois layers have seen their incomes rise over the past decade. They have become used to purchasing increasing amounts of imported goods from the United States, Japan, and Europe. They have gone into debt to buy houses and cars, and they have racked up credit card bills for washing machines, CD players, computers, and other consumer appliances. But now every borrower is feeling the squeeze that comes when interest rates start soaring.

If we tighten our belts, Zedillo and Co. are preparing to announce, then our friends in Washington and Ottawa and the International Monetary Fund have pledged to stand behind us 100 percent. Of course, these "friends" in Washington have no direct interest in "rescuing the peso." They intend to do what is necessary to defend the dollar and make sure that U.S. holders of Mexican bonds — the Yan-

---

gross domestic product fell by 7 percent in 1995. Some two million workers were laid off during the year.

kee ruling families — get paid. And that will undoubtedly bring Mexico's "friends" in Washington into conflict with Mexico's "friends" in Ottawa, London, and elsewhere, who have no interest in "rescuing" either the peso or the dollar.[6]

From Orange County to Mexico

When I began preparing for this meeting, I assumed I would probably open by saying a few things about an event closer even than Mexico — the bankruptcy of the Orange County government here in California earlier this month. It never occurred to me that we would have to start with Mexico instead. That shift is itself an apt reflection of the heightened volatility of capitalism and the growing insecurity this brings into the lives of working people and their allies the world over.

The world capitalist economy has entered a long-term deflationary crisis, a contraction that cannot be fundamentally reversed by the ups and downs of the business cycle. With their profit rates under long-term pressure, the capitalists are in their "lean and mean" period, their "just-on-time" period, their "downsizing," "computerizing," and "de-layering" period. They are laying off workers and other employees, speeding up production, and raking in short-term cash in the bargain.

But the one thing the capitalists are not doing, and are incapable

---

6. In return for a promised $50 billion in "loan guarantees" patched together by Washington, the U.S. rulers wrested agreement from the Mexican government that all Pemex export revenues would be deposited in an account at the Federal Reserve Bank of New York before being transferred to Mexico — or seized in the event of a loan default. Mexico's foreign debt to imperialist-owned banks and financial institutions at the end of 1997 remained at the staggering level of $150 billion. Substantial publicity was given to the Mexican government's early payback in January 1997 of its loan from Washington, including the whopping $580 million in interest extorted by the U.S. Treasury. Less attention, however, was given to the fact that this payback to the U.S. government was financed by other foreign loans, doing little or nothing to lessen Mexico's overall debt slavery to finance capital.

of doing, is expanding productive capacity to anywhere near the degree they need to fuel another gigantic boom, set industrial profit rates on a long-term upward course, and accelerate capital accumulation. Even as capitalists temporarily boost their returns by cutting costs and taking a bigger slice of market share away from their rivals, the long-run profit expectations of capital are such that they are still not investing in new plant and equipment that draws more and more workers into expanded production.

The money that *is* going into new equipment goes largely into ways to make us work faster to produce more with fewer co-workers. That does not expand productive capacity, however. It intensifies speedup and extends the workweek. But that alone does not create the basis for the rising profit rates and capital accumulation that marked the post–World War II capitalist boom until it began running out of steam by the early 1970s.[7]

In fact, instead of issuing stock to finance expansion — the classic source of "capital formation" extolled in standard economics textbooks — U.S. corporations for most of the 1980s and 1990s have actually bought more previously offered stock from each other than

---

7. This trend continued in the 1990s despite talk in the big-business press about an "investment boom." The total stock of industrial plant and equipment in the United States has grown at an annual rate of 2 percent since 1980, compared to an annual rate of 3.9 percent over the previous three decades. Investment as a share of national income has also fallen in the imperialist countries as a whole since 1980.

"There can be little doubt about the option that corporate America has chosen in the 1990s: downsizing has triumphed over rebuilding," wrote Stephen Roach, chief economist for the Wall Street investment house, Morgan Stanley, in November 1996. "Downsizing means making do with less — realizing efficiencies by pruning both labor and capital. . . . Historically, periods of accelerating productivity have been associated with *increased* employment."

Roach reports in a later article that computer hardware accounted for 57 percent of the growth in capital spending from 1994 to 1997. But the vast majority of such spending goes to replace obsolete equipment, not expand capacity. With the slowdown in the U.S. capitalist economy in late 1998, capital investment *excluding computers* was in fact declining.

they have issued in new shares. Capitalists have also issued large quantities of high-interest corporate bonds — gone deep into debt, in other words — to finance takeovers and buyouts.[8]

So, the world's propertied families have been fighting among themselves more and more to use credit to corner a bigger cut of the surplus value they collectively squeeze from working people. They have been blowing up great balloons of debt. But ever since the 1987 stock market panic, and at an accelerated pace since the onset of world depression conditions at the opening of the 1990s, the capitalists have been plagued by the problem that first one balloon, then another, and then yet another begins to deflate. And they have no way of knowing which balloon will go next until they start hearing the "whoosh," and by then it is often too late.

All of us were children once and have blown up balloons. They can expand very slowly, very gradually. But then try to let the air out. That is harder to control. Remember? The balloons can get away and ricochet all over the room.

With returns on investments in capacity-expanding plant and equipment under pressure since the mid-1970s, owners of capital have not only been cost cutting; the holders of paper have been borrowing larger and larger amounts to buy and sell various forms of paper securities at a profit. They blew up a giant balloon of debt in Orange County over a period of years; the bondholders

---

8. "One of the consequences of corporate restructuring," Wall Street economist Edward Yardeni told the *Barron's* financial weekly in March 1996, "has been to generate an enormous amount of corporate cash flow. . . . [Companies] have hesitated to build new plant and equipment. Instead, they are to a certain extent buying their competitors — and by doing so they are basically buying back stock." In the third quarter of 1998, according to U.S. government figures, the withdrawal of shares from the market via buybacks and corporate mergers and acquisitions reached record levels, for a net shrinkage in shares — after accounting for stock newly issued — at an annual rate of $234 billion. Since the early 1980s, the nearly $2 trillion in stock that has disappeared from the market through buybacks and corporate takeovers is greater than that newly issued.

thought they had died and gone to heaven. Then the balloon began to deflate, as they learned the hard way that interest rates go up as well as down. When the balloon international bankers had inflated in Mexico in the 1980s began to collapse, the bondholders stepped in and blew it back up for a while. But in Orange County, the more local officials borrowed to make a killing using public funds to gamble with bond merchants, the greater their vulnerability became. Earlier this year, when rates started rising and low-interest bond issues were suddenly no longer available, the moment of truth arrived.

Now the capitalists and their public representatives — and not just in Mexico or Orange County — have been given another warning of the long-run possibilities of an uncontrollable deflation.

Over the past couple of decades, upturns in the business cycle have relied on floating large amounts of fictitious capital — ballooning debt and other paper values. The capitalists are now paying the piper for the lack of sufficient economic growth during that period to keep rolling over the loans.

The financial press has a term for this explosive process; they call it "de-leveraging." Among other things, this means we will be seeing more breakdowns like the bankruptcy in public "trust funds" in Orange County. Now I will admit, if you had asked me which of the thousands of local and state administrations was most likely to go belly up, I would have been hard put to guess Orange County. The spiritual home of Ronald Reagan and site of John Wayne Airport, Orange County has a median income in the top 2 percent of households in the United States.

Remember those pieces of paper with the cute names we mentioned in "What the 1987 Stock Market Crash Foretold"[9] — the Fannie Maes, Ginnie Maes, Farmer Macs? They are interest-bearing securities supposedly guaranteed by quasi-government agencies that

---

9. This resolution, adopted by the 1988 convention of the Socialist Workers Party, is available in issue no. 10 (1994) of *New International*, a magazine of Marxist politics and theory.

buy up mortgages and second mortgages on homes and farmland. It was these bits of paper — cut apart, repackaged, and jazzed up as roulette chips labeled "derivatives" — whose declining prices imploded on Orange County and got it in such a jam.

Wall Street has already offered up Orange County's treasurer as a scapegoat. But their bottom line is going to be that it is working people like us who are really to blame. If we would accept fewer schools and hospitals, if we would agree to pay higher tuition, if we would demand less public transportation, if "illegals" could be kept off the public rolls, then there would not be so much pressure on poor fund managers to pour billions into high-risk investments. And public workers are already the first to suffer layoffs in Orange County.[10]

Municipal bonds, together with U.S. Treasury bills, are the prerogative of the very rich. Ross Perot, for instance, is one of the biggest individual holders of municipal bonds in the United States. And written on each and every one of these pieces of paper are the words "Full faith and credit." That means the only collateral they are ultimately backed up by is the "full faith and credit" of the government or agency that issued them. The "faith" derives from the guarantee to the wealthy bondholders that they are *always* at the head of the line to be paid out of taxes and other revenues. First comes the in-

---

10. Some 1,600 county employees were laid off by Orange County in 1995. The wages of other county workers were frozen, and sections of their union contracts were unilaterally annulled. In addition, the wealthy county fathers slashed health services, school funding, and social programs. In fact, the only county budget category to expand in 1995 was debt payments to the bondholders.

At the same time, the Orange County fathers compelled bondholders to "roll over" $1 billion in debt that came due in mid-1995. This "delay" in payments on interest and principal for at least one year was a de facto default — the first one on a major municipal bond issue in the United States since the depression of the 1930s. In late 1998, the effort by Orange County officials to recover more of their losses from Wall Street firms such as Merrill Lynch was stymied when a federal court rejected damage payments above and beyond the $740 million the county had already won in prior settlements.

terest — then, if there is anything left, the schools, roads, hospitals, and payroll. It is never the other way around.

No cuts! That is the bondholders' slogan too!

And since governments produce no wealth, *we* are the ones the debtors come to in order to demonstrate their "full faith and credit." The blood money is squeezed from us.

Imperialist debt bondage

Back at the opening of this century, Porfirio Díaz — the president of Mexico whose corrupt rule helped precipitate the Mexican revolution of 1910 — is said to have lamented, "Poor Mexico, so far from God and so close to the United States."

As recent events confirm, that fundamental relationship between U.S. imperialism and the rulers in Mexico has not changed. Moreover, what is happening to toilers in Mexico right now is not exceptional. It is just one variant of the future facing every country held in economic bondage to world finance capital. This relationship between oppressed and oppressor nations accelerates conflicts among the imperialist countries themselves. And it underlines the fact that, in the context of world capitalism's deflationary conditions, the stability of the imperialist countries is increasingly held in bondage to the effects of crises and breakdowns in the exploited Third World.

Just a few weeks before the peso's collapse, an article appeared in *Forbes,* a leading business magazine, by a top manager of the big U.S. stock brokerage firm Bear Stearns. He pointed out that Moody's, one of the two major Wall Street bond rating firms, had recently upgraded Mexican debt. The headline of that article, which appeared in the December 5 issue — the December 5 issue! — was "Take a chance on Mexico." The article begins like this: "If you are like a lot of bond buyers" — *Forbes* has a selective audience — "you have too many eggs in the U.S. basket. Mexico or Brazil could boost your yield and reduce your volatility."

Reduce your volatility! The Bear Stearns executive goes on to explain that according to academic "portfolio theorists" — many with Ph.D.s from Yale, no doubt — the yield on your bondhold-ings will not only be larger but also more stable if you spread your money around, including into bonds from "emerging mar-kets" that pay higher interest to compensate for greater risks.

Then he goes on to say: "Some of these off-brand coun-tries" — *off-brand* countries, how's that for Wall Street's respect-ful attitude toward semicolonial nations? — "will join the ranks of industrial nations. Still more will see their debt upgraded to a BBB or better."

That sounds funny now, but it is not an extreme view. For ex-ample, a recent article in the *New York Times* recalled the even wilder lunacy that Mexico — with the launching of the North American Free Trade Agreement a year ago — "was supposed to be inducted into the community of developed nations."

Just think back a few weeks ago to President Clinton's unre-strained hype about Mexico and NAFTA at the "Summit of the Americas" held in Miami December 9–11. "If current trends con-tinue," Clinton told heads of state from throughout the Americas, "within just a decade, our hemisphere will be the biggest market in the world — more than 850 million consumers buying $3 trillion worth of goods and services. These are remarkable, hopeful times." Capitalism in Latin America is "working wonders," Clinton said. Just not for every class in the same way, he should have added.

Until less than two weeks ago, Mexico was one of a handful of models pointed to by boosters of the so-called free-market sys-tem of how the entire "post–Cold War" world was now going to develop, grow, stabilize, and democratize together. They painted a radiant picture of economic growth, booming profits, national development, expanding democracy, better education, and rising incomes for all.

Far from capitalism becoming less volatile, the new debt crisis that will eventually emerge will make the one in the 1980s look mild.

The economics and the politics of all this cannot be untangled. Those who lend vast amounts of money to reap enormous interest payments, those who seek to take over whole parts of the Third

World to squeeze profits from superexploitation of workers and peasants — those same barons of finance capital simultaneously put their tentacles in every powder keg all over the world and add to its instability. They are ultimately held hostage by their own rapaciousness and by their own successes. Where have the capitalists ever had such success — on their own terms — as they have proclaimed in Mexico over the past decade?

And do not believe a word you read in the press about the irreversibility of the "trend toward democracy" in Mexico. Do not believe a word about how much the U.S. rulers and those around Zedillo in the Mexican bourgeoisie want to break up Bonapartist party rule there. Given the volatility and uncertainty in Mexico, what the bourgeoisie needs and wants is an even stronger Bonapartist state. But what is happening right now underlines both why they need a "stronger" state in Mexico and the problems they'll have in getting one.[11]

---

11. Originating in periods of deep social crisis, a Bonapartist regime relies on a centralized executive power that presents itself as standing above conflicting class interests in order to maintain the power of the dominant social layer. Karl Marx and Frederick Engels coined the term from the experience with Louis-Napoleon Bonaparte's regime in France from 1852 to 1870, as the bourgeoisie strengthened its dominance over the working class in the wake of the retreat of the democratic revolutions of 1848–49.

In Mexico the Institutional Revolutionary Party (PRI) has used Bonapartist methods of rule since 1929 on behalf of the rising capitalist class, claiming the mantle of the revolution as a political weapon against any challenge by workers and peasants to their rule. The PRI initially presented itself as the arbiter between, on the one hand, the rebellious peasantry that powered the 1910 revolution and its allies among a small but growing industrial working class, and, on the other hand, the traditional landowning class and commercial capitalists most directly tied to U.S. and British imperialism.

In midterm elections in July 1997, the PRI for the first time ever lost its majority in the House of Deputies, as well as the powerful post of mayor of Mexico City. Between 1997 and early 1999, the PRI also lost several more state governorships; until 1989 it had filled this office in all thirty-one of Mexico's states. This shift registers the Mexican bourgeoisie's growing difficulties in maintaining the stability of its Bonapartist rule.

We are just beginning to see the results in Mexico for working people and also for the newly arising professional and commercial petty bourgeoisie.

Zedillo can go on television next week and announce the "rescue plan" that capitalists in the United States and Mexico have worked out. But implementing it will be another matter. Even by the Mexican government's own figures, it was only two years ago that workers' real wages finally began to recover from a decade-long plunge. A lot of workers remember that as recently as 1987, prices were leaping by more than 150 percent annually.

Not everybody in Mexico is going to cheer when they hear the new president talk about permitting big U.S. banks to begin buying up Mexican banks. Millions will not look kindly on allowing Wall Street to seize more and more of the national patrimony as collateral to ensure payment of blood money on new loans. There are sure to be protests against beginning to give away little hunks of Pemex to the Yankee colossus — directly or indirectly.

Nor is Mexico the only country where such a crisis can build up. It is just the first among many as the celebration of the millennium approaches. Look at what has already begun happening in Argentina, despite the "market miracle" so loudly trumpeted in the big-business press since 1990.

A section of both the Argentine bourgeoisie and imperialist interests have raked in massive, bloated profits in recent years, including through the privatization of state-owned oil and other industries at bargain-basement prices. Polarization is accelerating within the middle class, which is still relatively small by standards of imperialist countries, but is expanding and rapacious. The expansion of these petty-bourgeois layers has spurred growing demands for imported consumer and luxury goods enjoyed by the middle classes in other countries. Partly as a result, a giant deficit in the balance of payments has opened since 1990. And all this has been paid for by foreign loans, including the sale of bonds and short-term notes to North American and British banks.

Now, with the reverberations spreading from Mexico, the

deflationary squeeze is already tightening in Argentina. The value of the Argentine peso is under pressure — despite its supposedly sustainable one-to-one parity with the dollar! Three days ago the central bank sold off the largest amount of dollars in four years in an effort to stem the tide. One Argentine investment bank is already on the ropes, and the government of President Carlos Menem is announcing new austerity measures. The timetable for Argentina's slide into a deep recession has been moved up, and the ax will fall hardest on workers and farmers.[12]

12. Argentina sank into a deep, eighteen-month recession in 1995, with official jobless figures shooting to 18.6 percent and still hovering over 13 percent in 1998. Figures released in January 1999 showed that 20 percent of the population lives on $2 per day or less.

As the moneyed classes sought to turn in their pesos for dollars during the 1995 crisis, there was a run on Argentine banks, which lost some 20 percent of their deposits in the first half of that year; capital flight amounted to some $8 billion all told. The Menem regime responded by going more deeply in debt to banks and bondholders in the imperialist countries. More than 50 Argentine banks have been closed or bought since that time, and foreign capital now controls some 40 percent of the banking system. Argentina's foreign debt stood at $105 billion at the close of 1997.

A social explosion erupted in early 1997, in the wake of harsh measures announced by the Argentine government the previous year slashing food allowances, health benefits, and wages of working people and increasing the legal workday. Teachers in Neuquén province waged a month-long strike in April 1997 protesting a 20 percent wage cut. Over the next several months, strikes, road blockades, and mass demonstrations were organized by working people across the country, especially in the devastated northern provinces of Jujuy and Salta, where official jobless figures stood at 33 percent. Workers in the oil-rich Neuquén region have been hit by massive layoffs since the initial privatization in 1992 of hunks of the formerly state-owned oil company, YPF Argentina.

At the opening of 1999, Menem signaled two further surrenders to imperialist encroachment on Argentine national sovereignty. First, in response to the sharp currency crisis in Brazil, Argentina's largest trading partner, Menem announced his support for abolishing the nation's currency, the peso, and replacing it with the U.S. dollar — "dollarization," as the degrading procedure is called. Simultaneously, Menem announced that his regime was holding talks with the government of the United Kingdom about renouncing Argentina's sovereignty over the Malvinas Islands (called "the Falklands" by

The story is much the same in Brazil. There, however, even the illusion of economic stability has been much more tenuous. Yesterday the central bank took over two of the biggest state-owned banks to prevent them from going under. The head of the central bank, who will be finance minister in the new government sworn in tomorrow, floated the idea of privatizing the two banks — in practice handing them over to imperialism. Brazil's soon-to-be-inaugurated president Fernando Henrique Cardoso has already discovered the real source of the country's economic crisis — too much spending on retirement benefits! Cardoso says it is necessary to raise the retirement age.

The ruling families of U.S. finance capital are showing their regard and concern for their fellow bourgeoisies in Mexico, Argentina, Brazil, and the rest of Latin America by pulling massive amounts of money out of these countries in recent days.[13] They

---

the British imperialist colonizers), in exchange for the right to fly the flag over the graveyard of hundreds of Argentine soldiers killed during the war.

13. According to the World Bank, foreign private capital flows into Latin America dropped 32 percent in 1995, to $33.2 billion. The boom in foreign money earlier in the 1990s, in Mexico above all, involved buying up mostly stocks and bonds, not new factories and equipment. Such so-called portfolio capital dropped especially sharply in 1995, and Latin American governments had to offer Wall Street coupon-clippers even more onerous interest rates to entice them to buy bonds.

After a two-year recovery of capital flows into Latin America, reaching nearly $90 billion in 1997, there was substantial capital flight in 1998 once again under the impact of the sharp world capitalist economic crisis that began in Asia. Stock markets across Latin America plummeted by 30 to 50 percent in the economically strongest countries in 1998. By the end of that year, Brazil had already slid into recession, and the average growth rate in Latin America as a whole had decelerated by more then 2 percent.

In January 1999, the Brazilian government devalued its currency, the *real*, which plunged more than 40 percent against the U.S. dollar over the following two weeks. The devaluation came on the heels of a year-long effort by the Cardoso regime to shore up the real — an effort that drained Brazil's foreign exchange reserves from $75 billion in January 1998 to $35 billion at the close of December. Since Brazil accounts for 50 percent of the population of South America and 40 percent of its economic output, and in the wake of the sharp

may have shifted a little of their capital to Chile — a place the imperialists trust a bit more, since the bourgeoisie there has used firmer methods over the past quarter century to bring workers and farmers to heel. It took a bloody rightist coup in Chile in 1973, and imposition of a fascist-like military regime for some fifteen years, to deal blows to the working class on the scale of dismantling the state retirement fund and privatizing pensions. The new president of Brazil will not have such an easy time of it as he tries to begin chipping away at social security there.

So it does not much matter what the presidents of Mexico or Argentina or Brazil may have been dreaming about up until the last few days. The message sent from Chiapas was the truth: "Welcome to the nightmare!"

Cuba, the Cordobazo, and the nightmare of the bourgeoisie

The biggest nightmare in Latin America is not what President Zedillo in Mexico, or President Cardoso in Brazil, or President

---

economic contraction in Asia, the impact of the currency crisis throughout Latin America and the capitalist world is potentially even greater than the Mexican crisis of 1994–95. In the aftermath of that earlier crisis, imperialist finance capital gobbled up Brazilian assets, expanding its ownership from $2 billion to $36 billion, in part by buying up formerly state-owned communications networks, utilities, and mines put on the auction block by Cardoso. Brazil's foreign debt in 1998 stood at a staggering $226 billion.

In collusion with the imperialist rulers, the Brazilian bourgeoisie has used the sharpening crisis to rationalize harsher assaults on the pensions and other social rights of workers and peasants in that country.

Menem in Argentina have been waking up to in recent days. The real nightmare is the economic and social reality that hundreds of millions of workers and peasants wake up to each and every morning. Actual nightmares, of course, are unpredictable, chaotic. But the one unfolding across the Americas and elsewhere is not born of chaos. It is the product of the lawful, predictable, irreversible, and unreformable inner workings — the "value relations" — of the world capitalist system.

No Third World country can or will develop today into an economically advanced industrial power with the class structure of the United States, Canada, the countries of Western Europe, Japan, Australia, or New Zealand. No new centers of world finance capital are going to emerge. That has been settled by history. That is one of the great lessons of the twentieth century. It hasn't changed since Bolshevik leader V.I. Lenin summed up the scientific conclusion of the communist workers movement seventy-five years ago. The imperialist world, Lenin said, has been "divided into a large number of oppressed nations and an insignificant number of oppressor nations, the latter possessing colossal wealth and powerful armed forces."[14]

It must have seemed unbelievable to many people when Lenin, Leon Trotsky, and other leaders of the Soviet Communist Party and Communist International insisted on this conclusion at the time. After all, it had not been true for that long. It had not been true in the previous century. Only seventy-five years before Lenin spoke those words in 1920, Germany was still one of the most economically backward regions in Europe; it wasn't even a united nation-state at the time. And even just a decade or so prior to the turn of the century, no one could have accurately predicted that

14. V.I. Lenin, "Report of the Commission on the National and Colonial Questions" to the Second Congress of the Communist International, July 26, 1920, in *Collected Works*, vol. 31, p. 240 (Moscow: Progress Publishers, 1966). It can also be found in Pathfinder's *Workers of the World and Oppressed Peoples, Unite! Proceedings and Documents of the Second Congress, 1920*, vol. 1, p. 212.

coal- and oil-poor Japan — just beginning to emerge from feudalism — would soon develop into an imperialist power, while
Argentina would end up among the oppressed not the oppressor
nations in the world.

Since the consolidation of imperialism at the opening of this
century, every action by finance capital in relation to the more economically backward countries ends up further warping the economies of the colonial or semicolonial countries. That is the effect of
every bank loan to their ruling classes; every investment in landed,
industrial, and commercial capital; every purchase of bonds issued
by a semicolonial administration; every trade pact; every scheme to
peg the value of weaker currencies to stronger ones. Every one of
these moves makes the oppressed nations of Latin America, Asia,
and Africa more, not less, dependent on capital, technology, and im-
ports from the imperialist nations. Their currencies are ever more
reliant on, and vulnerable to, the U.S. dollar, the British pound, the
German mark, the French franc, or the Japanese yen.

Capitalist classes do arise in these countries, and they do come
into conflict with the imperialist overlords over division of the
surplus value produced by the peasants and workers. But the national bourgeoisies are ultimately too weak to come out on top in
these conflicts, short of the kind of working-class and peasant
mobilizations that would threaten the privileged classes' own
wealth and power in the process. That is why as long as the bourgeoisie remains in power in a semicolonial country, national sovereignty cannot be achieved.

When you read or hear the terms "developing countries" or
"emerging economies," be sure to notice the "-ing" on the end of
the adjectives — "develop-*ing*," "emerg-*ing*." That is the tip-off
that not one of these "developing" countries has developed into an
advanced industrial power in the twentieth century. Not one
"emerging" economy has emerged from bondage to the big banks
and strong currencies of the ruling families of finance capital.
Emerging forever; emerged . . . never. Not one.

It is not surprising, in face of this reality, that many workers and young people initially conclude that the deepening crisis that surrounds them must be a symptom of chaos. Everything seems to be out of control. Everything seems unpredictable.

Others suppose there must be a conspiracy. I am sure all of us will be talking to workers over the next few weeks who will tell us something to this effect: "I didn't expect miracles in Mexico, but I thought things were getting a little better. I thought there would be some progress. What happened? How could it be so sudden? There must have been some kind of a plot."

That is not an unreasonable assumption. Workers know from bitter experience that the employers and their politicians scheme and plot all the time. They scheme to cut wages and extend the workday. They plan ways to cut social programs the working class has fought for and won to the benefit of all. They are always cheating on the edges; they are always plotting to one degree or another. They lie as a matter of course. And workers learn never to trust them.

But no plot is necessary to explain what is happening in Mexico — or in Orange County either, for that matter. Nor is what is happening chaotic. It is the outcome of the lawful workings of capitalism in the imperialist epoch. It can all be understood and explained to other workers. Our point — the point of the politically conscious vanguard of the working class — is not that something *didn't* work, but that this is *how* it works.

Capitalism by its very laws of motion operates to take tools and land away from working farmers and other small producers. It operates to amass the wealth produced by the toiling majority in the hands of the propertied minority. It operates to produce and reproduce not only commodities and the profits from their sale, but also the entire class structure and social relations of subordination that make this system of exploitation possible.

As I was leaving to catch the plane to come out here this morning, a comrade in New York handed me a copy of Lenin's *Imperialism*. He urged me to reread it during the flight. Given what had begun happening in Mexico, he said, I was bound to find something useful in preparing for this meeting. He was right.

When Lenin used the term "imperialism" — and Marxists still use the term the same way — he was not just speaking in a political and military sense about the aggression and oppression imposed by the rulers of a handful of wealthy and powerful nation-states on colonial peoples. He was not just referring to the colonial system and related forms of semicolonial exploitation. That is a permanent aspect of imperialism, but Lenin was referring to something more fundamental.

Imperialism, Lenin explained, is the final stage of capitalism. He described its features. Reading *Imperialism*, I discovered once again, is well worth the effort. The chapter that struck me in a new way this time is the one entitled "The Parasitism and Decay of Capitalism."

Lenin wrote the booklet in 1916, just a year before the Russian revolution. At that stage in the development of world capitalism, he explained, "The income of the bondholders is *five times greater* than the income obtained from the foreign trade of the greatest 'trading' country in the world [Britain].

"This," Lenin said, "is the essence of imperialism and imperialist parasitism."

For that reason, Lenin added, Marxists should not object to those at the time — including some bourgeois commentators — who had begun to refer to the major capitalist industrial powers of the day as "rentier states" or "usurer states." The rival imperialist powers remain industrial giants and fight over markets for their exports, Lenin said. But at the same time, "The world has become divided into a handful of usurer states on the one side, and a vast majority of debtor states on the other."

Since Lenin's time, of course, the absolute increase in the industrial output and exports of manufactured goods by the imperialist powers has been enormous. But Lenin would not have been at all surprised by the even greater relative increase, especially over the past two decades, in the income capitalists derive from interest, dividends, commissions, royalties, and returns on a widening range of paper securities — what Marx called "fictitious capital."

Lenin would not have been surprised that the world's quantity of bonds, stocks, and other paper values since 1980 has grown two and a half times faster than the national income of the major imperialist countries, and that the volume of trade in these securities has accelerated even more. He would not have been surprised that international sales and purchases of U.S. Treasury bonds alone shot up from $30 billion in 1983 to $500 billion in 1993, nor that the ratio of international currency transactions to world trade in actual industrial and agricultural goods rose from 10 to 1 in 1983 to 60 to 1 in 1992.

Nor would Lenin have been at all surprised by the much-talked-about proliferation of "derivatives" on Wall Street in recent years — basically, bets placed on the future rise or decline in the prices of stocks, bonds, or other pieces of paper — whose total value has now reached some $20 trillion. In fact, he would remind us that such speculative devices always become necessary to the capitalist rentier class at a certain point. When the total yield from their bonds goes down, they always attempt to float new kinds of paper that turn a heftier profit.

Yes, bonds are just pieces of paper. But as long as capitalism exists, they are the most important pieces of paper in the social world. And if you want to know what happens when you do not show the bondholders the proper respect, just ask the Mexican bourgeoisie or the officials of Orange County!

"The creditor is more permanently attached to the debtor than the seller is to the buyer." Lenin approvingly cites that assessment from a book on British imperialism by a bourgeois writer. And it remains true today.

Capitalism and its gravediggers

Isn't that what makes the deflationary conditions facing the imperialist countries so explosive? Doesn't that fact loom behind the increased dangers today of the use of imperialism's armed forces around the world?

The ultimate showdowns are not over trade primarily, and

never have been. Washington emerged from World War I as imperialism's great creditor, more than its great trader initially. Together with British and French finance capital, the U.S. rulers imposed onerous debts — packaged as "reparations" — on their defeated German rivals totaling the equivalent in today's currency of more than $400 billion, one and a half times Germany's entire national income in 1929. What's more, Washington demanded that its "allies" pay off their wartime debts as well. London owed the U.S. rulers some $90 billion in current dollars, about half its national income in 1929, and France owed the equivalent of about two-thirds of its national income. And when some voices in Washington floated the idea of forgiving these "inter-Allied" debts, President Calvin Coolidge spoke for bondholders the world over in snapping: "They hired the money, didn't they?" (In the end, not only Berlin, but London and Paris as well, defaulted on their wartime debts in the early 1930s.)

Today massive Third World debt remains the source both of enormous potential economic breakdowns of the world capitalist monetary system and of imperialist military interventions as well. The pressures that come down on bourgeois governments in the colonial world to devalue their currencies, or to impose sharp austerity measures in order to avoid devaluation, are enormous — wreaking havoc on the living standards of the toilers and broad layers of the middle classes.

Over the past fifteen years, a hammerlock has often been placed on the victims in the name of the International Monetary Fund and its "structural adjustment" programs. That seemingly appeared less crude than overt action by Wall Street backed by the Pentagon. But as we are seeing in Mexico, at some point in the capitalist crisis the niceties were bound to give way. Now it is the U.S. ruling class directly that is dictating the terms. The same Yankee bondholders and bankers who so eagerly thrust the loans on their Mexican "colleagues" to begin with will now demand a program of "frugality" and further inroads for U.S. finance capital into Mexico's national patrimony. And to pay off the new debts, there will be further loans down the line — and the cycle will start all over again. This is the plan, the anticipated pattern.

This is always the pattern. That is why what will "develop" and "emerge" in today's world are the conditions for new debt balloons and new collapses. This is the outcome of the lawful functioning of parasitic imperialism. This is the result of the rivalry among the ruling families of finance capital to intensify their exploitation of the toilers the world over, increase their market share, collect on their debts, and enhance their profit rates. There is no plot. There is no mystery to it; it is perfectly comprehensible.

What is less comprehensible to the rulers — and more comprehensible to workers — are the struggles these workings of capitalism will engender. What's more, this imperialist reality is also a damned good reason for the toilers to overthrow those who benefit from and defend the capitalist system.

The leadership of the Cuban revolution had absorbed the political implications of this reality in the 1950s. That helped make it possible for them to lead the workers and farmers to power in 1959 and organize the toilers to uproot capitalist property relations over the next two years. In 1962 Cuba's communist leadership, based on their own experiences, reaffirmed this fundamental lesson in a revolutionary manifesto for the Americas known as the Second Declaration of Havana. "Experience shows that in our nations [the national bourgeoisie], even when its interests are in contradiction to those of Yankee imperialism, has been incapable of confronting it," the declaration said, "for the national bourgeoisie is paralyzed by fear of social revolution and frightened by the cry of the exploited masses."[15]

I'd urge you to read this revolutionary document, or to reread it. The *Militant* printed the full text at the time. The predecessor of Pathfinder Press rapidly brought it out as a pamphlet in 1962, and

---

15. *The Second Declaration of Havana* (New York: Pathfinder, 1962, 1994). Pathfinder published a new French edition in 1995 as well, entitled *La deuxième déclaration de La Havane*, and a Spanish edition, *La segunda declaración de La Habana*, in 1997.

Pathfinder has kept it in print without interruption ever since.

The Second Declaration of Havana is a call by the leadership of the Cuban revolution to toilers throughout the Americas to confront what faces them everywhere. It explains why the only class that can point a way forward is the working class. That is because workers are the only class with no interest in exploitation of any kind — and with no stake in trying to make capitalism work. In fact, when our class gets suckered into trying to help the capitalists make their system work, the bosses always make sure that every step along the way is to their advantage and to our detriment.

So, the exploiters do have a nightmare. The nightmare is what began happening in Chiapas exactly one year ago, when peasants and rural workers said no to the accelerated pace at which they were being driven off the land.

The nightmare is what happened in Argentina, also about one year ago, when workers in the northern province of Santiago del Estero, seemingly out of the blue, rose up and took over government buildings for several days to protest that they had not been paid since the previous August. Smaller explosions then developed elsewhere in that region and in the province of Tucumán over the next month or so.[16] To the Argentine capitalists, these rebellions were completely unexpected. In fact, however, they were the product of the buildup of unbearable conditions over a period of years.

And if that is what the capitalists got a taste of in early 1994, when Argentina, Mexico, and Chile were still being heralded as the trinity of the market's miracles in the Americas, then we can wager they are worried even more about what is coming in the months and years ahead.

16. In response to intensifying government and employer assaults on living standards, strikes and demonstrations erupted across Argentina in the first half of 1995. Actions took place in at least twelve Argentine provinces, from Tierra del Fuego in the far south, to Córdoba, to renewed protests in Santiago del Estero. During a one-day general strike in Córdoba in June 1995, the offices of the Radical Civic Union, the governing party in that province, were set on fire after cops fired rubber bullets into a mass workers demonstration.

The Santiago del Estero events reminded Argentina's rulers of an even worse nightmare. That one exploded in 1969 when rising workers struggles, backed by students, culminated in a general strike in the country's second largest city, Rosario, and in a massive working-class uprising in the big industrial city of Córdoba. The *Cordobazo*, as that explosion came to be known, opened a prerevolutionary situation in the Southern Cone of South America. The capitalist rulers only succeeded in snuffing it out through savage military coups in Bolivia in 1971, Chile in 1973, and Argentina in 1976.

Anybody who was alive and politically aware in those times can never forget what happened, as the working class rose in major cities, not just in one country but in several — especially if you had comrades and knew revolutionists in Argentina and elsewhere in South America. For revolutionary-minded workers, such events confirm what our class is capable of and what we know is coming sooner or later in every country of the world. But for the capitalist rulers throughout Latin America, that memory is a recurring nightmare.

Because equally as lawful and inevitable as the workings of capitalism and its sudden breakdowns is the resistance, mobilization, and organization of its gravediggers produced by that very social system.

The capitalists are always surprised when their system begins coming unstuck. But they are even more surprised when working people finally stand up and say "No!" The rulers fear the working class, but they have also been bred to treat us with the utmost class contempt. So when we revolt, it comes as a shock. They try to convince themselves, and to convince us, that it's not really happening. But it is.

The specter of the Cuban revolution

You may have read stories about New Year's Eve in Havana exactly thirty-six years ago today. Even as armed fighters from the July 26 Movement were taking over the streets of Havana, big parties were in full swing in the casinos, swank hotels, and palatial homes of the wealthy. The beneficiaries of Fulgencio Batista's brutal dictatorship were celebrating, along with the cream — or what you might call scum — of Cuba's capitalist class, absentee landlords, and their dear friends flown in from the United States. They were wearing their tuxedos, their evening gowns, their imported orchids, their jewels and furs (yes, furs!). They were swilling champagne and pouring it over each other's heads. Just another typical New Year's Eve for that tiny layer in Cuba.

They were taken by surprise at the triumph of the revolution that night. Only three weeks earlier, a U.S. senator on a trip to Havana had boasted to the press, "Is there a revolution here? I hadn't noticed any trouble."[17]

When I was in Cuba in 1960, I remember being told a story about one of those New Year's Eve parties. A couple of young guys with beards walked into the Havana Hilton — soon to be the Havana Libre — and the wealthy partygoers hollered at the doorman to get the intruders out of there. The doorman went

17. Between December 29, 1958, and January 1, 1959, 300 Rebel Army soldiers under the command of Ernesto Che Guevara capped a series of rapid and spectacular victories in Cuba's central Las Villas province, taking Santa Clara, the country's third-largest city, aided by residents who impeded government troop movements. Over those same days Rebel Army troops led by Fidel Castro closed in on Santiago de Cuba, the second-largest city, in Cuba's easternmost Oriente province. As word of these victories spread in the wee hours of New Year's Day, armed workers and youth in Havana took to the streets, and Batista fled the country. On January 8 the main Rebel Army columns under Fidel Castro's command entered Havana, completing a cross-island march from Santiago. Evidence of Washington's surprise at the victory was an Associated Press dispatch run in U.S. newspapers New Year's day. It was headlined, "Cuba Rebels Driven From Santa Clara, 4,000 Casualties Reported in City; Batista Troops Pressing Attack." For an account of the military campaign and popular struggles that culminated in the triumph, see Ernesto Che Guevara, *Episodes of the Cuban Revolutionary War: 1956–58* (New York: Pathfinder, 1996).

over to them and one turned out to be his cousin!

Most of the revelers finally figured out the party was over. But until that moment, their class instincts had told them to order the servants to throw the trash out. Instead, the parasitic classes were themselves thrown out of power and, before too long, expropriated of the wealth and property they themselves had expropriated from Cuban working people.

Batista was caught off guard too. He had already stashed most of his wealth in the United States and Switzerland. But when he had to flee Cuba on a plane at 3:00 a.m. on New Year's Day, he uncharacteristically left behind large quantities of cash, jewels, stock, and bond certificates. That same night, other government officials and bourgeois families hightailed it out of Cuba on yachts. Some stayed around for a year or two in hopes that the revolutionary government could be tamed and corrupted. But to no avail.

That, above all, illustrates why this meeting tonight is celebrating the recent publication of issue number 10 of *New International* magazine that includes the article "Imperialism's March toward Fascism and War." Fascism and war *is* the logic of the march of finance capital. The operation of that social system, its unceasing drive to maximize profits, pushes the international capitalist economy into crisis, spawns savage rightist movements, and ultimately drags the toilers into worldwide slaughters. That is what imperialism has inflicted on humanity twice before in this century, and that is where capitalism is heading once again. That is the inevitable logic today of what the exploiters call "the free market system."

But the new issue of *New International* also features the article, "Defending Cuba, Defending Cuba's Socialist Revolution" by Mary-Alice Waters. Because as Cuban working people have shown, what is far from inevitable is that the outcome of the workings of capitalism will be triumphant fascism and a third world war. Along the road to such an unthinkable catastrophe, the ruling capitalist families all over the world must try to fight their way through hundreds of millions of working people and youth like us and like those in Cuba.

The exploiters' failure to defeat us in World War II and its aftermath set up the problems they face today.

We are their worst nightmare.

Immigration: Internationalizing the working class

The imperialists fight to open up every spot on earth to the free flow of their goods and the free flow of their capital. At a certain point, however, they start lashing out against the increasing free flow of labor that is an inevitable consequence of the needs of capital.

You have seen a prime example here in California, where the majority of the employing class recently pushed through Proposition 187, which seeks to deny immigrants schooling and social benefits available to other workers. But there was a fight against Prop 187, too. Some young demonstrators even took to the streets waving Mexican flags, embarrassing the liberals and other bourgeois politicians who opposed the initiative on grounds that it was unenforceable and that immigration could be stemmed more effectively by beefing up the border cops.[18]

18. Anti-immigrant measures on both state and federal levels, along with other attacks on the rights and dignity of the foreign-born, have sparked ongoing protests, as shown by the October 12, 1996, national march for immigrants' rights in Washington, D.C., which drew some 20,000 participants from across the United States. The action was initiated by forces in California active in the mobilizations against Proposition 187 in 1994. In April 1996, a few days after California police were videotaped savagely beating several Mexican workers, 6,000 people once again took to the streets of Los Angeles to demand prosecution of the cops and full rights for immigrants.

With overwhelming bipartisan backing, President Clinton in September

Despite their intentions, the propertied families the world over are internationalizing the working class. The capitalists do not set out to do most of the things that inevitably result from the way their system works. But from one end of the globe to the other, toilers are migrating in larger numbers than ever before in human history, drawn in by the changing needs of capital.

In the United States, it is relatively easy to make this case. Most of us understand to one degree or another the scope of the immigration from the rest of the Americas and from East Asia. This is also a worldwide phenomenon, however, as we can see from looking at the size and scope of movements from North Africa into France.

Civil war in Algeria and class struggles in France

The same kind of argument over immigration is going on among the rulers in France as here in California and across the United States. The rightists are beating the drums, and they are getting a

---

1996 signed into law the Illegal Immigration and Reform Responsibility Act that, among other things, aims to double the number of border police over the following five years. The law also authorizes some $12 million to build a fence along the U.S.-Mexican border south of San Diego; eliminates constitutional protections in order to speed deportations; and imposes other draconian measures against immigrants and those seeking asylum. The previous month Clinton had also signed new federal welfare legislation denying many social entitlements to both "legal" and "illegal" immigrants. Earlier, in February 1996, Clinton issued an executive order barring federal contracts to companies that hire undocumented workers, asserting that "America's jobs belong to America's legal workers."

In the two years following adoption of the new law, the U.S. Immigration and Naturalization Service stepped up deportations and anti-immigrant factory raids, expelling a record 300,000 immigrants — more than twice the number in the previous two years. With nearly a billion dollars earmarked by Congress for deportations, the INS has rapidly grown into the largest federal police agency — bigger than the FBI. It set public targets of 93,000 deportations for 1997 and 127,300 for 1998, surpassing both. Under the Clinton legislation, immigrants are now being deported within a few hours of being detained, with no right to an attorney or legal proceedings of any kind.

wider echo across the spectrum of bourgeois politics. Should Algerians and other immigrants be able to go to school? Should limits be put on their "foreign" attire?[19] Should they have access to hospitals and health care? Should they have pension rights and receive unemployment and welfare benefits?

These are the same issues you argue and discuss right here in southern California every week.

A civil war has been widening and deepening in Algeria since early 1992. We would never know this from reading the newspapers here in the United States, however, or from watching television. There has been a flurry of coverage this month about the hijacking of an Air France jet, which ended with French government commandos killing all four Algerians involved in the takeover. But that is about all we as workers in the United States are likely to find out.

Yet an average of *eight hundred people each week* have been killed in that conflict in the recent period — thirty thousand in all over the past three years. I find that figure mind-boggling — it is two-thirds the number of U.S. soldiers killed in action during the entire Vietnam war. But those are the figures reported in the *Financial Times* of London and elsewhere.[20] To the big-business press, nonetheless, it is thirty thousand Arabs, thirty thousand Muslims, thirty thousand fanatics. "Who's gonna miss 'em?" That is truly their attitude.

The civil war in Algeria, moreover, is in large part the product of the imperialist foreign policy of the capitalist rulers in France, the country's former colonial overlord. In December 1991, Paris collaborated with the government in Algiers to annul the results of the

19. In 1994 Paris barred Islamic girls from wearing headscarves in school. Later, in April 1995, the French government banned a book entitled *The Licit and Illicit in Islam* by Youssef Qaradhawi. The Interior Ministry said the book could "cause dangers for public order because of its clearly anti-Western tone and ideas contrary to the laws and fundamental values of the republic."

20. The human toll had reached an estimated 75,000 by mid-1998.

national elections there. The specter of "Islamic fundamentalism" sweeping across North Africa was used as the pretext. The French rulers were concerned because the bourgeois opposition party that had won the first round — the Islamic Salvation Front — was insufficiently deferential to the language and culture of Paris's propertied class. Such a regime promised to be less pliant and less subservient to the economic and political demands of French imperialism.

A military junta took command in Algeria, and France's Socialist Party president François Mitterrand acted on behalf of the ruling capitalist families to arm the new regime in Algiers with attack helicopters and other weaponry to use against its opponents. This was not a new departure for the social democrats in France. They were also the dominant party in the government just after World War II that dispatched troops to hold on to French colonies in Algeria and Indochina; the pro-Moscow French Communist Party, too, held posts in that government and backed its colonial policies. In the mid-1950s, a Socialist Party-led coalition regime again pressed the bloody but losing war to suppress Algerian freedom fighters. (Mitterrand, in fact, was the interior minister, or top cop, in that government.)

Because of the attraction by capital of accelerating labor flows over the past several decades, these civil conflicts and class tensions in Algeria come right into France, right into the former colonial power itself. There are one million Algerians or people of Algerian origin in France today. Immigrants from North Africa and other predominantly Muslim countries make up about 5 percent of the population, a substantially larger percentage in Paris and in cities across southern France, and a much larger percentage of the working class.

With official unemployment at around 12 percent in France, the same kind of anti-immigrant scapegoating is on the rise there that we hear from Patrick Buchanan here in the United States. "Save American jobs!" "Save French jobs!" Just as in the United States, such nationalist demagogy is on the increase in France, including in the officialdom of the social democratic- and Stalinist-led parties and unions.

The French rulers are also continuing to press their defense of the *franc fort* — that is, keeping interest rates high in order to keep the franc strong, pegged to the German mark. That deflationary policy puts the squeeze on anybody who works for a living in France or who needs a job, whatever their national origin. But it serves the class interests of most of those who own and control wealth, and all of those who own bonds and hold debt.

Borders more valued than ever by bourgeoisie

National boundaries are more important to the bourgeoisie today than at any time in history, just as they are becoming more porous than ever before. Forget the hoopla about European unity, the North American Free Trade Agreement, the World Trade Organization, and the United Nations. To the most powerful ruling families of world finance capital, borders are becoming more important, not less.

Why? Because national boundaries mark off two things the capitalist rulers need in order to maximize their wealth and protect it in face of rising competition.

One, boundaries define currencies. The borders of France define the area in which the franc is legal tender, backed by the full faith and credit of the state. The French bourgeoisie's effort to keep the franc strong is important if they are to keep capital flowing into their coffers, not out.

Second, boundaries define the home base of the bourgeoisies' armed forces. The French army stands behind the franc; that is the power that makes the franc more than a piece of paper when push comes to shove. French bankers do not want a devalued franc when it comes time to collect on their loans; the bourgeois state and its armed forces are the ultimate collection agency. It defends French finance capital against its rivals around the world and against the effrontery of working people from Paris to Rwanda, from Lyons to Martinique and Guadeloupe, and from New Caledonia to Marseilles.

The greatest single contradiction in world politics is the internationalization of both capital and labor, on the one hand, and, on the other, the growing conflicts among the most powerfully armed nation-states as a result of intensifying competition for profits. Marx and Engels explained this fundamental contradiction of capitalism many years ago, and Lenin and the Bolsheviks taught us why these conflicts are much more explosive and much more devastating for working people in the imperialist epoch.

We might look at the wars that have been fought in recent years and initially think: well, these all seem to be conflicts between imperialist powers and colonial countries, as in the Gulf War; or between big powers and oppressed peoples, as in Moscow's assault against Chechnya; or civil wars between rival ruling groups in colonial countries or weaker workers states, as in Angola or in Yugoslavia. If we look a little more carefully, however, we can also see the mounting social tensions in world politics that lead to growing nationalist demagogy and rightist movements in the imperialist countries. We can see the class polarization that can and will fuel the war party — the nonpartisan bourgeois war party — in all the centers of finance capital. And we can recognize the threat of interimperialist armed conflicts and wars that can set humanity on the path toward a world conflagration.

We must learn to spot the significance of occurrences that might at first seem accidental or unrelated to broader political developments. To cite one example, take the events this year marking the fiftieth anniversary of the atomic bombing of Hiroshima and Nagasaki — one of the most horrible crimes in the history of the U.S. ruling class. Stop and think for a moment about the decision by the U.S. postal service to issue a stamp depicting a mushroom cloud with the caption, "Atomic bombs hasten war's end, August 1945." The Clinton administration finally bowed to the outcry from world public opinion and withdrew the stamp. But it had already been designed and was ready to be issued in September 1995.

The stamp is not an isolated incident. In recent years, the U.S. rulers have been striving to reaffirm not only that the war with Japan was a just war, but also that unleashing nuclear terror against the populations of Hiroshima and Nagasaki was justified to save the lives of U.S. soldiers. There continues to be a firm bipartisan consensus to brook no retreat from Washington's official rationale for this heinous act.

But that rationale makes no sense without the assumption that the lives of the Japanese people are worth less than the lives of U.S. troops. Not only that, but this rationale assumes that civilian populations are fair game as the target of any holocaust those directing the imperialist war deem expedient. More than 200,000 Japanese were killed by those bombs, and 100,000 more died later from cancer and other effects of the bombings. Such reactionary arguments are used by the rulers not only to justify new wars tomorrow, but to undermine the international class solidarity of working people in the United States today.

Communist workers welcome the internationalization of our class. We welcome the breakdown of borders. (Along the more than 1,000 miles from Brownsville to Tijuana, are you in the United States, Mexico, or both?) Crumbling borders weaken the employer-fostered competition between workers of different nationalities and widen the cultural scope and world view of the working class. This process strengthens the fighting potential of labor's battalions and brings new experiences and militancy into the workers movement.

Workers recently arrived from "beyond the border" will make up a large and growing percentage of the cadres and leadership of the revolutionary party in every imperialist country.

Imperialism's new holy crusade

The television networks and daily newspapers gave a lot of play to various international conferences in 1994. There was the "Summit of the Americas" in Miami. There have been conferences of NATO, the European Union, the General Agreement on Tariffs and Trade, and others.

Another international conference this month did not get much coverage, however. The fifty-two-member Organization of the Islamic Conference met in Casablanca, Morocco, in North Africa, December 13–15. While we were being deluged with dispatches about other world gatherings, I only saw one mention of the Islamic Conference — a short item in the "World News Briefs" column of the *New York Times*.

This is hardly an organization of firebrand revolutionaries. It is made up of the heads of state of bourgeois regimes — from the king of Morocco to the prime minister of Pakistan. But these figures rule in the name of hundreds of millions of people who are convinced, with good reason, that racist and xenophobic attitudes toward their religion and culture are being promoted by the governments and leading politicians in the imperialist countries — France, Germany, the United Kingdom, Canada, the United States, and elsewhere.

I was struck by two decisions of this conference. First, the heads of state adopted a resolution condemning the "ferocious campaign to tarnish Islam" and associate it with terrorism. And they also voted unanimously to urge military aid for the embattled Muslims in Bosnia and Herzegovina.

I do not raise this because I expect these governments to start supplying substantial material aid to Bosnia. I do not — although we will see stranger things happen before this century is over. I raise it because class-conscious workers in the United States and other imperialist countries need to start paying more attention to the imperialists' aims in fanning the flames about "Islamic fundamentalism" or "Arab fanaticism" or whatever they choose to call it.

To workers here in the United States especially, this crusade has seemed largely external in the past. Yes, Washington has pounded away against the Iranian revolution and "the mullahs" since 1979. Yes, anti-Arab and anti-Islamic prejudice were used a few years ago to undergird support for the U.S.-organized war against Iraq — the so-called Gulf War. Yes, the U.S. rulers demonized Libyan head of state Mu'ammar Gadhafi and organized air strikes on his home and other targets. Yes, we were told by the U.S. rulers why "we" must support Israel in several wars against Arab governments and reject the call for a democratic, secular Palestine. Yes, above all, "we" must defend "our" oil resources in the Middle East.

But even if all these goals were important, we were led to believe, they largely had to do with events in the Middle East or North Africa. They did not touch directly on what happened in the United States or Europe. They were largely external to the daily lives of those living in the imperialist world.

That is what has changed quite recently. For the past three years, we have watched the first large-scale war take place in Europe in almost half a century. There has been massive, sustained artillery shelling. Air power has been used to bomb civilian populations in Europe for the first time since the bombings of Dresden, London, and other cities during World War II. Altogether U.S. jets, together with warplanes from the United Kingdom, France, and Holland, have carried out five bombing operations in Yugoslavia since February 1994.[21]

21. By late May 1995 U.S. and NATO forces had conducted eight bombing assaults. The most massive bombing came in August and September 1995, as some 60 NATO planes carried out some 3,200 sorties over a two-week period. The air strikes were combined with shelling from NATO positions on Bosnian hillsides and the launching of Tomahawk cruise missiles from U.S. warships off the coast. In October, in the wake of this sustained bombardment, Washington announced a cease-fire by Serbian, Croatian, and Bosnian forces. Talks at Wright-Patterson Air Force Base in Dayton, Ohio, later in the year laid the basis for Washington to spearhead sending an occupation army of some 60,000 NATO troops — including 20,000 U.S. soldiers — into Bosnia. As of early 1999, the U.S.-organized occupation force, initially scheduled to depart in late 1996, remained in Bosnia with no settled departure date.

Washington once again threatened NATO air strikes against Serbia in 1998. The Clinton administration backed off this threat in October 1998, after the

All this has been happening in Yugoslavia. It is a war that has brought to the surface the deepest conflicts among the imperialist powers in Europe and North America since the collapse of the Stalinist apparatuses at the opening of the 1990s. It is a war that has exposed the increasing contradictions in what continues to be called the NATO alliance.

And what do we find right at the center of this European war? We find that one of the combatants, the Bosnian government, presides over a majority Islamic population. We find the terror squads of Bosnian Serb leader Radovan Karadzic agitating against "Islamic fundamentalism" as the pretext to promote murderous "ethnic cleansing" along national and religious lines among working people who had lived and worked alongside each other for decades since the Yugoslav revolution in the aftermath of World War II. (Imagine what Karadzic could do to save the lives of "Serbian boys" with just a couple of small bombs the size of those U.S. president Harry Truman used to incinerate Hiroshima and Nagasaki!)[22]

Then you turn to the news about what is going on in Russia. The *New York Times* recently featured two photographs accompanying an article headlined, "Russian General Halts His Tanks As

---

Serbian-dominated Yugoslav government agreed to begin talks on the withdrawal of its military forces from Kosova, a territory populated by ethnic Albanians. The Serbian regime, whose forces remained in Kosova at the opening of 1999, has carried out a military offensive in that region, driving as many as 300,000 Albanians from their homes; in 1998 alone some 2,000 Albanians were killed or disappeared. While opposing the Kosovans' demand for national self-determination, Washington has exploited the conflict in Kosova — as it continues to do in Bosnia — as a pretext to maintain the NATO military occupation in Yugoslavia.

22. Among the major activities of the U.S.-organized NATO "Implementation Force (Ifor)" in Bosnia in 1996 was pressuring Bosnian Muslim authorities to deport volunteer fighters from Iran and other countries with large Islamic populations and to cut off further military aid and training from the Iranian government. The first widely publicized NATO military operation was a February 1996 raid on what Washington labeled an Iranian-run "terrorist training camp" near Sarajevo.

Qualms Over Rebellion Grow." One was of women from Chechnya on the road leading to the capital city of Grozny. They were appealing to Russian troops to refuse Moscow's orders and halt their advance. In this case, as in several others, the Russian soldiers and their officers were won over and refused to move their tanks any further.[23]

The other photograph was of U.S. vice president Albert Gore and his wife Tipper the same day with big smiles on their faces at the fancy GUM department store in Moscow. I guess this scene was supposed to be suggestive of budding capitalism. They were there to show Washington's backing for their man Boris Yeltsin. The Russian president has been having a hard time of it lately and evidently needed a public display of support.

To justify his bloody onslaught and imperial designs in Chechnya, Yeltsin is raising the specter of "Islamic fanaticism." And what did the grinning Gore have to say about all this while in Moscow? He repeated the assertion of his commander-in-chief, William Clinton, that Chechnya was "an internal affair" of Russia. The Clinton administration supports the suppression of any secessionist or other moves that would further destabilize the weak Bonapartist regime in Moscow.[24]

23. In December 1994 the government of Boris Yeltsin dispatched an invasion force of 30,000 Russian troops to crush the independence movement of the largely Islamic people of Chechnya in the northern Caucasus mountains, bordering Georgia. During the first year and a half of relentless Russian army bombing and shelling, an estimated 35,000 people were killed and the capital city of Grozny and dozens of Chechen villages were laid to ruin. The war was unpopular from the outset among broad layers of working people and others in Russia.

24. Standing beside Yeltsin at a news conference during an April 1996 summit meeting in Moscow, U.S. president William Clinton responded as follows to a question about the U.S. government's position on Moscow's assault against Chechnya and the death toll it has taken: "I would remind you that we once had a civil war in our country in which we lost, on a per capita basis, far more people than we lost in any of the wars of the 20th century, over the proposition that Abraham Lincoln gave his life for, that no state had a right

We should note that Gore and Clinton get no quarrel on this score from ultrarightist Patrick Buchanan, who has warned in his syndicated column about the dangers of the "nationalist virus" in places such as Chechnya "spreading to the West." "Look homeward, America!" Buchanan writes. "With the multinational empires torn apart, are the multinational nations next?" And in Russia itself, the most prominent voice rallying to the defense of Yeltsin's war against the Chechens has been that of the fascist Vladimir Zhirinovsky.

From the Caucasus and all along the Silk Road,[25] national groupings and minorities who are predominantly Muslim chafe against subordination to the Great Russian overlords and their agents. This chauvinist course makes a mockery of Moscow's claims of normalization and stability, let alone its hypocritical championing of the inviolability of borders.

This anti-Islamic crusade in Russia is not an innovation of the Yeltsin government, however. It is a product of the Stalinist counterrevolution in the Soviet Union some seventy years ago. Previously, under Lenin's leadership, the course of the Bolshevik-led workers and peasants government had been guided by one of its very first decrees, the "Appeal to All Toiling Muslims of Russia and the East," issued in early December 1917. Without lending an iota of credence to the progressive character of any religious beliefs or institutions, the Soviet republic declared:

> All you whose mosques and shrines have been destroyed, whose beliefs and customs have been trampled on by the tsars and the Russian oppressors! Henceforth your beliefs and cus-

---

to withdrawal from our union." The U.S. government, Clinton added, "has taken the position that Chechnya is a part of Russia, but that in the end, a free country has to have free association, so there would have to be something beyond the fighting, there would have to be a diplomatic solution."

25. The part of the world from Iran through Central and East Asia. The term derives from an ancient trade route for silk, spices, and other goods linking China with the eastern Mediterranean.

toms, your national and cultural institutions are declared free and inviolable. Build your national life freely and without hindrance. It is your right. Know that your rights — like those of all the peoples of Russia — are defended by the full force of the revolution and its organs, the soviets of workers', soldiers', and peasants' deputies.

And a few years later, at the 1920 Baku Congress of the Peoples of the East, leaders of the Communist International joined with other revolutionary fighters — from inside the borders of the old tsarist empire and beyond — in calling on all Muslim toilers in the region to join in a "holy war for the liberation of all humanity from the yoke of capitalist and imperialist slavery, for the ending of all forms of oppression of one people by another and of all forms of exploitation of man by man!"[26]

Three quarters of a century later, we can confidently assert that for communist workers in the United States, Europe, and elsewhere, reaffirming this clear pledge to oppressed and exploited toilers who may be Muslim, or who hail from parts of the world that are predominantly Muslim, is not a remote or external matter.

It comes directly into the fight against imperialist war in Europe.

It comes directly into the fight by the workers and peasants of Russia to defend the political space they carved out with the collapse of the Stalinist apparatus there.

It comes directly into the fight for democratic rights in the United States, where federal prosecutors will soon begin the first open sedition trial in many decades, this time against an Islamic cleric from Egypt and ten other defendants — a frame-up trial built around agents provocateurs.[27]

---

26. Both documents are contained in *To See the Dawn: Baku 1920, First Congress of the Peoples of the East* (New York: Pathfinder, 1993). See pages 251 and 231–32.

27. In 1995 Sheik Omar Abdel Rahman and nine others were convicted in a federal court of violating a Civil War–era seditious conspiracy statute. The prosecution case, linking them to the 1994 World Trade Center bombing, rested on testimony by an informer who admitted in court that he had lied

Communists and other class-struggle-minded workers combat every vestige of imperial arrogance and prejudice. We approach fellow toilers as equals who — through experience combating oppression and exploitation, and irrespective of beliefs they start out with — can be won to a scientific world outlook and communist organization. This conviction is a touchstone for those building a proletarian party and world movement.

Historic transformation in China

The massive migrations of toilers that are strengthening and internationalizing our class also include flows of labor *within* national boundaries.

In China the rapid and massive transformation of the toiling classes that is under way right now dwarfs anything that has happened since the early days of the industrial revolution in Europe. The Stalinist apparatus of the parasitic caste in China cannot and will not escape the fate of those from Belgrade and Budapest to Berlin and Moscow. But the pace and forms of such a crisis in China can be expected to be different, for reasons related to this historic transformation.

In the Soviet Union, the Stalinist regime exhausted its potential several decades ago to accelerate economic growth and raise labor productivity by opening up new lands to cultivation and

---

under oath and had received more than $1 million from the FBI. The defendants were not convicted of carrying out a criminal act, but of conspiring "to overthrow, or put down, or destroy by force the government of the United States." Rahman and one other defendant were sentenced to life in prison; eight others received from twenty-five to fifty-seven years.

drawing peasants in large numbers out of the countryside into mining, oil extraction, and industrial production. A similar pattern holds true for the deformed and degenerated workers states of Eastern Europe, despite their varying histories and class structures. Only in Albania is more than 50 percent of the labor force engaged in agriculture. Elsewhere the percentage is less than a third of the labor force, usually far less.

In China, on the other hand, nearly three-quarters of the population still live in the countryside, and more than 90 percent did so as recently as the opening of the 1980s. So it is still possible in China to draw toilers off the land into the cities and industry on a large scale, raising the productivity of labor in this way.

Central to the industrialization of every modern nation is a transformation of relations between town and country, such that labor power is pulled into the factories. Capitalism has a very brutal way of doing this. Peasants' land is taken away from them. Their fields are fenced in and turned into grazing lands for herds of cattle and flocks of sheep owned by capitalist farmers. They lose traditional rights to the use of common lands, to forage for firewood, to hunt and fish. This process is accelerating in parts of Mexico today and lies behind the Chiapas resistance, for example.

Marx provides a good summary of how this happened in Britain, in the closing part of volume 1 of *Capital*. He chose chapter titles like "The expropriation of the agricultural population from the land," "Bloody legislation against the expropriated," "The genesis of the capitalist farmer," and "The genesis of the industrial capitalist."

But doesn't China's class structure, then, make it much more like many other countries in the Third World, which also have huge reserve armies of labor in the countryside? The answer is no. That would be to ignore the central fact of history and the class struggle in China in this century: the revolution of 1949.

Coming out of World War II, China — above every country in the world — had been the apple of the eye of U.S. imperialism. In the wake of the Chinese revolution, an incipient fascist movement in the United States, spearheaded by Senator Joseph Mc-Carthy and then-U.S. congressman Richard Nixon, began agitating around the question: "Who lost China?" But it was the wrong question. No one lost China. The Chinese *took* it — that was the real answer.

Through the Chinese revolution, the workers and peasants eliminated imperialist pillage and expropriated the emerging capitalist class in both agriculture and industry. These conquests made possible China's centralization as a modern nation, with a massive network of production and distribution that operates to a significant degree on a national scale. This is true despite all the distortions from forced collectivization of agriculture and Stalinist methods of economic planning and management of industry.

India is similar to China in many ways — not the least in its size, some 900 million people compared to China's 1.2 billion. More than 70 percent of the population of India lives in rural areas. Both countries experienced centuries of colonial domination and superexploitation (even if China maintained its formal independence through most of that period).

But India never had a socialist revolution. And that is a big difference. There will undoubtedly be a large expansion of both imperialist and domestic capital in India over the coming decade. But the capitalists will confront the fact that India has still never truly been formed as a modern, centralized nation-state with a unified national market. Commodities sell at completely different prices from one region of the country to the next. Products are taxed as they are transported internally across state borders, as they were prior to the bourgeois revolutions in France, Germany, and elsewhere in Europe in the eighteenth and nineteenth centuries. India is still saddled with this legacy of precapitalist society and colonial exploitation that in China has been largely overcome through a massive workers and peasants revolution.

The manifestations of this class difference between China and India are tangible and dramatic. To this day, life expectancy in China is about ten years longer than in India; infant mortality is a third lower than in India; and the illiteracy rate in India is twice that in China.[28]

That is the framework in which to look at the gigantic migration from the countryside to the cities that is unfolding in China. As the regime has reorganized agricultural production over the past fifteen years, dismantling the giant collective farms forcibly imposed on peasants during the revolution's first decade, tens of millions of rural toilers are being pushed off the land year in and year out.

A friend from Minnesota recently sent me an article that first appeared in the *Baltimore Sun* and then in the *Minneapolis Star Tribune.* It reports that the percentage of China's population living in rural areas has declined by 20 percent just in the past fifteen years — that is, a shift of some 200 million people. Almost as large as the entire population of the United States!

Some 80 million of these former peasants, the article says, have migrated to big cities, especially along the coast, where many live in wretched conditions. In search of a livelihood, millions of toilers from the countryside in China continue to head toward the cities, to head toward the small towns, to head toward the factories and manufacturing establishments large and small.[29] What is happening to them is comparable in many ways to what happened to those pushed off the land in England several hundred years ago, described by Marx.

Because of the Stalinist "population policies" imposed in China, working people there are required to carry ID cards and are supposed to seek permission before moving. As a result, the

28. In a November 1995 commentary on China and India, three economists for Wall Street's Merrill Lynch investment house wrote that "during the past quarter-century, China's economy has grown considerably faster than India's, on average — roughly 8% a year vs. 4.5%. . . . Internally, China has built a more extensive infrastructure than India [and] has a healthier and better-educated workforce than India."

29. The estimated number of migrants reached 100 million by late 1998.

article reports that many of the rural toilers who have migrated to urban areas are denied legal residence in the cities and thus are not able to send their children to school or to use public health facilities. (These reactionary population measures also include forced sterilization and abortions, as well as economic and other penalties against families with more than one child.)

Horrible living and working conditions are being created in the swelling proletarian neighborhoods and in both the huge state-owned enterprises and rapidly expanding capitalist-owned factories in China today. Workers face low wages, extremely long hours, and often appalling health and safety conditions.

Because of the socialist revolution, however, workers and peasants in China have a different view of themselves, of what they are capable of, and of their social rights earned as part of the working class. Toilers in China have a different attitude toward their right to land; their right to a job; their right to a certain level of education and health care; their right to a place to live at a payable rent; their right to jobless benefits and a retirement pension.

This is what the imperialists confront in attempting to restore the dominance of capitalist social relations. This is not the China whose land, resources, and cheap labor the U.S. rulers lusted for coming out of their victory over Japan at the end of World War II. The U.S., Japanese, Taiwanese, Hong Kong, and other capitalists setting up shop in China today — as well as the expanding capitalist layers and wannabe capitalists within China's dominant social caste — are already meeting resistance from workers and peasants. As these class battles develop, we will see in practice why the socialist revolution in China and the fact that a workers state still exists — no matter how horribly deformed — remains the key to politics there.

Clashes are also bound to sharpen *inside* the Stalinist bureaucracy in China, which still dominates the country to a greater degree than in the Soviet Union and Eastern Europe, where these apparatuses have shattered since 1990. Big sections of the bureaucratic caste in China, including in the armed forces officer corps, are determined to maintain centralization and control over the departments and state enterprises from which they derive their power and privileges. This brings them into conflict not only with workers in these enterprises, but also with other sections of the bureaucracy trying to open up China more to capitalist relations and foreign investment.

Giant struggles are coming in China. And given the massive urban migrations, the coming history of the countryside there will be settled more than ever by what happens in the cities, not vice versa.

For communists, it will be a great pleasure to be part of the changes that hundreds of millions of Chinese workers on the march will bring to the world working-class movement.

The United Kingdom, devolution, and Ireland

Let's look at a final example of the contradictions between the internationalization of capital and the national borders and institutions that still divide the imperialist world — the United Kingdom. The uneven development of capitalism there, and the forms it inherits from previous periods of class society, are being thrust forward into politics in new ways by the crisis of the world imperialist system.

The weekend edition of the *Financial Times* of London, which came out today, carries a front-page headline, "Blair signals start of devolution battle and Lords' reform." Tony Blair is the recently elected head of the Labour Party. All the big-business press there says he is a new kind of Labour leader — one who does not even pretend very hard to be leading labor. Well, that may not be totally new, but it is certainly accurate.

Blair has presented two of the issues Labour intends to campaign on in its efforts to win the next parliamentary elections in Britain. The first is what is referred to there as devolution. Blair proposes to grant elected parliaments to both Scotland and Wales. Second, he proposes, according to the *Financial Times*, to "reform the House of Lords and trim the monarchy."[30]

On first blush, it might seem that Blair and other Labour Party leaders must be off their rockers. Given everything going on in politics in Britain and elsewhere, are these really among the issues that one of the two major bourgeois parties is picking to

30. In May 1997 the Labour Party won the parliamentary elections in the United Kingdom by a wide margin, registering the failure of the rulers to convince working people to accept British capital's demands for greater sacrifice in return for the will-o'-the-wisp of greater prosperity sometime in the future. Workers in Britain celebrated Labour's electoral victory as a break from nearly two decades of the anti-working-class, union-busting policies of the previous Conservative (Tory) Party governments of Margaret Thatcher and John Major.

In his first several months as prime minister, however, Blair made good on his pledge to the employing class that "New Labour" would not diverge fundamentally from the Tories' course in cutting the social wage won by working people, eroding union power, and defending the interests of declining British imperialism. Blair's initial budget proposal to Parliament shifted taxation even further onto the backs of working people; launched a "Welfare-to-Work" program forcing workers to either accept low-wage, menial jobs or lose their benefits; and included no mention of the modest minimum wage legislation included in Labour's election platform.

At the same time, Blair did press legislation through Parliament in 1997 setting a referendum in Scotland on establishing an elected parliament with devolved powers over schools, health, transportation, the courts, and police, as well as in Wales on an elected assembly with more limited powers. Both proposals received majorities; and elections are set for 1999. The demand among growing numbers in Scotland, and to a lesser degree Wales, for independence was not on the ballot. In January 1999, Blair also announced initial plans for a "constitutional reform" to take away voting rights in the House of Lords from its hereditary members.

start with? But if we stop and think about it for a moment, this makes perfect sense. What the central issues end up being when an election is actually called is a different matter, of course, but it's worth taking Blair at his word in order to see what lies beneath it.

Blair's statements are another reflection of the world picture we have been discussing. Think about Canada, for example, and the incapacity of the capitalist rulers there, despite all their efforts over decades, to put a lid on resistance to national oppression and demands for independence by the French-speaking majority in Quebec.[31] As the pressures of a world capitalist depression build up, bourgeois governments and ruling parties find it more difficult than ever to contain the aspirations of oppressed nationalities, remnants of national groupings, or economically backward regions. Under such pressures, borders and institutions patched together by the propertied ruling classes decades or even centuries ago, and imposed on peoples against their will, begin coming unstuck.

That is why we have said in recent years that we should stop using the terms "England" or "Britain" when, in reality, we are referring to the "United Kingdom." The United Kingdom was established almost 200 years ago, in 1801, when, under the so-

31. Tens of thousands of Quebecois working people and youth joined in rallies and took to the streets in 1995 in support of a "yes" vote on a Quebec sovereignty referendum. Expressing growing proindependence views, one of the most popular chants was "We want a country!" The "yes" position received more than 49 percent of the ballots cast, and 60 percent of those cast by members of the oppressed Quebecois nationality. A similar referendum fifteen years earlier received a 42 percent "yes" vote, including 46 percent of the ballots cast by Quebecois.

In late 1998 Canada's rulers suffered another setback to their hopes of "settling" the question of Quebec independence. In the November 30 elections that year, the campaign orchestrated by Ottawa failed to defeat the provincial government of the Parti Quebecois, a bourgeois party that combines support for sovereignty with assaults on the rights and living standards of workers and farmers in Quebec.

called Act of Union, the English Parliament and Crown abolished even the semblance of a separate parliament in Ireland. Wales had already been incorporated into England for hundreds of years through military conquest, and the English rulers had imposed an earlier Act of Union on Scotland in 1707. Scotland retained its own legal system and schools, as well as its own state church (Presbyterian), whose head is the Queen when she steps across the border into Scottish territory.

So there is more to Her Majesty's realm than just pomp and symbol. The United Kingdom is the form of the bourgeois state — today, of the imperialist state power — with its seat in London. That is why the issue of "reforming" and "trimming" the monarchy and the House of Lords can and does emerge as an issue in bourgeois politics. It is not just a matter of pruning the state budget. The stakes are bigger.

In a capitalist state that takes the form of a constitutional monarchy, as economic and social crises deepen, the crowned head of state remains important. It becomes one of the few institutions that can "speak for the entire nation." In a bourgeois republic without a monarchy, the president often assumes Bonapartist powers and authority under such conditions. But in a constitutional monarchy, remnants of feudalism preserved by the bourgeoisie with few intrinsic vested powers — the Crown, as well as an unelected House of Lords — grow rather than diminish in their importance for maintaining stability amid the increasing brutality of capitalist life and rule.

The Canadian bourgeoisie keeps trying and failing to write a constitution. Most major bourgeois politicians in Canada have not yet challenged Queen Elizabeth as head of state — although that will happen too (as it already has among bourgeois politicians in Australia).[32] But Canada's bourgeois rulers have tried

---

32. Former Australian Labor Party prime minister Paul Keating campaigned in the 1996 elections to abolish the constitutional monarchy and establish a republic. The Labor government was defeated at the polls by the Liberal Party,

twice over the past decade to write a new constitution and failed both times.

Canada never had a successful bourgeois revolution, so it never had a real bourgeois constitution. But it is too late in history now. No constitution can be drafted for Canada that will satisfy the demands of French-speaking workers, farmers, and youth in Quebec for their unconditional right to national self-determination. No constitution can be drafted that will satisfy the demands of oppressed Native peoples. Nor can a constitution even be drafted that will resolve conflicts among capitalist interests in Canada who have greater or lesser amounts of capital at stake in various regions and provinces of the country. It is too late in history for that.

Many of us in the United States do not even know there is still a monarchy in Sweden. But now we'll start finding out. With the demise in recent years of "the Swedish miracle," the economic and social conditions of working people there are beginning to undergo qualitative changes like nothing they have lived through since World War I. With less leeway to grant concessions, the officialdom of the Social Democratic Party and trade unions needs additional help in the effort to become more effective tools for the bourgeoisie in Sweden in maintaining capitalist stability. So, we will begin seeing prominent capitalists there, too, trying to use the Swedish monarchy "to speak for the nation."

Under the same kinds of pressures in the United Kingdom, the bourgeoisie has begun to divide. Blair is speaking on behalf of those who think they have to present some answer to growing nationalist agitation in Scotland, fueled by regional disparities

---

whose leader, John Howard, opposes the constitutional change. Faced with ongoing pressures around this issue, including among most leading members of his own government, Prime Minister Howard in early 1997 called for a delegated "people's convention" later in the year to debate the question. That convention, held in February 1998, voted overwhelmingly to hold a referendum on the republic, and in December 1998 the Howard government announced that the vote would be scheduled for late 1999.

and inequalities that have widened in the depression conditions gripping the United Kingdom. That is why, off and on, there is even pressure around the issue of devolution for Wales, where the rapid decline of the capitalist coal industry has brought economic devastation and increased nationalist sentiment among tenant farmers and industrial workers.

According to the *Financial Times* article I cited earlier, Tory prime minister John Major responded that Blair's devolution proposal is "one of the most dangerous propositions ever put before the British nation. . . . It is done for short-term political advantage to the Labour party because they are seeking to cash in on the innate pride in being Scottish that the Scots feel, and they have given no thought whatsoever to the future unity of the UK" — that is, the United, or not-so-United, Kingdom. Major acknowledged that British capitalism is having "a bumpy ride."

What I found most striking of all about the *Financial Times* article, however, is that one word never appears anywhere in it — *Ireland.* Blair didn't have a single word to say about the most intractable and explosive of all the unresolved national questions in the United Kingdom. The Irish battle against English tyranny, of course, is centuries old. In the modern class struggle it goes back to the earliest days of the rising English bourgeoisie. The seeds of the current conflict were sown by the forcible and bloody partition of Ireland in 1920. Today's Irish Republic had been established that year following a national-democratic revolution, but bourgeois forces in the Republican movement acquiesced in Britain's retention of the Six Counties of Northern Ireland.

Ever since, the Catholic population in the North has been kept in a caste-like oppression, ghettoized and facing official and unofficial brutalization at every turn. The ruling layers among the majority Protestant oppressor population retain a separate educational system, courts, and cops — the notorious Royal Ulster Constabulary. And they had a nominal parliament, too, the Stormont, until 1972, when London asserted direct rule in the wake of a new rise of Irish Republican resistance. British troops have occupied Northern Ireland for a quarter of a century, since 1969, carrying out martial-law repression against the rebellious Catholic population.

Blair may have little to say about Ireland right now. But resistance in Belfast and Derry will prove no more yielding to a future government with him at the helm than it has been to current and prior regimes, whether Tory or Labour. In fact, London's weakness in face of its failure to force Irish toilers down on their knees accounts for Major's inability to take any initiatives in response to the Irish Republican Army's announcement of a cease-fire four months ago and Sinn Fein's repeated offers to begin negotiations.[33]

So, if you take Westminster's problems in Ireland, Scotland, and Wales, and then you add in the historic decline of the British

33. Both Major and Blair failed in their efforts to block Sinn Fein from negotiations until the Irish Republican Army "decommissioned" its weapons. A turning point in pressing London to change course came in July 1997, as nationalist forces in Northern Ireland organized militant mass protests and erected barricades following Blair's decision to protect a march through a Catholic neighborhood by the rightist Orange Order, forcing the reactionaries to back down and reroute their provocative parades the following weekend. In face of its inability to break the resistance of the Irish Catholic population, the British government in April 1998 signed an agreement with the Republic of Ireland and a broad range of political parties in the northern six counties, including Sinn Fein.

In May 1998 that agreement was approved in a referendum by substantial majorities both in the Irish republic and British-occupied counties. A 108-member Northern Ireland assembly was elected in June (Unionist parties won 58 seats; Sinn Fein won 18 seats; the Social Democratic and Labour Party, a reformist party based in the oppressed Catholic population, won 24 seats; and other parties won 8).

As of the end of 1998 London, in collusion with Unionist forces, was stalling on implementation of central aspects of the accord. Meanwhile, Irish Republicans continued using the political space they had conquered to mobilize around demands for the complete withdrawal of British troops (tens of thousands still occupy the six counties); the lifting of all repressive legislation and release of all political prisoners; and affirmative-action measures to redress the discrimination faced by the Catholic population in all aspects of social and political life.

pound and the state of world capitalism, you begin to see the strains pulling at the seams of the United Kingdom — seams that could begin to rip with a new rise in labor struggles and sustained social mobilizations, and the capitalists' inevitable need for tightened not loosened state centralization.

The historic forced retreat of the United Kingdom from acting as an effective world power continues.

❖

Class-conscious workers need to be able to recognize that all the things we have been discussing so far are not isolated events, as they are normally presented.

The collapse of the peso in Mexico. The destabilizing effects this is already having in Argentina. A municipal bond default in California. The transformation of the working class in France and its relationship to the civil war in Algeria and to the growth of French rightist forces. The first war in Europe since 1945 breaking out in the Balkans, in which Belgrade and its allied terror squads in Bosnia portray themselves as crusaders against "Islamic fundamentalism." A brutal war launched by Yeltsin against the people of Chechnya and the support he is winning from Clinton to Buchanan to Zhirinovsky. A massive migration from countryside to city in China, transforming the class composition of the toilers more rapidly than any time since the Industrial Revolution. The fight for equality and national independence by the Quebecois, by the Irish; growing national aspirations among the Scots and the Welsh.

What ties all these developments together is the instability and growing deflationary pressures that mark the entire world capitalist system.

What ties them together are the inevitable workings of the law of value.

What ties them together is the degree to which the most economically advanced capitalist powers — through the internationalization of flows of both capital and labor — increasingly spread their tentacles into every powder keg around the world.

What ties them together are the ways in which this explosive mixture combines contradictions from the most modern forms of capitalist production and exploitation with those unresolved over centuries, even millennia, of class society.

And teetering on top of it all is the final dominant imperialist power in history — with a reach and a currency too weak to shoulder the burden, but too strong to be replaced by an imperialist rival. And with national borders more needed than ever, but more porous with each passing day.

The last dominant imperial power; the last international reserve currency — both find it harder and harder to maintain a firm footing in today's world. That is what the U.S. rulers face. And it is all to our advantage.

The world war they could not launch: The 'Cold War' they lost

When the Stalinist apparatuses began falling like dominoes in 1989–90, most bourgeois politicians and commentators announced that "the West," or "the United States," or "democratic capitalism" — they were all supposed to mean roughly the same thing — had "won the Cold War." Then, in 1990–91, when Washington cobbled together an unstable international coalition as cover for a war to impose an imperialist protectorate on Iraq, the U.S. rulers went even further; they proclaimed a New World Order — briefly.

As time passes, we hear less and less of such triumphalist language. The coalition assembled for the murderous assault on Iraq shattered the moment the fighting ended. The principal players have been sharply divided over the war in the Balkans. Washington will never be able to put such a coalition back together again.

The yellow brick road to the restoration of a stable capitalism in the former Soviet Union and Eastern European countries has vanished, too. Experience has shattered the illusion that the breakup of the old Russian empire rebuilt by Stalin and his heirs could produce in those regions a durable balance of forces advantageous to imperialism.

We can already see the fault lines along which Washington's hoped-for political stabilization in Russia could rapidly fracture. To wage war against the Chechens, Yeltsin has to reinforce the Bonapartist character of the regime. He has to advance more and more demagogic rationalizations for further centralization of executive power. He has had to reach out more openly to Great Russian ultrarightists and fascists such as Vladimir Zhirinovsky. As sections of the armed forces at first turned their guns aside and refused to fire on Chechen civilians, we could see the prospect of future clashes between the army and the palace guard built around the secret police and special elite units. Just think for a minute about the conclusions working people throughout Russia and the former Soviet Union must draw from what has been revealed about Moscow's armed forces as they have tried to take Chechnya.

Despite all the problems the capitalist rulers face, however, isn't it still true that Washington won the Cold War? That is the question we keep running into, voiced in many different ways, including among fighters who try to think and act as communists in the world. Yes, there is no New World Order around the corner, many people now acknowledge. Yes, it is proving much more difficult than anticipated to integrate the fragmented Soviet and Eastern European workers states into the capitalist system. But didn't imperialism still come out on top in the Cold War? That is the myth that holds on the longest.

But a myth it is, nonetheless. And to dispel it, it is useful to remind ourselves what the Cold War was all about to begin with. The

Cold War was not a clever strategy to win a war. The Cold War was the term used by the U.S. rulers to put a good face on what they were reduced to by the mid-1950s, once they had shelved the hot war they could not fight and did not think they could win.

We should remember that the term Cold War was not a common one in the first years after World War II. U.S. imperialism came out of that war fully intending to use whatever military might was necessary to maintain and consolidate what it had won. Having successfully completed the "trial run" of the atomic bomb against the peoples of Hiroshima and Nagasaki, the U.S. rulers planned to keep their armed forces strong in Asia. They intended to block the Chinese revolution and establish U.S. dominance in the Pacific region over the weaker and retreating British, French, and Dutch colonial powers. The U.S. government was also preparing to finish the job German imperialism had failed to achieve — the big task of overturning the gains of the Bolshevik revolution, initially by at least preventing the spread of Soviet property forms anywhere else in the world.

Washington and its allies were marching toward a third world war. Our movement was deeply convinced of that. We campaigned against the imperialist war drive in the *Militant*, in the unions, and through our election campaigns. And we were right. We were not exaggerating. What's more, that march toward war — plus the war economy, restrictions on democratic rights, and the "national security state" put together under the liberal administration of President Harry Truman — put wind in the sails of an incipient fascist movement associated with Senator Joseph McCarthy of Wisconsin. The militarization drive strengthened Bonapartist currents and other reactionary forces in the U.S. government, two-party system, and armed forces officer corps.

World War II: three wars in one

By 1953, however, it had become clear to the U.S. rulers that much of what they had fought World War II to win — and initially thought they *had* won — had not in fact been achieved. We often read that the United States "won" World War II. But that is not quite accurate, because what is commonly called World War II was actually at least three wars in one.

World War II was a war among rival imperialist powers to redivide the world. In that war, the U.S. ruling class triumphed over the capitalist rulers in Tokyo and Berlin who led the Axis powers — and over its own "allies" as well. That's a fact, and one with very important economic, political, and military consequences we continue to live with. That victory set up the fundamental relationship between the U.S. capitalist rulers and their rivals in Europe and Japan that still shapes world politics half a century later.

Intertwined with those interimperialist conflicts, World War II also became a war by the imperialist powers to overturn the Soviet workers state, drown the toilers in blood, and block any extension of the socialist revolution. From June 1941 the workers and peasants of the Soviet Union — at a staggering cost in deaths and destruction of material resources — fought to turn back the invasion by German imperialism. Washington and the capitalist Allied powers hoped to defeat their Axis rivals, while weakening the Soviet Union to such an extent that it too would go under — if not in the process, then soon afterwards. But that was not what happened. The imperialists lost that war. Not only did the USSR survive the onslaught. Even more importantly, in the aftermath of that colossal fact, capitalist social relations were overturned during the postwar years in Yugoslavia, Albania, and across Eastern Europe; in China, Korea, and Vietnam; and then, a decade later, in Washington's "own backyard," Cuba. The working class was the winner in that second aspect of the war.

World War II had a third aspect as well — it was a war by the colonial peoples against their imperialist overlords, of both the fascist and "democratic" stripes. That war, actually, was already under way by the mid-1930s, with the resistance of the Ethiopian people against occupation by fascist Italy, and of the Chinese and Korean toilers against Japanese imperialist occupation. The colonial peoples then took advantage of the wider war — the falling out among imperialist bandits — to begin shoving out all the oppressing powers. In the course of the war and the years following it, countries throughout Asia, the Pacific, Africa, the Middle East, and the Caribbean won their independence not only from German, Japanese, and Italian domination but also from British, French, Dutch, Belgian, and U.S. — yes, U.S. — colonial rule.

This struggle by workers and peasants to free themselves from colonial bondage went much further in China, in Vietnam, and in Korea than the imperialists ever dreamt it could go. And that example of socialist revolution was then picked up in Algeria and Cuba and began inspiring revolutionists throughout North Africa and the Americas.

Wall Street and Washington recognized the embryo of these defeats even as they were celebrating the "American Century" they had proclaimed at the outset of U.S. entry into World War II. No serious bourgeois political figure in the United States or any other imperialist country had any illusion between 1946 and 1950 that capitalism could be defended and spread throughout the world by peaceful means. The Chinese workers and peasants had to be stopped by force. The Korean and Vietnamese toilers had to be dealt with. The Soviet Union had not only to be contained but eventually the revolutionary conquests had to be rolled back and overturned. And the pushy colonial masses had to be taught some respect; they had to be taught to accept the exploitation and oppression necessary to the fortunes of capitalism.

Drive toward a third world war fails

But the U.S. rulers began bumping into obstacles as they wrapped up their last war and prepared for the next. Beginning in 1943 — right in the middle of the great patriotic war itself — the U.S. capitalists bumped into the labor movement at home. First, the coal miners said, "We won't go into unsafe mines anymore. We don't care about your wage freeze and so-called price controls. We won't live with shrinking paychecks any longer." And they went on strike. The government responded by ordering the miners back to work and saying it would take over the mines if the strikers didn't cave. "You can't mine coal with bayonets!" the miners shot back, and they won.

The miners' victory spurred other labor battles in the closing years of the war. These included increased determination by workers who were Black to combat job discrimination in the war industries and against Jim Crow segregation in the armed forces itself. And in 1945–46, as the war came to an end, the biggest strike wave swept the United States since the battles that built the industrial unions a decade earlier.

The Yankees also ran into obstacles among U.S. workers and farmers in uniform — American GIs. Several months after the war ended in early September 1945, tens of thousands of soldiers and sailors in the Philippines, Korea, China, and elsewhere in the Pacific still had no discharge dates. So they began to march, rally, and circulate petitions demanding to be brought home. They said, "Enough of the war! We were told we were fighting so the people of China could do as they choose. We're not going to be used now to fight a war against them." A "going home" movement spread throughout the region, as well as in France among GIs who Washington sought to maintain as a bridgehead against revolutionary developments in Europe. You can read the chronicle of this truly inspiring and hidden chapter in the U.S. class struggle in the article by Mary-Alice Waters entitled "1945: When U.S. Troops Said 'No!'" in *New International* no. 7.

To have launched a war so soon after World War II, the U.S. rulers would have had to fight their way through the working class and deal it some stunning blows. And that they were unable to do. The strike wave subsided by 1947, and the bosses launched a witch-hunting drive to divide the union ranks and undermine labor solidarity and combativity. But the rulers failed to crush the labor movement or stop the reemergence of the Black struggle. The working class was weakened but not defeated.

When the U.S. government launched the Korean War in 1950, it met with little enthusiasm among workers and farmers in the United States, including those drafted to fight; it never became a popular war.

Some of us are from a generation that remembers the Vietnam War and the movement against it quite well. But we should never forget that the U.S. rulers were dealt their first terrible defeat not in Vietnam but in Korea. They went into that war in 1950 to teach a lesson to the toilers not only of Korea, but to others anywhere in the world who challenged imperialist domination and capitalist exploitation. The U.S. rulers went into Korea to reverse the revolutionary struggle by workers and peasants that had already ripped the northern part of that country out of the capitalist sphere. And they went into Korea to begin the showdown with China's workers and peasants, aiming to find a pretext to push beyond the Yalu River and at least punish if not crush the revolution that had swept to victory in 1949.

Instead, by 1953 the U.S. rulers and their allies — waging war, for the first but not the last time, under cover of a United Nations "peacekeeping" operation — had been defeated. They were fought to a draw by the Korean toilers and Chinese Red Army who came to their aid. Moreover, the mobilizations by working people in China to defend the revolution in face of imperialist threats culminated in the expropriation of the last big capitalists in the cities and brought a workers state into being.

Communists at that time assessed this turning point in a series of articles published in the *Militant* newspaper between late August and the end of October 1953. Socialist Workers Party leader Joseph Hansen wrote:

> The Korean war appeared to give American Big Business the final clinchers in its war preparations: an excuse to convert a huge sector of the economy into war production, an excuse to vastly expand the armed forces and stockpiles of armaments, an excuse to get into a conflict which had every prospect of expanding into a general conflict in which the Soviet Union would be sucked in.
>
> Above all, it seemed to be the perfect means for finally convincing the American people about the justice and inevitability of war with the Soviet Union.
>
> But this war, which appeared to offer such a favorable open-

ing for carrying out the plans of American Big Business, turned into its opposite.

The fighting capacity of the North Koreans shocked America's rulers. And when the Chinese Armies took up the challenge that Gen. [Douglas] MacArthur flung at the Yalu river, it quickly became apparent that Wall Street had taken on far more than it bargained for. Truman's 'police action' turned into a war of completely unexpected scope. . . .

Korea turned out to be the most unpopular war in American history. This is admitted by every serious observer. It became a key issue in American politics. It helped bring a landslide defeat to the Democratic Party [in the 1952 presidential elections]. . . .

The popular opposition to the war in Korea is a tremendous new fact in American politics.

Concluding the series, Hansen warned that interpreting the U.S. rulers' postponement of war "as the opening of a prolonged period of peace would prove fatal. The task is to take advantage of the difficulties Wall Street faces in plunging our planet into another war. That means utilizing the breathing space to fight for the establishment of a Workers and Farmers Government in the United States. There is no other way to win enduring peace."

In addition to the U.S. defeat in Korea, 1953 was also the year the Soviet government announced it had developed and tested its own hydrogen bomb. In the United States, the McCarthy movement peaked in early 1954, as leading figures in both capitalist parties joined in slapping down the aspiring fascist demagogue when he attempted to extend the witch-hunt into the top brass of the U.S. Army. With the restabilization of world capitalism, the kind of depression conditions in the United States that would have fueled the development of a strong fascist movement did not come about. The accelerated capitalist expansion spread during the 1950s from North America to Europe and then Japan, continuing for some two decades.

So, by the mid-1950s it had become clear to the U.S. rulers that the war they really wanted — one that could accomplish what they failed to settle in World War II — had to be postponed. It was then that they reconceived and repackaged their foreign policy course as the Cold War. That became the name for everything they had to do because they could not do what they needed and planned to do. But the truth is, there never was a Cold *War*. Everybody knows a war cannot be won "coldly." The U.S. imperialist rulers, of all people, know this! They have butchered millions in pursuit of their class interests over the past century.

There *were* some real hot wars, like Korea and Vietnam, both of them lost by Yankee imperialism.

The U.S. and other imperialist powers used military force — real "hot" force — to try to stop colonial rebellions in Malaya, Indonesia, Algeria, the Congo, the Dominican Republic, the Middle East, Angola and Mozambique, and many other parts of the world.

There was a socialist revolution in Cuba. And Washington brought the world to the brink of nuclear war in the early 1960s before it became convinced that the communist-led workers and farmers would not lose their nerve and were determined to make the Yankee government pay an enormous military and political price for an invasion. That price stays the hand of the U.S. rulers to this day.

Washington built a counterrevolutionary army — the "contras" — in the 1980s that tried and failed to crush the Nicaraguan revolution in what threatened at several points to become a Central America–wide war. While the contras lost that war, the toll was devastating. Unlike the Cuban leadership under Fidel Castro, the leadership of Nicaragua's Sandinista National Liberation Front lost its nerve and shifted course. By the closing years of the 1980s the workers and peasants government had fallen. Anticapitalist revolutions have also been turned back and defeated in Algeria and Grenada in the years since World War II.

These were all hard-fought class conflicts, not manifestations of a so-called Cold War.

Decline of Stalinist apparatuses

Presenting this history accurately is important, because it is the opposite of how the "Cold War" is almost universally portrayed in the press, in the schools, and by capitalist politicians. When the Berlin Wall fell at the end of 1989, they assert, everything "the democracies" sought to achieve coming out of World War II suddenly became possible in the not-too-distant future.

This is all nonsense. But our movement was virtually alone in the world when we said, right from the start, "No, U.S. imperialism *lost* the Cold War." That was at the heart of the resolution we discussed and adopted at the 1990 SWP convention.[34]

By the mid-1950s the U.S. rulers had been pushed back to the point where they were reduced to relying on some force other than their own military might to help them accomplish their goals. They had to rely on something else to keep the workers in Russia and in the Soviet bloc under control, to drive them off the stage of world politics. They had to rely on some other force to promote bourgeois values and social norms that would weaken the workers states. And that force was the privileged social caste in the Soviet Union, with its massive entrenched apparatus, police-state control, and the international extensions of that bureaucratic machine through the world Stalinist movement.

Washington counted on Moscow to put the arm on the Stalinist regime in Beijing, in order to contain the international impact of the Chinese revolution. U.S. imperialism counted on Moscow to use its international apparatus and its cash to diminish the attraction of revolutionary-minded workers and youth to the example set by the Cuban revolution in the Americas and throughout the world.

"Washington versus Moscow" — the phrase permeated bourgeois propaganda for so long during the so-called Cold War that it can blur our vision. We need to keep two opposite things clearly in focus.

---

34. See "U.S. Imperialism Has Lost the Cold War," by Jack Barnes, in *New International* no. 11.

There *is* a fundamental conflict between world capitalism and the Soviet workers state. Washington built a massive strategic nuclear arsenal and conventional armed forces with the aim of blocking any extension of the socialist revolution and eventually crushing the Soviet Union by military might. The historic contradiction between imperialism and the conquests of the October 1917 revolution remains unresolved.

But that historic class conflict is not the same thing as "Washington versus Moscow." To the contrary, the U.S. ruling class maintained the hope that, in all the above ways, the "Cold War" could wear down the working class and weaken the workers states enough to make it possible over time to move in for the kill. But they failed.

The bureaucratic caste was not an adequate surrogate. It had contradictory, not identical, interests to those of the imperialists. Most important, it could not defeat the working class in the workers states. With brute force the caste held the working class down, but, at the same time, it parasitically derived its privileges and power from the social conquest of the working class — the workers state itself.

The Stalinist regime in Moscow, moreover, could not permanently limit the degree to which the colonial peoples encroached on the prerogatives of capital. Regardless of setbacks, the colonial toilers were becoming more proletarian and more politically experienced.

Unable to weather the combined effects of the growing crisis of world capitalism and the hatred of millions of working people excluded from political life by the bureaucracy for decades, these regimes finally disintegrated. And now imperialism, in a much weakened position compared to half a century ago, finds itself still confronting the working classes in these horribly degenerated workers states, as well as the communist-led socialist revolution in Cuba — but without the ability to rely on the massive counterrevolutionary apparatus of Stalinism as a buffer against uncontrolled forces in the world class struggle.

Communists have known all along that the bureaucratic castes were not a new class; they fulfill no historically necessary function in production in the workers states. We knew that the despotic regimes based on these petty-bourgeois layers were brittle and that because of their parasitic character they were bound to fall long before history had settled the struggle for socialism.

For many years, nonetheless, we anticipated that the Stalinist regimes would fall in the course of a political revolution by the working class. But by the mid-1950s if not before, what remained of the proletarian vanguard had been decimated and demoralized by the combined terror and corruption of Stalin and his cohorts. The political continuity of communism in the Soviet republics had been broken. The working class had been isolated from revolutionary fighters around the world. Under these circumstances, it had become highly likely that the shattering of the castes would occur more rapidly than the reemergence of conditions for a political revolution.

But one thing was always beyond doubt: the only statement more foolish than publishing magnate Henry Luce's 1941 prediction of a dawning "American Century" was Soviet premier Nikita Khrushchev's boast to the imperialists in 1956 that "We will bury you!" Not only was it precluded that the Stalinist-dominated workers states could surpass the industrially advanced capitalist powers economically, it was certain that at some point these regimes would start falling further and further behind.

To rationalize the bourgeois logic of their counterrevolutionary course, Stalin and his heirs began explaining that societies in the transition to socialism were governed by their own laws of motion. But this is false. It has nothing to do with Marxism. Trotsky explained this thoroughly, with little need for amendment, in works such as *The Revolution Betrayed: What Is the Soviet Union and Where Is It Going?* and *In Defense of Marxism.* The only blind laws governing social relations in the modern epoch are those of the capitalist system. Once the working class has expropriated the bourgeoisie and established a workers state, all advances toward or away from socialism — toward or away from the domination of commodity production and circulation — are the product not simply of lawful mechanisms but of the conscious political organization and leadership of the working class by its communist vanguard, as they join with toilers in other countries to advance the world socialist revolution. To the degree blind laws begin asserting their dominance once again, they can only be the laws of capital.

This is what Che Guevara understood and explained so well — including how difficult it can seem not to depend on such laws. That's one of many reasons to read and study Che's writings and speeches.

One thing the imperialists had going for them by the early 1950s was that they could make a case that capital's blind laws seemed to be working. A capitalist expansion was under way, and it continued for a couple of decades. It was built on the ashes of destruction — big sections of Europe, Japan, and other parts of the world had been obliterated — as well as the massive growth of wartime industrial production in the United States. It is described, among other places, in "What the 1987 Stock Market Crash Foretold," in issue no. 10 of *New International*. That expansion gave the employers a cushion for concessions to layers of the working class in the imperialist centers and postponed the emergence of a social crisis and big class battles.

But that has begun unwinding since the early 1970s, and doing so in an accelerated way in the deflationary conditions of the past half decade. In order to reverse this decline and open a sustained new period of rising profit rates and capital accumulation, the U.S. rulers once again have to do exactly what they set out to do after World War II — and failed to accomplish. They have to take on the working class and defeat it, both at home and abroad.

What's more, workers in Russia, workers across Eastern Europe, and workers in China are not going to travel along some different line of march from the rest of our class. They are less likely to do so as we enter the twenty-first century than ever before. There is not some separate set of social laws that will determine the outcome in these grotesquely deformed workers states. What happens there, like everywhere else, will be determined by the dialectic of the crisis and decline of the world imperialist system and the class battles unleashed by its pressures. The workers will become the decisive actors. But the action — including the growth in the size and social weight of the working class — will be produced and precipitated by the inevitable workings of the capitalist system on a world scale.

Ruling-class institutions weaker than they seem

From one point of view, this outcome to what has been called the Cold War is a frustrating one for revolutionary-minded workers and youth. We can see all the doors that have been opened. Stalinist calumnies and political prejudice are less effective than at any time since the mid-1920s in closing the minds of fighters and revolutionists to communist ideas. We take full advantage of these open doors. We distribute books, pamphlets, and newspapers presenting a revolutionary perspective in parts of the world where only five or ten years ago it was nearly impossible to do so without being arrested or worse.

Communist workers see the hunger for ideas everywhere we go abroad, whether it is along the Silk Road in Iran or Azerbaijan, or at a conference of the African National Congress in South Africa, or to young people we meet at a gathering somewhere in Asia. We find that same interest among workers and young people we meet in Cuba and fellow revolutionists we collaborate with there.

But there is frustration as well. The fact that world capitalism has been weakened does not translate into a burst forward of working-class struggles or an advance for independent labor political action and organization. It does not mean that the working class conquered new ground.

Similarly, the collapse of the Stalinist apparatuses does not, on its own, increase the size of the communist movement. It is one thing to celebrate the collapse of these oppressive regimes and to recognize that this tears down the greatest obstacle to drawing workers into world politics and leading the best of them to communist conclusions and organization. But it is another thing to say the working class in these countries has been strengthened politically or organizationally; it hasn't been. In order for communist leadership to be qualitatively expanded, the class struggle must first sharpen and expand.

The most important thing for class-conscious workers to understand, however, is that communists are in a better position today than at any time since the opening years of the Russian revolution to fight for proletarian leadership of revolutionary struggles as they develop. And the worst mistake we can make is to think that the rulers, that the enemies of the working class, are stronger than they are. To the contrary, they are weaker than they appear.

Everything we might think is strong — if we believed the bourgeois propaganda — is actually weaker than it seems. The rulers' moves are moves from weakness, not strength. They are moves marked by the extended, deflation-biased wave of capitalist development since the opening half of the 1970s.

This closing month of 1994 has been a particularly good one for illustrations. The peso was weaker than it seemed, wasn't it? NAFTA was weaker than it seemed. The U.S. dollar is weaker than it seemed (and at the same time *relatively* stronger compared not only to the Mexican peso or Canadian dollar but to the currencies of its rivals in Europe and Japan). The Russian army is weaker than it seemed.

What about NATO? NATO is not only weaker than it seems; it is not even an organization, contrary to what the name North Atlantic Treaty Organization implies, and it is less of an alliance than ever before. For most of the political lives of many of us, we thought of NATO as a thing. Even at its strongest, however, NATO was never a thing; it was the registration of a certain international relationship of class forces. It was a name for a collection of imperialist nation-states, each with its own government, its own armed forces, its own currency, and its own class interests. But we used shorthand, as human beings do, and fetishized the NATO alliance (with no substantial damage to our political orientation, in this case, I should add).

With the collapse of the Soviet bloc and Warsaw Pact, however, the rulers of the various European and North American capitalist powers no longer have any commonly perceived threat greater than their own diverging interests that would impel them to pay the price they once did to huddle under Washington's strategic nuclear umbrella. At the same time the imperialist rulers, and the masters of U.S. finance capital above all, want to place themselves in the strongest position militarily under these new conditions to someday roll back the remaining conquests of the Bolshevik-led revolution in Russia and reimpose the unimpeded dominance of capitalist exploitation.

If we recognize that fact, then we can understand what is behind the current tussle among various imperialist powers about how rapidly to extend NATO membership to certain former Warsaw Pact members in Central Europe, especially Poland, the Czech Republic, and Hungary. The debate over that aggressive move represents a further weakening, not a strengthening, of NATO. It deepens the divergence among NATO members, with the U.S. rulers in their big majority at the head of those pressing for eastward expansion. And, of course, it sharpens tensions between Moscow and Washington and other NATO governments.[35]

---

35. At Washington's initiative, the April 1999 NATO summit meeting scheduled for Washington will celebrate the 50th anniversary of the imperialist alliance by adding Poland, the Czech Republic, and Hungary to the current sixteen members. U.S president Clinton initiated the proposal for an eastward expansion of NATO at a summit meeting four years earlier. In pressing this course, Washington has flatly rejected Moscow's repeated protests, including the Russian government's proposal that NATO pledge not to deploy nuclear weapons or build military bases in the new member countries. Clinton's second-term secretary of state Madeleine Albright pulled few punches in stating Washington's aim in an article written for the weekly *Economist* of London on the eve of her first European trip in February 1997:

Let's look at another ruling-class institution: the Catholic Church. The Holy Apostolic Church of Rome is today weaker than at any time in the modern period. Pope John Paul II is *Time* magazine's man of the year for 1994; the issue is on the stands at grocery counters right now. That should tell us something right there. I'm sure some of us can remember when Richard Nixon was *Time*'s man of the year, or a while later Mikhail Gorbachev!

But bourgeois propagandists have sought to create an image around John Paul of a new church militant, a church on the march. The first Central European pope, a Polish pope who allegedly brought down communism. A church that will not only speak its mind but will mobilize the faithful and wage a fight against abortion rights and contraception.

But the truth is that the Catholic Church is weaker than ever

---

"Now that democracy's frontier has moved to Europe's farthest reaches, what logic would dictate that we freeze NATO's eastern edges where they presently lie, along the line where the Red Army stopped in the spring of 1945?"

It has been over the corpses of Yugoslav workers and peasants, first and foremost, that the U.S. rulers have asserted their position as the world's dominant "European power" since the early 1990s. As rival capitalist governments in Europe wore themselves out seeking to emerge the winner in the new Balkan wars, Washington sabotaged their various "peace initiatives" in Yugoslavia. Then, in 1994–95, the Clinton administration organized several rounds of sustained bombardment of Serbian forces, culminating in the NATO military occupation of Bosnia since late 1995 under the terms of the so-called Dayton Accords. Washington is pushing for the April 1999 NATO summit to formalize the U.S.-dominated alliance's authority to deploy military forces beyond the borders of its member states.

These U.S. moves have sharpened conflicts between Washington and its European rivals. In December 1998, on the eve of the NATO summit in Brussels, Paris and London announced agreement on a course toward giving the European Union for the first time the authority to deploy combat forces abroad. Given the British government's post–World War II "special relationship" with Washington, the U.S. rulers were especially alarmed at London's concurrence in this initiative. In response, U.S. Secretary of State Albright warned that "European decision making" must not come "unhooked from broader alliance decision making."

in its modern history. Never before has there been such a gap between the real views, the real practices, and the real doubts of the faithful, on the one hand, and the doctrine of the hierarchy, on the other. The hierarchy cannot get a majority of the faithful to agree with their line on birth control or with their line on abortion. And this phenomenon is not limited to the United States; even in Ireland the grip of the hierarchy has slipped, and perhaps the greatest gap of all is in Italy, the Vatican's home base.

Why is it, then, that institutions that are actually so weak can be presented as so strong? What allows such illusions to persist?

The answer, above all, is that the international labor movement has gone for so long without any mass revolutionary leadership that speaks and acts in the interests of the working class and challenges the petty-bourgeois misleaders who parrot and trail after the bourgeoisie.

The bipartisan framework of U.S. bourgeois politics

How is the pattern of world politics we have been discussing reflected concretely in the class struggle in the United States today? What do workers and youth in this country confront, and what can we do about it?

Right after the 1992 presidential elections, a public meeting was organized in New York City in conjunction with a conference of the Socialist Workers Party's National Committee and communist leaders from several other countries. At that public meeting, we said that what was most important about the bourgeoisie's election campaign was the fact that it was not going to end with the counting of the ballots. "America First," the "culture war," building a wall along the border with Mexico — the themes of the ultrarightist Republican primary candidate Patrick Buchanan — continued to resound. The campaign of Ross Perot — who ended up getting 19 percent of the popular vote — and his demagogic appeal to an insecure middle class was not a fleeting phenomenon in bourgeois politics, irrespective of Perot himself. In the course of the 1992 campaign, Clinton had already begun speaking Perot's language, probing measures to erode the social wage won through the labor struggles of the 1930s and civil rights battles of the 1950s and 1960s. The Democratic nominee campaigned on the pledge to "end welfare as we know it."

Across the bourgeois political spectrum, this coarsening rhetoric — aimed at heightening resentment in the middle classes and undercutting social solidarity among working people — continued after the election, as we said it would. Two years into the Clinton presidency and two months after the election of a Republican majority in the U.S. Congress, an ideological battle still rages within the bourgeoisie, packaged in demagogy directed to the broader population.

How should the capitalists operate politically in this new period of economic crisis and growing instability? Why are the employers still so far from accomplishing what they need to do, even after more than a decade of assaults on real wages, employment levels, job conditions, and working hours? How can they break through obstacles to take qualitatively more? How can the bourgeoisie start marshaling arguments that will enable them — even if ever so cautiously at first — to chip away more significantly at the assumptions underlying Social Security itself? These are among the questions at the center of bourgeois politics in the United States today.

The bipartisan framework of bourgeois politics continues to move to the right. What is the net result, for example, of a Democratic president coming into office and pledging to do something about national health care? Two years later, working people are further away from the socialization of medical coverage than before — *further away*. That is the reality. But the same direction is true across the board. There is a bipartisan move-ment to the right — and in some important respects a conver-gence — in the economic and social legislative agendas of both bourgeois parties.

Advancing along this trajectory inevitably breeds rightist dema-gogy, because the efforts by the Democratic and Republican politi-cians to rationalize their policies end up feeding reactionary biases, fears, and resentments. No matter how particular politicians try to package their anti-working-class moves, it is rightist views that are given the biggest impulse by the fact of these moves itself.

Newt Gingrich, the new Republican speaker of the House of Rep-resentatives, doodled a box during an interview with a columnist for a magazine called *The New Republic*. One end of the rectangular box was labeled "January 4" — the day the next session of Congress con-venes — and the other end "August 4" — the day Congress is set to recess. Underneath the box were the words "contract" — that is, the Republican's "Contract with America" — "budget," and "appro-priations."

According to the columnist, "Gingrich's rule is, as he put it, 'Don't go outside the box.' That means only issues in the Con-tract with America or ones involving spending will be consid-ered. Abortion, school choice, school prayer — these split Re-publicans (along with everyone else) and will be put off until next fall or 1996." Gingrich will supposedly concentrate between January and August on adopting the "contract" and cutting budget appropriations.

But, try as they will, they will not be able to "stay in the box." Gingrich himself jumped out of it right away by suggesting that the government begin opening up orphanages everywhere once again for children to be seized from "welfare mothers." More important, the right wing of the bourgeois forces does not even intend to pay lip service to "staying in the box."

Capitalism over the past couple of decades has at least doubled the official jobless rate that is considered "natural" in the United States, Europe, and most other imperialist countries. The numbers of workers no longer even counted as part of the labor force still continues to grow. At the same time, the capitalists have reduced unemployment benefits, held down the minimum wage, diminished the buying power of take-home pay, denied government funding for child care, and allowed welfare benefits to fall further and further behind price increases. Working people are being driven out of affordable housing, and medical and retirement benefits are being cut.

This is what capitalism is imposing on growing numbers in the working class today. And then politicians from both parties start branding those forced to live under these conditions as outlaws. They start talking about putting the children of the "underclass" into orphanages. They start denying workers unemployment benefits or welfare unless we accept jobs at a minimum or subminimum wage. They draw immigrants across the border to exploit cheap labor and then begin organizing to deny them schooling, medical care, and social benefits.

In a long-term deflationary period such as we are living through today, the bourgeoisie does not even have to do anything for most of these conditions to worsen. It is not primarily a matter of government policies. Under such depression-marked circumstances, all the propertied families and their politicians have to do is let capitalism operate. As it does so, both economic and social conditions, and the relationship of class forces, shift against the workers and their allies.

We should never forget that for substantial periods during the initial years of industrial capitalism in England in the eighteenth and nineteenth centuries, conditions in factories and mills — and in the working-class districts of Manchester and London and Liverpool — plunged to such a level that fertility and birth rates threatened to fall below levels necessary to replace living labor. This was especially the case during the second quarter of the nineteenth century — a period of protracted deflationary pressures across Europe. As this devastation deepened, the first unions and working-class organizations began to agitate and fight for change. Under this pressure, sections of the bourgeoisie themselves began calling for reforms, fearing that the reproduction of the working class was being called into question. Marx and Engels describe this in detail in their writings.[36]

Propagandists for the "market system" tell us such things cannot happen again in industrialized countries as we approach the twenty-first century. But the bitter truth turns out to be that it cannot *not* happen. In fact, it is happening *right now* in parts of the former Soviet Union and Eastern Europe, including in the eastern half of Germany — birth rates are declining, and mortality rates are on the rise. And more and more workers sense it

---

36. In his early book *The Condition of the Working Class in England in 1844*, Frederick Engels pointed out that in the industrial and port city of Liverpool in 1840, the average life expectancy of urban workers was fifteen years, compared to thirty-five years for the middle and upper classes. In Manchester, a major factory center, 57 percent of children from working-class families died before the age of five, versus 20 percent for the upper classes. Engels's firsthand observations of workers' wretched conditions during an extended stay in England as a young man — as well as his experiences there with the Chartist movement and other forms of working-class resistance — had an important political impact in making him a communist for the rest of his life. (For Engels's description of health and sanitary conditions in working-class areas, see especially the chapter entitled "Results.")

Conditions improved in the wake of the capitalist expansion that began in the 1850s and the political results of the 1848–49 revolutions in Europe and stepped-up working-class organization and agitation in England. Nonetheless, nearly a quarter-century later, Marx wrote in volume 1 of *Capital* that "the consumption of labour-power by capital is so rapid that the worker has already more or less completely lived himself out when he is only half-way through his life.... Under these circumstances, the absolute increase of this section of the proletariat [those in large-scale industry] must take a form which swells their numbers, despite the rapid wastage of their individual elements. Hence, rapid replacement of one generation of workers by another.... This social requirement is met by early marriages, which are a necessary consequence of the conditions in which workers in large-scale industry live, and by the premium that the exploitation of the workers' children sets on their production." (For Marx's discussion of these questions, see especially chapter 10 on "The Working Day," chapter 15 on "Machinery and Large-Scale Industry," and chapter 25 on "The General Law of Capitalist Accumulation.")

could also begin happening in the United States, Britain, Germany, Japan, New Zealand, and other imperialist countries, as depression conditions deepen.

The battle has opened up around all these questions in bourgeois politics in the United States. And it should come as no surprise that the right wing is firing the opening shots. The street battles will come later, after a fighting labor movement has begun to take shape and threaten capitalist rule. But the political initiative, to begin with, lies with the rightist and fascist forces that emerge out of the right wing of the bourgeois parties themselves, linking up over time with elements within the cops and officer corps of the armed forces.

Working-class currents, on the other hand, do not come out of the radicalization of a left wing of the bourgeois parties. They come out of a sharp and sustained rise in working-class struggles. And class battles on that scale will only begin later in the crisis; that is what the historical experience of our class has demonstrated. So it is the radical right that gets the first shot, and whose nuclei begin to grow earlier and faster.

That is why in the mass media today we already hear the voices of ultrarightists — a Patrick Buchanan, for example — but we do not hear communists.

That is why Yeltsin leans on a fascist like Vladimir Zhirinovsky as the crisis deepens in Russia, while there are still no substantial revolutionary workers organizations there (and why when Yeltsin is replaced, even if not by Zhirinovsky, it will not be by forces to the left of the current government).

That is why an openly fascist party can be given a cabinet portfolio in the government of Italy, a NATO country.[37] And it is also why that coalition can then receive the blessing of the president of the United States. On a visit to Rome in June 1994, Clinton said the Italian government "from top to bottom is une-

---

37. Italian prime minister Silvio Berlusconi formed a coalition government in May 1994, appointing leaders of the fascist Italian Social Movement to head five ministries. The government fell at the end of December 1994.

quivocally committed to democracy," adding that this remained so despite the fact that many parties "have their roots in a less democratic past." What a delicate touch, offering an Ozark howdy to some fascist friends!

During the 1992 U.S. presidential campaign, the bourgeoisie's two-party setup already began to show its tendency to disintegrate around the edges under the pressures we have been describing. And this process will continue. The first manifestations will not necessarily be recognizably fascist. Perot, for instance, is a Bonapartist demagogue who presses a generally right-wing political agenda, but his movement does not have the incipient fascist thrust of what Buchanan is trying to put together.

Whether it is Perot, Buchanan, or other figures and currents that carve out a niche in bourgeois politics, their initial target will not be to take the labor movement head on, or to go after revolutionary-minded workers and communists. In fact, many will demagogically speak on behalf of "the ordinary working man." Right now the ultrarightists are largely going after the Clinton administration, as well as those in their own milieu soft on these "New Deal–influenced" "globalist elites." They rail against those who are selling out "America" and "American workers." They condemn the "corrupt and decadent pretenders" to leadership of the nation among the spokespeople of the existing bourgeois parties, government institutions, and federal bureaucracy.[38]

---

38. In announcing his bid for the 1996 Republican presidential nomination in March 1995, Patrick Buchanan said: "This campaign is about an America that once again looks after its own people and our own country first.... Why are our people not realizing the fruits of their labor? Because we have a government that is frozen in the ice of its own indifference. A government that does not listen anymore to the forgotten men and women who work in the forges and factories and plants and businesses. We have instead a government that is too busy taking the phone calls from lobbyists for foreign countries and the corporate contributions of the Fortune 500."

This combination of American chauvinism and anticapitalist demagogy was a growing theme of Buchanan's primary campaign. "For whose benefit was that

This is how political radicalization begins, as evidence of political weakness and moral bankruptcy mount in capitalist politics. And we should remember that forces coming from different directions in bourgeois politics can and do converge around radical demagogy of this kind. Buchanan and Perot, for example, converge with those such as the so-called consumer advocate Ralph Nader and *Nation* columnist Alexander Cockburn to rail against the North American Free Trade Agreement — all of them speaking more or less openly in "America First" terms, while shedding crocodile tears over the conditions of Mexican workers and farmers.

Aspects of what incipient fascist forces say can sound like they are addressed to radicalizing workers and youth. Clinton has no respect for the ordinary working person, they say, or for the little guy in the middle class. Social conditions in the country just get worse and worse. But we should never be fooled for even a minute. What they say and what communists say have nothing in common — nothing at all. Theirs are the voices of a current in bourgeois politics, a current alien to everything the line of march of the working class leads toward.

The bourgeoisie itself places sharp limits on rightist forces, as long as the social crisis is not so deep that it must rely on them to maintain capitalist rule. We have seen a couple of examples of that in 1994, especially with the Oliver North campaign for the U.S. Senate seat from Virginia against incumbent Democrat Charles Robb.

$50 billion bailout of Mexico City?" he asked participants at an August 1995 conference sponsored by Ross Perot. "It wasn't the workers of Main Street, it was the bankers of Wall Street. Citibank, Chase Manhattan, J.P. Morgan, and Goldman Sachs all got off the hook, and they put us on." In a campaign speech in early 1996 he said: "When AT&T lops off 40,000 jobs, the executioner that does it, he's a big hero on the cover of one of those magazines, and AT&T stock soars."

"Watch the establishment," Buchanan jubilantly told supporters two days before winning the New Hampshire primary in February 1996. "All the knights and barons will be riding into the castle, pulling up the drawbridge, because they're coming. All the peasants are coming with pitchforks after them."

Throughout most of that campaign, North seemed like a shoo-in for the Republican right. But when North said in a public statement in October, broadcast on television, that "Bill Clinton is not my commander in chief," from that moment on there was no way he could win the election. In fact, it will be difficult for North to regain much weight in capitalist politics. Because the bourgeoisie, in their overwhelming majority, do not take kindly to public challenges to the military command structure, which they depend on the populace to accept unconditionally in the event of a "national" crisis.

Demise of the 'labor-liberal' coalition

Since at least the end of World War II, there has never been a time in the United States when the employing class thought they needed the trade union bureaucracy less than they do today. Thus the top AFL-CIO officialdom has less leverage in the Democratic Party and capitalist two-party system. Never have prominent bourgeois politicians of either party made less pretense of concessions to the top AFL-CIO officialdom. Never has less attention been paid to their wish list of "labor legislation." They get fewer invitations to the White House, to testify before Congress, or probably even to play golf at country clubs of the rich. They more and more try to merge their unions, capable of doing little else. Their slogan seems to be "One Big Dues Base" — almost like a cruel parody on the old Wobblies.[39]

39. At the same time, growing sections of the labor officialdom are collaborating with employers to maintain a relatively stable even if smaller dues base among better-off and higher seniority workers. In January 1999, for example, the top officialdom of the United Auto Workers joined with General Motors management in seeking to sell UAW members at two plants in Ohio and Michigan on a deal that would cut the workforce by 60 percent. According to the *New York Times*, UAW officials "said in interviews today that so many of their workers were ready to retire that the unions were willing to accept sharp cuts in employment. In exchange, the new factories would provide long-term job security for the workers who retired." No individual or current in the U.S. labor officialdom has the perspective of a fight to win jobs

The labor bureaucrats argue among themselves more these days as well, accusing each other of responsibility for their fallen estate. And since they accomplish so little, they live in mounting fear and hatred of the ranks, who might at any time elect someone else to replace them in office.

That is why, among other things, trade union officials have begun to approach workers such as yourselves, whom they peg as activists and radicals, to try to draw you into union structures they dominate. They need you more right now. They are looking for activists who have authority in the ranks. They count on militants being frustrated and thus initially seeing any change as perhaps a step forward. And they count on the petty-bourgeois radical left in the labor movement doing their bidding for a very small fee, and hopefully bringing some militant-minded workers along with them.[40]

The officialdom's overtures are a diversion from what class-conscious workers need to be doing, and from what we have substantial political space to accomplish in the unions today. We need to be working together in whatever ways possible with others *in the ranks*. That is where the power and the determination will come to make real changes in the labor movement as struggles pick up — changes that go well beyond the plans of the more left-talking officials.

In times like these, the officialdom goes after the soul of class-conscious workers. Union militants, for example, have always insisted to the general public, to other working people, and to the

---

for all by cutting the workweek with no cut in pay and promoting a federally funded program of public works to build housing, schools, hospitals, roads, and other goods and services needed by working people.

40. The union tops seek to draw not only militant workers behind their bandwagon, but radicalizing student youth as well. In 1996 the AFL-CIO recruited some 1,200 students to a "Union Summer" to train them in "community and labor organizing," i.e., first and foremost, helping to get out the vote for the Democrats in the November 1996 elections.

middle class that strong unions mean safer conditions — not just for workers in the industry, but for the general public as well. That is what we and other class-struggle-oriented workers have said about unions in the airlines, on the railroads, in the refineries, in other industries. And we mean it. It is not public relations; it is not hype.

So, what should we say about the startling increase in airline deaths and disasters over the past year or so? Yes, it is a product of the downsizing and cost-cutting drive by management. That is all true. But our responsibility, as the political vanguard of our class, is to recognize that at the same time, until labor's retreat is reversed, a breakdown begins to take place in the labor movement too. As conditions of work get worse, as hours increase, as wages go down, some workers begin to say: "I don't give a damn. It's not my job. Let somebody else take care of it. The devil take the hindmost."

The union officialdom's example in life encourages such cynicism among a few in the ranks. The bureaucrats are complicit with the bosses in encouraging the divisions among workers that breed atomization and demoralization. They have no intention of leading the kind of fight necessary to improve working conditions, shorten hours of work, and increase wages. They cannot imagine a union that puts itself in the front ranks of a fighting movement for universal social security protection, real health and safety enforcement, and effective protection of the environment, regardless of the consequences for any boss or any bourgeois party or politician.

But class-conscious workers *must* take questions such as safety seriously. Labor must convince broad layers of the population as a whole that it is the working-class movement above all that cares about these questions. We must be able to assert with complete confidence and integrity that the stronger and more militant the union, the safer the operations of the industry, whatever it may be. This is a fundamental matter of class pride, of self-respect, of the morale of the working class. It is a question of the working class taking the moral high ground in the battle against the exploiting class and for human solidarity.

Karl Marx put it this way nearly 130 years ago in the final sentence of the resolution "Trade Unions: Their Past, Present, and Future" that he proposed for adoption by the International Working Men's Association, the First International. The unions, Marx said, "must convince the world at large that their efforts, far from being narrow and selfish, aim at the emancipation of the downtrodden millions."[41]

Think about the people you admire and seek to emulate: take, for instance, Farrell Dobbs, the greatest communist class-struggle leader of the labor movement in the United States; or Malcolm X; or Nelson Mandela.[42] The true leaders of the oppressed and exploited have never addressed themselves to the bourgeoisie, to the oppressors, to complain about what *they* are doing to us. Leaders talk to fellow workers, fellow fighters about where *we* are messing up; what *we* have to do; what *we* have to prepare for. Leaders explain how *we* have to increase our discipline, change our view of ourselves, and much more in order to accomplish our ends.

The bourgeoisie puts on a pretense of being the class that bears intelligence, culture, politeness, civility. But in volatile times such as these, their pretense turns to ashes in their mouths.

41. This resolution drafted by Karl Marx is included in *Trade Unions in the Epoch of Imperialist Decay* by Leon Trotsky (New York: Pathfinder, 1990), p. 35.

42. **Farrell Dobbs** (1907–1983) was a leader of the 1934 Minneapolis strikes and eleven-state organizing drive that transformed the Teamsters in much of the Midwest into a fighting industrial union in the 1930s. Won to the communist movement in the early stages of these labor battles, he was Socialist Workers Party national secretary from 1953 to 1972. **Malcolm X** (1925–1965) was among the outstanding leaders of the oppressed Black nationality and working class in the United States. A founder in 1964 of the Organization of Afro-American Unity, he championed revolutionary struggles against oppression and exploitation around the world. **Nelson Mandela** (b. 1918) is the central leader of the African National Congress and, since 1994, president of South Africa. He was imprisoned from 1962 to 1990 for his leadership in the struggle against the white supremacist apartheid system and for a nonracial democratic republic.

Writings and speeches by Dobbs, Malcolm X, and Mandela are published by Pathfinder.

They are in fact only the parasitic bearers of surplus value — of a part of the fruits of the working day they steal from the labor of our class! And we begin to understand that the most important idea that revolutionists such as Farrell Dobbs, such as Malcolm, can teach us is not about *them* — not about the exploiters — but about what *we* can accomplish together, and about what weaknesses we need to overcome in order to do so. As Malcolm once put it, that is why his goal in building a revolutionary organization was not to awaken Afro-Americans to their exploitation but "to their humanity, to their own worth."

Those of us who grew up in the postwar period are acquainted with what has been known as the Democratic Party "labor-liberal coalition." It grouped together — under the political awning of the Democratic Party — the AFL-CIO officialdom, the leaderships of the NAACP and other major civil rights groups, and executive officers of public and private welfare agencies. Today, that coalition is scarcely a shadow of its former self. Nor does it have the appearance of any substantial weight in bourgeois politics. For the Communist Party and the rest of the petty-bourgeois left in the working-class movement in the United States, this is cause for great sorrow and lamentation. But for communist workers, it is grounds for celebration.

The so-called labor–liberal–civil rights coalition was never a fighting alliance of workers and youth. It was never an alliance of the ranks of the massive battles that built the industrial unions in the 1930s and then advanced Black rights in the 1950s and 1960s. It was a coalition of apparatuses and officialdoms who derived their authority from the concessions those working-class struggles had wrested. It was a coalition of those who sat on top of the unions and civil rights organizations and prevented them from effectively defending or extending those gains. It was a coalition that blocked all advances toward political activity independent of the party structures that serve the exploiters and oppressors. As such, it was very useful to the capitalist parties and politicians for many decades.

This so-called coalition was built on the lie that if working people in struggle would support this or that wing of the exploiters, staying within their two-party system, then a way could be found to make progress and improve conditions of life for workers and farmers. So long as the postwar capitalist expansion gave the rulers a margin for concessions, that class-collaborationist illusion could be portrayed by the labor officialdom as having some basis in reality. Given capitalism's current deflationary conditions, however, the bureaucracy finds it harder and harder to produce on that lie. But with the help of parts of the left, growing sections of the officialdom will work overtime to try to give that coalition an appearance of renewal.[43]

The fight for jobs and class unity

The cadres of a revolutionary working-class movement will not come out of the breakup of the "labor-liberal coalition" in the Democratic Party. They will not emerge around the edges of bourgeois politics and institutions. Radicalized working-class currents will begin to develop only as a conscious, fighting labor movement grows. Only the actions and combat experience of workers, and the self-confidence such activity brings, will fuel a working-class radicalization and propel the emergence of new leadership from the ranks of those who are fighting.

43. In October 1995 a slate headed by John Sweeney, president of the Service Employees International Union, unseated Lane Kirkland and other top officials of the AFL-CIO. The Communist Party USA hailed the change in personnel, as did most centrist groups, at least initially. The AFL-CIO convention, said CPUSA leader Gus Hall, "did away with a 100-year policy of class collaboration, corporate partnership, concessions and mainly defensive battles. The trade union movement voted to pursue policies of class struggle. . . ."

During its first months in office, the Sweeney team's main initiative was a special convention in March 1996 to levy a 15-cent-a-month dues increase on union members to help raise $35 million to campaign for Clinton and for a Democratic Congress in the November elections. Sweeney says the federation will also raise $20 million to organize the unorganized, something the officialdom has pledged to do every so often since the AFL merged with the CIO in 1955.

Class-conscious workers must never fall for the bourgeois propaganda that the government ever *gives* us anything. They do not *give* us what they call welfare benefits, or Social Security pensions, or workers compensation, or unemployment benefits, or public schools, or Medicare, or anything else. Whatever workers win in expanding the social wage is simply taking back from the exploiting class a portion of the wealth our class has produced with our social labor.

The labor movement has to fight to replace the stingy, means-tested, tax-your-paycheck programs that the bosses call welfare, that they call Social Security, with *real* welfare, *real* social security. Labor must fight for compensation at union wages for all those who cannot work, have been laid off, or cannot find a job. Labor must fight for retirement pensions, disability benefits, and lifetime public education.

This is not "the dole," "handouts," or "giveaways." These are *universal social rights* for a class, participating in the culture the wealth they produce makes possible. These entitlements are distributed out of a part of what that class — and only that class and its toiling allies — produces. The working class is taking back a portion of those resources so our class *as a whole* can be stronger, can make it between jobs, has some protection from the ravages of inflation, and has some precious time to do the things the bosses' system prevents us from doing. This is an essential part of fighting for the unity, the morale, and the combativity that the labor movement needs to wage a successful revolutionary struggle. These are part of what the working class fights to establish as human rights.

The demand for jobs is becoming more and more important throughout the capitalist world, as well. There is more than 12 percent unemployment officially in France today. This is during an upturn in France and across capitalist Europe. It is 8.9 percent in Britain — a couple of years into the upswing there. Canada is 10.0 percent — there is a recovery there too. Italy is 11.9 percent. Sweden is 7.4 percent officially — a level not seen for decades there. And Spain is 24.3 percent!

Here in the United States, the Clinton administration is boasting that unemployment dropped below 6 percent in recent months for the first time since the 1990–91 recession. The official figures released by the government, however, don't count those in our class who have either given up looking for work for the time being — "discouraged workers," in the lingo of bourgeois economists — or those who have involuntarily taken part-time jobs because they are unable to find full-time work.[44]

Bipartisan convergence

Today, bourgeois politics in the United States is more of a one-party system than it has ever been in the lifetime of anyone in this hall. Not just in foreign policy, where the rulers have followed a bipartisan strategic course since the end of World War I, but in domestic economic and social policy as well.

I do not mean to exaggerate — the two-party face of the one-party system remains decisive for the bourgeoisie in fooling

---

44. In 1995 the U.S. Bureau of Labor Statistics, with little or no fanfare, began keeping track of a jobless figure called "U-6" that includes so-called discouraged workers and involuntary part-time workers. That figure, roughly 11 percent at the time this talk was presented, stood at 7.6 percent in September 1998. In fact, job growth during the first six years of the 1990s was the slowest of any decade since the end of World War II.

In Europe, the situation was only marginally better by the closing months of 1998. Joblessness in the European Union has been above 10 percent since the opening months of 1993. "[U]nemployment is the crucial issue for the future of Europe," said German central bank president Hans Tietmeyer in an interview in the January 20, 1997, issue of the *International Herald Tribune*. "I am not sure how long societies will accept this level of unemployment." In Germany, Europe's economically strongest capitalist power, government figures released in February 1997 showed the "jobless total at a level last seen around the time Hitler took power in 1933," reported the *Financial Times* of London, citing public remarks by Chancellor Helmut Kohl. As of early 1999 the official figure was still above 11 percent for the country as a whole, and nearly 20 percent for eastern Germany (an understatement of the true situation in the east, since the figure excludes tens of thousands in government-funded make-work and "training" programs).

working people, and there is an extreme right wing within capitalist politics that shows substantial strength at each new turning point. But on defense of the dollar; on preparing for economic war against U.S. capital's competitors; on cutting back social spending; on laying the basis to erode the social wage and limit universal entitlements; on "reviewing" and where necessary reversing affirmative action; on strengthening repressive legislation and the cops, including the border cops; on weakening the power of the unions to resist — on all these fundamental questions there is a common direction, regardless of the different voices in which Clinton and Gingrich speak.

I was struck in this regard by the speech Gingrich gave at the beginning of December to a gathering of Republicans in Congress, accepting their nomination as Speaker of the House. "If you truly love democracy and you truly believe in representative self-government, you can never study Franklin Delano Roosevelt too much," he said. "He did bring us out of the Depression. He did lead the Allied movement in World War II. In many ways he created the modern world. He was clearly, I think, as a political leader the greatest figure of the 20th century," Gingrich said.

"[A]nd if you go back and read the New Deal, they tried again and again. They didn't always get it right, and we would have voted against much of it, but the truth is we would have voted for much of it."

Then Gingrich turned to Winston Churchill, who, he sermonized, "in 1940 in the darkest and grimmest days said, 'I have nothing to offer but blood, sweat, toil and tears.'"

Roosevelt and Churchill. The two most prominent Allied war leaders during the second world imperialist slaughter. Both of them often portrayed as decisive individuals who in abnormal times stood above normal government functioning and got things done. That is who Gingrich offered up as models.

It is not that the Republicans are setting the line in Washington. It is that under today's crisis conditions, a bipartisan imperialist political lodestar keeps being followed to the right. And the initiative increasingly comes from those who claim to speak directly to the American people, over and above workaday partisan politics. More and more of the initiative comes from those politicians who say the people must be mobilized against all those who have lost touch with the average American — against the insiders, against the elites, against the bureaucrats, against the politicians!

It makes no difference that their proposals are sheer demagogy. It is such voices within bourgeois politics that have held the initiative since the 1992 election and continue to do so today.

Building a proletarian party

The working class in the United States, as throughout the world, will resist the horrors the declining capitalist system has in store for the vast majority who must labor for a living, produce all social wealth, and create the basis for the advance of culture. The fights we see and take part in today — from the strike against Caterpillar by members of the United Auto Workers, to strikes and massive street mobilizations by workers and youth in France this year against the government's antilabor moves, to responses to attacks on women's rights and racist assaults, to the protests sure to come in Mexico against Zedillo's plan to "rescue" the peso at working people's expense — waves of resistance like these will at some point cross a threshold in one or more countries and pass over into a period of more sustained class battles.[45]

45. In November and December 1995, millions of workers and youth in France conducted another round of strikes and mobilizations against Paris's auster-

As those struggles break out and develop — and we have no way of foreseeing the place or the timing — communist workers are not only going to be part of them from day one. They, as well as their party and their newspaper, are also going to be already known by many fellow fighters from having gone through earlier struggles together.

Unlike in the 1930s — during the last major capitalist crisis and rise of working-class battles and revolutionary opportunities in many countries — this time around it is not foreordained that the big majority of working-class fighters and youth attracted to revolutionary political conclusions will end up being misled into believing — and acting on the belief — that to be a communist is to be a Stalinist. That false consciousness, which facilitated either corrupting or demoralizing millions of revolutionists, became weaker in the second half of the 1950s following Moscow's revelations of some of Stalin's crimes. It was further weakened in the wake of rebellions by workers and youth in Eastern Europe in the 1950s and 1960s. The Cuban revolution and its internationalist course dealt Stalinism even bigger blows. But the barrier nonetheless remained largely intact.

Today this poisonous confusion of a counterfeit of communism for the real thing can begin to be remedied. In the heat of coming class battles, the door will be open as it has not been

---

ity moves. The mass protests, backed by all three major union federations, succeeded in slowing down aspects of the government's assault on jobs and retirement benefits of rail workers and other public employees. In the spring 1997 parliamentary elections, the Socialist and Communist parties won a majority and formed a new government, registering the rejection by workers and substantial layers of the middle class of the austerity course being pressed by the previous regime amid jobless levels exceeding 12 percent.

On May Day 1996 hundreds of thousands of unionists and other workers demonstrated in Mexico City against the austerity pact imposed by the Zedillo regime and agreed to by the progovernment officialdom of the Confederation of Mexican Workers (CTM). The CTM officials had called off all May Day activities and told workers to stay out of the streets.

since the early days of the Bolshevik-led Russian revolution to win the most revolutionary-oriented and self-sacrificing workers and youth to communism. They can be won to the scientific conclusion that the working class must get rid of a social system that relies on the monopoly of productive property by a tiny minority of ruling families who grow wealthy off the fruits of what the toiling majority produce with our labor. Revolutionists can and will be won to the only accurate conclusion from the experience of our class in this century — that unless we build proletarian parties and a communist world movement capable of leading workers and farmers to make a socialist revolution, capitalism will repeat its descent toward fascism and world war, and under even more horrible conditions than before.

Communist workers who have internalized the lessons of the modern class struggle never pay any attention to the doomsayers. Why speculate or argue about the prospects for a world conflagration that might set back human civilization for centuries, or perhaps even destroy the basis for life on earth? Who knows what horrors might become possible if conditions reach such a stage?

The important thing is that without taking on the working class and our organizations in gigantic battles *that we will have the opportunity to win*, the exploiters cannot use their enormous military might to unleash a third imperialist world slaughter. Don't fall for the rulers' bluff. Long before such a war becomes possible, the capitalists must cow the workers and defeat us in struggle. They will ultimately finance and support growing rightist and fascist movements, because the capitalists cannot defeat the working class using "normal" methods. There will be massive street battles between fascist legions and the forces mobilized by the class-struggle-minded labor movement.

That is the nightmare for the world's capitalist classes and their temporary political spokespersons — the Clintons, the Gingriches, the Majors, the Blairs, the Zedillos. In their big majority, they do not want to confront those class battles, because they are far from confident they can win. They try to put off the confrontations and finesse them. They buy off this or that middle-class layer in order to weaken our class organizations and try to con us into accepting more and more sacrifices for the good of the "nation."

But a point is always reached where working people can be conned no longer and struggles begin to mount. And with revolutionary leadership, forged and tested in coming struggles, the international working class has the numbers, the social power, the culture, the values, and the program to defeat the reactionary forces loosed by finance capital. We can organize victorious revolutions and open the construction of socialism on a world scale.

That is what we are preparing for. That is what is so important about political weapons such as the new issue of *New International* that we are celebrating here. That is why it is so important to get this magazine — along with the *Militant*, the Spanish-language *Perspectiva Mundial*, and our entire arsenal of revolutionary books and pamphlets published and distributed by Pathfinder — into the hands of workers and young people who are fighters and aspire to be revolutionists.

The right wing in this country puts a lot of time and money into TV talk shows and radio call-in programs. The Rush Limbaughs, and others far to the right of him, mix suggestive coarseness and cynicism with saccharine sentimentality. The radical right trades in demagogy. They seek to tap fears and anxieties. They try to whip you up emotionally. They treat sex as a commodity and gender as a joke. They debase and corrupt politics, life, and civil discourse — as do their counterparts in the United Kingdom, France, Germany, Japan, Russia, and all over the world.

But the one thing they do not do is urge those to whom they are appealing to read books — to really read books. They want you to scapegoat two or three layers in society — immigrants, welfare mothers, labor unions, the "femi-nazis," whatever — and blame them for all the problems created by capitalism. The last thing the rightist demagogues ever want you to do is to read and work at understanding sober, scientific explanations of the capitalist system. They do not want you to learn from history and draw the political lessons. The radical right will never call on anybody to read more — because they have no respect for those whom they seek to mobilize as a mass social base. They have no confidence in the worth of human beings, no sense of social solidarity.

Disgruntled middle-class layers, enraged bourgeois youth, thin strata of demoralized workers — these social layers are radicalized by mounting fear, envy, and resentments. They respond to prejudice and demagogy. Their growing radicalization is reinforced and focused by the rhetoric of a Patrick Buchanan, telling them how much they are being mucked over by the degenerate elites, the illegal aliens, the un-Americans. That is why no fascist movement is ever going to have a serious education program. They never have; they never will.

The opposite is true of the revolutionary workers movement. What the working class needs is not demagogy, not scapegoats, not crank theories, even if spun by Ph.D.s from Harvard or Yale. As workers, farmers, and youth organize to resist the assaults and probes by the capitalists, we need in the process to develop a clearer understanding of the entire world picture. We are confident that those who work at studying the past experiences of our class and who take the time and effort to think about and discuss what we are facing today will come to communist conclusions.

We know that only by fighting *and* by reading can the working class prepare itself to do what it must to ensure the future of humanity. We know that reading, discussing, and coming to understand the truth is the road to more effective working-class action and organization. It is working people's most powerful weapon in charting a revolutionary course that can take on the imperialist war makers and win.

These are the communist conclusions that best fit the facts of how history has actually unfolded in this century. And these communist conclusions are thus the best guide to action for vanguard workers and revolutionary-minded youth.

There is no way for any individual or group of individuals to arrive at these lessons from their involvement in any one struggle in their factory, city, or country — or even from a number of such struggles. Nobody can come to these conclusions just from good trade union work, for example. Nobody can do so just from effective participation in a Cuba defense coalition, an abortion rights fight, or other social protest activity. It is not even possible to draw communist conclusions from any single revolution in this century, even the most important ones such as the Russian and Cuban revolutions. We cannot just follow how the socialist revolution is developing in Cuba, look forward to the working-class resistance we know is coming in Mexico, and from that derive a proletarian orientation in world politics.

Fighters can draw very militant, very revolutionary conclusions. They can become very determined, very steadfast in their commitment, and very courageous in their actions. But on the basis of experience from a limited number of struggles in any single place or time, it does not necessarily follow that the only way for the working class to win and permanently consolidate its gains is to overthrow the political power of the capitalists, establish a workers and farmers government, wrest productive property out of their hands, and join in the worldwide construction of socialism.

It is only when we begin to understand the world capitalist system as a whole that we can draw the communist conclusion that there is no way to reform any one piece of that system. It is only when we begin to dissect the relations among all the classes in society — looking not just at the workers and our exploited allies, but also at the exploiters and the middle-class and professional layers — that we begin to absorb the true history and lessons of the international working-class struggle. Only then do revolutionary conclusions become unavoidable.

To be a communist means recognizing that the capitalist system in its totality must be overthrown by the working class and replaced by the conscious organization of the great majority. It means actively participating alongside others in struggles to win immediate and democratic demands, while doggedly maintaining our independence from all attempts that count on reforming capitalism and from all bourgeois political forces and petty-bourgeois misleaderships inside our class that act on their behalf. That is the beginning of communist consciousness, of real class consciousness. And it can only come along the road of struggle and study we have just described.

It is always possible to hope that even if progress seems unrealizable within a capitalist framework in a particular country, and under specific circumstances, perhaps something different will happen somewhere else in the world. And that will make the gradual reform of capitalism possible.

For experienced communist workers, rejecting such a reformist outlook is the most basic of all conclusions. We take it for granted. In fact, however, it is the most difficult of all conclusions to come to. But it is also the most liberating to finally reach, and the most rewarding around which to organize a lifetime of struggle.

DISCUSSION

The church and counterrevolution

COMMENT: I want to ask a question on your remarks about *Time* magazine naming Pope John Paul its man of the year. Didn't they honor him for having destroyed communism in Europe? Didn't he play the same role there as Cardinal Obando y Bravo did against the Sandinista revolution in Nicaragua? Don't these church figures work together with Western spy agencies to do this? A few weeks ago, the Catholic Church named a new cardinal in Cuba. Does this imply that the church is now looking to build a base of social support there to destroy the Cuban revolution? Those are my questions.

RESPONSE: Let me start with Cuba. We should begin by reminding ourselves that the church hierarchy is part of the world's propertied classes. The Catholic Church itself is one of the big property holders in the world.

The hierarchy has the same view toward the Cuban revolution today that it has had from the outset. It wants to help any social layer in Cuba that is seeking to slow down or reverse the revolution.

The church is not trying to build a base of support *for itself* in Cuba. That puts the cart before the horse. Church officials are trying *to support* those middle-class-inclined layers in the bureaucracy of the state, economic enterprises, and party who want to push in a capitalist direction and toward an accommodation with U.S. imperialism. The church hierarchy will do what it can to provide ideological — even theological! — justifications and lend its reputation among the faithful to that effort. It will be careful, however. The Cuban revolution remains strong, and the Holy Apostolic Church of Rome is headed by competent and disciplined tacticians. A spirit of Jesuit discipline has not wholly disappeared and can even be usefully emulated by proletarian revolutionists.

The church and church hierarchy in today's world are no longer a social force in and of themselves. They have not been for a long time — not since the rise and consolidation of industrial capitalism. At one time, "the church militant" was an economic power, a ruling-class force in its own right. In whole sections of feudal Europe and later in other parts of the world, the church was the dominant holder of landed property. It was the single most powerful force among the landed estates.

That is no longer true, however. It is not true of priests, of bishops, of archbishops, of cardinals, or of the pope. They are not an independent social force; they do not have the power to overthrow social revolutions or reverse mass proletarian struggles. The church remains a ruling-class institution. But church officials function in the class struggle primarily by seeking to lend their moral authority to powerful bourgeois political forces or their agencies. They often offer ideological support to rightist movements, helping to give them a veneer of morality, of eternity, of ritual, of stately pomp. They try to anoint the counterrevolution.

But the church fathers are effective only if the working class and other toilers have no capable revolutionary leadership of their own to help clarify political questions and lead them forward. The church hierarchy in Cuba has been hostile to the revolution from the very beginning. But it has never been a big problem for the revolutionary leadership and isn't going to become one now. The Catholic Church, with or without a new cardinal, will not be an independent problem unless counterrevolutionary forces among professional, middle-class, and bureaucratic layers reach the stage in Cuba where they can begin steering the government away from a revolutionary course.

But the working class in Cuba and its communist leadership have continued fighting to keep the revolution on course, and in face of some daunting obstacles in recent years. Should the Cuban revolution be overthrown at some point, neither Fidel Castro nor other communists would ever blame it on the church. That will be decided in struggle by the advances or retreats in the political organization, consciousness, and morale of working people in Cuba, along with revolutionary developments throughout the Americas and the rest of the world.

Did the pope destroy communism?

On your other point: I have not read the article in *Time*, but I can easily believe that it explained its choice of Pope John Paul II as man of the year partly on the basis that he destroyed communism in Eastern Europe. But he *didn't* destroy communism in Eastern Europe. Because there was no communism in Eastern Europe — either before or after he became pope.

John Paul and others in the Catholic Church hierarchy in Poland took advantage of the disintegration of the Stalinist apparatus to throw support behind forces they hoped would reopen the country to capitalism. They hoped they could help reverse the gains workers had achieved through the overturn of capitalist property relations nearly half a century earlier, in the aftermath of World War II. At times, John Paul sounded like the old Socialist Revolutionaries and Mensheviks in the early years of the Russian revolution when they became so murderously anticommunist but still pretended to speak for the toiling poor.[46]

46. The peasant-based Socialist Revolutionary Party and the Mensheviks, a reformist workers party, were two of the main opposition forces to the tsarist regime in Russia in the early 1900s. Following the Bolshevik-led workers and peasants revolution in October 1917, the petty-bourgeois leaderships of both parties joined with Russia's capitalist and landlord classes, and with the imperialist powers, to launch a savage but unsuccessful civil war. As cover for their counterrevolutionary course, they claimed to be acting on behalf of the downtrodden in Russia.

There was not a socialist revolution in Poland like there had been in Russia in 1917 under communist leadership — or even like those that triumphed despite Stalinist leaderships in Yugoslavia, Albania, China, or Vietnam following the war. But neither was capitalism overthrown in Poland and other Eastern European countries by the occupying Soviet army, as bourgeois sources tell the tale. It took revolutionary action by the peasants to throw out the landlord class and by the working class in the cities to expropriate the capitalists — even if these mobilizations were tightly controlled by the Stalinists.

Once it became clear to the Catholic Church hierarchy in Poland in the late 1940s that the ruling capitalist and landed classes were not likely to regain power any time soon, the bishops and cardinals came to an accommodation with the new Stalinist regime. They supported the bureaucrats' efforts to keep the working class out of politics and isolated from contact with anti-imperialist and working-class revolutionists in other countries.

The massive privileged petty-bourgeois social caste that dominated the apparatus of the government and Communist Party in Poland did succeed in atomizing, depoliticizing, exiling, or killing the communist vanguard of the working class. But it was never able to break workers' will to resist social injustice and oppression. Working people despised the new icons and rituals that replaced the old ones. What was called communism in Poland had become in fact a form of religion — and it got about the same observance and respect from thinking workers. When the Stalinist regimes collapsed there and elsewhere throughout Eastern Europe at the opening of this decade, workers got the same joy from tearing down some of the "Marxist" statues and icons as they have gotten during previous uprisings and revolutions from knocking down symbols and turning their backs on rituals that had long been used to justify their oppression.

By the time Karol Wojtyla had become a well-known figure in the church hierarchy in Poland, let alone when he was elected pope in 1978, there were no organized groups of communists left anywhere in Eastern Europe. Communism had been betrayed well before he was even ordained into the priesthood. There has been no continuity of communism in Poland at any time during his career in the hierarchy. So he did not destroy communism in Poland or anywhere else.

But neither John Paul nor any other church figure will be able to block a new generation of workers in Poland from rebuilding the communist movement as developments in the class struggle not only there but also in the rest of the world make it possible to do so. Nor to win them to social positions they have come to doubt. In modern times, no *rising* proletariat is "priest-ridden" — Polish, Irish, or any other.

There was a time during the 1970s and 1980s when anyone or any institution that seemed to stand up to the police repression, to the social regimentation, to the tyranny, to what was grotesquely presented as socialism in Poland gained an element of popularity and credibility among those who were the victims of this regime. That included the Catholic Church and some of its officials. Under that umbrella of credibility, they were able to promote all sorts of reactionary views and activities.

But today the church in Poland has begun to be hated by many workers and even sections of the peasantry in the countryside. It has even begun to be hated by many of those who came to support it as a symbol of resistance to the Stalinist regime and thus ended up buying into much of the hierarchy's reactionary rhetoric.

Many working people in Poland today detest the church's support for slashing health care and other social gains they had come to view as rights. They despise the church's unqualified support to the presidency. They hate its opposition to a woman's right to abortion and contraception and its vigorous support earlier this year for President Lech Walesa's veto of parliament's mild attempt to ease Poland's antiabortion law. They dislike the periodic eruption of Jew-hatred among members of the hierarchy. They reject the church's opposition to the right to divorce and its other reactionary positions on women's rights.

The promised flowering of democracy, of plenty, of peace, of economic expansion, of successful capitalism in Poland turned out to be a lie. And millions of workers blame those who were the biggest peddlers of this lie, including the hierarchy of the Catholic Church and this pope in particular. Even if all you know is what you read in the big-business press, it is clear that the church is more distrusted and even despised among broad masses of people in Poland today than it has been for decades. That's positive, one more consequence of the collapse of the Stalinist apparatuses that will strengthen the working class.

The implosion of the Stalinist regime in Poland at the close of the 1980s was the product of a *social* struggle. There are no *religious* struggles. Some social struggles take religious forms, just as some take national forms and other forms that to one degree or another conceal the underlying class conflicts. But that is not what happened in Poland.

All attempts in the modern period to turn religion into some kind of revolutionary ideology are bound to fail. During feudalism, popular movements that rose against oppressive conditions in the countryside and scattered towns and cities — and thus in part against the dominant class power of the church hierarchy — universally adopted a dissenting religious form. Secular revolutionary ideas found the beginnings of a popular echo only in the decades leading up to the American and French revolutions.

With the rise and consolidation of capitalist states and the growth of a modern proletariat, however, all that has changed. That is why liberation theology could never be the dominant outlook of a revolutionary movement. It is *not* a Marxist form of religion; it is a form of religion whose proponents, involved in various social struggles, attempt to graft onto it all kinds of ideas, including some borrowed from Marxism. But to the degree a worker or peasant or young person who starts down this road gets more deeply involved in revolutionary politics, to that degree they will sooner or later begin looking for clearer ways to explain the class forces they are confronting and more effective ways to advance the struggle and win. And to the degree anybody remains faithful to the church, to that degree they will over time prefer sticking to the Roman rites without all the political add-ons.

The revolutionary workers movement opposes attempts to combine religion and politics through the back door. There is no way to carry the day in the church hierarchy for such an effort either. That is not how the bishops, archbishops, and cardinals got where they are. They are not a social force in their own right, but they *are* bourgeois figures in the epoch of imperialist decay.

Of course, communist workers will work and fight shoulder to shoulder with any individual as an equal in a common struggle, no matter what his or her beliefs or other views. We never quiz fellow fighters about their religious beliefs, nor do we push to be quizzed about ours. And we never let any such beliefs be a barrier to practical work together.

What's more, communists are absolutely opposed to the coarse and cynical measures taken by Stalinist regimes to attempt to force people to drop their religious beliefs, or change them through "ideological struggle" or "reeducation." Over time, as people go through a range of experiences in the class struggle, many come to change their views on religion and other questions. In the future, during the transition to socialism, as all human relations undergo revolutionary change, the social conditions that gave rise to religion will wither away along with private property, the state, the family, and other institutions of class-divided society. There will no longer be a social basis for institutions, beliefs, and forms of regimentation and moral authority inherited from earlier class society in order to maintain a propertied minority in power.[47]

---

47. In a 1909 article on "The Attitude of the Workers' Party to Religion," Lenin wrote: "No educational book can eradicate religion from the minds of masses who are crushed by capitalist hard labor, and who are at the mercy of the blind destructive forces of capitalism, until those masses themselves learn to fight this root of religion, fight the rule of capital in all its forms, in a united, organized, planned and conscious way.... A Marxist must be a materialist,

If any individual is to be credited with destroying communism, it is Joseph Stalin not Karol Wojtyla.

The Sandinistas, the church, and the CIA

Finally, the Catholic Church had very little to do with the demise of the Nicaraguan revolution either. Nor was the CIA the decisive force. Both the church hierarchy and imperialist police agencies worked overtime from the outset to try to help reverse that magnificent revolution, of course. From 1979 on, the U.S. rulers, operating in large part through the CIA, armed and financed counterrevolutionary military forces that waged a war against the revolutionary government. The contra war took a horrible toll in human lives and the destruction of productive resources. But the Sandinista-led workers and peasants defeated the contras in combat.

The Nicaraguan revolution rose, it conquered, it declined, and it fell through living social forces whose leadership — the leadership of the Sandinista National Liberation Front — weakened at a decisive point and was no longer able to lead the working class forward on an anticapitalist course.

There is a broader lesson here for revolutionists and other fighters. We'll be badly disoriented, and can end up doing grave damage to the goals for which we are fighting, if our eyes become

---

i.e., an enemy of religion, but a dialectical materialist, i.e., one who treats the struggle against religion not in an abstract way, not on the basis of remote, purely theoretical, never-varying preaching, but in a concrete way, on the basis of the class struggle which is going on *in practice* and is educating the masses more and better than anything could." V.I. Lenin, *Collected Works*, vol. 15, pp. 406–7. Also see Lenin's 1905 article, "Socialism and Religion," in *CW*, vol. 10, pp. 83–87.

As for the Stalinists' attempts to forcibly "reeducate" religious believers, Frederick Engels had pointed out long before, in 1874, "that persecution is the best means of promoting undesirable convictions! This much is for sure: the only service that can be rendered to God today is to declare atheism a compulsory dogma." See "Programme of the Blanquist Commune Refugees," Karl Marx and Frederick Engels, *Collected Works,* vol. 24, (Moscow: Progress Publishers, 1989), pp. 12–18.

fixated on the church hierarchy, or even on spies, cops, and other direct agencies of the ruling classes. They are always there doing their dirty work; that is a given to class-conscious workers. But the most destructive and paralyzing harm to the workers movement and struggles of the exploited and oppressed can only be done from within our own leadership and ranks.

We'll never know, for example, whether the FBI, CIA, or other police agencies would have assassinated Malcolm X. What we do know is that they hesitated to do so, fearing the political consequences that would follow. And we know that the intensifying drive to kill Malcolm organized by the leadership of the Nation of Islam starting in the latter half of 1964 accomplished the vile deed in February 1965 — and that the New York City and federal cops were able to hide in the shadows of this operation.

The destruction of the Grenada revolution in 1983 is another example. The murder of Maurice Bishop and dozens of other revolutionary leaders and cadres was organized and carried out by the Stalinist faction led by Bernard Coard; all that was left for Washington to do was to send in its troops a few days later to mop up the situation and install its handpicked regime.

Similarly in Nicaragua, it was the accelerated retreat from a proletarian political course by the Sandinista leadership following defeat of the contras that increasingly shifted the relationship of forces against the toilers, eroded their fighting morale, and led to the demise of the revolution. This retreat included the disingenuous posturing as "good Catholics" by some Sandinista leaders, every bit of which backfired and strengthened the class enemies of the revolution. For a detailed analysis of these events, I'd urge you to read the articles in issue no. 9 of *New International* on "The Rise and Fall of the Nicaraguan Revolution." They are based on more than a decade of working-class journalism that followed the course of that workers and peasants revolution from the inside, as partisans and participants.

Far from protecting the workers movement against setbacks and defeats, efforts to search out spies and class enemies within our own ranks only opens up our organizations to greater disruption and provocation. Attempts to explain away setbacks or failures as the product of plots or conspiracies by outside forces is not only a source of political disorientation, but can even open up wings of the movement to right-wing crankism and demagogy. What workers and our allies need is an independent working-class political orientation and revolutionary proletarian organization. With that, we can get the job done.

So, we cannot put primary blame on the church or the archbishop in Nicaragua, either. Neither churches nor secret police have ever determined the outcome of any real social revolution or struggle. Those questions are settled on secular, social, and political grounds, no matter how many believers are involved on either side. If we build a solid proletarian communist leadership, and the revolutionary opportunity is ripe enough, no church or secret police or agents provocateurs can block the workers and farmers from victory. That is true of every struggle we have ever seen and every one that will count in any of our lifetimes. History's bloody lessons have taught us to have confidence in that.

How communists prepare

COMMENT: From your talk I drew that we've entered a different kind of period now. The attacks on the working class are much broader, much more widespread. The collapse of capitalism is accelerating. And there is going to be a response by the working class.

So my question is, do you conclude from this that communists also need to begin taking a different approach from that of the last decade — a more agitational approach? Not just explanation, but more agitation, in your press and in your other political work?

RESPONSE: I don't think I would call it a new stage. I am cautious about "stages." And I am cautious about a global acceleration of a capitalist collapse. But what is unassailable is this: the long-term deflationary bias and instability of capitalism are increasing. The enemy is showing more vulnerable spots, even as they deliver blows to our class. Conditions are more volatile. They affect working people and broad layers of the middle classes all over the world in more unexpected ways, bringing greater insecurity and uncertainty into their lives.

Ten days ago, none of us in this room expected what was going to happen in Mexico. But at the same time, we also knew it was bound to happen, didn't we? That is a sign of the times we are living in.

Nobody can predict the "when"; that is unpredictable. Revolutionary workers do not hold ourselves accountable for that. But we can make one ultimately fatal mistake. We can wait until conditions "reach a new stage" before getting serious about building a disciplined proletarian party. By then it is too late. By then, it is no longer possible to redeem the time that has been lost.

The history of the twentieth century teaches us that during periods of rising class battles and revolutionary struggles, a small communist nucleus can grow into a large political force very rapidly. But that is only possible if an initial communist nucleus has been built beforehand. It has to be a nucleus that is proletarian not only in its political program and continuity, but also in the composition of the big majority of its membership and leadership. It has to organize not only through rounded, self-confident, political branch units, but also through structured groups of communist workers in the major industrial workplaces — what we call union fractions in the communist movement.

The worker cadres of such a communist organization need to have gone through substantial experience in the working-class movement beforehand. They must have engaged in strikes and social protest activity with others and gained confidence in debating counterposed strategies and perspectives. They must have experience in talking socialism with co-workers and organizing around a weekly rhythm of political activity. They must be pros in getting revolutionary newspapers, books, and pamphlets into the hands of other fighters and winning workers and revolutionary-minded young people to the communist movement.

Once big class battles and revolutionary struggles break out, it is too late to start building from scratch. If the time beforehand has been redeemed, then the cadres of a communist organization will have had enough experience to have internalized revolutionary proletarian politics in their gut. They will provide self-confident leadership and fight alongside other workers with a bolshevik discipline that comes from within themselves: from years of experience, education, and preparation. They will have developed the habits of discipline, including the habits of study and the discipline to think systematically. They will not be dependent on the formulas of sects. They will not rely on or trust any bureaucratic apparatus ultimately beholden to the exploiting classes.

Revolutionary-minded workers must learn to read broadly, to take complicated questions seriously and work at them — and to study together with co-workers, youth, and newly won members of the communist movement. The capitalist rulers do everything they can to confuse workers, to make us believe we must rely on experts, wizards, and pollsters. They try to obfuscate — about economics, about stocks and bonds, about the monarchy in Britain, about the church in Poland, about class relations in the United States, about education and wage differentials, you name it.

It is always difficult, for example, for workers and revolutionary-minded young people to accept that the bourgeoisie has *no* strategy of any kind. None. We have to learn that through experience. The employing class has no long-term plan. They seek to cut their costs and maximize their profits. They take back what they are strong enough to take. They pragmatically try new tactics and policies when the old ones do not work. They plan to refight the last war.

There is a classic quote in this weekend's *Investor's Business Daily*. Right after Zedillo announced the devaluation of the peso, the managers of one of the big Wall Street mutual funds released a public statement complaining: "The timing of the move was not good, coming at the end of the year when brokers were trying to square up positions and when liquidity was low due to the numbers of investors on vacation for the holidays."

The imperialist bloodsuckers supreme! We were on vacation! But we'll be back on Tuesday to take the fruits of your labor.

The unexpected consequences of the peso's devaluation were not some "Mexican thing," however. We will see more such breakdowns and panics in today's deflationary conditions. The imperialist bourgeoisie in its decline has no plans, no overarching strategy. But at the same time, everything we see beginning to unravel is also the inevitable outcome of the lawful workings of the capitalist system.

What is important for communist workers is to begin preparing now — not to wait for *it* to happen. There is no way to prepare for *it*. Because neither we nor anybody else knows, or can know, what *it* is going to be.

Workers have to fight to get out of the framework the capitalists try to impose on every social and political question. It is not possible for workers to come to the necessary revolutionary conclusions alone, without exchanging experiences and ideas with other revolutionary workers and without reading and studying and discussing what the lessons of our class have been over more than a century of struggles in scores of countries all over the world. We have to think, to discuss, to plan, to organize — to broaden our scope. It takes time and work — and it takes a revolutionary party.

This is the kind of organization the Socialist Workers Party set out to build from the beginning, as you can document for yourself in books such as *The Struggle for a Proletarian Party* by James

P. Cannon, and the four-volume Teamsters series by Farrell Dobbs. The best single guide to party-building in the world our class has been facing since the mid-1970s is *The Changing Face of U.S. Politics: Working-Class Politics and the Trade Unions*. All these books are the heart of the revolutionary political arsenal kept in print by Pathfinder Press.

Yes, we also have to agitate when it's timely to do so. But we do not counterpose agitation to political explanation — which communist workers will continue to do, and to do more of, as the pace of the class struggle picks up. We should never forget that it was during the biggest revolutionary situation in this century, in the months just after the collapse of the tsarist regime in Russia in February 1917, that Lenin taught the ranks of the Bolsheviks that their task above all was "to patiently explain"; their task was to convince the working class of what it was capable of accomplishing by organizing for the conquest of power and breaking politically with all the misleaders who stood in the way of doing so.[48]

Today, we have to work to understand and to explain to other workers why capitalism is becoming more unstable, why this will not be reversed by reforms, why big class battles are inevitable, and why we must organize collectively — as an international class — to overturn this exploitative social system.

If the nucleus of the revolutionary working class does not prepare beforehand, if we do not effectively use the time we have right now, then the odds shift against our class being successful when revolutionary situations develop. If we understand this, then we can see the truth of what the communist movement has said ever since the rise of fascism in this century: that before reaction can conquer, the workers get the first chance.

The capitalist class does not need the fascists, and it will not let them conquer, unless the working class is in a position to contend for power and has lost that opportunity as a result of inade-

48. See the April 1917 articles, "The Tasks of the Proletariat in the Present Revolution" and "Letter on Tactics" in Lenin's *Collected Works,* vol. 24, pp. 19–26, 42–54.

quate leadership. Fascism gains momentum when the working class is putting the fear of God into the exploiters but has not yet removed them from power. If we do not prepare now by building proletarian communist organizations, however, then the upshot of such revolutionary situations will be defeats — and the disastrous consequences such failures will bring not just for working people but for humanity as a whole.

The 'Bell Curve': The scandal of class privilege

COMMENT: You had some things to say earlier today about Yale economists. I wonder what your opinion is of the Harvard professors who came up with *The Bell Curve*. I'm especially interested in why it is that *The Bell Curve* has made such a splash in the public debate in the media. Why it is that every decade or so, it seems, this theory of genetically determined intellectual superiority or racial superiority gets regurgitated and debated and debunked, and then comes back in another form? And in *The Bell Curve*, the form isn't even that different from the past. So why does it seem to have such staying power?[49]

RESPONSE: If my memory serves me right, I think only one of the authors — Richard Herrnstein — was a Harvard professor; he

---

49. Richard Herrnstein and Charles Murray, *The Bell Curve: Intelligence and Class Structure in American Life* (New York: The Free Press, 1994). Much of the debate around the book in the bourgeois press and academic circles is collected in Russell Jacoby and Naomi Glauberman, *The Bell Curve Debate: History, Documents, Opinions* (New York: Times Books, 1995).

just died. I think Murray is currently hired by one of the reactionary think tanks in Washington, D.C. — the American Enterprise Institute.

First, I do not think *The Bell Curve* is as big a deal as it is made out to be. I do not think the debate around it is going to last all that long. Let me ask a question: Will all those in the audience who have read *The Bell Curve* raise your hands? Well, it is pretty much as I thought — a couple of people have read it. I have read about 450 pages, including the last few chapters, and I do not intend to read any more. Yes, there's a lot more.

The recurring debate the questioner referred to is over a political matter, not a scientific one. The debate is not about the bell curve, neither the statistical concept nor the book by that name. What is at issue is the attempt to provide yet another rationalization for the wealth and class privilege of a social layer — "the cognitive elite" is the euphemism chosen by Murray and Herrnstein.

I had hoped to deal with this in the talk, but I did not have time. I expected the question might come up anyway, however, so I brought my copy with me.

Let me read you the first few sentences from the second to the last chapter of *The Bell Curve*, chapter 21, entitled "The Way We Are Headed."

"In this penultimate chapter" — Herrnstein and Murray could have written "second-to-last" chapter, but they had to justify their parents having spent $42,000, or whatever, to send them to Harvard or Yale — "In this penultimate chapter we speculate about the impact of cognitive stratification on American life and government. Predicting the course of society is chancy, but certain tendencies seem strong enough to worry about."

"Worry about" — that's interesting language in what is supposed to be a scientific study. Then they go on to list these "worrying" tendencies:

"• An increasingly isolated cognitive elite.

"• A merging of the cognitive elite with the affluent.

"• A deteriorating quality of life for people at the bottom end of the cognitive ability distribution."

So, that is the opening paragraph of the penultimate chapter. Now let's say it another way:

We're rich. We're rich because we're smart. You can tell we're smart because we're rich. Because we're smart and rich, our kids are smart, and are going to be rich too. But there are a lot of people who aren't getting rich, and they can't seem to accept the fact that this is simply because their forebears were dumb. The liberals — those who are rich and those who aren't — know this and live by it, but are embarrassed to say so. Most people, however, mistakenly think there is some connection between what *we're* doing to get rich and their own deteriorating quality of life. We're getting more isolated in that sense, and a little nervous about anyone wanting to take our privileges away. But we want to enjoy being rich. There is nothing to feel guilty about. We're rich because we're smart.

That is about the long and the short of it.

Then the book ends up with some proposals about what to do with all of us "at the bottom end of the cognitive ability distribution" — orphanages and so on, some of the things we have discussed already. If we can "face reality about the underclass," the book says, then we can provide "the opportunity for everyone, not just the lucky ones, to live a satisfying life." That is, you can learn to like being poor (or be made to pretend to like it).

But this is only possible, the book says, if we get rid of all the social programs and legislation that fly in the face of accepting this reality, such as the minimum wage; affirmative action; more money for public education ("For many people, there is nothing they can learn that will repay the cost of the teaching" — my favorite sentence in the book); the extension of Social Security protections; welfare payments; and so on.

The book *is* a retread of discredited views, but not primarily pseudoscientific ones about IQ, genetics, and so on. It has that too, but that is not the main point. The book is subtitled, "Intelligence and Class Structure in American Life." That is what it is about. It is about *social class* above all, more than it is about race.

The Bell Curve is a rehash — not explicitly, or even consciously, but in fact — of views such as those presented in the 1930s by a man named Bruno Rizzi in a book called *The Bureaucratization of the World*. Similar views began to be developed by James Burnham in the 1940s. Following a fusion in the mid-1930s of communist forces with the American Workers Party, in which Burnham had been a prominent figure, he had become a member of our National Committee. He was a leader of the petty-bourgeois currents in the party that bent to patriotic pressures in the buildup toward U.S. entry into World War II and broke with communism; they split with the party in 1940. Burnham carried his position to a logical conclusion and wrote a book called *The Managerial Revolution* in 1941. He subsequently became one of the most prominent editors and writers on the staff of William Buckley's magazine, *National Review*. Others — prominent New Dealers and so on — have presented their own variants of the "managerial revolution" as well.

All of these writers do the same thing. They project their own professions as a world-organizing force, and as a justification for incomes well above those of working people. And they resent the bourgeoisie at the same time.

Our movement has had decades of experience answering such views. Communist leader Leon Trotsky dealt with their political implications in 1939 and 1940, for example, in articles and letters collected in *In Defense of Marxism*. The book is published by Pathfinder and available on that table at this conference.

According to Murray and Herrnstein, capitalism achieved a wonderful thing by the opening years of the twentieth century. In the United States it happened even a bit earlier, they say. Before then wealth and social position had for centuries been passed on from one generation to the next through a rigid class structure — through aristocratic elites. Those in the ruling classes — from the kings and queens right on down — were often not very smart, notoriously slothful, and morally dissolute.

With capitalism, however, came "the career open to talent." Anyone, they say, from any class background or of any nationality or skin color, could now rise to positions of political power and material comfort — on the basis of merit, intelligence, hard work, and moral virtue.

But today something further is happening, as the level of capitalist technology and computerization advances, they add. The intelligence and competence required to keep modern society up and running is inevitably concentrating wealth and power more and more in the hands of a relatively small layer of middle-class professionals, technocrats, managers, and academics — people, coincidentally, much like themselves. They call this "the cognitive elite." There is nothing that can, or should, be done about this. That is just the way it is, and has to be, due to modern technology.

This is why the book has produced a bit of a scandal in bourgeois public opinion, across the political spectrum but especially among liberals. The furor is not primarily because of what the book says about race. The scandal is its open self-rationalization of the class inequality and privilege benefiting a growing middle-class layer, and its justification for the rightward bipartisan convergence around economic and social policy.

Admit it, Murray and Herrnstein say to middle-class liberals, isn't this what all of us really think? Isn't it how all of us really act? Isn't this why we all live where we live? Isn't it why more and more of us send our kids to private schools? Isn't it why we hire round-the-clock private cops to patrol our neighborhoods? Don't feel guilty. We're rich because we deserve to be rich.

In fact, in the chapter I have been describing, Murray and Herrnstein directly say that during "the Bush and Clinton administrations, the old lines began to blur" between liberals and conservatives. They talk in *The Bell Curve* about the "cognitive elite" versus those who "aren't very smart." Labor secretary Robert Reich, Clinton's house liberal, talks in his book, *The Work of Nations*, about the "symbolic analysts" at the top of the income ladder versus the "in-person servers" and "routine producers" who comprise the majority of the population. What is the difference?

This is also why a layer of ultrarightists in bourgeois politics like Patrick Buchanan have given thumbs down to *The Bell Curve* (and to *The Work of Nations*). Murray and Herrnstein and Reich glorify the "elites" who the rightists rail against. "I think America is a land of opportunity where B students and C students have had A students working for them for generations," Buchanan said in response to *The Bell Curve*. "In America it is not IQ that is destiny; it is character, courage, ambition, drive, personality, all of these things."

That is the kind of demagogy Buchanan aims at sections of the middle class, and receptive and disoriented layers of the working class, who are under growing economic pressure as a result of capitalism's deflationary squeeze. But it is closer to reality, and closer to the gut reactions of the resentful, than *The Bell Curve*, so Buchanan gets a wider hearing than Charles Murray and Richard Hernnstein.

Mounting bourgeois worries
But the scandal around *The Bell Curve* is just one small, and I believe relatively fleeting, reflection of concerns voiced by some in the bourgeoisie about the potentially explosive consequences of what is happening in the world capitalist economy, including the effects of the employers' "successes" in downsizing and cost cutting. Some of them are taking a look at what is building up among the working classes in the United States and other parts of the world and it is beginning to scare them. It is not just communists who can see developments ultimately heading toward intensified class struggle.

A couple of weeks ago, the former editor of the *New York Times*, A.M. Rosenthal, entitled one of his regular op-ed page columns "Lean and Very Mean." He ended with this paragraph:

> If leanness-meanness goes on too long and American opti-

mism finally dies, workers may one day fill the streets again. There will be no F.D.R. to rescue capitalism. . . . American business will find out how very mean life can get.

A.M. Rosenthal is not what they used to call a "bleeding-heart liberal." He is a social conservative, with openly reactionary positions on a few questions. He has been praising big business for being lean and mean for a decade or more. But this is the unexpected outcome he now fears.[50] (By the way, Rosenthal still uses the initials "A.M.," because when he started with the *New York Times* during World War II, if you were Jewish and had a name like Abraham, you weren't allowed to use it on articles or columns and had to go by your initials. The capitalist family that owns the *Times* is Jewish, and that was one of the ways they accommodated to their niche in the U.S. ruling class, where anti-Semitism is the rule, not the exception. Rosenthal has reason to be slightly more concerned than some others in the "isolated cognitive elite.")

About a month earlier, there was an opinion column in the London business daily, the *Financial Times*. The column is called the "Global Investor," and the headline last November 14 was "Work Harder, or Not at All." Think about that for a while — "Work Harder, or Not at All." I'm not making it up.

The column is accompanied by a chart, with three lines tracing indexes economists use to measure productivity in the United States. One line is labeled "manufacturing output" — with a couple of dips,

50. In a subsequent column headlined "American Class Struggle" in March 1995, Rosenthal wrote: "Inevitably Americans who find themselves poorer or more frightened, with nothing between them and the ground, will look to business, a big beneficiary and supporter of the cuts [in federal social spending], to erect a new net. . . .

"If they destroy too much of the government safety net, Republicans will be loading business down with a job it cannot do, with working-class expectations it does not want to meet and cannot. As a bleeding-heart conservative, I believe that will be not only the prescription for class struggle but the beginning of its reality. . . . Left unrecognized or ignored, class struggle creates divisions that can undermine society — any society."

it goes up since 1991. The second line is labeled "hours worked" — it goes up. Then there is the third line, labeled "compensation per hour" — it slides down. There is nothing like a chart to confirm what every working person knows and feels in our bones!

The columnist opens by pointing out that over the previous three months in the United States, profits were "up strongly," sales were "also up sharply," and "many manufacturers said they were still shedding labour." And then he adds: "Here is productivity and no mistake. If this is what the peak of the cycle looks like, God help the workers in the next downturn."

This is what many spokespersons for the bourgeoisie are beginning to worry about — including the "scientists" who wrote *The Bell Curve*, by the way. Yes, we want to push profits up. Yes, we want to be wealthy. Yes, that means we have to keep wages down, push hours up, and speed up production. But isn't this all heading toward some fights by workers? The *Financial Times* article even mentions *The Bell Curve*, commenting that "one does not have to accept the argument to take the point: one way or another, the technological revolution is social dynamite." Leave aside the foolishness that it is "technological revolution" — not the effects of the bosses' cost cutting and downsizing, the effects of the social relations of capitalism — that is "social dynamite." But the *Financial Times* columnist does take the point.

While we're at it, Rosenthal gives a bit too much credit to the power of New York bourgeois aristocrats in stating that "F.D.R. saved capitalism" during the depression of the 1930s. Once workers are engaged in concerted struggle, few of them, especially class-conscious workers, listen to much of anything most capitalist politicians have to say, including Franklin Roosevelt. What Rosenthal leaves out of the story of the 1930s are the union bureaucracy, the Communist Party, and the social democracy. These class-collaborationist forces are the ones who, from within the workers organizations, derailed the social power of the rising industrial union movement by diverting it into support for the capitalist two-party system.

But it is not only thinking workers who can see what is building up under today's deflationary conditions. So if what we see happening all around us — declining real wages, longer hours, deteriorating safety conditions, growing impoverishment — is what is happening in the third year of an *expansion* in the business cycle, then what is in store with the next not-so-soft landing? And what kind of struggles by workers will that lead to when the cycle turns up a little bit and there is some more room to resist? That is what some in the employing class are beginning to worry about.

Politics, not science

So these are the real questions to keep in mind when we are discussing *The Bell Curve*. There are undoubtedly many legitimate criticisms that can be, and have been, made about the book's genetics, its reading or misreading of all kinds of studies, its statistical methods, and so on. To cite just one example, average IQ levels in the industrially advanced countries have gone up substantially since World War II. But if that is what the figures show, and it is (as cited even by Murray and Hernnstein), then this cannot possibly be the product of genetic shifts; it cannot have anything to do with evolution. It is much too short a period of time. These figures reflect changes in social relations, in human beings' concept of themselves, in how they spend their time, and so on. They register the growth in the size of the working class, the drawing of more women out of the home into the labor force, the growing numbers of toilers who have access to primary education, improved nutrition, and other social factors.

But good science or bad is not primarily what is involved with *The Bell Curve*. Charles Murray is not a geneticist. He is a political propagandist. He got a big name during the Reagan administration for writing a book saying that the government should get rid of welfare programs — a book called *Losing Ground: American Social Policy 1950–1980*. The Reagan administration praised it but was not about to follow its advice. Reagan cut some taxes for the rich, and that was about it. The Reagan White House actually increased federal spending across the board, including for welfare payments. Clinton, by the way, also said last year that Murray's writings on the social effects of welfare payments were "essentially right."

Murray says, yes, we have to get rid of welfare. That is the necessary first step toward slashing the social wage. Get rid of welfare and let the chips fall where they may. That is the only way "we" are ever going to get to the point where "we" will be able to walk around safely again in our cities, he says.

Nobody in the ruling class has any solution to the crisis of the capitalist system, and none of them, of course, has any alternative to doing what is necessary to maximize profits. What could they propose? To stop competing? To raise wages and cut hours while their rivals are cutting wages and extending hours?

But more of them are beginning to see what is coming as the decline accelerates and as they press harder and harder against the working class. Some of them are old enough to remember earlier periods in the history of capitalism, or have read enough about them, to know what begins happening when growing labor battles and other social struggles start overlapping and interconnecting. They know that the employers find out that the working class too can get mean as well as lean.

This is the problem some employers are just beginning to anticipate. The hype around *The Bell Curve* has already peaked, but workers' resistance to what the capitalists are trying to impose will not go away.

Most of the debate around the book in the bourgeois press was never serious to begin with. Most of it did not amount to much more than scolding the authors that no matter what they think about these questions, they just shouldn't say it. Now is not the time. It's too explosive.

There is no basis in bourgeois politics right now for some new rise of a reactionary eugenics movement. There was nothing scientific about the Nazis' racial theories. They could not come into their own until the working class had been defeated and fascism had triumphed in Germany. That was a political, not a scientific question.

Anyway, *The Bell Curve* says it is the Jews and Japanese who are the really smart ones, not the Aryans. So, that nixes its appeal straight away with the "America Firsters" and white supremacists. They aren't interested in any eugenics program that could end up phasing out white folks and putting Jews and Asians on top! Hell no, we won't go! They prefer Buchanan to Murray and Herrnstein — you can bet the farm on that.

Human beings, of course, have a genetic structure. But we are not computers. It is not just our hardware that changes. Our software changes, too, as soon as we start doing things with our hands and eyes when we are still just tiny infants. Social practice and experience make us what we are. There are also some things about human beings, of course, that do not change, no matter what happens to us socially. We come in two different sexes. We have different skin pigmentation. And there are many other examples. The world would be awfully boring if this were not true.

But none of this is reducible to some built-in limit to the potential of human beings, or of any socially defined group of human beings. Because that is what both classes and races *are* — they are historically determined social constructs, the product of the rise of class-divided society. The concept of race, in its virulent and pseudoscientific forms, in fact, is the product of only the most recent stage in class society — the rise and consolidation of capitalism.

All the great Marxists have gloried in how the building of socialism will enable working people to transform ourselves — to transform who we are and what we are capable of. Read the Communist Manifesto and other writings by Marx and Engels. Read what Lenin, Trotsky, and other Bolshevik leaders had to say about this. Read the articles and books by James P. Cannon and Farrell Dobbs. Read the books by George Novack and by Evelyn Reed recounting humanity's millennia-long ascent. Read Malcolm X. Read *Socialism and Man* and other works by Ernesto Che Guevara, as well as those by Maurice Bishop.

It is labor that makes possible all civilization and the advance of culture. Working people begin to transform ourselves and strengthen bonds of human solidarity in the very process of building the fighting social movements and disciplined proletarian organizations without which the capitalist rulers will plunge the world into fascism and war.

The transition to socialism is not possible without the organization of working people to begin transforming ourselves and our attitudes toward life and work and each other as we fundamentally transform the social relations of production. We are convinced that what collective human labor will make possible under communism will put humanity so far above the shoulders of those whom we today consider the great thinkers and doers of history that we cannot even conceive the terms of comparison.

CONFERENCE SUMMARY

The following summary talk was presented on behalf of the conference organizers to the January 2, 1995, closing session of the three-day gathering in Los Angeles.

On the lookout for fights and the fighters

For every revolutionary-minded worker or young person today, not just in the United States but the world over, the biggest frustration is the gap that still exists between the assaults by the capitalist rulers and the beginning of any sustained counterpunching by the working class. The entire history of the workers movement teaches us, however, that the aggressive initiatives by the bosses will themselves, over time, begin breeding the counterpunches.[51]

51. Such counterpunches had begun to be landed by working people by early 1997. Over the next two years strikes, resistance to employer lockouts, and other forms of defensive struggles increased in the United States and other imperialist countries.

The Socialist Workers Party and Young Socialists joined in these battles, helping to organize solidarity in the unions and on campuses, getting out the truth about these fights in the pages of the *Militant* and *Perspectiva Mundial*, circulating socialist books and pamphlets, and linking up politically with vanguard workers and farmers engaged in struggle.

As explained by Jack Barnes and Mary-Alice Waters in "Ours is the Epoch of World Revolution," the introductory article to issue no. 11 of *New International* magazine: "The evidence continues to accumulate that the working class in the United States and most other imperialist countries has emerged from the period of political retreat that followed the short, brutal — and demoralizing, because largely uncontested — imperial assault on the people of Iraq in 1990–91. Signs of renewed defensive action are all around us — more numerous strike actions reflecting the tenacity and resistance of the

This conference has helped clarify for all of us that as this process occurs, the preparation by the working-class vanguard that preceded these fights will reap rich rewards. Every day, every week, every month is precious time that revolutionists must use to the fullest to prepare. We must redeem the time we have right now to study the lessons of previous struggles by our class and understand the sources and consequences of capitalism's growing volatility. And we must improve our skills at explaining all this clearly and concretely to other working people and youth as we fight alongside them in every battle that erupts and seek to win them to communist conclusions.

As the working class does start going into action, the numbers, political training, initial combat experience, and even geographical spread of class-conscious workers who are cadres of disciplined proletarian organizations will make the decisive difference in the outcome. In the course of such class battles, a mass communist movement can be built.

While we have been taking part in this conference over the New Year's weekend, a demonstration has been called for Boston later this month to protest the murders of two volunteers at two women's health clinics a few days ago. This lays the basis for solidarity demonstrations that same day here on the West Coast and around the country.[52]

---

embattled ranks; a noticeable growth in the confidence and determination of women in industry; the increased weight of Black leadership in labor battles and struggles of working farmers; an upswing in the Puerto Rican independence movement; more actions in defense of immigrants' rights. Such developments prepare the strengthening of working-class leadership in these struggles and increase the potential of the unions 'to act deliberately as organizing centers of the working class in the broad interests of its complete emancipation.' "

52. On December 30, 1994, Shannon Lowney and Leanne Nichols were murdered while at work at two clinics in Brookline, Massachusetts, near Boston. Five other volunteers were seriously wounded. In March 1996 John Salvi was sentenced to life in prison for first-degree murder.

Within hours of the killings, hundreds of people had mobilized in front of

The murders in Brookline are signs of the weakness of the enemy, not its strength. These killings, like several others over the past two years in Pensacola, Florida, and elsewhere, are acts of terrorism by a handful. Their cause has shown itself incapable of sustaining popular support, let alone shifting bourgeois public opinion against the right to choose.

This is important, because the fact that the right wing today has the political initiative, for the reasons I explained in the opening talk, does not mean they are strong. And it does not mean that workers and youth and anybody with an ounce of human decency cannot respond rapidly and effectively to each and every reactionary probe by the bourgeois parties or rightist outfits. To the contrary, there will be no progress if the vanguard of the working class hesitates when action is urgently needed.

Ever since a rising radicalization and a fundamental shift in the balance of class forces obliged the U.S. Supreme Court to hand down the *Roe v. Wade* decision decriminalizing abortion in 1973, there have been moves by federal, state, and local courts and legislative bodies that have in practice limited access to this medical procedure, especially for working-class women. Federal funding has been cut off; abortion is frequently not covered in medical plans; and numerous state governments have imposed waiting periods and parental consent provisions. There are fewer and fewer counties and fewer and fewer hospitals in the United States today where abortions are in fact available.[53]

---

one of the clinics to protest the murders and defend a woman's right to choose. A few days later a January 22 Action for Reproductive Freedom was called by the Massachusetts National Organization for Women. The action drew 2,500 people from across the East Coast, and hundreds participated in actions elsewhere in the country as well. On April 9, 1995, up to 100,000 people participated in a NOW-sponsored Rally for Women's Lives in Washington, D.C., that raised demands in defense of abortion rights, against domestic violence, for affirmative action, and around a range of other questions.

53. According to a 1998 study, 86 percent of counties in the United States and

At the same time, the majority of working people continue to support abortion rights, and most bourgeois politicians in both parties recognize that prospects to roll back *Roe v. Wade* right now are dim.

It is useful to remember what happened just a few years ago when Operation Rescue launched its nationwide offensive to mobilize right-wing cadres from around the country to shut down clinics and deny women access to abortions. These right-wingers were outmobilized and defeated by counterdemonstrations across the country — from Buffalo, New York, to Baton Rouge, Louisiana. There was a huge demonstration in support of a woman's right to choose in Washington, D.C., in April 1992. Operation Rescue and outfits like it have not recovered from that blow.

When a doctor was murdered outside a clinic in Pensacola in 1993, and when another doctor and clinic escort volunteer were gunned down there just a few months ago in July, there wasn't much in the way of immediate protests.[54] Supporters of women's rights were stunned; some were initially frightened; the fight was momentarily shoved back.

Many of us remember this well, because the second round of murders had happened in July 1994, a few weeks before a socialist conference in Ohio that August where we discussed it. But

---

one-third of U.S. cities have no abortion providers.

54. Dr. David Gunn was killed outside a clinic in Pensacola, Florida, on March 10, 1993. Michael Griffin was found guilty of first-degree murder and sentenced to life in prison. James Barrett, a clinic escort, and Dr. John Bayard Britton were shot to death outside another Pensacola clinic on July 29, 1994. Paul Hill was found guilty on two counts of first-degree murder and sentenced to death. Several years later, in October 1998, Dr. Barnett Slepian, a physician who performed abortions at a clinic in Buffalo, New York, was murdered by sniper fire in the kitchen of his home. Protests were organized over the next several weeks in the Buffalo area, New York City, Boston, Toronto, Vancouver, and other cities in the United States and Canada. As of early 1999, nobody had been arrested in connection with the killing.

the evidence from what has already begun happening the past few days in Massachusetts and elsewhere indicates a different response this time around. There are going to be mobilizations by those who represent the real majority view on this question in the United States.

At least momentarily, the terrorist action in Brookline is already further dividing, and weakening, right-wing forces opposed to women's rights. The cardinal in Boston canceled a planned anti-abortion-rights protest there and called for a moratorium on further actions at clinics. On the TV news this morning, on the other hand, I watched an interview with several ultra-right-wingers. One priest explained that "innocent life" must take precedence over life that is "not innocent." While not condoning murder, this rightist said, what happened in Brookline was a justifiable response to a much greater evil — the slaughter of innocents that goes on every day.

Such views will never carry the working class in the United States. They cannot carry young people. They cannot carry women. The 1973 Supreme Court decision registered what had been won in struggle by the mass civil rights battles and the rise of a women's liberation movement over the past several decades. It cannot be taken back without big battles and a major defeat to the labor movement and fighters for democratic rights.

Participants in this conference from Houston, from Seattle, and from Vancouver have already come up to me over the past two days to tell me that the weekly meetings of the Militant Labor Forum in those cities next weekend will protest the Boston killings and discuss their meaning in U.S. politics. I'm sure there will be other such meetings here on the West Coast and around the country. Public forums where workers and young people can get together to analyze, discuss, and better understand these events and the political questions raised by them are a form of protest in their own right. People come to meetings like that as a way not only to discuss the issues but to stand up against acts that disgust and outrage them. These public forums will also help alert activists to the protest picket lines, clinic defense activities, and demonstrations that are scheduled for Boston and other cities.

The events in Brookline and the initial response to them confirm many of the political themes we have been discussing at this conference over the past three days.

It's important not to exaggerate what is happening in politics. As revolutionists, we are always looking for action; we always want struggles to advance. So we should also work to be objective in our judgments about the degree of resistance taking place. Not cautious in responding in a timely way to developments in the class struggle, large or small. Not cautious in the political initiatives we take in reaching out to broader forces. But we should be prudent in exactly what we say about political developments as they begin unfolding and how we assess them.

It is often better to be a day late about what is coming than to jump the gun and end up disappointing ourselves and others unnecessarily. Young revolutionists need to learn to fight and operate in politics, not to speculate on exactly how fast our class will be able to conquer this or that particular goal.

But I think the facts before us from the past couple of years — the facts we discussed at the convention of the Socialist Workers Party in August 1994 and that were reported in the *Militant* newspaper, the facts that are presented in issue no. 10 of *New International*, and that we have discussed some more here at this conference — justify drawing a number of conclusions that revolutionists need to act on. Young people who are being repelled by the horrors capitalism is producing, and by the growing voice of rightism they hear in political life, need to hear these conclusions. They need to be explained to the growing numbers of workers who — regardless of what the unions are or are not doing right now — are convinced that something is terribly wrong with the way this system works and are willing to discuss, read, and think about radical ideas as to why and what can be done about it.

Out here in California, Governor Wilson evidently thinks the results at the ballot box in November justify a total transformation of class relations in the state. According to an article I read in the *Los Angeles Times* on the opening day of the conference, Wilson still thinks he is riding high from the adoption of Prop 187 and now plans to go after affirmative action. "I don't think that it's fair to give preference based upon race or gender," Wilson says. "I think what we should do is make those judgments based upon merit" — here comes the cognitive elite, the managerial revolutionaries, the symbolic analysts again! — "after affording real equality and opportunity of access." (And Wilson knows individuals rise on the basis of merit, because he rose! What else could explain it! QED.)

The article goes on to describe efforts by a Republican state assemblyman here to get an amendment passed to the state constitution barring affirmative action laws. He says he will either take the amendment directly through the state legislature or launch a petition drive to get it on the ballot in 1996 like Prop 187.[55]

But Wilson is deluding himself if he thinks he can keep pressing without a fight. The ballot box poses every question in bourgeois

55. First elected governor of California in 1990, Wilson was returned to office in the November 1994 elections in which the anti-immigrant Proposition 187 also received a majority of the ballots cast. Opponents of affirmative action succeeded in placing a so-called "California Civil Rights Initiative" (Proposition 209) on the ballot for the 1996 elections. In July 1995 the University of California Board of Regents, including Wilson, voted to end affirmative action programs in admissions and hiring in the state university system. In response to these moves, supporters of affirmative action organized meetings and protest actions in cities and on university campuses across the state.

Proposition 209 was adopted by 54 percent of votes cast in the November 1996 elections. Enforcement of the reactionary measure was upheld by a federal circuit court in April 1997, and the U.S. Supreme Court allowed that ruling to stand. The very next year, the percentage of Blacks, Latinos, and American Indians accepted into the 1998–99 freshman class at the University of California at Berkeley dropped to 10.5 percent from 21.9 percent the previous year; the percentage fell to 14.1 percent from 21.8 percent at the University of California at Los Angeles; and it dropped to 15.2 percent from 17.6 percent for the eight campuses in the University of California system as a whole.

terms, and the results it produces can be misleading. Those who turn out to vote — and large numbers of workers do not — are given a choice between bourgeois parties.[56] If there happen to be referenda on the ballot, the choice is usually between alternative poles of bourgeois "solutions" to dilemmas they confront, and are often demagogically packaged as well.

A conference participant brought to my attention something else that appeared in the *Los Angeles Times* just yesterday — one of the year-end photos of a massive demonstration in opposition to Proposition 187. And there have been other demonstrations, school walkouts, and protests of various kinds both before the elections and since. These are a much more reliable gauge than Wilson's ballot box of what is building up here in California and throughout the country.

Citizens of the world

What we have been discussing the last several days are not phenomena that affect working people just in Mexico but not California, or that shape politics just in Russia and China but not Canada and Britain. These are all international phenomena, and that fact is very important to communist workers. Because we are citizens of the world, and that is not just a metaphor!

Walk into a factory in the United States — or in France, or Sweden, or Germany, or Australia, or even to a smaller but growing degree in Japan. You will find workers from throughout the world. You will find more and more people from different nations and na-

---

56. Voter turnout in the 1996 elections dropped to 49 percent of the voting-age population, the lowest in any modern U.S. presidential election.

tionalities working side by side. They draw strength from each other when any resistance to the boss class flares. They exchange experiences from the class struggle in their countries of origin. They initiate discussions with each other about what is happening all over the world and bring to bear their different experiences and perspectives.

All this is the product of the workings of capital, accelerating for a quarter century or more.

Communists preclude any lasting progress toward transforming social relations unless the experience, energy, and talents of toilers all over the world are drawn into that process. "Socialism in one country" has been a counterrevolutionary notion from the time it was first championed by Stalin in the mid-1920s to rationalize the retreat from proletarian internationalism by an increasingly privileged apparatus. But it is even more of a reactionary utopia three-quarters of a century later. No single country can surge ahead and build socialism, turning its back on the rest of the world, any more than we can transform social relations and ourselves "at a snail's pace."[57]

Of course, capitalism from its origins has been a world phenomenon in its tendency and effects. That is one of the things discussed by those of you who went to this weekend's class on the Communist Manifesto. "The need of a constantly expanding market for its products chases the bourgeoisie over the whole

---

57. Stalin initially combined the call for "socialism in one country" with support for Soviet leader Nikolai Bukharin's call for building socialism in the USSR "at a snail's pace." This was a rationalization for the emerging caste's political bloc with developing capitalist layers and commercial "middlemen" in the countryside. Trotsky and other opponents of Stalin's counterrevolutionary foreign policy also advocated an alternative domestic policy of accelerated industrial development to strengthen the worker-peasant alliance. At the end of the 1920s, when the emerging petty capitalists withheld grain from the Soviet government to drive up prices, Stalin turned on a dime. Moscow launched a brutal forced collectivization of the peasantry and heavy industrialization, at the cost of a drastic decline in needed food, fiber, and quality manufactured goods for working people. Bukharin was purged by Stalin from the party leadership in 1929 and executed following a frame-up trial in 1938.

surface of the globe," Marx and Engels explained in the Manifesto. "It must nestle everywhere, settle everywhere, establish connections everywhere.... It compels all nations, on pain of extinction, to adopt the bourgeois mode of production; it compels them to introduce what it calls civilization into their midst, i.e., to become bourgeois themselves. In one word, it creates a world after its own image."[58]

We learned a little more about this from another angle during Tom Leonard's class on "Racist and Anti-Immigrant Discrimination and the Trade Unions: The Case of the Maritime Unions." Over the decades, class-conscious workers on the merchant ships have been able to see firsthand in many countries — from Korea to Guatemala to South Africa — just how capitalism "creates a world in its own image." And they also experienced how a tiny microcosm of those oppressive social relations was recreated in the composition and command structure of the crews themselves.

This internationalization has been under way for several hundred years, since capital set out to conquer the earth and bring everything — from textiles and handicrafts in India, to slaves from Africa, to gold and silver from the New World — into an expanding world market. From the very origins of the modern communist workers movement 150 years ago, Marx and Engels and other revolutionary leaders insisted on approaching toilers in every corner of the globe as comrades and equals, not as "socialist" liberators, missionaries, or lecturers. There were fights and divisions over that communist course between revolutionists and reformists from the very beginning of the modern workers movement.

But even with the growing international penetration of capital, there was still not a single world politically. The communist movement from the days of Marx and Engels through World War I and the Russian revolution was overwhelmingly a Euro-

58. Karl Marx and Frederick Engels, *The Communist Manifesto* (New York: Pathfinder, 1995), pp. 26–27.

pean and North American movement, with a few scattered organizations in parts of South America and Japan.

But with the October 1917 revolution, the call was sounded by the Bolshevik leadership that the toilers of the entire world could emulate what their brothers and sisters had begun in Russia and other parts of the old tsarist empire. When the Communist International held its founding conference in 1919, it brought into being for the first time a *world* movement in every sense — not only in its internationalist perspectives, but also concretely by drawing proletarian revolutionists from the colonial world, especially Asia, into its ranks *and into its leadership.*

Lenin and other Bolshevik leaders insistently pointed out that nowhere in the world — even in the most economically backward countries — did the toilers any longer have to accept the imposition of some necessary stage of political rule by the bourgeoisie and brutal exploitation by them. Everywhere in the world the toilers were capable of following the example of the workers and peasants in Russia and overturning the power of the landlords and capitalists. Everywhere in the world it was possible to establish revolutionary governments based on soviets — that is, councils — of the exploited producing classes themselves.

Lenin would not have been surprised that a popular revolutionary government could come to power in a very poor country such as Burkina Faso in West Africa; that it could produce a world-class communist leader such as Thomas Sankara; nor that the working people of that country — overwhelmingly peasants, with a small urban working class — could set an example that young revolutionists across Africa and beyond into the imperialist metropolises would begin to look toward.

Lenin would not have been surprised that a workers and farmers government could come to power on a small Caribbean island such as Grenada under the leadership of a proletarian revolutionist such as Maurice Bishop.

Lenin would certainly not have been surprised that a communist leadership of the caliber of Fidel Castro, Ernesto Che Guevara, and others could lead the workers and farmers of a relatively economically advanced semicolonial country such as Cuba in a victorious socialist revolution.

The new period opened by the Russian revolution and Communist International did not mean, of course, that the concrete character and priority of economic, social, and political tasks was the same in every country or region of the world, nor that the socialist revolution was on the agenda in each of them. Until the decades following World War II, as we discussed during the opening session of the conference, the majority of the world's toilers lived under direct colonial subjugation, and the combined fight for national independence and land was the axis of revolutionary struggles in most of these nations.

The peasants and workers formed the backbone of the movements that fought for and won national independence, in most cases under bourgeois or petty-bourgeois leaderships. These battles, in turn, often spurred further struggles to take back the national patrimony — natural resources, ports, transportation, and utilities — from direct imperialist ownership and control.

In one of the sessions earlier in this conference, we had an extensive and useful discussion of the eyewitness report back by Greg McCartan on the unfolding democratic revolution in South Africa, which over the past half decade has been led to a new stage by Nelson Mandela and the African National Congress. The victory there earlier this year in holding the first-ever one-person, one-vote elections in that country, in which the ANC won a decisive majority, is opening up new prospects to forge and strengthen proletarian leadership in that country and elsewhere in Africa.

With all these particular forms and complexities, however, the fight for revolutionary governments of the toilers has truly become a world phenomenon since the October 1917 revolution. In China following World War II, for example, the rotting of landlord and capitalist rule was so advanced that the workers and peasants there triumphed even under Stalinist leadership. And the U.S. rulers' effort during the Korean War to deal a deathblow to the Chinese revolution ended up unleashing the defensive actions by working people that culminated in the establishment of a workers state in China in 1953.

The Chinese revolution shattered racist lies and assumptions about the oppressed peoples of color that had been perpetuated for centuries by the major colonial and then imperialist ruling classes of Europe and North America. Malcolm X deeply appreciated what that revolution meant to oppressed and exploited peoples around the world. He had many wonderful things to say about it during the last year of his life.

"There was a time in this country when they used to use the expression about Chinese, 'He doesn't have a Chinaman's chance,'" Malcolm told a rally in Harlem in November 1964, just after returning from a trip to Africa and the Middle East. "Remember when they used to say that about the Chinese? You don't hear them saying that nowadays. Because the Chinaman has more chance now than they do.... It was not until China became independent and strong that Chinese people all over the world became respected.... It's the same way with you and me."[59]

I vividly remember sitting with some other comrades in the King Solomon Baptist Church in Detroit earlier where Malcolm was speaking and hearing him say that what frightened Washington the most about the Chinese getting the atomic bomb was not that they might develop advanced missiles, but the knowledge that hundreds of millions were ready to hand-carry the bomb if need be to defend their revolution.

But the Stalinist regime headed by Mao Zedong made it impossible for the Chinese toilers to become as powerful a force as they could have been to advance the struggle for national liberation and socialism in Asia and throughout the world. To the degree the Maoist regime did influence fighters, it turned them away from proletarian internationalism toward petty-bourgeois

59. "The Homecoming Rally of the OAAU" in Malcolm X, *By Any Means Necessary* (New York: Pathfinder, 1970, 1992), p. 136.

nationalism. Nowhere was there a greater gap than in China between what the working class and peasantry had shown themselves capable of accomplishing and what they were blocked from
doing by Stalinism. The Stalinist apparatus in China is still in
place today, but the influence of the Beijing variant of Stalinism
is qualitatively weaker in the workers movement in Asia than at
any time since the 1950s.

As we have been discussing throughout this conference, never
since the rise of Stalinism has there been a better time than today for
revolutionary workers to share experiences with other workers and
youth in other countries and sell them books, pamphlets, and other
communist literature. The breakdown of the bureaucratic apparatuses, capitalism's ceaseless internationalization of our class, the
worldwide spread of communication and news — all this allows
workers who are becoming political and young people who want to
fight to be drawn together as never before. Just a few years ago, we
would have been prevented by force of arms in many countries such
as the German Democratic Republic and the USSR from traveling
and openly discussing communist politics as we do today. The limit
is no longer where we are not able to go but our own political initiative, experience, and resources.

The example I find most striking is the anti–Vietnam War
movement in the 1960s and early 1970s. It became a very large and
broad social protest movement, and it spread internationally
throughout Western Europe, Asia, and many countries in the
Third World. There was an ongoing Vietnam solidarity campaign
in Cuba.

But we utterly failed to draw workers and youth from the Soviet Union and most of the workers states in Eastern Europe into
the real battle in the streets against the Vietnam War. (A few actions in Czechoslovakia and Yugoslavia were the exceptions.)
Revolutionists and many others active in the antiwar movement
would have loved to do so, and efforts were made. But it was not
a goal we could achieve under prevailing conditions. Stalinism
weighed too heavily.

The Soviet Union and Vietnam were allies. The Soviet government was the main source of military aid to Vietnam. But it was next to impossible to have discussions and make connections with any individuals or political forces in the Soviet Union or elsewhere in Eastern Europe who could be drawn into common anti-war activity. The Stalinist apparatuses that rigidly controlled all political activity were afraid to mobilize or allow the mobilization of large numbers of young people in the streets against imperialism. Where would it lead? The official "solidarity" organizations suffocated any genuine solidarity with living revolutionary struggles. The handfuls of young people there who did try to initiate meaningful protest actions against the Vietnam War quickly found themselves in jail.

Moreover, the fact that the regimes and Stalinist parties professing "bonds of proletarian internationalist friendship" with Vietnam were themselves the hated oppressors of working people in city and countryside dampened enthusiasm. All these factors stood in the way of any active solidarity in these workers states with the Cuban, Nicaraguan, or Grenada revolutions as well.

These conditions are now changed. And while there is no royal road to international solidarity, the obstacles that less than a decade ago walled off toilers in a number of countries from political winds sweeping the rest of the world have now been greatly weakened.

Aren't all of us influenced and inspired by the human courage displayed by Chechens who have blocked the roads around Grozny and appealed to the Russian soldiers? That is a matter of human courage, not technology. There is no doubt that the capital of Chechnya could be taken by an all-out ground assault, at a great cost in human life. Where there *is* room for doubt, however, is the price Yeltsin will have to pay over time to organize the Russian army to carry out such an operation. That is still not settled.

Moscow is starting to see the limits of raw force. Because ultimately raw force has to be carried out by human beings, and human beings can be transformed by deep-going social and political processes. People watching television around the world saw a group of women standing in a road and then saw a Russian officer start weeping and order his tanks to turn back. That refusal to carry out Moscow's orders cost the regime much more politically than it stood to gain militarily from making those orders stick.

If ever there was a time when workers need to think of ourselves as citizens of the world, and make that the starting point of politics, it is now.

Winning new forces to the communist movement

During the session on South Africa earlier in the conference, I was struck by something Greg quoted from Nelson Mandela's closing speech to the convention of the African National Congress that took place a couple of weeks ago. Mandela stressed how much the ANC, at every level, needs "new blood."

We, of course, can say the same thing. In fact, I think every revolutionary organization in the world can say the same thing.

This conference over the New Year's weekend here has confirmed that new blood is coming toward the communist movement. Earlier today, a leader of the Young Socialists reported to us that a number of young people here have expressed interest in becoming YS members. We have heard reports throughout the conference about the people we meet who want to get involved with us in activities in defense of the Cuban revolution, in support of abortion rights, against Prop 187 and other attacks on immigrants, and around a range of political questions. We have collaborated closely with fellow unionists active in the Caterpillar strike and other labor resistance we have taken part in over the past year.

In all these different ways, we are meeting workers and various young people who get involved in actions, who begin to resist what capitalism is producing. And we find that a growing number of them become interested in broader political ideas and decide to join the communist movement. We should glory in this process. Because it is the heat lightning of much bigger class battles.

Young people are being radicalized. Youth become sensitive to the political, social, cultural, and moral implications of capitalism's breakdowns earlier than other layers of society. They react to the injustices, and they are ready as individuals to make commitments to do something about them.

The important question for the communist movement is this: How do these radicalizing youth find their way to the working class? This is not a question of class origins. We are talking about how radicalizing young people in general can be won to the working class, not just youth from the middle class. Being born and raised in a working-class family does not by itself bring anybody to the working class *politically*.

Lenin expressed a very radical view that was disliked by some "orthodox Marxists" of his time. He said that students — what we would today call high school and college youth — are going through a period in their lives when their class is not a settled question; they are to some degree determining what class they will be part of. Of course, no one can choose to become part of the bourgeoisie. Wealth and class privilege in capitalist society are passed along through blood lines. The working class, too, is a hereditary class, with only relatively small numbers climbing into the middle class (and even smaller numbers during periods of social crisis like today, with growing numbers from the lower middle class being pushed into the working class as well).

That was not Lenin's point, however. He was making a *political* point about student youth. He was not talking about the thin, privileged layer being trained in special, elite institutions for their roles in the ruling class. Lenin's point was that if you take student youth as a whole, in the high schools and universities, those individuals most open to politics are not blocked by their class origins from coming to revolutionary proletarian conclusions if they find the revolutionary proletarian organization.

Even if a young person is open to politics, of course, it is not until they become active that they begin to understand what politics really is. That is, they discover they must decide which class's line of march is worth fighting to advance. Which class provides effective social and political answers worth committing their lives to? Which class has the program, strategy, and social power to wipe the filth, the unconscionable relations among human beings produced and reproduced by capitalism, off the face of the earth and begin reorganizing society on new foundations?

It is not unusual, nor should it be surprising, for young people to ask questions about whether workers can actually build a socialist world. In fact, the correct answer is: "No, we can't; not as we are today. We make no pretense otherwise."

But there is a much deeper truth, which has been at the heart of Marxism from its origins and which Che Guevara endeavored with such clarity and eloquence to salvage from decades of Stalinist muck. That is, in any true social revolution, workers begin the process of transforming themselves as they collaborate, mobilize, organize, and educate themselves to transform the exploitative class relations they inherit from capitalist society.

That fact is the root of the greatest contradiction that has, since the Stalinist counterrevolution, confronted the workers states in the former Soviet Union, across Eastern Europe, and in China. That is why Khrushchev's boast "We will bury you!" could only be a reactionary fantasy. Through the expropriation of the bourgeoisie and establishment of the foundations for a planned economy, the indispensable base had been laid for workers to begin collectively transforming themselves and their social relations, becoming thinking human beings of a new type as they advanced the transition to socialism — at whatever pace and with whatever detours the course of the world revolution made necessary.

But thinking, self-acting workers are a deadly threat to any entrenched bureaucracy. And so at the point that economic output in the Soviet Union and across Eastern Europe could no longer be expanded by drawing another layer of rural toilers into the factories, progress began slowing to a crawl. Because only a politically class-conscious and motivated working class could organize under those conditions — outside the domination of the law of value — to advance labor productivity. But a class-conscious working class was precisely what the petty-bourgeois Stalinist regimes could never tolerate, let alone encourage.

Workers, however, *can* organize ourselves to revolutionize society and begin our own transformation in the process. This is what young fighters, young revolutionists can be won to. As Farrell Dobbs often explained, young people at any time can come to the working class *politically* through the revolutionary party.

What the communist movement has to offer young fighters is not riches, not a powerful apparatus to become dependent on, either politically or financially. What the communist movement has to offer above all are the generalized lessons, the truthful written record, of the experience of the modern working-class struggle over the past century and a half. It is only by reading, by doing the hard work of studying, and then collectively discussing these lessons that we can redeem what others before us have fought for and won, often at great sacrifice. That is the only way we can learn from their successes, avoid their mistakes, and put ourselves and our class on a stronger footing to fight effectively and win.

I think many of us over the weekend were struck in particular by Tom Leonard's two classes, the one on immigrants I mentioned previously and the one on the unions and the fight against imperialist war. For the majority of us, this was an opportunity to learn from the experiences of a veteran revolutionary worker, from how he personally discovered some of the biggest transformations in world politics as he traveled the seas as a maritime worker during and after World War II. For many in this room, it was an opportunity to draw lessons from a period of time when you were not yet even on the face of this earth. At the same time, there is also one participant in this conference, Harry Ring, who will soon celebrate his sixtieth year in the communist movement. And we have others here who are well into their fourth decade in the movement, or their third, or their second.

So, the political continuity of the communist movement exists not only through books — nor can it ever, solely — but also through a living web of practical political work and experience. That is why we place such importance on forging a cadre and a leadership that braids together these generations and their overlapping experiences and transforms them into a disciplined combat organization and world communist movement.

It is not just youth, not just thinking political workers, who are attuned to the elemental shifts in politics and the class struggle, even before sustained mass action gets going. These rumblings are detected, if not fully understood, by the most alert spokespeople for the bourgeoisie as well. More and more of them are worried by signs that working people are being pressed too hard, signs that unexpected fights may be brewing.

Remember the brief excerpts I read during the discussion period the day before yesterday from a *New York Times* column by A.M. Rosenthal, a column from the *Financial Times* of London, and the closing chapters of *The Bell Curve*. We are breeding a class war, these bourgeois voices are saying, and we must either prepare for it or try somehow to slow it down. But the capitalists can never prepare sufficiently for the uncontrollable and unforeseeable forces their declining system is producing. Moreover, the crisis itself places ever-sharper limits on the concessions they can make to the toilers, if not to slow down the decline then at least to buffer its consequences.

In their own fashion, sections of the trade union bureaucracy sense these changes too. These bureaucrats are social parasites,

1 (RIGHT) RALLY IN DECATUR, ILLINOIS, IN SOLIDARITY WITH MEMBERS OF AUTOWORKERS UNION ON STRIKE AGAINST CATERPILLAR, INC., RUBBERWORKERS ON STRIKE AGAINST BRIDGESTONE/FIRESTONE, AND WORKERS LOCKED OUT BY A.E. STALEY, OCTOBER 1994. OUT OF THESE STRUGGLES IN THE MID-1990S A CADRE OF "ROAD WARRIORS," CATERPILLAR "BLUE SHIRTS," AND OTHER WORKERS EMERGED THAT CONTINUES TO BE ACTIVE IN LABOR STRUGGLES AND SOLIDARITY TODAY. **2** (BELOW) WORKERS IN ARGENTINA PROTEST UNEMPLOYMENT, INTOLERABLE SOCIAL CONDITIONS. LIBERTADOR, JUJUY PROVINCE, MAY 1997.

"The nightmare unfolding across the Americas and elsewhere is the product of the lawful, predictable, irreversible, and unreformable workings of capitalism. But equally as lawful and inevitable is the resistance, mobilization, and organization of its gravediggers."

3 (TOP) WORKERS IN PUERTO RICO DURING GENERAL STRIKE AGAINST PRIVATIZATION OF TELEPHONE COMPANY, JULY 1998. SIGN SAYS, "NO TO THE BIGGEST ROBBERY IN HISTORY. NO TO THE SALE OF TELEFONICA." **4** (BOTTOM) COAL MINERS ON STRIKE AGAINST FREEMAN COAL AND SUPPORTERS MARCH IN VIRDEN, ILLINOIS, OCTOBER 1998.

5 (TOP) FARMWORKERS AND SUPPORTERS, YAKIMA, WASHINGTON, APRIL 1997. **6** (MIDDLE) UNEMPLOYED WORKERS IN PARIS DEMAND WORK, INCREASED BENEFITS, JANUARY 1998. **7** (BOTTOM) PALESTINIAN YOUTH CONFRONT ISRAELI SOLDIERS IN BETHLEHEM, DECEMBER 1998.

"The consequences of the capitalists' declining rate of profit will have decisive weight in determining the course of the class struggle. There will be no return to a sustained growth of investment in capacity-expanding plant and equipment that can draw wave after wave of labor into increased production."

8 (RIGHT) UNSOLD HYUNDAI AUTOMOBILES SIT IN STORAGE AT PORT NEWARK, NEW JERSEY. **9** (BELOW) UNEMPLOYED WORKERS LINE UP TO APPLY FOR JOBS, DETROIT, MICHIGAN, 1993.

10 SINCE THE 1994-95 "PESO CRISIS," U.S. CORPORATIONS HAVE BOUGHT OUT MEXICAN BANKS AND OTHER ENTERPRISES. CITIBANK ASSUMED CONTROL OF CONFIA, MEXICO'S ELEVENTH LARGEST BANK, IN AUGUST 1997. (RIGHT) CITIBANK BRANCH IN GUADALAJARA. **11** (BELOW) FIFTEEN THOUSAND PROTEST IN MEXICO CITY AGAINST GOVERNMENT PLANS TO SELL PART OF STATE-OWNED OIL COMPANY, MARCH 1996.

"The essence of imperialism is that the world has become divided into a handful of usurer states on the one side, and a vast majority of debtor states on the other."

"Some in the bourgeoisie are getting worried. It is not just communists who can see developments ultimately heading toward intensified class struggle."

12 (TOP LEFT) WORKERS IN BERLIN PROTEST
UNEMPLOYMENT, MARCH 1998. SIMILAR
RALLIES TOOK PLACE IN OVER 200 CITIES
ACROSS GERMANY. **13** (BOTTOM LEFT)
MEMBERS OF UNITED STEELWORKERS ON
STRIKE AGAINST TITAN TIRE IN DES MOINES,
IOWA, NOVEMBER, 1998. **14** (TOP THIS PAGE)
DOCKWORKERS IN AUSTRALIA CELEBRATE
VICTORY AFTER COMPANY IS ORDERED TO
REINSTATE 1,400 WORKERS IT HAD DISMISSED
TWO WEEKS EARLIER, APRIL 1998. **15** (RIGHT)
CANADA'S RULERS ARE LOSING GROUND IN
THEIR ATTEMPT TO STOP THE FIGHT FOR
INDEPENDENCE IN QUEBEC. 100,000 PEOPLE
PARTICIPATE IN JUNE 1998 CELEBRATION OF
QUEBEC'S NATIONAL HOLIDAY.

"These clumps of vanguard workers and farmers who are resisting in the *present* also have a political and collective *past*. They have established relations of mutual trust with other fighters, and have a political *future*, as well. They are the cells of a class-struggle cadre that will grow into the millions as battles accelerate."

16 (RIGHT) UAW MEMBERS ON STRIKE AGAINST TAZEWELL MACHINE WORKS IN PEKIN, ILLINOIS, DECEMBER 1998, SUPPORTED BY AUTOWORKERS FROM CATERPILLAR PLANT IN NEARBY EAST PEORIA. **17** (BELOW) WORKERS LOCKED OUT BY CROWN CENTRAL PETROLEUM IN PASADENA, TEXAS, AND ALABAMA SUPPORTERS PICKET CROWN GAS STATION IN BIRMINGHAM.

"The accelerating crises and breakdowns in the exploited Third World are good reason for the toilers to overthrow those who benefit from and defend the imperialist system."

18 (TOP) THOUSANDS DEMONSTRATE IN ALGIERS, ALGERIA, OCTOBER 1997, TO PROTEST RIGGED ELECTIONS. **19** (BOTTOM LEFT) DEMONSTRATION IN BOGOR, INDONESIA, DEMANDS RETURN OF FARMLAND STOLEN BY GOVERNMENT, SEPTEMBER 1998. **20** (BOTTOM RIGHT) STARK CONTRAST OF WEALTH AND POVERTY IN RIO DE JANEIRO, BRAZIL.

"The U.S. rulers' yellow brick road to the restoration of a stable capitalism in the former Soviet Union and Eastern Europe has vanished."

21 (TOP LEFT) WORKER IN ALBANIA GUARDS FIGHTER JETS SEIZED DURING 1997 POPULAR UPRISING AGAINST U.S.-BACKED REGIME OF SALI BERISHA. **22** (TOP CENTER) WOMEN NEAR GROZNY, CHECHNYA, CONFRONT OCCUPYING RUSSIAN SOLDIER, DECEMBER 1994. **23** (TOP RIGHT) 3,000 MARCH IN SARAJEVO, DECEMBER 1995, AGAINST THE DISMANTLING OF THE MULTINATIONAL STATE FORGED DURING THE YUGOSLAV REVOLUTION OF 1945. **24** (RIGHT) COAL MINERS IN RUSSIA BLOCK THE SIBERIAN RAILWAY DURING MAY 1998 STRIKE DEMANDING PAYMENT OF BACK WAGES BY YELTSIN GOVERNMENT.

"Immigration strengthens the fighting potential of labor's battalions and brings new experiences and militancy into the workers movement."

25 (TOP LEFT) MARCH IN SOLINGEN, GERMANY, CONDEMNS ATTACKS ON TURKISH IMMIGRANTS, MAY 1998. SIGN SAYS, "FIGHT NEO-FASCISM AND RACISM. EQUAL RIGHTS FOR ALL." **26** (BOTTOM LEFT) WORKERS ON STRIKE AT FOSTER FARMS POULTRY PLANT IN LIVINGSTON, CALIFORNIA, OCTOBER 1997. **27** (TOP THIS PAGE) HIGH SCHOOL STUDENTS IN LOS ANGELES, CALIFORNIA, PROTEST ANTI-IMMIGRANT LEGISLATION, NOVEMBER 1994. **28** (BOTTOM THIS PAGE) MARCH 1993 DEMONSTRATION IN JERSEY CITY, NEW JERSEY, PROTESTING FRAME-UP ARRESTS FOLLOWING WORLD TRADE CENTER BOMBING IN NEW YORK EARLIER THAT YEAR.

"The scandal of the 'Bell Curve' in bourgeois public opinion is its open self-rationalization of the class inequality and privilege benefiting a growing middle-class layer."

29 (ABOVE) GAP IN LIVING STANDARDS BETWEEN UPPER MIDDLE CLASS AND PROFESSIONALS, AND THE VAST MAJORITY OF WORKING PEOPLE, WIDENED THROUGHOUT THE 1980S AND 1990S. **30** DEATH PENALTY IS USED BY RULING CLASS TO INTIMIDATE WORKERS. RICKY RAY RECTOR (LEFT) WAS EXECUTED IN ARKANSAS DURING 1992 PRESIDENTIAL CAMPAIGN. WILLIAM CLINTON, THEN GOVERNOR, RETURNED FROM CAMPAIGNING AS A SHOW OF SUPPORT FOR EXECUTION.

"Cops mete out punishment on the spot. That is the class reality of cop harassment and brutality."

31 "BRUTALITY IS THE CONDUCT TAUGHT IN POLICE DEPARTMENTS IN CITIES AND TOWNS ACROSS THE COUNTRY." (RIGHT) LOS ANGELES, JULY 1995.
32 (BELOW) AUGUST 1997 PROTEST TO DEMAND JUSTICE FOR ABNER LOUIMA, WORKER FROM HAITI TORTURED BY NEW YORK COPS.

"The exploiters' failure to defeat us during World War II and its aftermath set up the problems they face today. The Cold War was the term used by the U.S. rulers to describe the hot war they could not fight and did not think they could win."

33 (TOP) MASSIVE PROTESTS BY U.S. TROOPS IN EUROPE AND ASIA AT CLOSE OF WORLD WAR II PREVENTED WASHINGTON FROM FOLLOWING THROUGH WITH ITS PLANS TO CRUSH THE ADVANCING CHINESE REVOLUTION. **34** (RIGHT) WORKING PEOPLE OF ZAGREB GREET YUGOSLAV PARTISAN TROOPS AS THEY LIBERATE THE CITY, MAY 1945.

35 (TOP) STUDENTS WELCOME SOLDIERS
FROM THE KOREAN PEOPLE'S ARMY AS THEY
ENTER SEOUL IN THE SUMMER OF 1950.
KOREAN AND CHINESE TROOPS HANDED
U.S. IMPERIALISM ITS FIRST MILITARY DEFEAT.
36 (RIGHT) SAYING "YOU CAN'T MINE
COAL WITH BAYONETS," COAL MINERS
REJECTED BOSSES' "NO STRIKE" LAWS
DURING WORLD WAR II. **37** (BOTTOM)
1942 NEW YORK PROTEST AGAINST RACIST
FRAME-UP AND DISCRIMINATION BY
BOSSES AND GOVERNMENT.

38 NINETEENTH CENTURY POORHOUSE IN ENGLAND. FIGHT FOR GOVERNMENT-FUNDED UNEMPLOYMENT INSURANCE, DISABILITY BENEFITS, HEALTH CARE, AND PENSIONS HAS BEEN AND REMAINS CENTRAL TO UNITING THE WORKING CLASS AND ITS TOILING ALLIES.

"For workers in the United States, Social Security was the beginning of the attempt to moderate the dog-eat-dog competition imposed on the working class under capitalism. For the working class, there is no real social security that does not cover the entire lifetime of a worker."

"The battle for jobs, the battle for solidarity, against racism and the oppression of women, the battle against immigrant-bashing, the battle for social protection are battles for the life and death of the labor movement."

39 (RIGHT) MARCH FOR AFFIRMATIVE ACTION AT UNIVERSITY OF CALIFORNIA IN LOS ANGELES, OCTOBER 1995. **40** (BOTTOM) DECEMBER 1994 PROTEST AGAINST MURDER OF TWO HEALTH WORKERS THE PREVIOUS DAY AT CLINIC NEAR BOSTON THAT PROVIDED ABORTIONS.

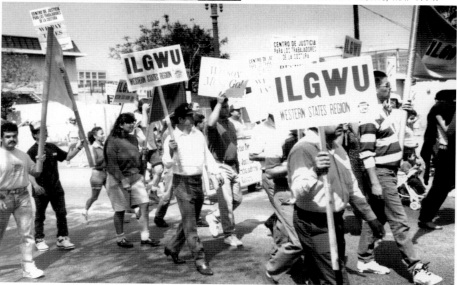

"**The unions must convince the world at large that their efforts, far from being narrow and selfish, aim at the emancipation of the downtrodden millions.**"

41 (LEFT) STRIKING MINERS FROM JEDDO COAL CO. IN EBERVALE, PENNSYLVANIA, HELP LEAD COMMUNITY FIGHT AGAINST TOXIC WASTE DUMP, FEBRUARY 1998. **42** (BELOW) GARMENT WORKERS CONTINGENT AT LOS ANGELES MARCH FOR IMMIGRANT RIGHTS, MAY 1994.

even if in a different way from the bondholders and other capitalists. The officialdom makes its living by trying to make sure you do what they want you to do, so they can keep collecting your dues and at the same time maintain the backing of their masters in the employing class. Daniel DeLeon was an old socialist from the turn of the last century who got a lot of things wrong, but among the things he got right was a name for the labor bureaucrats — a name that Lenin loved. DeLeon called them "the labor lieutenants of the capitalist class."

They are ultimately a very weak layer, whose berths will be quickly threatened in the course of any substantial upswing in labor struggles. So out of an instinct for self-preservation, some of them have developed a nose for when class equilibrium is becoming unsettled and things could start getting dicey.

At such times, the officialdom starts reaching out to radicalized workers — including to many like you in this room — to try to get your eyes off the ranks of the working class. They want you instead to collaborate with them to pressure the bosses and the bosses' parties. They want your help in refurbishing in the eyes of the ranks — without altering — the union structures as they currently exist. These officials sense the deadly logic for themselves if the gates are swung open and the ranks burst forward to wield union power against the bosses and the government.

That is why there are few errors worse for class-conscious workers to make right now than to allow ourselves to be drawn into taking responsibility, under whatever guise, for the formal mechanisms of the trade union movement. To do so, as this molecular process of change begins to become palpable in the working class, can only aid the officialdom in cleaning up their image and derailing any breaks toward a fighting labor movement.

Many young people who become sensitive to these changes, however, do so for reasons diametrically opposite to those of the bourgeois commentators or trade union hacks. Young people want to take action against the horrors bred by the capitalist system. And as they do so, some are attracted to a communist workers movement that not only understands and can explain the social and political roots of these horrors, but that looks forward to a good fight and aspires to build on and add to the legacy of all the revolutionary struggles of the past.

Above all, we must never forget what it is that we are preparing ourselves for. We are preparing for the consequences of the inescapable logic of capitalism in its decline, summed up in the feature headline of the new issue of *New International* — "Imperialism's March toward Fascism and War." It is not a logic just toward greater use of military power. It is a logic that breeds more, and more virulent, fascist formations aimed at crushing the world workers movement. And it is a logic that heads toward a third, unthinkable world conflagration.

But the outcome is not inevitable. Because, as we have discussed this weekend, before the exploiters can inflict these horrors on humanity, they have to go through the working class; they have to defeat the working class. That was the truth in Italy at the opening of the 1920s. That was the truth in Japan in 1931–32, and again in Germany in 1933. That was the truth in Spain in the closing years of the 1930s.

The working class was horribly defeated in those class battles, paving the way for imperialism's second world slaughter, and the accompanying horrors from Buchenwald to Hiroshima. But coming out of World War II — despite the bloody defeats that led up to it and the infamies it encompassed — U.S. imperialism failed to overcome the obstacles to their renewed war plans. Working people in many corners of the earth — from their own GIs and labor movement, to workers and farmers in the Soviet Union and throughout Asia, the Middle East, Africa, and the Americas — remained an unexpectedly strong barrier to the U.S. rulers' goals.

If you think about the world we have been describing over the past three days, this is quite some ending to the twentieth century! We are living through the consequences of what the imperialists failed to accomplish, because they could not defeat the working class. As we have said, the seeming chaos our class faces today — here in the United States, in Mexico, and around the world — is *not* chaos. What we face can be understood. It is lawful. It should be sobering, but it does not have to be frightening. If we think it through, it will help us understand why our class enemies — despite their wealth, their military might, and their brutality — are acting from weakness.

What is described in *New International* is the honest, historical truth. What we have been discussing here this weekend, to use the words of the Communist Manifesto, is nothing more nor less than the "actual relations springing from an existing class struggle, from a historical movement going on under our very eyes."[60] And it is truly the best reason to join the communist movement.

60. Marx and Engels, *The Communist Manifesto*, p. 36.

CAPITALISM'S DEADLY
WORLD DISORDER

The following talk was presented April 10, 1993, to participants in a regional socialist educational conference in Greensboro, North Carolina, and the following day to a similar gathering in Des Moines, Iowa. The talk reported the decisions of a meeting the previous weekend in New York City of the Socialist Workers Party National Committee, youth leaders of the SWP, and leaders of communist leagues in several other countries.

The brevity of the 'New World Order'

The *Militant* has been running an ad for this weekend's conference entitled "Challenges Facing the Working Class." That's fine. But in this talk I want to alter the focus to, "Challenges *and Opportunities* Facing the Working Class." I would like to open discussion here on the proposition that communists confront fewer obstacles in spreading revolutionary ideas today — in working together with other working-class and revolutionary-minded fighters who are not yet communists, and distributing communist literature on a wider scale in this country and around the world — than we have faced for decades.

We not only need to see these opportunities in their longer-run context, but to grasp — and accept — the responsibilities they imply. I have had some help in preparing this presentation, since I was fortunate enough to have just spent four days in New York at an international meeting of leaderships of communist leagues from around the world and of youth who are leaders of the Socialist Workers Party. We came to agreement at that meeting that the idea of a "New World Order" — with which global bourgeois opinion was so enamored right after the war against Iraq — is now behind us, and that a pattern of disintegration of the capitalist world order is starting to emerge.

Think about the world we have practiced politics in since late 1987 when panic swept stock markets from New York to Hong Kong.

Think about the events that have transpired since then — from the Soviet Union, to China, to South Africa, to Cuba, to Europe (East, West, and Central), and to the United States. It has been a very unusual six years.

The evidence is, however, that the changes that caused the greatest surprises are behind us. That is, we can now better anticipate the character and the broad response of different classes to the world conflicts that are unfolding and will continue to unfold. We can begin to describe — and then analyze — this pattern.

We know what is going to happen with the capitalist economy. Regardless of conjunctural ups and downs, the reality of the opening of a world depression and its deflationary bias will not go away. Cyclical capitalist recoveries, regardless of their duration, will be marked by that deflationary reality. It will mark the assaults on the working class and the increasing economic, and even social, differentiation within our class. And it will mark the character of the contest between the working-class vanguard and the capitalist rulers over how badly our class will be damaged by the workings of the market system before large-scale resistance begins.

Just a few months ago, the new Democratic Party Clinton administration took office. Clinton is a war president. That includes international economic and financial wars that will end up destabilizing capitalism and threatening real wars, as they always have throughout the history of capitalism. It will include the cold-blooded use of assaults against oppressed and exploited peoples and nations, in order to further advance Washington's dominant position in the imperialist feeding chain. A striking feature of the comments by communists from other countries at last weekend's meeting was their emphasis on the degree to which the big-business press in those countries was startled — even stunned — by the economic and political offensive of the Clinton administration.

True economic aggression has been declared against Japan, against Germany and other countries in capitalist Europe. Clinton came into office and announced to the Canadian and Mexican governments that it was very nice that they had negotiated and signed initial accords for the so-called North American Free Trade Agreement, and now it would be very nice before signing the final one for them to make a few more concessions his administration deems just.[1]

U.S. imperialism will use its weight — be it police power, be it economic coercion, be it grinding pressure on the job, be it threats abroad, be it organizing direct military intervention or precipitating bloody struggles in other countries it pretends to stand above — in order to try to compensate for the disintegration of the stability of an expanding, self-confident capitalist social and economic order. How it does so, and the effects, dominate the patterns of world politics. Economic instability, social dislocation, and political radicalization — right and left: that is what all of us are slowly but surely being pulled into.

There are only two forces on earth today that face up to this reality. And even though both are relatively small, to a large degree what they do — including what they do relative to each other's successes, forcefulness, and political clarity — will have a great deal to do with how the growing world crisis of capitalism is resolved.

One of these are forces on the ultraright. They at least see what is coming in the sense of realizing what liberal, parliamentary democracy *cannot* produce. They have few illusions in normal bourgeois politics, its rituals, and its established elites. Day after day, month after month, opportunities are increasing for the ultraright to denounce capitalist politicians and political parties — the parties their leaders are members of — for failing to "do something

---

1. The North American Free Trade Agreement, signed by Washington, Ottawa, and Mexico City, went into effect January 1, 1994, with the additional concessions negotiated by the U.S. rulers. On that same day, an uprising in the southern Mexican state of Chiapas opened a simmering peasant-based rebellion that has continued since that time.

effective" about the recurrent manifestations of the economic and social crisis. The rightists point the finger of blame at scapegoats, including those who suffer the most from the effects of the crisis. That process has begun inside the capitalist two-party system in the United States. It has begun on the streets of Germany and inside the bourgeois parties in France, in Italy, in Japan. It has begun inside Russia and throughout most of the world.

The communist movement is the other force that understands what is coming. We understand the implications of how world politics is unfolding. And we fight to take advantage of every single opportunity to explain this world outlook to the vanguard of the working class, to work together with other fighters, and to draw forces toward the communist movement and toward its written legacy from a century and a half of class-struggle experience.

Revolutionists are often accused of wanting economic and social conditions to get worse, because we supposedly think "the worse, the better." We are accused of predicting crises that do not occur, or of expecting events in the class struggle to develop more rapidly than they do. The latter has an element of truth, perhaps. There is a tendency among those who want to change the world to be impatient. That is not the worst trait in the world; being "laid back," let alone cynical, is much worse. But revolutionists do have to work hard if we are going to be accurate and if we are to deserve the confidence of working-class fighters. It takes work not to misjudge, not to jump too far ahead, not to oversimplify; it takes genuine analysis.

I think the danger we face today, however, is not one of impatience or exaggerated expectations. The danger is being unable to face up to the implications of where the social crisis is headed. The crisis is heading toward the kinds of struggles, toward a shift in the pace of political life, that practically no one in this room has ever seen. It is heading toward battles with the kind of explosive character and violence that are seen only infrequently in the development of class society.

Thinking workers and other fighters sense that a corner has been turned. As pressures from the rising class tensions build, they sense that today's deepening crisis — at whatever pace it unfolds, and with whatever twists and turns — will not be resolved short of battles in which reactionary forces will be unleashed in the streets against the labor movement and its allies. If communists do not clearly and forthrightly explain what is coming, then the anticipation of these developments can drive us away from the line of march of the working class and even make cowards of us over time, to our belated surprise.

It is often said that great historical crises are always and only resolved in struggle; you do not have to be much of a historian to know that makes sense. But what is not said as often is that the odds in these class struggles — the probability of victory or of loss — are determined long before the battles themselves break out. The odds depend on the self-confidence, political clarity, and previous combat experience of vanguard forces who see the political trends and who are already among the fighters on one side or the other of the class barricades. It depends on the preparations by cadres of disciplined proletarian organizations who know that what they have done *beforehand* will be decisive when the working class moves toward revolutionary action.

The best example, of course, is the October 1917 revolution in Russia. Prior to the revolution, the Bolsheviks were a relatively small force many of whose leaders, above all V.I. Lenin, had worked for nearly a quarter-century with a very clear idea of the character, inevitability, and depth of the crisis that was coming. Every "legitimate" force — including in the broad left wing of the international socialist labor movement of that day — considered the Bolsheviks to be an irksome minority of extremists doomed to inconsequentiality. But it was the Bolsheviks who were able to lead the workers and peasants in putting an end to the horrors and the bloodshed of World War I, and of capitalist and landlord domination in the tsarist empire.

That kind of political preparation, for those kinds of coming class battles, remains the central task of small communist organizations today.

Crisis of the market system is worldwide

To get an accurate understanding of the unfolding crisis of the world capitalist order, it is useful to review what the Socialist Workers Party and our co-thinkers in communist organizations in other countries have discussed and come to agreement on since the worldwide stock market crash of October 1987.

The crash was confirmation that we have entered a sharply defined segment in the historic curve of capitalist development. The outlines of everything we are living through now, and are going to be living with in the foreseeable future, came into sharper focus. We presented our assessment of this turning point in the resolution discussed and adopted at the party's 1988 convention, "What the 1987 Stock Market Crash Foretold."[2]

We said we had entered an extended period in which the consequences of the capitalists' long-term declining rate of profit will have decisive weight in determining the course of the class struggle. There will be no return to a sustained growth of investment in capacity-expanding plant and equipment that can draw wave after wave of new labor power into increased production. That is, we will not see the kind of prolonged economic expansion that could allow the capitalists — as they did for several dec-

---

2. The resolution is available in *New International* no. 10. See also the 1923 article "The Curve of Capitalist Development" by Bolshevik leader Leon Trotsky, printed in that same issue.

ades after World War II, and during certain other periods since the latter half of the last century — to buy off, even corrupt, better-off layers of working people and to stabilize their social system on that basis. The capitalists will not be able to dominate major areas of the world in such a way that — while repressing, oppressing, and exploiting growing hundreds of millions — a surface stability nonetheless reigns in the economically developed capitalist powers and in the relations among them.

A world depression had become inevitable, we said. We refused to predict when the depression would come, and we kept saying, "Be cautious; don't jump to identify a crash and stunning social crisis with the opening of depression conditions." But when it did come, we said, it would prevent normal conjunctural upturns in the capitalist business cycle from substantially reducing unemployment. For the first time since the 1930s, we explained, workers would experience the deflationary effects of growing domestic and international price competition among capitalists. The capitalists would continue their assault on real wages. Attacks would broaden and mount against the social wage, against the social rights and entitlements that working people have won through struggles earlier in this century to defend ourselves as a class. And attacks would escalate against the political rights workers have wrested from the rulers that facilitate action in the streets to press for their needs.

Out of the conflicts engendered by such a social crisis, we said, growing political polarization was inevitable. Rightist forces would become more bold, as the failures of the traditional bourgeois parties and leaders to produce solutions became more obvious to increasingly insecure layers of the middle class and working people.

The Berlin Wall tumbles

Two years later, in 1990, we discussed the developments taking place in Central and Eastern Europe and the Soviet Union and drew broader conclusions about world politics.

The United States ruling class has lost the Cold War, we said. What the bourgeois press and spokespeople were initially hailing as the U.S. victory in the Cold War was in fact ordained to become an enormous new burden for world capitalism. The capitalists in Germany and some other European countries who were greedily investing in Central and Eastern Europe and in Russia, in order to consolidate their supposed great victory, were "live ones," we said. They were suckers — nothing like the salvation they were reaching for would come out of this profit-seeking lurch to the east.[3]

The imperialist rulers face an enormous problem in attempting to reestablish the capitalist system in the former Soviet Union and other workers states, we said. There is no capitalist class in these states, and it takes a long time for historic classes to be created. It takes a long time for a bourgeoisie to consolidate ownership of banking, industrial, and landed capital, and for bourgeois

---

3. Imperialist investment in Russia, minuscule relative to capital flows to Asia and Latin America throughout the 1990s, virtually collapsed following the Yeltsin government's default in August 1998 on some $40 billion in domestic debt. Coming on top of the credit and currency crisis in Asia, Moscow's default sent shockwaves through the holders of some $150 billion in Russia's foreign debt. Apparently in hopes of buffering a panic ever more costly to imperialist creditors, Standard and Poor's — one of the Wall Street firms that assigns ratings of creditworthiness to various countries and corporations — invented a new category in February 1999 just for Russia: "Selective Default"!

Between 1991 and 1997, $9 billion in foreign investment in plant and equipment flowed into Russia, compared to $160 billion to Latin America over that same period, and $181 billion to China alone. Overall foreign direct investment into the Central and Eastern European workers states (including Russia) during these same years totaled a little more than $50 billion. At the same time, there was an estimated $150 billion in capital flight from Russia between 1991 and the end of 1998.

The world capitalist crisis whose manifestations spread from Asia in 1997 to Latin America and beyond resulted in a sharp decline of more than $100 billion in imperialist capital flows to the Third World and European workers states as a whole in 1998.

values, legal systems, and money and credit networks to become dominant, let alone stable. A rising exploiting class can only accomplish this through accumulating capital, entrenching its own power, and imposing on a propertyless proletariat the social relations that go along with that power. But every serious step in this direction involves massive assaults on the working class that will meet resistance and threaten social stability, we explained.

Every other political current, not only in the world bourgeoisie but throughout the workers movement, said that the fall of the east German Stalinist regime would lead to a great economic burst forward for German capitalism. We said no. German finance capital would become a dysfunctional boa constrictor: the west would swallow the east whole but would find the indigestion worse than the meal. Unemployment and social differentiation would increase in the west. Class tensions and political polarization would increase in Germany, and the myth of a coming conflictless "united Europe" would be further undermined.[4]

---

4. As of the end of 1998, the German imperialist government had poured some $625 billion into the eastern half of the country since 1990. With two-thirds of industrial workers in eastern Germany having been turned out of their jobs over that period, most of Bonn's funding goes to social transfer payments, not investment in infrastructure or plant and equipment. In early 1999, the official unemployment rate in the eastern half of Germany was still nearly 20 percent, and over 11 percent for Germany as a whole — the highest level since the early 1930s — and living standards in the east remained well below the national average.

By 1998 large-scale discontent coming out of rising class tensions was propelling a leftward shift in bourgeois politics in Germany, as in most of Europe and North America, resulting in the election in September of a Social Democratic Party–Green Party coalition government, with Gerhard Schröder as the new chancellor. The Christian Democratic Union–Christian Social Union (CDU-CSU) coalition, headed by Helmut Kohl — the self-proclaimed "father" of German unification — was swept from office for the first time in sixteen years.

At the same time, the accelerating social crisis fueled ongoing political polarization, as registered by the CDU's successful state election campaign in Hesse in February 1999 on a rightist platform targeting the rights of Germany's 7 million immigrants. Only hours after this electoral setback, the So-

Moreover, what was opening up as a result of the collapse of the Stalinist apparatuses in Eastern Europe and the Soviet Union was the possibility, for the first time in half a century or more, of collaboration between workers in these countries and workers facing similar assaults on their rights and living conditions in other countries. About a week ago, I watched on the TV news a mass demonstration in Germany of metalworkers and their supporters from other unions. All the workers there — from the western and eastern parts of Germany, from Sweden and other countries who had come to show their solidarity — were above all protesting one thing: the decision by the German government and employers to renege on the public promises to bring together the living standards, wages, and working conditions of workers in the two parts of the country. That kind of Germany-wide working-class action could now begin to happen again, after more than sixty years. It will take time, but it is now possible.

All this sounds less surprising today. But just two years ago when we insisted on this perspective, it sounded wild to almost everybody else. Even other fighters we knew — capable, committed revolutionists and communists from Cuba, South Africa, and elsewhere — thought this view was literally nonsense. What will become today's common sense among a growing layer was then still seen as outrageous.

Trade rivalries and interimperialist conflicts would sharpen, we said, and new ones would develop. Without their old anti-Soviet, anticommunist shibboleths, the imperialists would wage a new ideological fight to justify military intervention when they needed it around the world, and that would increase nationalism

---

cial Democrats said they were reconsidering proposed legislation granting dual citizenship rights for the first time to some immigrants. The Greens followed suit, saying they too were ready to compromise further on immigrants' rights; the Greens had previously watered down their call for shutting down nuclear power plants in Germany. In addition, the government coalition has announced its readiness to dispatch 2,000 combat troops to Kosova in Yugoslavia as part of any NATO "peacekeeping" force.

and feed into the "culture war" of the rightists.

The rulers would launch a new ideological assault to blame the working class for the catastrophes caused by the capitalist crisis. They would target entire layers of the working class — immigrants, workers receiving social welfare payments, working women raising children on their own, and others. The rulers intend for these workers to be blamed by other workers for their troubles and targeted by an increasingly insecure middle class. The capitalists' goal is to deepen economic and social divisions in our class and in the process weaken human solidarity within the proletariat. In face of these pressures, at a certain stage the working class will begin to find a way to unite itself and start probing common struggles — out of which a fighting political vanguard will grow. Either that vanguard will prove capable of charting a class-struggle course toward power, or the toilers will suffer their worst defeat in history.

While we were sizing up these major new developments in the world class struggle, we were also engaged in important fights in *this* country, including the 686-day strike by Eastern Airlines ramp workers, cleaners, and mechanics in the International Association of Machinists and the eleven-month-long strike by United Mine Workers–organized miners against Pittston coal company and other mine owners. These fights confirmed that if worker-bolsheviks keep our eyes on the right place, on the *ranks* of the working class and labor movement, then we can find political space to step up our political work. Communist workers can find individuals to talk socialism to and, together with them, can more easily see the possibilities for a way out of the growing social tensions bred by the disintegrating capitalist world order.

U.S.-organized war against Iraq

Then, after several months of building up a massive military machine in the Arab-Persian Gulf, Washington launched a climax to the war against Iraq at the beginning of 1991. U.S.-organized air assaults inflicted massive death and destruction, and 150,000 or more Iraqis were cold-bloodedly massacred during the one-hundred-hour invasion and "turkey shoot" that culminated the war. Saddam Hussein, Iraq's bourgeois military dictator, had simply refused to organize a fight, setting up the country's troops and civilian population for the slaughter. Nonetheless, we said, the outcome of the Gulf War was not the big victory that Washington initially pretended. Instead, its consequences would accelerate the coming world political fiasco for U.S. imperialism.

Contrary to dominant opinion, across the spectrum from right to left, we insisted that the kind of alliance cobbled together by Washington for that war would not be put together again, and could not be put together again. An alliance of all the imperialist powers and many bourgeois governments in the Gulf region and Middle East, with open backing in the United Nations Security Council from Moscow and Beijing, had come together to support Washington. But such a combination of powers would never again come to agreement on a war or similar major military operation.

Far from the Gulf War alliance being the clearest example of the New World Order trumpeted by the U.S. rulers, we pointed out, conflicts will accelerate internationally and open up the next stage of world capitalist *disorder.* In fact, we did something we usually should not do; we predicted something very specific. We predicted that well after U.S. president George Bush, Soviet president Mikhail Gorbachev, and other heads of state in the U.S.-led alliance were long gone, Iraqi president Saddam Hussein would be like the Eveready Rabbit — he'd keep on going and going and going. And we were right.

We argued the U.S. rulers face a fundamental dilemma, which is not being confronted by the mainstream of either major imperialist party. Either they use the kind of military force abroad that over time leads to resistance to their wars among working people and youth in the United States and begins to transform politics in this country. Or they are unable to use the kind of force they need to resolve political and social crises that will threaten U.S. imperialist interests and undermine acceptable, stable conditions for capitalist world trade and investment. The first Iraq war was far from the last time the U.S. ruling families will face this dilemma in the years ahead.

The accelerating conflicts in the world mean there is greater danger of the use of nuclear weapons today, we said. There will be greater proliferation of nuclear weapons, and the missiles and planes capable of delivering them will become more and more unsophisticated and cheaper to acquire.

Just two weeks ago, we had the public confirmation by [then] South African president F.W. de Klerk that the apartheid regime gave up its nuclear weapons program when it lost to the Cuban internationalist volunteers and Angolan army at the battle of Cuito Cuanavale in the late 1980s.[5] That was the end for all time of the dream of becoming a strategic nuclear power that would dominate Africa, from the Cape of Good Hope to the Sahara. (De Klerk's announcement also gives you an insight into the mentality of the racists in power there. The need to stop "them" from getting the bomb, now that "they" are going to dominate the government, was what carried the day in the cabinet.) Contrary to Pretoria's denials, we found out that everything we had deduced since the 1970s had been correct: the self-proclaimed representatives of the two "chosen

---

5. In 1975 the South African apartheid regime, with Washington's support, invaded Angola in an effort to overturn the government of that newly independent country, formerly a Portuguese colony. The invasion was blocked with the help of Cuban internationalist volunteer troops, who responded to the Angolan government's appeal for assistance. The white supremacist regime continued its war against Angola until 1988, when it was decisively defeated at the battle of Cuito Cuanavale by Cuban, Angolan, and Namibian forces.

The victory at Cuito Cuanavale propelled a new rise of struggles against the apartheid regime within South Africa itself. In 1990 the white minority regime of de Klerk was compelled to unban the African National Congress and release ANC leader Nelson Mandela from prison after more than a quarter of a century. The racist forces were unable to stop the rising revolutionary struggle against apartheid, and in April 1994 the first-ever one-person, one-vote elections were held, in which the ANC won a decisive victory. Mandela became the new president of South Africa.

peoples" — from Tel Aviv and from Johannesburg — *had* cooperated to set off nuclear test explosions in the South Atlantic, and to jointly advance the strategic nuclear war program of each.

It has also recently been admitted for the first time that the governments of India and Pakistan came closer than anybody ever knew to using nuclear weapons against each other a couple of years ago.[6]

The outcome of the Gulf War did not bring the government of Iran closer to Washington, but it strengthened the position of Iran's capitalist rulers vis-à-vis other ruling families in the Gulf region. This includes the rulers of Saudi Arabia, who will be economically devastated — and less internally stable and more dependent than ever on Washington — as a result of their expensively purchased victory in the war against Iraq.

The war both exposed and furthered the exhaustion of bourgeois nationalism in the region. In countries from Egypt to Syria, the war weakened bourgeois forces and political figures that claim to speak for the interests of the entire oppressed nation, including working people. These forces are no longer able to play the role some did even a few decades ago in presenting themselves as effective defenders of sovereignty and the national patrimony against imperialist domination and plunder. Egypt's president Hosni Mubarak can turn over information to Washington about a sheik and allege to have evidence he was involved in a conspiracy to blow up the World Trade Center. But Mubarak cannot pretend to lead the toilers in Egypt forward or to do anything to improve their standards of life.

---

6. In the spring of 1990 the government of Pakistan placed its nuclear weapons arsenal on alert as it amassed tank units along its border with India. Four years earlier, in December 1986, the Indian military integrated tactical nuclear weapons into maneuvers staged near the Pakistani border. Ever since India and Pakistan won their independence from the United Kingdom in 1947, the governments of the two countries — formed as a result of British colonialism's divide-and-rule tactics — have disputed sovereignty over Kashmir. India controls two-thirds of the region. In May 1998 the Indian government detonated five underground nuclear weapons. Pakistan carried out six nuclear tests two weeks later.

The war did nothing to bring the imperialists nearer their goal of imposing a solution denying the right to national self-determination to the Palestinians. At the same time, we said, the Palestine Liberation Organization leadership dealt itself a political blow during the Gulf War when Yasir Arafat and other PLO leaders publicly backed Saddam Hussein's demagogic linkage of Iraqi withdrawal from Kuwait with Israeli withdrawal from the occupied Arab territories.[7]

---

7. In the wake of the 1987–92 Palestinian uprising (the *intifada*) in the Israeli-occupied West Bank and Gaza strip, the PLO signed a series of agreements with Tel Aviv in late 1993 and the first half of 1994. The accords established limited Palestinian self-administration over pockets of land in the West Bank of the Jordan and Gaza (only some 2 percent of the West Bank), with the Israeli government retaining overall sovereignty, control of all borders, and veto power over questions of land and water usage. In January 1995 elections were held for president and a legislative assembly of the Palestinian National Authority (PNA), which would function as the municipal administration for Palestinian-controlled areas of Gaza and the West Bank.

Over the next several years, both Labor- and Likud-dominated regimes in Israel reneged on implementing additional small-scale withdrawals from Palestinian territory in the West Bank, while provocatively encouraging further Israeli settlements there. In face of ongoing Palestinian resistance, Washington brokered an agreement signed in October 1998 by Arafat and Israeli prime minister Benjamin Netanyahu at the Wye River Plantation in Maryland, under which Tel Aviv pledged to proceed with the withdrawals by early February 1999 in return for additional Palestinian concessions. These concessions included agreement that the Palestine National Council would reaffirm its vote of two years earlier removing clauses from the PLO charter calling for the overthrow of the Israeli state and establishment of a democratic, secular Palestine. (Implementation of that agreement involved the degrading spectacle of Clinton actually checking out from the platform the nearly unanimous show of hands by PNC members during his December trip to the region.) In the spirit of the Wye Accords, PNA police also banned protests in the West Bank and Gaza against Tel Aviv's refusal to carry through on its agreed release of Palestinian political prisoners and against Washington's renewed bombing of Iraq in the closing weeks of 1998.

As of February 1999, the Netanyahu government, for its part, had refused once again to meet Israel's agreed-on deadlines for additional troop withdrawals and release of Palestinian prisoners.

Finally, during the Gulf War and its onset, communist workers here in the United States, like those around the world, proved that if we stuck to our guns and said what we believed, we could have civil discussion and political arguments with other workers about the war and imperialism. We got a hearing from other workers, even as U.S. soldiers were carrying out military operations in the Gulf in January and February 1991.

We sold the resolutely anti-imperialist, antiwar, and defeatist *Militant* newsweekly and socialist books and pamphlets on the job right through the war preparations and the brief war. Pathfinder rapidly produced a book to gain the widest possible hearing for the only government in the world that was telling the truth about Washington's war preparations and seeking to mobilize international opposition to it. The book was entitled, *U.S. Hands Off the Mideast!: Cuba Speaks Out at the United Nations*, and we sold it to co-workers, outside factory gates, on campuses and street corners, and at protest picket lines and demonstrations against the war.

In doing so, we demonstrated the political space that exists for communist workers to carry out politics in the labor movement. This only has meaning, however, if we work together with other workers to use that space, whether in peacetime or in wartime.

These are the political conclusions that communist workers in the United States and other countries drew from our experience campaigning against imperialism and war, and we discussed and codified them in several reports adopted by the party's June 1991 convention. Those lessons are accessible in a special issue of the magazine *New International*, issue no. 7, titled "The Opening Guns of World War III: Washington's Assault on Iraq." They are also contained in the opening article of Pathfinder's expanded 1994 edition of *The Changing Face of U.S. Politics: Working-Class Politics and the Trade Unions*.

A worldwide crisis

At the beginning of 1992, we were able to put one more piece in place. We pointed out that the economic factors we had observed since the 1987 crash and the trends that led up to it, *plus* the collapse of the Stalinist apparatuses and the consequences of the war in Iraq, coincided with and reinforced the entry of the world capitalist economy into the early stages of a long-term deflationary crisis. These events precipitated the opening of depression conditions. Everything that happens in world politics will now happen under its pressure, with increased financial instability and unpredictability. It narrows the economic policy options of the big capitalist powers and imposes further economic pressures on the working class and social differentiations within it.

The crisis of the market system had become worldwide. And its mounting impact, its grinding character and duration, would increasingly shake the illusions among more and more working people the world over that capitalism is strong and destined to deliver a better future for all.

What we had seen happen in the Soviet Union, what we saw throughout Central and Eastern Europe, the economic and social pressures we see building up in China — these are not the breakdown of socialism. Instead, they register the disintegration of Stalinist regimes and the growing contradictions facing all those who believe the capitalist system can be imposed on the toilers of these countries without massive class conflict. Late 1991 and the beginning of 1992, you may remember, was the heyday for all the professors from Harvard, all the economists from Cambridge, and so on who were prescribing their various theories — shock treatment in Poland and Hungary, nonshock treatment in Romania; deflation in Russia, loans to Georgia, inflation (a little) in Azerbaijan. People facing terrible conditions had become experiments for economists strutting like demented professors who had been given a piece of the real world to manipulate.

What we began noticing was that the United States government was more and more using its weight and pressure to force its allies to do what the U.S. rulers themselves began getting nervous about. The German government had lent so much to Russia in the orgy of the original Gorbachev days, for example, that they were stuck out there on the front lines with truckloads of debt. But try to collect on it! And try to say "no" to the United States when Washington starts talking about everybody "renegotiating" reduced interest repayments from Russia and providing more loans. We are going to see an example of this next week, when the finance ministers of the seven major imperialist powers meet in Tokyo, and Germany is going to be forced to pour more money into Russia. The result will be that interest rates will go back up in Germany, they will not be able to collect on all their loans, the French franc will decline sooner, and "Europe" will come apart just a little bit more. That is the next step we are going to see in capitalism's "victory."[8]

Those who came before us in the Socialist Workers Party and our world movement had taught us that what exists in the so-called socialist countries is not socialism. There are not two different historic social and economic systems confronting each other in the world. What exists in the Soviet Union, Central and Eastern Europe, and

---

8. In addition to Moscow's August 1998 default on some $40 billion in ruble-denominated domestic debt, the Yeltsin government by early 1999 had budgeted payment of barely half the $17.5 billion in interest payments on foreign debt owed to Bonn, Paris, Rome, Washington, the International Monetary Fund, and the World Bank. Bourgeois opinion throughout the imperialist world feared not even that much would actually be paid.

Russia's gross domestic product fell 6 percent in 1998, leaving national output 45 percent below its level in 1989. (Only three Central or Eastern European workers states had regained their 1989 output levels at the end of 1998 — Poland, Slovakia, and Slovenia.) Net investment in new plant and equipment is close to zero. Russia's grain harvest reached its lowest point in nearly half a century in 1998, and milk and meat production are plummeting. The human consequences of this deepening economic crisis are devastating. Almost half the population in Russia live below the poverty line (defined as income below $120 a month). Some 40 percent of workers in Russia have gone weeks or months without pay — with wage arrears standing at $11 billion in mid-1998 — leading to a wave of strikes beginning in mid-1998 by miners, rail workers, oilfield workers, and others. Average life expectancy in Russia for men plummeted from 64 years in 1990 to 57 in 1995 and from 74 to 72 years for women. Since 1985 the birth rate in Russia almost halved, resulting in a population decline of nearly a million a year.

China is the terrible deformation and degeneration of the first step by the workers after getting rid of the capitalists — taking state power out of their hands and expropriating their property in the means of production. In the SWP's 1990 resolution, which I mentioned earlier, we reviewed our political and theoretical foundations on this question, going back in this century to V.I. Lenin, Leon Trotsky, and other leaders of the communist movement.

Two things have happened with the collapse since late 1989 of the Stalinist regimes — regimes that always tried to balance politically between imperialism and the working class, and that were always the transmission belt of imperialist pressures and bourgeois values in their antagonism to the workers of those countries.

First, a crisis for *capitalism* has now opened up. Every failure in Poland, every failure in Hungary, every failure in Czechoslovakia, every failure in the Ukraine will not be a failure for "socialism," as the propagandists for capitalism have falsely sought to portray the degenerated workers states for as long as any of us can remember. More and more workers and youth will be experiencing firsthand the failures of world capitalism's promises, its possibilities, its "reforms." It will become clearer to millions that what we are living through is far from a world in which liberal democracy is expanding, as successful, stable, capitalist social systems are brought into being from the Berlin Wall to the Great Wall of China.

Second, the greatest *obstacle* within the workers movement to advancing toward socialism — the Stalinist apparatuses in the Soviet Union and Eastern European workers states, along with their mass Communist parties abroad — have been qualitatively weakened in a way they cannot recover from. The Stalinists used the power and resources of the state to fight — ultimately by mass terror — every attempt by the workers to link up and act in solidarity with each other's struggles and move forward along a road of class independence. The Stalinists used their power to combat the legacy of the Bolshevik-led revolutionary government and Communist International, no matter how attenuated after decades of political counterrevolution.

Now that these apparatuses have collapsed, it is easier for communists to explain to other workers that the laws of the class struggle determine the laws of motion of every nation-state, and that we must always look at the world as a political whole. It is easier to explain that our job is to bind together the struggles and fortunes of the workers of the world, to go to each other's fights.

So, despite the U.S. rulers' initial triumphalism at the opening of the 1990s, it is already becoming clear that their butchery in the Gulf ended up not stabilizing world capitalism, but instead exacerbating conflicts among the rival imperialist powers, as well as Washington's relations with bourgeois regimes in the region. The collapse of the Stalinist apparatuses, as it turned out, has not blazed a trail to reintegration into the imperialist system of the one-third of the earth's population who have overthrown rule by the bourgeoisie.

What is posed for the bourgeoisie — for the families who own the banks, the factories, the mines and who control large agricultural production — is the necessity to take on working people around the world in the attempt to defeat their resistance to the worsening conditions of life and labor they face. This is the only way for the rulers to establish even the preconditions to try to open up a new wave of capitalist expansion.

Buchananism: What it is and how to fight it

At the June 1991 Socialist Workers Party convention, where we assessed how communist workers had responded to the challenge of Washington's war against Iraq, we also began taking a closer look at another aspect of the accelerating political polarization in the United States and other imperialist countries.

In the opening political report to that convention, I pointed out that given the relative prosperity and social stability that had prevailed in most imperialist countries for almost four decades following World War II, it had become easy for most working people to think that the spectrum of politics runs from liberal to conservative, all within a normal bourgeois parliamentary framework. But as crisis conditions ripen under capitalism, the true political spectrum changes: it begins first to encompass incipient fascist organizations — with one foot in and one foot out of the spectrum of normal bourgeois politics — and then a developing fighting workers vanguard.

It is wrong to think of fascism as an extension of bourgeois conservatism. Fascist currents do originate, in part, within the right wing of existing bourgeois parties under crisis conditions, but they are not simply an extension of two-party politics as we have known it for the past few decades. They are *radical* movements that base themselves on the popular grievances of increasingly economically insecure and devastated small business people, other middle-class and professional layers, and sections of the working class. They are *street action* movements in their trajectories.

American fascism
Sometime in 1990, Patrick Buchanan — a former speech writer and aide in the Richard Nixon and Ronald Reagan White Houses, and a newspaper columnist and talk-show host — had issued a second edition of his autobiographical political tract, *Right from the Beginning*. I had picked up a copy of the book and started reading it, and I brought a copy with me to the convention that year. That was very much on my mind as I took some time in the report to begin raising the connection between the deepening social crisis we had been living through, the opening guns of renewed interimperialist conflicts, and the inevitable emergence of incipient fascist currents and demagogues in the United States and other imperialist countries.

I had been struck in particular by a chapter in Buchanan's book entitled, "As We Remember Joe," a nostalgic account of why his father had held Senator Joseph McCarthy in such high esteem. Among the other family heroes, Buchanan explains, were General Francisco Franco, leader of the fascist forces during the Spanish civil war in the late 1930s, and right-wing U.S. general Douglas MacArthur. MacArthur was the commander of U.S. forces in Korea who pressed for an invasion of China even after the U.S. rulers, despite their initial plans, concluded in their majority that this would be a fiasco. To understand why people such as his father admired these ultrarightist figures, Buchanan wrote, "is to begin to understand not only his generation but ours."

In the early 1950s, Buchanan said, America was "ready for Joe McCarthy's boisterous, bellowing call for the overthrow of its reigning establishment." The "war of legitimacy that Joe launched had undertones . . . of class warfare," Buchanan said. Behind the controversy around McCarthy "were warring concepts of morality, of legitimacy, of patriotism," he said. "Who is the legitimate moral authority in America? Who, by conviction, background, character, and belief, should rightly determine the destiny of the Republic, and which is the illegitimate usurper, incompetent to identify and protect America's true interests from her real enemies?"[9] (Notice how "communists" are absent here as direct targets!)

In November 1991 Buchanan announced his intention to wrest the Republican nomination for president from George Bush. We immediately began campaigning to explain the true political significance of Buchanan's announcement. What most of the big-business media was initially treating as a sideshow inside the Republican Party, we said, was not at all funny. It was not idiosyncratic. Instead, it marked a revival for the first time since McCarthy of a demagogic ultrarightist strand in bourgeois politics in the United States — a strand that would eventually spill over into the streets, and that would not go away until the fate of humanity was

9. Patrick Buchanan, *Right from the Beginning* (Washington, D.C.: Regnery Gateway, 1990), pp. 91–95.

decided in struggle in those same streets.

By early 1992 a few bourgeois commentators were beginning to take seriously what Buchanan was setting out to do. One example was an article by conservative columnist Charles Krauthammer that had been run in the March 1 issue of the *Washington Post* and syndicated in daily papers throughout the United States. He had written that the central problem with Buchanan is not his anti-Semitism — which several other commentators had accurately pointed to — nor various other of his particular reactionary views. (Krauthammer cataloged some of these: Buchanan's exhortations against "a morally cancerous welfare state"; his racist alarm bells about the "flood tide of immigration"; his warning that "white Americans will be a minority by 2050"; his question, "Who speaks for the Euro-Americans?"; his hero-worship of Franco and the butcher of Chile, Gen. Augusto Pinochet; and his euphemistic reference to the apartheid regime in South Africa as "the Boer republic.")

"The real problem with Buchanan," Krauthammer wrote, is that his views are "in various and distinct ways, fascistic."

That bald characterization of the Buchanan campaign marked a new departure in the respectable daily press in the United States. Until then, the big-business media had been doing their best to slide over the fact that a fascist program was being advanced as a "legitimate" perspective within the two-party system by one of the leading contenders in the 1992 presidential primaries. But Krauthammer's characterization was correct, as far as it went. Buchanan's "America First" demagogy is indeed not only a variety of an incipient American fascism, but the most prominent organizing center for it today.[10]

10. In an interview in the July 17, 1995, issue of the *New Yorker* magazine, the conservative Republican politician and former Bush administration official William Bennett warned that Buchanan is "flirting with" fascism. "This Fortress America stuff, this You the People stuff — I think it's tricky." Bennett is, like Buchanan, a Republican, a Roman Catholic, and a prominent bourgeois campaigner for "family values" and around many of the themes at the

But fascism is a special kind of extreme nationalist movement, something that Krauthammer, as an apologist for capitalism, did not and could not explain. A fascist movement above all seeks to mobilize the emotional energies of masses of people who hate the liberal capitalist democracy that is failing so horribly but can find no way forward to replace it with something historically progressive.

We called this new development in U.S. politics "Buchananism." And we printed a special issue of the *International Socialist Review* supplement to the *Militant,* headlined, "Buchananism: What It Is and How to Fight It," that supporters of the Socialist Workers Party presidential ticket of James Warren and Estelle DeBates sold thousands of copies of last year as a central piece of campaign literature. We joined with others around the country in picketing events where Buchanan was proselytizing for his reactionary cause.

Incipient fascist movements, demagogic "popular" ultrarightist movements, are often identified with an individual: McCarthyism ("Nixonism" would have served as well at the time), Huey Longism, Father Coughlinism, and there are many more examples from the United States and other countries.[11] It is useful to note this fact, to show the variety of forms rightist movements can take and where they come from. The individuals or "movements" such currents are named after are accidental. They have no scientific ideas, or materialist analysis of the crisis of capitalism. But they do have a real "solution" to offer desperate and resentful people.

While Buchanan keeps one foot firmly planted in "normal"

---

center of Buchanan's "culture war." Also like Buchanan, Bennett's family roots are not in the ruling class or its exclusive private prep schools.

11. As a young U.S. congressman from California, Richard Nixon was the most prominent other U.S. political figure in the leadership of the incipient fascist current associated with McCarthy. Father Charles Coughlin, the so-called radio priest, led the fascist "Social Justice" movement, which began to gain momentum in the United States during the renewed sharpening of the Great Depression in 1937–38. Huey Long, governor and later U.S. senator from Louisiana, built a base for his Bonapartist control of state politics in the late 1920s and early 1930s under the demagogic slogan, "Share the Wealth."

bourgeois politics, he at the same time appeals to those who will increasingly seek to function outside that framework and to fight in the streets to impose radical solutions to stop the descent into a "new Sodom." In the Buchanan phenomenon, we could see a pincers movement: one flank came out of the "respectable" Republican Party, including the middle-class areas of Washington, D.C., where Buchanan himself was born and reared. It converged with the cowards trying to block the abortion clinics, with the thugs who simply put the white sheets aside for a while, with all those attracted to taking out their insecurity and hatred against sections of the working class.

Buchanan's hero, Joseph McCarthy, also set out to galvanize a fascist movement in the United States in the aftermath of World War II. And right-wing presidential campaigns were organized in 1964 by Republican candidate Barry Goldwater and in 1968 by Gov. George Wallace of Alabama. But none of these figures arose in conditions of an economic and social crisis that was bound to get worse. None arose in depression-like conditions under which the radical social demagogy and aggressive nationalism necessary to inspire a cadre would have enabled a mass fascist movement to get organized and grow.[12]

The 'culture war'

In the 1990s, however, political polarization is deepening, and class

12. For a discussion of the 1964 Republican presidential campaign of Arizona Senator Barry Goldwater, see "What Goldwater Represents" by Joseph Hansen in the July 31, 1964, issue of *World Outlook* magazine. Given the capitalist boom at the time, and the impact on U.S. politics of the Black rights struggle and colonial revolution, Hansen wrote, "America is not ripe for a fascist takeover. On the contrary, the ground is being prepared for an enormous push in the opposite direction." George Wallace gained national prominence as governor of Alabama in the early 1960s as a demagogic defender of Jim Crow segregation and "states' rights." In 1968 he ran for president on the American Independent Party (AIP) ticket on a platform aimed at rolling back the conquests of the mass civil rights movement. Wallace received 13 percent of the popular vote. The AIP disappeared shortly following the election.

tensions are increasing within that polarization. If the war Buchanan has declared — what he calls "the culture war" — is serious, then communists and, in fact, all those mindful of the democratic rights we have wrested from the rulers, ignore it at our peril.

As with other tribunes of incipient fascist movements in this century, Buchanan does not begin by taking on the working class directly. He begins by targeting other bourgeois politicians in both parties — those part of, or soft on, the "establishment elite" — both liberals and conservatives. He goes after the dominant ruling circles in the bourgeois parties, accusing them of letting America down; tolerating corruption in the hallways of power while failing to maintain law and order on Main Street; and living privileged lives while more and more "ordinary American working people" are pushed to the wall. He presents himself as the voice of those working men and women — "the folk."

Buchanan aggressively defines who "Americans" are — and (more venomously) who they are *not*. This is the aim of his obscene anti-immigrant demagogy. This is the content of his calculated and thinly veiled anti-Semitic forays, aimed especially against Jews on Wall Street or in top government posts. Buchanan is a master of the politics of resentment and the coarsening of civil discourse, often with a smile.

The polarization in the "culture war" declared by Buchanan and other ultrarightists takes many forms: chauvinist anti-foreigner agitation, racist assaults on affirmative action, vulgar attacks on women's social equality, half-hidden but virulent outbursts of Jew-hatred, fearful prejudice against homosexuals. These incipient fascist forces are vocal advocates of the cops, like those currently on trial in Los Angeles for brutally beating Rodney King; fascist movements always draw many of their cadres from the cops.[13] There will be no

13. Los Angeles policemen Theodore Briseno, Stacey Koon, Laurence Powell, and Timothy Wind were on trial in federal court for violating the civil rights of Rodney King, a Black worker whom they had been videotaped brutally beating in March 1991. Following an earlier acquittal of the cops by an all-white jury in state criminal court in April 1992, anticop riots broke out

limit to the pornographic overtones of their demagogy, as they claim to offer a road to bring a "decadent" society out of its crisis.

These reactionary positions have no logical evolution or rational content. They are a collection and recombination of refuse from the past, floating out from the backwaters of class history. It can be ancient religious ideas, pagan symbols, age-old prejudices, regional attitudes, beliefs about women born of economic and social conditions from millennia past. It does not make any difference; it is accidental. But these come together in various mixtures. They are patched together into partial truths from the myriad forms of exploitation and oppression and pressures under capital. They are invested with emotional energy and declared to be the banner of a movement.

These are not religious movements; it is not "the religious right," "the Christian right," "the fundamentalist right." These are not movements about art or culture; they are not movements about schools or education. Those just provide some of the words that emotional energy is invested in. It is a reactionary, demagogic, petty-bourgeois *social and political movement*, one that over time becomes increasingly brutal and murderous in its methods.

As the capitalist social crisis deepens, and the working class and labor movement begin to engage in battles to defend our living standards and our unions, growing numbers within the ruling class, often reluctantly, will begin to provide financial and political support to the fascists. They will unleash the energy of the ultraright in the streets, against striking workers, labor gath-

---

across much of Los Angeles for more than four days. On orders from the Bush administration, some 1,100 U.S. marines, 600 army infantry troops, and 1,000 Border Patrol and other federal cops joined 6,500 California National Guardsmen and thousands of Los Angeles police in occupying large areas of the city's Black and Latino communities. Fifty-eight people were killed over the four days, more than 80 percent of them Black or Latino; some 17,000 people were arrested; and immigration cops used the dragnet as an excuse to deport several hundred detainees.

erings, social protests, and organizations of the oppressed. They will use whatever force and violence is necessary to deny enough democratic rights to the majority of working people, eventually, to preserve the privileges of the upper middle class and maintain capitalist rule.

Last year, some of you will remember, we underlined something in particular about Buchanan's speech at the Republican nominating convention in August. Everything else at the convention we had heard before — until Buchanan shoved Reagan aside for an hour during prime time and, not to put it more politely than it was, gave the finger to the entire respectable Republican bourgeoisie.

Think very carefully about one phrase in Buchanan's speech. As he had done throughout his campaign, he invoked religious expressions, railed against gay rights and "radical feminism," and called for "a religious war," a "culture war," a war "for the soul of America." Then he came to the windup of the talk. "We must take . . . back our culture and take back our country," Buchanan said, *"block by block"* — just as the called-up National Guardsmen had done in Los Angeles a few months earlier. (Buchanan's description of the L.A. events was a gross exaggeration, but that is not the point.)

Block by block — that was the banner Buchanan raised to bring to their feet his partisans watching him live on TV around the country. That was Buchanan's summation. That fight was his promise. And that day will come.

You'll sometimes see Buchanan referred to in the bourgeois press as an "isolationist," or "antiwar." He opposed U.S. government policy during the Gulf War and speaks out against committing U.S. troops to the United Nations military operation in Bosnia. But class-conscious workers could make no more deadly mistake than failing to recognize — and to act on — the political fact that Buchananism is part of the imperialist war drive today.

Buchanan will mobilize the rightist movement he is building to demand that Washington use *all* its military might to back "our boys." But he's determined to first win the war *at home* against the working class, to hamstring *us*, and he urges his followers to act in the image of his heroes, Franco, MacArthur, and McCarthy. That's a precondition *to really do the job*, Buchanan holds, but then America has to do it!

A radical movement

I think many of us, for most of our political lives, have been used to using the term "radical" in a sort of positive way. It begins when you are young: "Are you radical?" "Yeah!" "That's a radical movement," or "Those are radical youth."

But all of us will now learn more thoroughly that "radical solutions" and "radical movements" have no social content in and of themselves, outside concrete connection with classes and the class struggle. The traditional bourgeois parties and parliamentary democracy are increasingly being exposed as bankrupt. As the capitalist social crisis deepens, layers of the increasingly insecure middle classes in particular, as well as sections of working people, will start looking for alternative solutions they hope can work, "radical" solutions.

The workers movement must explain that capitalism is the source of the crisis; it must organize the toilers in a revolutionary struggle to take power out of the hands of the exploiters and establish a workers and farmers government. It must present convincing answers, a working-class alternative, to the demagogy of the Buchanans and the others. Because if labor does not do so — if it offers those being crushed by the capitalist crisis no effective way to fight, and then seems to flub the chances we have to win — we will shove potential class allies into the hands of the rightists. And the working class will be divided and defeated in blood.

This polarization will accelerate the seriousness of workers and youth who come into politics. Young fighters despise the assaults on human solidarity by the ultraright, assaults that stand *against* everything they are reaching *for*. And growing numbers of workers, regardless of their own current political views, will see the need to guarantee space for fellow workers with whom they are fighting shoulder to shoulder — whether these workers are communist or whatever — to raise and discuss their ideas and for all workers to consider where the crisis is heading and what we can do about it.

The bourgeois campaign continues

Following the U.S. presidential elections in November 1992, the National Committee of the Socialist Workers Party organized public forums in New York and several other cities to discuss what the election showed. We subtitled these presentations — accurately, if wordily — "How the 1992 Elections Hid the Real Political Issues and Prepared Deepening Aggression by Washington."[14]

Remember the "analysis" promoted on TV and in the daily papers at the time about why Clinton won the election? Taking their cue from the Clinton campaign's spin doctors, they explained how Clinton's election "strategist" James Carville had put up a sign in the campaign headquarters in Little Rock, Arkansas, saying, "It's the economy, stupid!" — and they had all been guided by that credo to the letter. (By the way, how is that for working relations among equals? "It's the economy, *stupid.*" "That's not the way to do it, *stupid.*") We said we disagreed with that arrogant sign and the importance it was being assigned by the big-business media. The elections were *not* about economic policy.

What was behind the outcome last November were the defeats

14. The New York talk, with a shorter subtitle, is included as chapter 4 of this book.

that had been dealt to Washington internationally, and the Bush administration's incapacity to provide even the semblance of a stable political way forward for U.S. capitalism. Bush had lost the confidence of the majority of the U.S. ruling class coming out of the Gulf War. Despite the initial victory hype only months earlier when White House approval was at its zenith in opinion polls, Bush lost the bourgeoisie's confidence as the resulting fiasco became clear to them.

The most important political fact in the elections was the vote for a Bonapartist-type candidate. Ross Perot, a person few people had even heard of shortly before, had gotten nearly 20 percent of the votes cast. Perot moved into bourgeois politics from a different angle than Buchanan; his campaign did not have the direct thrust toward an incipient fascist movement. But he converged with Buchanan's "America First" demagogy and tried to tap the same kind of fears and insecurities in the middle class.

All the political trends we had seen during the elections, we said, would continue after the election. In fact, one of the best ways to look at politics today is that the election campaign is continuing.

Domestic politics during the Clinton administration is deepening the bipartisan assault on the social wage of the working class that marked the Bush White House and other Republican and Democratic administrations going back to the mid-1970s. This is proceeding along the lines argued by all the bourgeois candidates during the election campaign but pounded at most insistently by Perot. Just last month, *New York Times* correspondent B. Drummond Ayres pointed out that "some parts of Mr. Clinton's speeches are beginning to sound like Ross Perot clichés. These days, the President talks almost as much as Mr. Perot about program cuts, bureaucratic bloat and government waste."

Every adaptation to Perot by the Clinton administration, we noted earlier, will further embolden Perot and his supporters. Each time Clinton says to his critics on the right, "I've done a tremendous amount of what you're arguing for," the rightists take heart and reply: "Not enough. It's not working, and you're at fault." Clinton has a disadvantage: he eventually has to *do something*. The right-wing demagogues, on the other hand, have a great advantage — they never have to do anything. Their aim is not to get their program carried out, not yet — they really have no short-term program in that sense. Their long-term aim is to shove aside the other bourgeois forces and bring themselves to political dominance playing on the battered hopes of the middle class for stability and security.

What is happening in U.S. politics today is not that rightists like Patrick Buchanan or Ross Perot are pushing Bush, Clinton, and other Democratic or Republican politicians to the right. To the contrary, it is the failure of capitalism and the rightward drift of the two parties that provides these demagogues with the themes of their campaigns and makes other capitalist politicians so vulnerable to them. They simply state forthrightly the reactionary presumptions behind the politically more right-wing direction that politicians in *both* parties are taking, even as they spar with each other over how fast and how far to go right now in their assault on the freedoms and living standards of working people and the oppressed.

How many politicians, Democratic or Republican, for example, are willing to answer Buchanan's rightist demagogy by saying that they are for quotas when necessary to combat racist and anti-woman discrimination and move toward equality in hiring and education? Or that they welcome all those who choose to immigrate to the United States? Or that they are not for "America First"? The truth is that regardless of platitudes about world peace and cooperation, a harsher and harsher bourgeois nationalism increasingly marks the language of capitalist politics across the board in the United States (and throughout the imperialist world).

That is why we said Clinton will be a war president, that the elections prepared expanding world aggression. His administration, we said, will be marked by efforts to find new ways of threatening to use, and if necessary using, U.S. military force. The U.S. rulers try to use their small allies as surrogates in some cases. During the National Committee meeting last week, communists from

New Zealand, Australia, Canada, and Sweden listed the places around the world where troops from these countries are currently stationed: Lebanon, Cambodia, Bosnia, Somalia, and elsewhere.

But when push comes to shove, it is the U.S. armed forces that will dominate any sustained, large-scale military operation. And after initial enthusiasm and grudging support for our boys, a fight at home will open that will begin to transform politics in this country, as happened during the U.S. war against Vietnam.

Communist analysis and the test of events

This is the world — its accelerating disorder, its lines of disintegration, its class struggles — whose dialectics the Socialist Workers Party and our co-thinkers in other countries have brought into focus since the 1987 stock market crash. Each time we have confronted a new turning point, we have gotten together at international leadership gatherings, evaluated how our analysis has stood up, made any indicated adjustments, and used that assessment as our guide for what to do next, as our guide to action.

I have taken the time to review this record to try to make the case for one conclusion: new turning points like these are not what is in store for us now. What is on the agenda is the further unfolding of this world pattern: growing class tensions, political polarization and radicalization, and class differentiations and conflicts within all nations and nationalities. Communists have to clearly and confidently present this world and explain it. That is what thinking workers and revolutionary-minded fighters want to hear about and discuss. Because if this description is true, then it has historic consequences for every fighter, everywhere in the world.

I tried to write down just some of the things I have read in the papers the last few days that illustrate this world picture.

Both Bonn and Tokyo have taken new steps toward becoming stronger strategic military powers, for example. Two days ago the German Supreme Court interpreted the constitution to rule that German soldiers could fly on NATO missions in Yugoslavia even though these could become combat missions. It is not that things like these are ever decided by a constitution. But under these conditions, the court made a formal constitutional ruling on an appeal by a government party to approve doing what the German rulers want to do and would have done anyway.[15]

Three days ago, you may have assumed from what you were reading in the papers that the Japanese government might pull its troops out of Cambodia because a Japanese civilian in the so-called United Nations peacekeeping forces had been killed there. But if you read the papers this morning, you would have seen that Tokyo is instead sending in fresh troops.

The Swedish government has announced plans for cuts in health care, pensions, child support, and sick leave benefits. Listen to Swedish workers explain what these "reforms" mean for their conditions of life and work. The "Swedish miracle" surely is disappearing quickly! In a matter of two and a half years, Sweden has gone from being the country that remained the model of social welfare, to being a harbinger of what is coming for workers throughout the imperialist world. The Swedish government, for example, has recently cut unemployment benefits — at a time when joblessness has leapt, by official figures, from 3 percent to 12 percent in the last two years.

Capitalist instability, outmoded forms of rule

We even have to stop and think about things that seem inconsequential or silly at first. Who can possibly follow the ups and

15. Some 3,000 of the 31,000-soldier NATO intervention force sent into Bosnia at the end of 1996 were German troops, authorized by Bonn to engage in combat.

downs of the royal family in Britain, for instance? Who can take it at all seriously? Well, if we stop always using the word *Britain,* and start saying the *United Kingdom* sometimes, then perhaps we can begin to see that we have to take it seriously.

We should ask ourselves the question: Why doesn't London get its troops out of Ireland? Almost twenty thousand British soldiers occupy Northern Ireland, a remarkably high percentage of the active armed forces of the United Kingdom. Proportionally that is comparable to nearly 100,000 American troops. Given what this occupation costs them economically and socially, it can seem almost irrational.

But the British rulers have a problem — one that is made worse by the Prince of Wales, by Lady Diana, by "Fergie," by this quasipornographic soap opera that goes on and on. Their problem is that the queen of England is *the head of state.* That may sound strange: What could that possibly mean? The queen of England has no power, does she? The House of Lords has no power, does it? But that is not quite true. Power is vested in these institutions by the fact that Britain's rulers have had to preserve these forms, and use them when necessary, to try to reinforce the centralization of the state and some public continuity beyond the internal bureaucracy of the parliamentary system. All politics takes place with the inherited national institutions at hand. New forms and institutions cannot simply be *created*; existing institutions must be *transformed.* They have to be taken from what the past offers up, or changed by revolution. And the United Kingdom is, after all, a constitutional monarchy, not a republic.

Look at it this way: the United Kingdom is one state, three governments, and four countries. Neither Scotland nor Northern Ireland has its own parliament, but there are governments of a kind in both of them. Northern Ireland has its own special police force, a notoriously repressive one. And those residing in the north of Ireland who are citizens of the United Kingdom can be barred from traveling across the Irish Sea to the rest of what is supposed to be their country.

The English and Scottish crowns were united nearly 300 years ago. But Scotland still has its own legal system, its own educational system, and its own cops, and Scottish banks issue banknotes that are used as money there. Scotland has its own established state church, too (in fact, as the queen crosses into Scotland to vacation at Balmoral Castle, I believe, she is transformed from head of the Anglican Church of England to head of the Presbyterian Church of Scotland). There is still a substantial movement that wants to take Scotland out of the United Kingdom.

And there are actually *four* countries in the United Kingdom, when one adds in Wales — as quite a number of Welsh do.

But there is only one head of state: the queen. She is also head of state of several countries in the Commonwealth — Australia, Canada, and others. And as recently as 1975 the crown was used by Australian finance capital to exercise that power to bring down the Labor Party government, put the opposition party in office, and call new elections. These Commonwealth governments can formally go over to a republic any time they choose, but doing so is not nearly so simple as a Yankee might assume. The ruling classes must weigh whether dumping the crown contributes more to bourgeois national identity than it threatens to lose them by legitimizing discontinuity — and how such archaic forms can be used in crisis situations to increase executive power in ways more acceptable to "public opinion."

What are the possible political consequences for London of withdrawing from Ireland — of coming up with a historic compromise, thereby knocking down the United Kingdom by one piece? The rulers fear that such a move could give impetus to further challenges to capitalist order. How could the ruling class then take an unyielding stand against self-determination for Scotland? And, beyond the national question, against the labor movement? Against the miners? Could this threaten the state's stability?

That is why anything that shakes the monarchy, while certainly not the biggest problem confronting the rulers of the

United Kingdom, is nonetheless a serious one. It is a reflection of the weakness, heterogeneity, and loss of nerve and self-confidence in the British ruling class. And the queen (and tomorrow the prince of Wales) *is* the head of state of the United Kingdom. That is to whom the prime minister goes to form a government. That is supposedly what cements Scotland, Northern Ireland, Wales, and England into a United *Kingdom.* That is what they have not found a substitute for, even as the popular view of these institutions coarsens over time.

(While oblivious to the actual significance of the monarchy in the United Kingdom, the titillated petty-bourgeois left often revels in the latest salacious "leaks." The "pornographication" of politics, whoever its alleged target, ultimately redounds to the detriment of the rights of the working class. The fight for the moral high ground, and against the coarsening of political discourse, is a fight by the working class both for allies and for the space to practice politics free from harassment by the government, the bosses, and rightist thugs.)

The Church of England seems to be becoming more of a destabilizing than a stabilizing influence. This year it has split into two warring churches — one *with* women priests, one *without* women priests. The most modern of struggles — like the struggle for women's rights — the most advanced ideas, intersect with the oldest forms, which go back a thousand years or more into feudalism. And suddenly they add to the instability of a major imperialist power as we approach the twenty-first century.[16]

Under the crisis conditions of world capitalism today, all these factors help limit the options of the British rulers in the class

---

16. Over the following year, the House of Commons and the General Synod of the Church of England voted to ordain women priests. In February 1994, 712 Anglican priests and 7 bishops announced their intention to join the Roman Catholic church; several hundred had already done so. Commenting on the ordination, one of these shepherds of the flock, a vicar in Lincolnshire, told reporters that "priestesses should be burnt at the stake because they are assuming powers they have no right to. . . . I would burn the bloody bitches."

struggle. Even in their weakened condition, union coal miners and their supporters have mobilized over the past year against massive pit closures and layoffs announced by the government, which has already reduced the workforce to some 15,000 miners from more than 200,000 a decade ago. Rail workers have gone out on strike in solidarity with the miners and to advance their own demands.

The capitalist rulers in the United Kingdom have also backed off from imposing the kinds of economic austerity measures demanded by their rivals in France and especially Germany to be part of a new historic alliance within the framework of the European Union. The British rulers have instead clung all the more tightly to their postwar "special relationship" with Washington — a relationship of dependency. This further relative weakening of British imperialism will open up new possibilities for the Irish, for the Scottish, for the miners, for the rail workers, for others who resist. It will lead to the end of the Thatcher-Major interregnum and open up more political space for working people and the oppressed.

These are the kinds of combined developments and historical unevennesses we are seeing now. I picked what I thought was one of the extreme examples: Ireland, the monarchy, and how the British imperialist rulers are frozen in various ways in relation to these problems. But comparable anachronistic and ultimately destabilizing combinations mark most capitalist countries.

It is only a revolution that can write new constitutions, that can put together new forms of government. Every place where the bourgeoisie tries to declare a new constitution, a new form of government, *without* revolutionary developments, the proposed changes end up in a fiasco that just make the crisis deeper.

Over the past year we all read about and watched on TV the preparation of a new constitution in Canada. The commentators and bourgeois politicians said it was going to give everyone rights. It was going to solve substantial numbers of the conflicts in relations between Quebec and the other provinces. It was going to give the native peoples rights. But all this was the opposite of the truth. All the talk about a new constitution was intended to shut up the Quebecois and their demands for national self-determination; to shut up the native peoples; to shut up the women demanding full equality; to shut up local capitalists, small business people, and farmers in the western provinces. It was an attempt to invent some stability, and then get back to business. But stability cannot be invented, it has to be won, and won by a rising class. The effort disintegrated and these crises continued.

These are not "constitutional crises," as they are sometimes portrayed in the daily press. Any more than big political movements in parts of the world today are "religious movements." Any more than the monarchy in the United Kingdom is a question of lords and ladies. Outmoded forms that the bourgeoisie has not been able to replace begin to crack under the pressures of crisis conditions. Even in the historically newest imperialist countries, like the United States, existing bourgeois forms and institutions will begin to fracture as capitalist disorder accelerates and class battles mount.

This is something most of us have never seen in our lifetimes. Every single imperialist power, without exception, confronts declining respect for its state institutions, government, and leading personnel today. Governments from London to Tokyo, from Bonn to Ottawa, from Wellington to Washington are less stable, and more vulnerable to rightist demagogy from within bourgeois politics itself.

Growth of rightist forces worldwide

Under these conditions, rightist forces the world over are growing. They are fueled by a deepening unease among middle-class layers about the incapacity of liberal democracy to deliver, socially or economically. They are fueled by the rightward course of bourgeois politics across the imperialist world. The ultraright pounds away at the lies and corruption in high places. They rail against the institutions of liberal democracy — in order to target scapegoats and restrict the democratic rights that provide the best conditions for workers to organize and defend the interests of the toiling majority.

We have been hearing a lot in the daily press about a new "prognosis" recently: Either we support Yeltsin, or there will be fascism in Russia. There are two things to note about this.

First, it is not "we" but *they*, the U.S. capitalist class, who support Yeltsin. And they do so for one reason: at least he is a known quantity. It is that simple: the unknown frightens the U.S. rulers. If Yeltsin falls, what is going to happen?

Second, their "prognosis" leaves out the workers in Russia, as the capitalist rulers usually do. In August 1991, when the abortive coup attempt occurred in the Soviet Union, the workers intervened because their rights were threatened. Why aren't workers intervening now in the so-called constitutional crisis in Russia? Because they recognize that there is no showdown between contending forces today that threatens their rights.[17]

The ultraright will not win without a struggle, not in Russia nor anywhere else. As resistance grows workers will have the chance to

---

17. Over the course of 1993 a struggle over constitutional powers sharpened within Russia's governing bureaucratic caste between President Boris Yeltsin and the leadership of the parliament. The infighting culminated several months following this April 1993 talk, when Yeltsin ordered the dissolution of parliament in September and called new elections for December. The parliamentary leadership refused to dissolve, and in early October there were armed clashes in Moscow over control of the central television building and the parliament building. On October 4, tank units loyal to Yeltsin shelled the parliament for some ten hours; nearly 200 people were killed in the fighting. The leadership of the opposition surrendered and were jailed.

At the time of the August 1991 coup attempt in Moscow, hundreds of thousands of Russian working people and youth had poured into the streets to help block what they recognized as an attempt to roll back the expanded space they had won for political organization and activity over the previous several years. During the yearlong constitutional crisis in 1993, however, the working class in Russia did not identify defense of their political rights and living standards with any of the conflicting bureaucratic factions.

mobilize our allies and impose a working-class solution to the capitalist crisis. As workers seek to prevent democratic rights from going down to defeat, and space to struggle from being foreclosed, a battle for the allegiance of millions will take place. It will be waged with demagogy and thuggery on one side, and political clarity and class-struggle methods on the other.

Social Security and labor unity

For more than fifteen years, the American working class has suffered from a particular kind of assault with a particular result. That assault has left growing millions facing conditions that make them part of what Karl Marx called the industrial reserve army of labor. From the beginning of the 1950s up through the middle of the 1970s, every time there was a recession in the United States, no matter how deep, real wages continued to rise. Even when unemployment was growing, the buying power of workers' take-home pay still rose, even if slowly.

But this climb in real wages began to reverse with the 1974–75 world recession, the downturn that confirmed that the post–World War II capitalist expansion had peaked. The wage trend did not reverse because of some inexorable economic law, however. It began to reverse because the working class was becoming more divided. Larger and larger layers were excluded from any meaningful protection from the growing vicissitudes and pressures of the workings of capitalism. The working class itself became more polarized socially, as inequalities in income and living conditions widened. Oppressed nationalities became polarized, as a substantial middle class arose in the Black population alongside an ever-expanding layer of jobless and very poor workers who are Black.

That is why we need to take a careful look at the connection between the employers' broader war on labor and their assault on welfare and various public programs that provide income security for the working class — unemployment insurance, workers' compensation, pensions, and health care insurance such as Medicare and Medicaid. These programs help make it possible for workers to make it through a lifetime. They help make it possible for workers to provide care for the young, to get an education, to have a retirement pension. They help tie the working class together as a class.

As workers today face fewer possibilities of getting jobs and holding them, the capitalists' attacks on social welfare programs take a bigger toll. If workers have unemployment benefits, if we have workers' compensation, if we have supplemental unemployment benefits, and we get laid off after working for three or four years someplace, we don't go out to look for a job the next morning. We don't want to. We don't have to.

But the more workers' comp is eroded, the less often unemployment benefits get extended, the smaller those benefits are as a percentage of a living wage, the larger the proportion of medical bills workers and our families must cover without government programs — the less confident we are. The more likely we are to rush right back out, begin looking for work, and take a job for one, two, three, four dollars an hour less. This is not an unusual experience for many people in this room.

The so-called culture war is at the heart of this assault. Its aim is decisive to the right, and ultimately to the class dominance of the entire bourgeoisie: to single out the layers of the working class who suffer most from this assault and blame *them* for the social crisis of capitalism. Point to *them* as an infection in the social order. Go after human solidarity. Go after everything we have won *as a class*. And by doing so, drive down the wages and conditions of the class as a whole. That is what the employers and their politicians in both parties aim to do.

The rulers try to convince people, for instance, that the conditions faced by the elderly are not the problem of the middle-aged or the young. The capitalist does not care about the first thirteen years of workers' lives; then he cares about our ability to work hard for the next fifty years; then he hopes we die quickly. That coarse attitude is what the rulers try to get layers of the working population to accept as well.

The most revealing explanations of what the bipartisan assault on Social Security is all about are those made by some of the more boldly forthright statisticians and economists. They say: when we passed Social Security legislation in the mid-1930s, when we conceded to the rising industrial union movement there was a need for it, we never expected to have to pay out most of it, because average life expectancy in the United States was lower than the retirement age of sixty five. (Yes, *lower*, by about five years on average, much lower than that for workers, and more than ten years lower for Blacks.) But now workers live some ten years longer than retirement age, on average. So our lifespan has become a big problem for the rulers. Why won't you people face this? the "experts" ask.

Read their economic articles; read their debates and arguments about the Social Security fund. This is the capitalists' complaint. To them, Social Security was a concession. It might ameliorate some problems that could otherwise become destabilizing, but they never intended for workers to live off it for very long. The insurance specialists, the actuaries had it all figured out: Look at the averages, they said; few will get much of anything for more than a year or two. We can handle that; don't worry.

Workers had a different view. For us, Social Security was the beginning of the attempt to moderate the dog-eat-dog competition imposed on the working class under capitalism. Social Security was an initial step by our class — by those who produce wealth — toward conquering the social organization of conditions necessary for life, such as education and health care, *for a lifetime.* Workers think of each other in terms of a lifetime. We cannot think of each other the way capitalists think of us. We cannot make ourselves think of other human beings as though they do not exist up to the age of thirteen or after the age of sixty-five. That is not how workers function. We have a different class view, a different moral view of society. Elementary human solidarity is in our interests, not in conflict with them.

For the working class, there is no real Social Security that does not cover the entire *lifetime* of a worker. For the working class, there is no real education that is not *lifetime* education.

That is what the battle for Social Security was and remains. It was never just about pensions. What we won in 1935, with all its inadequacies, nonetheless encompassed the first federal-guaranteed universal unemployment benefits and the first guaranteed disability compensation. It established the Aid to Families with Dependent Children program that politicians in both parties are talking today about dumping.[18] Out of the Black rights battles of the 1950s

---

18. Acting on his 1992 campaign pledge "to end welfare as we know it" and "move people from welfare to work," Clinton in the fall of 1996 signed into law the bipartisan "Personal Responsibility and Work Opportunity Reconciliation Act," eliminating federally guaranteed Aid for Families with Dependent Children. AFDC payments were replaced by federal "block grants" to each individual state — a shift that both reduced the overall funds for such payments, and transferred to state governments the power to disburse. The so-called welfare reform act also cut off food stamps and Medicaid to many working people.

In early 1999 Clinton boasted that welfare rolls in the United States were down 44 percent from 1994, failing to mention that up to 50 percent of those denied payments had no jobs at all and the majority of the rest were employed at makework jobs paying minimum wage with no benefits. A federal study released in early 1999 also revealed that one-quarter of the $12 billion allotted to state governments for welfare payments in 1998 had actually been used for other purposes.

In his remarks during the 1996 Senate debate on the legislation, Democratic senator Daniel Moynihan of New York said that the Clinton proposal "is not 'welfare reform,' it is 'welfare repeal.' It is the first step in dismantling the social contract that has been in place in the United States since at least the 1930's. Do not doubt that Social Security itself, which is to say insured

and early 1960s, the working class won the extension of Social Security to include health benefits like Medicare for the elderly and Medicaid for workers with very low incomes.

To the political vanguard of the working class, Social Security has always been about the battle to bring *all* welfare payments, *all* medical claims, *all* supplemental payments for education and child care into a comprehensive, nationwide, government-guaranteed entitlement. That is why the term "the social wage" is a useful one. We are talking about something that goes beyond the wage any individual worker receives from an employer. We are talking about something that the working class and labor movement fight to establish as social rights *for all.*

But for the capitalists, Social Security was about making the smallest concessions necessary. It was about looking at actuarial tables to make sure that payments would never take much out of their potential profits or reduce their power over a divided and insecure working class. That is how the exploiters still look at it.

Workers should never present today's crisis of the propertied classes and their social system as primarily an economic crisis. No, it is the great *political and moral crisis* of our time. It is proof that only the working class has a chance to resolve this crisis and begin transforming society in a truly human way. Because only the working class, the propertyless class, has no interest in turning like dogs on *any* of the victims of the crisis-ridden capitalist system.

---

retirement benefits, will be next." In fact, politicians in both big-business parties — from the Clinton administration, to the Republican leadership in Congress — are increasingly preparing the ground to erode the universal and federally financed character of pensions. To rationalize this course, the employing class is promoting the notion that the Social Security system will be bankrupted early in the next century unless working people and worse-off layers of the middle class recognize that they cannot depend on federal pensions to make it through retirement — and must "supplement" these payments through private savings and investment accounts that they finance themselves, and for which they must individually bear the "market risk."

That is why the battle for jobs, the battle for solidarity, the battle against racism and the oppression of women, the battle against immigrant-bashing, the battle for social protection — why all these are a battle for the life and death of the labor movement. *They are the battle for the time and space to prepare a socialist revolution!* That is what is at stake in pulling the working class together.

Consider the political implications of the capitalists' assault on entitlements here in the United States over the past decade or so. Thinking workers must explain this to other working people: "Look at what they're doing to our class. Look at what they're doing to the social wage, to the entitlements we have fought for and won. Our class is under assault. They're pitting us against each other and tearing us apart."

The stakes for free labor
The working class is being torn apart in the plants, too — literally. There are industries where thousands of immigrant workers and other workers who have become desperate for a job offer their limbs in exchange for a weekly wage. That is the bargain in more and more meatpacking plants in this country. The frequency of carpal tunnel and other repetitive motion injuries is staggering. Normal use of hands, shoulders, necks, vertebrae, and tendons is lost — sometimes forever. Not to mention injuries from knives and machinery. It is not just selling your labor power; it is selling life and limb.

The working class fought bloody battles over the last two centuries, as industrial capitalism expanded, to make sure we would not face these kinds of conditions as a norm. We built unions and fought to end all forms of physical bondage. We fought for laws that took away the "right" for anyone to sell themselves — or any little piece of themselves. It was *working people* who fought for this: for human beings not to be treated like commodities.

Throughout most of history, where the toiling majority worked, how long we worked, under what conditions we worked, how our physical being was used for the production and reproduction of commodities — including human reproduction, the production of new labor power! — was outside our control. Working people were simply chewed up, mauled. Think of the life expectancy in the mines in Roman times, in the mills in the opening decades of industrial capitalism, on plantations under the slavocracy.

What a gain it was for humanity when working people had to offer only our power to labor as a commodity on the market — arduous as the work often is — not ourselves or any part of us. What a gain it was when our contractual agreement to work for somebody else was brought under civil law, instead of criminal law with penalties ranging from imprisonment to mutilation or death. What a gain it was when we could walk out of a workplace at any time and the only thing the boss could do is fire us. All this registered the end of bonded labor, of serfdom, of slavery, of peonage, of domestic indentured service.

It was only as free workers took up the fight to eliminate bonded labor and joined together in trade unions and fought that we pushed back inhuman hours, conditions, and wages. It has only been a couple hundred years — much less than that in some parts of the world, including most of the United States.

In many parts of the world today, in fact, this victory remains far from complete. This is true especially where capitalist industry is still in its early stages of development and is growing rapidly by drawing labor off the land. That is the reality in parts of Latin America, in India, Pakistan, and elsewhere in Asia, in big parts of Africa, and in the Middle East. That is the reality in the capitalist enclaves in China — the ones right across the border from Hong Kong, and others.

The exploiters under crisis conditions always attempt to push back the clock of history. It was only a little more than a century ago that chattel slavery was swept away in the Civil War, the second American revolution. The door was opened to a vast expansion of free labor, on the land and in the factories. Under the momentum of the political reaction following the defeat of Radical Reconstruction, however, the capitalists pushed back rural labor in the U.S. South toward forms of peonage. That was part of the social counterrevolution that imposed Jim Crow segregation on the oppressed Black nationality and left the toilers of this country weakened and divided. It took the rise of the industrial union movement and then the mass Black rights battles in this century to begin reversing the consequences of that historic setback.

This is what the broader historic struggle for Social Security is all about. It is about whether workers have a *lifetime* right to medical care; to workers' compensation if we are injured; to unemployment insurance for as long as needed. It is part and parcel of the fight for affirmative action to combat racist and anti-woman discrimination, so we can unite our class and strengthen the labor movement. It is about the fight to ensure jobs for all; to raise the wages and shorten the hours of the working class; and to defend health and safety on and off the job.

It is a fight to keep the capitalists from tearing the working class apart.

All politics is class politics

Every time some politician pontificates about the "culture war," workers should remember it is really about justifying reactionary assaults on our rights and conditions on and off the job. It is about justifying the cop beatings of workers every night. It is about justifying assaults on women's rights. It is about *dignity*. It is about getting us to accept that since we are working people, we should expect a lesser standard of dignity than is accorded those who sanctimoniously preach to us about dignity. It is about getting us to accept being treated as commodities.

Labor's answer to the "culture war" must be to build a leadership capable of acting on the conviction that every time the capitalists say "we" — "we" Americans, "we" at General Motors," "we" family people, "we" who speak English — they are lying. Every time the capitalists blame *part of us* for what *they* are trying to impose on *all of us*, they are trying to turn us against each other. They do not want *us* to be able to effectively fight *them*. They want us to become the kind of people they say we should aspire to be. Beneath their moralizing pronouncements, the capitalists promote ever more reactionary, ever more antihuman attitudes in their drive to undermine social solidarity and crush the ability of the working class and our organizations to organize struggles and win.

That is why communists insist on looking at everything the employers and their government do as *class* questions. That is what lies behind all their policies. But the rulers do everything they can to stop us from recognizing politics as class questions. They do all they can to stop us from acting politically as a class. They do not want us to think about each other as workers. They want us to think about each other as employed or unemployed, Black or white, "American" or immigrant, men or women, young or old. But we have to cut through the way they present things and explain the class realities they are covering up.

'Single mothers'

Politicians talk a lot these days about the "problem of single mothers," for example. But what about women in the capitalist class, or even the surviving remnants of the feudal aristocracy? Aren't they all single mothers? Isn't the queen of England a single mother? Such ruling-class women may or may not be connected with a husband through some legal, financial arrangement. That is irrelevant, however. Their husbands certainly do not build their lives around their families. Talk about "deadbeat dads"!

Men and women in the ruling class are very busy people; they have *things to do.* They have professions to engage in, hobbies to enjoy, money to make, governments to run, charities to organize, employees to keep an eye on. They *hire* people to raise their children. The children are raised very well. They are taught to read and write when they are very young. They receive good educations. They are given self-confidence and taught that they have an important place in the world.

So, women in the ruling class, and many upper-middle-class women too, are single mothers; the difference is in the economic and social arrangements these mothers have.

That is what was behind the crises earlier this year over Clinton's nomination of Zoë Baird and then Kimba Wood for U.S. attorney general. The problem the White House ran into was not what got played up in the daily press; it was not that these two upper-middle-class women hired undocumented immigrants and did not pay their Social Security taxes. That may be how some liberals looked at it. And a lot of workers thought these women and their husbands were sort of cheap, but that is what workers expect from people with money. That is not why it became such a scandal in this country — and it did become a scandal.

No, the problem was that these cabinet appointments inadvertently exposed the simple truth: there are two classes of families in this country and in the world, and thus two classes of women. There are those who raise their children the best they can under the conditions they face, and there are those who hire other women to raise their children. And the women who are hired are often also raising children of their own.

The people in the class that hires other women to raise their children think this setup is natural so long as they pay $4.64 an hour, or $5.50, or maybe even $6.70. In fact, they consider it so natural that the problem never even occurred to Clinton and his advisers when they proposed Zoë Baird. They were blind to how the vast majority of workers would look at this. In fact, they were so blind they did it twice (twice, that is, where it became a public issue).

That is the social reality behind the Zoë Baird and Kimba Wood scandal. It is a class question. The mounting social pressures, the economic breakdowns, the difficulties in getting jobs, the assaults on our rights and entitlements — they are all class questions. To say "no" to all this — to stand up and fight — is the battle for dignity. Just say "no" is step one, although not the step that former first lady Nancy Reagan had in mind.

Whenever the capitalist politicians and their defenders seek to justify their reactionary policies, we have to go deeper to the class question behind every single one of them. Take the widely publicized protest organized in February by this new right-wing group "Lead or Leave" outside the American Association of Retired Persons headquarters, for example. When leaders of this self-proclaimed youth organization rail demagogically against the cost of Social Security, we have to explain that it is not "the elderly" they are attacking. It is an assault on a section of the working class — those who depend on Social Security. Many elderly people in this country have no need for Social Security and actually agree with Lead or Leave. The minute we reduce this to an attack on "the elderly" we begin losing the battle.

Vanguard workers want "the elderly" to have an equal opportunity to participate fully in social life as part of their lifetime of creating social wealth. We are for being generous to the "high net worth" elderly in this regard too. Ross Perot's demagogy about the "outrage" of billionaires like himself receiving Social Security checks is simply designed to soften up public opinion to begin unraveling retirement pensions as a social entitlement. The working class must fight for universal Social Security, regardless of class or income.

The trap of liberal 'reforms'

Or take the attempt to use a "sin tax" as economic pressure. Clinton, for example, is putting an increased tax on cigarettes in his budget proposal to Congress. Think about what such taxes mean in class terms. One class can afford to pay the "sin tax" without even stopping to think about it. The other class is punished economically for buying certain things and then scolded by their inferiors in the bargain.

I believe that cigarettes cause cancer and do all kinds of harmful things to your health. But under a workers government, there will be not one penny of tax on cigarettes. Or on beer. That is the pledge of a workers government. Not one penny. If the workers movement is going to educate adults on the health effects of different habits, it has to do so without combining such education with differential economic punishments. That is the only road to free women and men remaking themselves.

The Clinton administration's national health care proposal is another example. It is all well and good for Hillary Clinton, the head of the White House health care task force, to say that everyone will stand in the same lines for limited medical resources and everything is going to be fair. Most workers would be ready to fight for the principle that if William or Hillary Clinton got on line as number five at a Health Maintenance Organization and somebody else got on line as number seven, one of the Clintons has a right to the prior appointment. But most workers also know this is not how it works in the real world, even if they do not explain it in clear class terms. Most workers know that the members of the entire class whose interests William Clinton represents do not have to stand on line, ever.

The truth is that the Clinton administration's so-called national health care program is a fraud. It is a way to further the *class* organization of medicine. It is a scheme to subsidize the ruling class and their giant insurance companies, HMOs, and other big businesses. It is the institutionalization of class differentiation in health care rationing in the name of "reform."[19]

19. In his January 1995 State of the Union address, Clinton dumped the proposed health care plan, saying his administration had bitten "off more than we could chew." Meanwhile, the percentage of the U.S. population with no health insurance coverage increased to 16 percent in 1999 from 13.6 percent in 1990. The share of employed U.S. workers covered by employer-sponsored health plans has fallen by nearly 10 percent since the late 1980s, while more and more workers are being forced to pay an increasing share of the costs of job-linked insurance plans.

Communist workers are also against what is broadly referred to as "prison reform." That, for sure, is a class question. We are *for* defending any con against any brutality or arbitrariness, and we are *for* prisoners taking as much space as they can get to break down the barriers that separate them from the rest of society and deprive them of their rights.

But we are *against* education being organized *by the prisons*. We are *against* therapy being organized by the prisons. Because anything organized through the prison system and imposed upon a con, even if supposedly "voluntary," is an attempt to control them, to break them, to make them complicit with the horrors of how prisons are organized and run under capitalism. It is a degrading reflection of the values and brutalities of declining bourgeois society.

Better alcoholic treatment programs, *better* sex offenders programs, *better* substance abuse programs, *better* job training programs for prisoners — these reforms are all designed to do the same thing as gangs in the prison yard and corruption in the cell blocks. Everything is organized to turn cons against one another, to reinforce the worst, dog-eat-dog values of bourgeois society, to differentiate the incarcerated. The fight of the working class is the opposite. Not to organize anything through the prisons, but to break down every barrier we can between the life of prisoners and life beyond those walls.

None of these prison programs have anything to do with education or medical treatment. None have anything to do with raising the self-confidence and affirming the dignity of anyone. All are part of "owning up" to your own supposed inhumanity, instead of reaching beyond the bars to productive work and revolutionary activity as free men and women with dignity intact.

The expansion of supposedly voluntary sexual offenders programs in the prisons in recent years is part of the hysteria the rulers have had some success in whipping up around this question; it is one of the most effective pretexts they have found so far to justify pushing back democratic rights. These programs are of a piece with repressive laws like the one passed in Washington state three years ago allowing juries to indefinitely jail — and inflict "therapy" on — individuals convicted of violent sex crimes who have already served out their terms.[20]

The clarity that Mark Curtis, who is himself in prison on frame-up sexual assault and burglary charges, has helped bring to these questions is a model of worker-bolshevik leadership. He has set an example in life, by continuing to carry out political activity behind bars. And many workers who have not yet heard of Mark Curtis will be convinced on these issues as experience in the class struggle deepens.[21]

Rodney King beating: standard cop procedure

The events surrounding the brutal cop beating of Rodney King in Los Angeles two years ago illustrate another aspect of the class divisions in capitalist society and their consequences. Anybody who has ever watched even a portion of the videotape knows that

20. Although the Washington state law was ruled unconstitutional by a federal judge in August 1995 on grounds that it violated due process by punishing individuals twice for a single crime, a similar Kansas state law was upheld by the U.S. Supreme Court in June 1997. In May 1996 Clinton signed into law a federal statute making it mandatory for state governments to notify communities when a person previously convicted of a sex offense moves into a local neighborhood; the 1994 Federal Crime Bill had already required state and local authorities to register and track these persons for at least ten years. While neighbor notification provisions in several states have been ruled unconstitutional in federal court, the highest U.S. appeals courts to rule on the constitutionality of such laws upheld the New Jersey legislation (the so-called Megan's Law) and a similar law in New York in August 1997.

21. Curtis was released from prison on parole in June 1996. He had served seven and a half years of a twenty-five year sentence, substantially longer than average in Iowa for individuals convicted on similar charges. A central pretext used by Iowa authorities for denying Curtis parole for so long was his refusal to enter the state prison system's Sex Offenders' Treatment Program, which requires participants to "own their own crime," that is, to acknowledge their guilt. Curtis maintains his innocence. See Naomi Craine, *A Packinghouse Worker's Fight for Justice: The Mark Curtis Story* (New York: Pathfinder, 1996).

the cops who beat King almost to death should go to jail for a long, long time. The Bill of Rights to the U.S. Constitution is a higher authority than the L.A. Police Department regulations the cops used in their defense. Workers have fought long and hard to win and defend those rights.

But when Stacey Koon and the three other cops testified they were carrying out L.A. Police Department guidelines, working people have every reason to think the cops, to that degree, were speaking the truth. Such brutality *is* the implementation of the manual of conduct as taught in practice for sergeants of the LAPD, as it is for police departments in cities and towns across the country. It is reinforced by every aspect of the training the cops receive. It is reinforced by the brutal, racist language that is considered not only acceptable but a badge of honor.

This is what cops do. *They mete out punishment on the spot.* Only this time they were caught on tape; that is the only difference.

Communist workers do not accept the "Nuremberg defense" employed by the four L.A. cops. We do not agree that those in the Nazis' Gestapo and SS units who killed communists, trade unionists, Jews, Gypsies, or others in the concentration camps were not accountable for their crimes, because someone higher up ordered them to do it. We hold the Los Angeles cops — like every cop — 100 percent responsible for their actions.

At the same time, we do not let the capitalist state off the hook. This was *not* a question of rogue cops; it was a question of established policy, in fact. These cops acted like cops act all over the country — like they are trained to act, like they are conditioned to act. Unless we can explain this in clear class terms to co-workers and others, we will never be able to get beyond the seemingly endless courtroom testimony about how Rodney King reacted when his car was stopped. What is the difference how he reacted? How do other workers react to the class reality of cop harassment and brutality? How might any of us react if it had happened often enough to us and our friends and relatives?

If what happened in Los Angeles were an isolated, rogue action, then it would just be a conflict between individuals that got out of hand. But that is not what happened. We are talking about a *social* phenomenon, the product of a *policy* that trains, coarsens, and makes it profitable for cops to mete out such brutal punishment.

Mark Curtis, too, was beaten up by the cops in the Des Moines police station the night they framed him up. That is standard operating procedure for cops everywhere. It's just that there are no video cameras in the Des Moines precinct house elevators and "interrogation" rooms, or other spots like them all over the world.

One final example: We have to explain the class realities behind the attempts of capitalist politicians to defend discrimination against gays and lesbians in the U.S. armed forces. The U.S. Constitution-guaranteed rights of citizens, including citizen-soldiers, are a higher law than the Uniform Code of Military Justice, just as the Bill of Rights is a higher law than the LAPD handbook.[22]

The defenders of the government policy talk about fears of "sexual abuse" in the bunks and showers if the policy is scrapped. We have to tell the class truth about sexual abuse in the armed forces. There is sexual abuse all the time. Abuse of female enlisted personnel by their officers. Abuse of female cadets at military academies. And systematic sexual abuse is *organized* on a mass scale

---

22. During his 1992 election campaign, Governor Clinton said he would end the ban on homosexuals in the armed forces. After his inauguration, however, Clinton reneged on the pledge, instituting instead what has become known as the "don't ask, don't tell" policy. Recruits are no longer supposed to be questioned about their sexual orientation, but soldiers who are known to be homosexual either by their own statements or in other ways are still subject to dismissal. According to an April 1998 review of the Clinton guidelines by the Defense Department itself, "the number of service members discharged for homosexual conduct has in fact risen since the new policy became effective in 1994." Pentagon figures indicate that 4,374 soldiers were discharged in the years 1994–1998, hitting a record 1,145 discharges under the new guidelines in 1998.

by the United States armed forces throughout the world. We need to explain the horrifying, degrading sexual slavery the officer corps organized in Korea during the Korean War; that they organized in Vietnam, in Thailand, in the Philippines during the Vietnam War; and that they organize to this day wherever there are U.S. bases. There is organized mass prostitution, rape, and always, inevitably, murder. On the rare occasions that an officer is called to order for degrading sexual brutality, the offense is explained away as uncondoned excess, a "crime of passion" by a man under "terrible pressure." We have to explain that class reality, too.[23]

There must be *some* social or political question that is *not* a class question, isn't there? Single mothers, psychological counseling in prisons, something? The answer is no. If we do not start with the class questions, we cannot explain any of them.

Working-class leaders, not social engineers

The biggest lie supporters of capitalism tell about socialists is that we are trying to create a utopia, mess with people's lives, and engineer a massive social experiment. You want to play God with the lives of other human beings, they charge. Big governments and bu-

---

23. The actual view of much of the army brass and many ruling-class politicians toward sexual abuse in the armed forces was expressed with unusual frankness by Fred C. Ikle, undersecretary of defense for policy in the Reagan administration. Ikle told a writer for the *New York Times* Sunday magazine in 1997 that, "You can't cultivate the necessary commitment to physical violence and fully protect against the risk of harassment. Military life may *correctly* foster the attitudes that tend toward rape, such as aggression and single-minded self-assertion."

reaucracy are proven enemies of common people — why can't you socialists ever learn? That is the opposite of the truth. In fact, communists are less inclined in that direction than any group of people on the face of the earth. As Marx put it, when writing about the Paris Commune of 1871, revolutionary-minded workers "have no ready-made utopias to introduce. . . . They know that in order to work out their own emancipation, and along with it that higher form to which present society is irresistibly tending by its own economic workings, they will have to pass through long struggles, through a series of historic processes, transforming circumstances and men."[24]

Communists are materialists, dialectical materialists. We start with facts, with social realities, and how they develop and change over history — how they are shaped by shifting productive relations, social labor, and revolutionary activity. We know that our class and its toiling allies, who make up the majority of humanity, cannot organize the world on new foundations *as we are.* And a state bureaucracy cannot do it for us, either. We must change ourselves. On this, we are "Guevarists" to the core.

"To build communism it is necessary, simultaneous with the new material foundations, to build the new man," Che Guevara wrote in his 1965 article "Socialism and Man in Cuba."[25] We agree. Workers can and will change ourselves as we go about changing the material foundations of our relations to each other. But this cannot be done without tearing down the brutal class divisions that underlie all social relations today and that will lead through war and fascism to a culmination too horrible to even imagine — unless our class organizes to take power out of the hands of the capitalists.

There is only one real equality possible in today's class-divided

---

24. Karl Marx, "The Civil War in France," in Marx and Engels, *Collected Works,* vol. 22, (Moscow: Progress Publishers, 1986), p. 335.

25. Ernesto Che Guevara and Fidel Castro, *Socialism and Man in Cuba* (New York: Pathfinder, 1989), p. 6.

world — *political* equality. And it only becomes possible in the revolutionary workers movement. It only becomes possible as those who make up a fighting workers vanguard collectively prepare ourselves for the battles to rid society of every vestige of exploitation, oppression, and discrimination.

The socialist revolution is not the end of recorded history, as Stalinist ideologues have tended to present it in order to rationalize the counterrevolutionary course of the parasitic caste and its claim to have established socialism in a single country. No, the workers revolution is the *beginning* of truly human history.

What is most important about the workers revolution is not the particular property changes that will sweep society directly in its wake — although without them, nothing further would be possible — but the fact that its victory opens other revolutions, such as the historic revolution for women's emancipation. That will not be settled just by overthrowing the capitalist state and declaring the class struggle over. The new possibilities opened by a revolutionary victory, however, will lay the material foundations on which women's liberation can be achieved and precipitate an explosion in the fight for real economic and social equality by the millennia-long oppressed sex. Similarly, all the manifold forms of class oppression bequeathed by thousands of years of property systems will for the first time be open to being vanquished.

Resistance will mount

Despite the refusal of the labor officialdom in the United States or in other imperialist countries to organize the working class to use union power, workers continue to press for ways through their class organizations to mount resistance to the capitalists' assaults. I asked comrades from the United Kingdom last week about the actions by coal miners over the past few months against the government's planned pit closures and layoffs. Members of the National Union of Mineworkers (NUM) have organized two one-day work stoppages, one of them just last week in collaboration with the rail workers union. And there were two big miners demonstrations in London last October. Comrades say miners tell them it is better taking some action than just accepting the government's assault and doing nothing, and we've had good sales of the *Militant* and of Pathfinder books and pamphlets at these protests. Resistance always increases broader political interests among workers.

That same attitude can be seen among miners at the Thorseby mine in Nottingham, comrades say. Thorseby is one of the three largest mines organized by the anti-NUM union — the Union of Democratic Miners — that was built up during the Thatcher period to weaken the NUM. Paul Galloway, a comrade in the communist movement in the UK, has been a union fighter in that mine for a long time. During the great 1984–85 miners strike in Britain, coal was cut at the Thorseby mine every day. At the conclusion of that year-long strike, the NUM was finally forced back to work by the failure of the rest of the union officialdom in the United Kingdom to organize decisive solidarity action. That was Thatcher's greatest victory during her years in office. The other stuff she is credited with — strengthening the economy, the privatizations — that is all nonsense. But the British rulers notched up a real victory in 1985. And throughout that entire strike, the hardest fought in Great Britain for more than a decade, coal was cut at Thorseby every day, despite every effort by the NUM to stop it.

Well, a week ago, when both the coal miners and the rail workers across the United Kingdom were engaged in a one-day stoppage against the pit closures, the NUM put up a picket line at Thorseby that was respected by members of the Union of Democratic Miners. Not one miner went into that mine and not one piece of coal was cut!

I do not raise this example because I expect such actions to lead to massive class battles right now in Britain, or even to short-run labor victories. No single group of workers can jump that far ahead of the rhythms of resistance of the broader working-class vanguard. Nor do I have such expectations from the resistance we have been seeing here in the United States: the fight by the drywallers in southern California to defend their union hiring hall; the strike by members of the United Steelworkers union against Trinity Industries in Bessemer, Alabama; or the strike earlier this year by 7,000 United Mine Workers members against Peabody Coal, and the fight looming next month between the UMWA and the Bituminous Coal Operators Association.

But these acts of resistance are all part of human beings changing, of refusing to be coerced into acquiescence regardless of the rulers' efforts. It is in these struggles that workers find space to practice politics, and that people of all ages gain experience.

We should not talk about these struggles primarily in terms of economics. In depression conditions, with the working class facing the kinds of social assaults we have discussed, the important questions are not economic — because workers cannot reorganize the economy yet. The working class must organize a victorious socialist revolution before that becomes possible.

But workers today *can* fight to defend ourselves and other working people against employer and government attacks. We *can* fight for protection against the ravages of capitalism. The questions confronting the working class are *political.* What kind of attitudes, what sense of dignity, what kind of class perspective can transform individuals and better prepare us to fight to take political power out of the hands of the rulers? That is important to people involved in demonstrations and strikes, and they want to talk about it. That is what they want to read about. They want to read about other workers who are resisting. They want to know what other workers are thinking, and how they are organizing to wage an effective fight.

A growing and changing working class

Enormous changes are taking place that are improving the odds that the international working class can become a social force able to transform and salvage the future. The working class makes up a larger and weightier component of the population in countries the world over than ever before in history, and it continues to expand. In a growing number of countries, moreover, the working class is more international in its makeup than ever before too. And these trends will continue and deepen as the crises of world capitalism unfold in coming years.

Communists often explain that there is no "Europe"; there are only a number of capitalist states and their rival national ruling classes. That is true, but I have learned that leaving it at that is not the best way to help people understand the political point we are making. It is more accurate to say that *their* Europe is *disappearing* — the capitalists' Europe. Their idea of a Europe of a single currency, of a single fiscal and monetary policy, of converging or at least compatible foreign military policies — all of this still widely talked about in ruling circles in Europe — is a bourgeois utopia.[26]

Our Europe is slowly coming into being, however. Think about the expansion of intra-European travel. What comes along with expanded flows of capital and commodities worldwide is greater migration by workers to get jobs. In every single capitalist country in Europe today there is a higher percentage than ever before of workers from other countries and other nationalities who are part of the working class. The working class in every imperialist country — and this will even begin to include Japan — is more multinational than at any time in its modern history.

On a leadership level, the importance of the political fights under way in Cuba and in South Africa deserves our attention.

---

26. On January 1, 1999, eleven governments in Europe did begin using a common currency — the "euro" — to denominate stock, bond, and banking transactions. Actual "euro" notes are to replace German marks, French francs, and other national currencies in circulation in 2002. Compared to its eleven separate predecessors, the euro will put up stiffer competition to a relatively weakened U.S. dollar as a store of value in national treasuries around the world, and later perhaps even as a unit of account. From birth, however, the euro's stability was undermined by the conflicting interests of the rival imperialist bourgeoisies it pretends to yoke together. As the onerous effects of capitalist overproduction bear down in differential ways on countries and regions across Europe — and working people press demands for jobs, against farm foreclosures, and for livable wages and government-funded social benefits — the fissures in the new currency union will widen.

Since you spent yesterday evening's session discussing Mary-Alice Waters's report on the Cuban revolution today, and will spend tomorrow morning discussing Sam Manuel's talk on South Africa, I will not say much about them tonight. But the increasing interest in genuine communist literature in these countries, and the degree of interest in discussions with revolutionary-minded workers and youth from other countries, indicates the possibilities of a way forward.

Not since the early days of the 1960s has there been the kind of political openness in Cuba that is developing there today. I am not talking about the new layer of hotel managers with gold chains and Rolex watches; I am not talking, of course, about those in Cuba who aspire to be like the pimps of the capitalist world. They may number in the hundreds of thousands. What I am talking about — and what I know was at the center of your discussions last night during the conference session on Cuba Today — are the millions of workers in Cuba, and their tested political leadership within the Communist Party, who are determined not to allow what they fought for, what they believe in, and what they have accomplished to be destroyed. They are determined to defend the socialist revolution. The working class and its communist vanguard are who ultimately count in Cuba, and they will have the final say in a real battle.

To understand the potential power of our class, we also must take account of the growing numbers of women workers the world over. Never in history has there been anything comparable to the position and political weight of women in the workforce and labor movement today. The place of the fight for women's rights as part of the political battle to transform the workers movement compares to nothing experienced by previous generations of revolutionists.

Another powerful advance for our class is registered by the fact that over the last several decades, for the first time in history, world-class communist leaders — looked to by thinking workers everywhere — have emerged from the most economically backward countries and parts of the world. Communists like Maurice

Bishop in Grenada and Thomas Sankara in Burkina Faso were genuine products of the class struggle in their own countries and became leaders of world stature.

And someday a small book will be written about the place of Nelson Mandela in the history of the class struggle in the imperialist epoch. Mandela has not only educated us all to better comprehend the dynamics of the class struggle in South Africa, but also helped transform the capacity of workers everywhere to recognize world-class revolutionary leadership when we see it in action. Here is a man who, during his visit to South Africa's Natal province in March of this year, stood up before a big audience, mostly of Indian origin, and frankly explained the weaknesses and mistakes of the African National Congress in relation to that community. Those mistakes, he said, are reflected even in the ANC's very popular anthem, which, he said, is "purely based on the history and the aspirations of the African people" and contains "no reference to the culture, the history, the contribution of the Indian and the Coloured communities."[27]

Workers the world over can learn a lot about class solidarity, too, from reading the speeches of Nelson Mandela. Time and again, he hammers away at the importance of the battle against the grinding social conditions and divisive racist oppression facing the working class in South Africa — the battle for employment; the battle against violence, against the coarsening of how society values life itself; the battle against racism, race-baiting, and scapegoating of any kind.

The greatest obstacle in the working-class movement that has faced all workers and all revolutionists — the worldwide Stalinist murder machine that caused the bloody defeat of so many revolutions — is weaker than at any time since its consolidation in the first half of the 1930s. The combination of fear and horror, of corruption and confusion that Stalinism brought into our class;

27. See "Speech to Members of the Indian Community," in *Nelson Mandela Speaks* (New York: Pathfinder, 1993), pp. 222–25.

the substitution of the needs of a small, privileged national caste for the international needs of working people — all this has taken historic blows.

Crises like those of the Stalinist apparatuses in the Soviet Union and Eastern Europe are still ahead of us in China. They will take different forms there, because the huge pools of labor in the countryside create different openings for economic development that no longer exist anywhere in Eastern Europe or the former USSR. But pushing rural toilers from the land and rapid, brutal industrialization will produce big class struggles in China, in different combinations and at a different pace, just as they did in Europe and America over the past one hundred and fifty years. That is all coming further down the road. The world bourgeoisie's dreams of the great miracle — a billion Chinese consumers and value-producers — will bring such struggles! And communist leadership in China will come in exactly the same way it will come everywhere else, from fighters in the working class and among revolutionary-minded youth.

We take it for granted now that young communists from the United States, or Sweden, or New Zealand go to the Philippines, or go to a conference of Asian youth in India, and mix it up with other young fighters from the region and sell communist literature. But for decades this was almost unthinkable. Such exchanges were largely blocked off by the virulence of Stalinism in Asia, which marched under the banner of Maoism and produced the horrors of Pol Potism, among other things.[28] In the so-called

28. Pol Pot was the top leader of the former Khmer Rouge regime that inflicted a murderous reign of terror on the peasants and working people of Cambodia for nearly four years following the collapse of the U.S.-backed rightist government there in April 1975. The Khmer Rouge, which combined the Maoist variant of Stalinism with xenophobic Cambodian nationalism, was driven from power by the combined forces of the Vietnamese armed forces and Cambodian oppositionists in January 1979.

In June 1997, after years of virtually complete clandestinity, Pol Pot was put on public trial in the military redoubt of a faction of the Khmer Rouge

Western world, there was a lot of petty-bourgeois romanticizing of this Maoist variant of Stalinism, as if a worker in Asia could not be an equal, could not be expected to rise to the same level of political consciousness as a worker elsewhere in the world.

But there is not a single political organization or current anywhere in the world today that looks politically to the Beijing regime or draws tribute from its trough. And only a handful of organizations in Asia or elsewhere, splintered among themselves, still cling to one or another variant of Maoism. Given the disintegration of these Stalinist obstacles, new energies, capacities, and creativity among millions of workers and youth can be opened throughout Asia and beyond.

The primordial fact that communists have insisted on over the past few years is being confirmed: It is *not* new wellsprings of capitalist expansion and power that are being created as the twenty-first century draws near. To the contrary, the size of the hereditary proletariat worldwide is growing, as are new possibilities for workers to cross borders and work together to find ways to move forward. And as this process unfolds, young people and workers looking for dignity — who are inspired by militant resistance and a growing desire to give as well as to receive solidarity, and who aspire to true political equality — will find their place in the ranks and leadership of the communist movement.

---

and sentenced to "life imprisonment" for ordering the execution of a top aide. The Stalinist-trained butcher died under house arrest in April 1998. In December 1998, the last remaining Khmer Rouge forces surrendered to the Cambodian government. A few weeks later, two remaining senior Khmer Rouge officials, Khieu Samphan and Nuon Chea, also turned themselves in, appealing at a press conference in Phnom Penh to "let bygones be bygones."

DISCUSSION

Crisis of capitalism,
prospects for communism

COMMENT: You seemed to be saying in your talk that what is happening today is not a crisis of communism but a capitalist crisis. That is certainly not what we've been reading in the newspapers or hearing on television since 1990, and even for a year or so before then. Could you say a bit more about why you are convinced that capitalism, not socialism, is in a world crisis?

RESPONSE: The increasingly universal character of the capitalist crisis can be seen from the fact that the attempts to continue organizing social and economic life through the market system are registering horrendous failures for the majority of toilers in growing parts of the world.

In the semicolonial countries, despite substantial industrialization in a number of areas, not a single nation has the prospect of catching up with even the weakest of the imperialist powers. The economic and social disparities within the semicolonial countries are widening, while the conditions of life for the majority of toilers are growing more, not less, desperate. Likewise, the disparity between the "underdeveloped" and "developed" countries continues to grow. I just noticed an article on the annual report of one of the big, Swiss-based imperialist financial agencies, called the Bank for International Settlements. It reported that the average income in Third World countries as a whole has fallen from 25 percent of the average income in industrially advanced countries in 1960 to 20 percent in 1990. These trends, the report said, "cast doubt on the widely held assumption that poor countries will generally gain relative to more advanced countries through the spillover of technology and capital inflows."

In the industrially advanced countries where capitalism is supposed to have demonstrated its power and glory, more and more working people live with a deepening sense of insecurity and foreboding. And in the workers states where government leaders, many of them formerly "Communists," are now bending over backwards to accommodate imperialist demands and introduce capitalist economic forms, the devastating social consequences — unacceptable to the majority — are mounting. It ties their hands, preventing the imperialists from pressing forward in the manner they had dreamed of.

It is not hard to convince people of this picture when we present the facts and explain the deadly logic of the workings of capitalism.

The problem with the term "the crisis of communism" is that the word *communism* is used in two different ways. It is commonly used to describe the world Stalinist movement, which has been the enemy of communist workers and an enormous obstacle to a socialist future. That movement, which owed allegiance to the privileged ruling caste of the Soviet Union above all, fostered the reactionary view that bureaucratic structures and social engineering — propped up by brutal police violence when necessary — is how workers should be organized, instead of workers organizing themselves to transform society. It bred illusions in alliances with the capitalists.

There truly is a world crisis of Stalinism. Reemerging Stalinist formations — and many of them will reemerge — can have only a shadow of their former power and influence. The parasitic castes, unlike social classes, had no necessary historical function. They rose as a counterrevolutionary excrescence — a parasitic growth weakening the social forms originally thrown up by a powerful socialist revolution. They were a barrier to workers transforming themselves, so they could organize the economy and govern the workers states more effectively. The castes had a profoundly depoliticizing weight. They were a transmission belt of capitalist pressures, ideas, and values into the workers states and international labor movement.

What might more accurately be called a crisis of communism is something quite different, it seems to me. Genuine communist forces worldwide remain small, above all because of the decades-long consequences of Stalinism. The Stalinists gave world capitalism opportunities to recover from its greatest social crisis of this century, the Great Depression of the 1930s, and to triumph over revolutionary uprisings by workers and peasants before, during, and after World War II. The Stalinists helped imperialism strengthen its global domination. They dealt terrible blows to the workers vanguard for more than six decades. How many millions who started off as fighters and revolutionists were fooled, corrupted, and demoralized by them!

While all this is true, however, I do not think calling it a crisis of communism helps clarify much. This has simply been a political fact of life for a very long time. In a genuine social and political crisis, when workers have the opportunity to fight, and revolutionary struggles develop, small communist formations can grow rapidly if they have prepared beforehand and if they are deeply a part of the mass workers movement — in composition, program, and fighting experience. This has been proven in practice, including by the Bolshevik-led October Revolution itself.

But if somebody insists, nonetheless, on describing the last sixty years as a crisis of communism, then the shattering of Stalinism's power, of course, does open the way to resolving that crisis. The outcome depends, however, on the rise of the world workers movement, of which communists form a politically organized part — and on what communists do in politics *right now* to prepare for such a rise.

Attempts by imperialism and national bourgeoisies to strengthen the domination of capital in each part of the world are deepening the crisis in all of them. If you want to watch this process unfold in a single country, watch Germany. It is like a boa constrictor that has swallowed a massive animal that it cannot digest. The German rulers will not be able to restore their prior, more stable conditions without struggles that have unforeseen consequences for them. And the workers, east and west, now have much better conditions to uproot capitalism in Germany as a whole — something much more difficult so long as Stalinism was able to disorient so many in both halves of the country.

The decades are now behind us when Stalinism alone guaranteed that the odds against any revolutionary workers struggle succeeding were very high — or, that if it did succeed, from the outset the odds were high that it would be corroded from within and ultimately overthrown. The working class still confronts a multitude of challenges. But the enormous obstacle of Stalinism as we know it is behind us, even though its political legacy and miseducation are not.

For most of this century, the word *communist* has been used primarily by those who largely monopolized speaking for the workers movement and who put an equal sign between communism and Stalinism. The Stalinists portrayed the bureaucratic caste of Mother Russia as the wave of the future and the salvation of humanity. They used the vocabulary of communism to cast the red glow of the history of revolutionary workers struggles on themselves and their lodestar.

Others in the workers movement — the social democrats, anarchists and anarcho-syndicalists, various centrist currents and sects — also identified Stalinism with communism, in order to cover up their own collaboration with the capitalists, with the imperialists, at home and abroad. Most of these currents gave fulsome support to U.S. finance capital's onslaught in World War II, and either open or tacit support to Washington's bloody wars against the Korean and Vietnamese people and aggression against Cuba to roll back the socialist revolution.

So, whichever way the term *communism* was being used by

others inside and outside the workers movement, it was confusing and disorienting to broader layers of workers and youth. Now, workers in countries where the road to communism was seemingly blocked for so long by mammoth statues of Lenin and Marx, and by giant mausoleums with mummies under glass, have the chance to discover communism as they gain class-struggle experience and meet embattled workers from other countries. And as they find their way back to the unvarnished Lenin, Marx, and Engels, they will need neither embalmed bodies nor grotesque statuary.

Some workers in eastern Germany will find out the truth about the *German* revolution of 1918–19 for the first time at a demonstration in Berlin, where they will meet workers from Britain who have brought with them the Pathfinder book in *English* that tells the story.[29] Things like that, seemingly paradoxical but delightful to revolutionists, become possible now, and they will happen more and more in coming years.

If we want to understand what these changes open up for revolutionists today, there is no better place to start than the Cuban revolution. It has survived as a socialist revolution for more than three decades. And its further advance both depends on, and will help speed, new steps toward resolving the crisis of working-class leadership on an international scale.

We should not have our eyes on bureaucrats in Cuba. We should not have our eyes on people who are no longer capable of fighting under the current difficult conditions. Instead, take a look at those who have shown, in often extraordinary ways, that they are able to fight, those who are genuine revolutionists. Remember that they and hundreds of thousands like them in Cuba — actually backed by millions — have in many ways carried the world on their shoulders for almost thirty-five years.

---

29. *The German Revolution and the Debate on Soviet Power: Documents, 1918–1919* (New York: Pathfinder, 1986). Part of Pathfinder's series, The Communist International in Lenin's Time.

When a door was opened by the collapse of the Stalinist apparatuses, discussion of *real* communist politics increased in Cuba. Previously, communists there were often preoccupied with the taboos on what could and could not be discussed openly while still maintaining relations with those who called themselves communists in the Soviet Union. Those concerns have receded since 1990.

If someone had told me even two years ago that universities in Cuba would be competing for which one gets the next donation of books published and distributed by Pathfinder Press, I don't think I would have believed it. The complex workings of history are something to behold. Over the past few years, supporters of Pathfinder have set up literature tables not only at the Havana book fairs in 1990 and 1992, but at several university-sponsored conferences in Holguín and Matanzas provinces. They report that if they do not have something available in Spanish, and if the Cuban they are talking to does not read much English, often that person will say, "But my *Russian* is excellent. I spent seven years studying in the Soviet Union." So there are people in Cuba right now who are reading the *Bulletin of the Opposition*,[30] or Leon Trotsky's *History of the Russian Revolution*, in Russian. They are reading communist material — written by those who fought the murderous counterrevolution against Lenin's course — in the original Russian.

A few supporters of Pathfinder last year prevented a substantial number of volumes by Marx, Engels, and Lenin from being pulped in Moscow and salvaged them to be read and studied as a guide to action by young fighters. That rescue operation is a popular story

30. The *Bulletin of the Opposition* was the Russian-language magazine of the communist opposition to the Stalinists' reversal of Lenin's proletarian internationalist course. Many of it leading articles were written by Bolshevik leader Leon Trotsky. Produced from 1929 to 1941, the banned magazine was circulated hand to hand by worker-bolsheviks in the Soviet Union in face of stiffening murderous repression. It is available in a four-volume facsimile edition published by Pathfinder.

in Cuba. It was reported in the weekly magazine *Bohemia*.

Examples like these are both new and are a pledge for the future.

The bourgeoisie, with its allied landed and titled aristocrats, is the class that claims to be so magnificently educated. But the class that is truly interested in ideas is the working class. Ideas are decisive for the working class, because ideas are necessary to forge a self-confident proletarian leadership and chart a course for humanity. We have said before that if all the political books were to disappear from the world tomorrow, it would not really hurt the bourgeoisie that much. The workings and reproduction of value relations would continue pumping out profits for them. And pragmatism would be the totally sufficient "philosophical" complement to social power.

But if every such book in the world were to disappear — if all the continuity, if all the lessons from the rise of humanity and struggles by the toilers were erased from the written record — the workers movement would be set back an indescribable distance. That is why we place such importance on the opportunities that are opening up to distribute books and other literature by revolutionists and communists more widely than ever before.

Lifetime education for all

COMMENT: One of the things I sometimes have a hard time explaining to interested students when I set up literature tables on campus is why they should support union struggles. Some of them say, for instance, that a lot of workers take home higher pay than some college graduates end up making. They ask: "Why should I go to school, pay $30,000 or whatever before graduating, and then get a job making $7 or $8 an hour, while mine workers, autoworkers, and other union members make $12 or $15 an hour? Workers don't have a college education and I do. Why should I support their strike when they make so much money already?" I find that some young people think there is no future for them once they graduate, and are swayed by these kinds of bourgeois, right-wing antiunion positions. Could you say something about this?

RESPONSE: Among other things, the students you describe have an exaggerated notion about what the average worker earns, including the average unionized worker. They are also mystified by two false notions. First that there is some connection between actual skills imparted in a college education and the income of college graduates. There is none. Second that there is some kind of "income pie" that is fixed, whereby a group of workers winning higher wages means lower incomes for everybody else. That is a myth promoted by the capitalists to protect their profits and profit rates.[31]

These, too, are class questions, not "educational" questions.

---

31. The truth is that wages have nothing to do with the value of the commodity a worker produces or the service he or she performs. To a substantial degree, wages are determined by what the working class, through organization and struggle, has been able to establish and defend over time as the socially acceptable minimum standard of living. In contrast with "other commodities," Karl Marx explained in *Capital*, "the determination of the value of labourpower contains a historical and moral element." (*Capital*, Penguin edition, vol. 1, p. 275.) A fight by the labor movement to increase wages, including the federal minimum wage, creates a better relationship of class forces for all workers to win better pay and safer job conditions. "The law of wages, then," Frederick Engels wrote in 1881, "is not one which draws a hard and fast line. It is not inexorable within certain limits. There is at every time (great depression excepted) for every trade a certain latitude within which the rate of wages may be modified by the results of the struggle between the two contending parties. . . . Without the means of resistance of the Trade Unions the labourer does not receive even what is his due according to the rules of the wages system." ("The Wages System," in Marx and Engels, *Collected Works*, vol. 24, pp. 380–81.)

The purpose of education in class society is not to educate. The purpose of education is to give "the educated" a stake in thinking they are going to be different — slightly better off, slightly more white collar — than other people who work all their lives. In the process, the rulers hope to make those who manage to get a college degree a more dependable supporter of the status quo. They want you to be comfortable supervising, "orienting," and testing workers — directly and indirectly. They want to be able to count on you as a stable supporter of the capitalist system. It is not education, it is confusion and corruption.

At the same time, entire social layers — lawyers and other so-called professionals — live off massive rents just because they can hang a piece of paper on the wall, a piece of paper kept scarce by the action of the state. That diploma becomes a justification for living off part of the fruits of the exploitation of workers, working farmers, and other toiling producers. That is another function of education under capitalism. It gives certain social layers a license to a higher income, to a portion of the surplus value workers produce with our labor.[32]

So the relationship between education and income in capitalist society has nothing to do with college graduates knowing more, let alone making a greater contribution to human welfare (or necessarily even a greater direct contribution to capitalist wealth,

---

32. Surplus value is the portion of the value workers create through their labor, above and beyond what the capitalists pay out in wages to the working class. The propertied owners of industrial, banking, commercial, and land-owning capital compete among themselves to maximize their share of surplus value in the form of profits, interest, and rent. The capitalist rulers also pay out part of this surplus value to layers of professionals and supervisory personnel whose services help maintain and reproduce the class relations, privilege, domination, and rule of the bourgeoisie. Analogous to the rent extorted by landlords because of their monopoly over a parcel of soil or ownership of a building, these professional layers collect a rent out of surplus value because of their monopoly over a relatively privileged position in the class structure and pecking order of capitalist society.

for that matter). Instead, it is a small price the propertied rulers pay for a middle class that helps them maintain social stability, hold off working-class demands, and rationalize the polarizing social consequences of the relations of production under capitalism.

Liberals, for example, have recently made a great deal of figures showing that the gap has grown over the past fifteen years between the average annual incomes of high school and college graduates. According to government figures, men with a university degree today take home on average about 90 percent more than those with a high school education, up from about 50 percent in 1979; for women the figure has gone up to about 75 percent from some 45 percent. Does that mean college graduates have gotten that much smarter over the past decade and a half, or that their skills are in that much greater demand by the capitalists? Does it mean that hi-tech society today has a greater need for "symbolic analysts" than it does for "routine producers," as Clinton's new secretary of labor, Harvard professor Robert Reich, would have us believe? (I concede that Reich is not a "routine producer." In fact, he is not a producer of any kind, except of a product I should not mention at a public gathering. Those who have spent time on a farm will be acquainted with it, however.)

No, this growing income gap means the union movement has gotten weaker and real wages have been pushed down. The price of our labor power has been driven down by the bosses. That is all it means.

Nor is there a fixed income pie. Higher wages won by workers mean less profits for capitalists; they don't come out of a "wage pool" that is depleted to the detriment of other workers and the lower middle class. In fact, as we have explained many times, higher wages and better conditions won in struggle by the labor movement put the working class as a whole — together with farmers and other toiling allies — on a stronger footing to fight for better living standards and conditions of life and work. That is why the capitalists carry out an ideological offensive to convince the middle class and layers of workers of the reactionary, nonscientific view that wage hikes are the cause of everything from inflation to unemployment to outright impoverishment.

None of this is true. Marx explained this many years ago in his pamphlets *Wage-Labor and Capital* and *Wages, Price, and Profit* (subsequent editions changed the title to *Value, Price, and Profit,* but I am using Marx's title; it is more accurate). On this point, there is nothing to add to the basic analysis he offers in those pamphlets, written as political weapons for the workers movement at the time.

Until society is reorganized so that education is a human activity from the time we are very young until the time we die, there will be no serious education. There will only be the pretensions to education or to technical expertise of a small group of people. That is the historical truth.

Not a 'youth' question

Capitalist society promotes the myth that education is a youth question. But any society that sees education as a question just for young people can never have education that is meaningful for human beings, including youth. Social solidarity will never exist in such a society.

The working class cannot begin with how to change things so that *youth* get a better education. We have to begin with how to transform the values of society, not just the economics; it cannot be reduced simply to an economic problem. To be meaningful, education has to create the possibilities for society as a whole to advance, instead of reinforcing the exploitation of the majority by the few. Until then, the only "liberal education" available to any fighter who wants one is political education within the workers movement.

What is taught in most schools today is largely worthless. There are a handful of skills that provide some preparation for life — learning to read, learning to write, learning to compute, practicing to increase our attention spans, learning the discipline necessary to study and use our minds. Reading and studying are extremely hard. It takes discipline to sit still for three hours, two hours, even one hour — not moving, not jumping up — and to work through ideas. Working through ideas is hard; we all have to learn how to do it. But it is part of taking ourselves seriously. It is part of taking humanity seriously. We have to learn how to read and study by coming to better understand how other people live and work, whether they are older or younger than we are.

But most everything else we are taught in school, especially in the so-called social sciences and related "disciplines," are things we need to unlearn. Civics courses, social studies courses — these are all obfuscation. There is technical training of certain kinds, and applied sciences, that can be OK, with some luck. But these are forms of apprenticeships, not liberal education in the meaningful, universal sense.

Many young people wonder why they should go to school for twelve years in this society. Most never learn anything of value past the sixth or seventh grade. I went to a working-class elementary school in southern Ohio in the forties and fifties. I never had to write a single essay or do anything like that my entire time in school; I was never given a reason to concentrate on doing so. But I had some teachers who were fine people and who taught me to read, taught me grammar and spelling, showed me by example how to at least sit quietly and work for a while, and encouraged me to do so. They displayed some social solidarity. That is all I can say I ever got from going to school. But that part turned out to be valuable. It was an accident. But because of this accident, I learned to read, for *life.* At the same time, I hated reading what they crammed down my throat in high school. I hated Shakespeare then; I hated *Macbeth* the way it was taught.

Most young people never get taught they have anything to look forward to after their compulsory schooling is over. They never get taught in such a way as to make them believe the educational system is based on the assumption that their lives are worth a damn. (Many of us can remember teachers and principals who reeked of this attitude, I'm sure.) Instead, young people learn they have nothing to look forward to. They do not need to be told this in so many words; all they have to do is just watch other workers older than themselves. They just watch people like themselves who are above seventeen or eighteen years of age. Between ages six and seventeen young workers go to school six or seven hours a day; they are supposed to read books, work for good grades, study things, turn in homework. They are supposed to "just say no." Then, all of a sudden they turn eighteen and they never do it again. They are supposed to just say *yes* to whatever an employer asks.[33]

Don't underestimate young people's moral yearnings, their openness, human solidarity, and sensitivity. Perhaps they cannot put what they see into words. Perhaps they cannot theorize it. But they *know* a lot about what's going on. What does this kind of education have to do with the human race?

To really discuss education is not to discuss how to reform the seventh grade in Canarsie. The seventh grade in Canarsie *is not going to be reformed.* Or in Louisville. Or anywhere else. I guarantee it, because the rulers have no need, and thus no desire, for workers to be educated in this society. It is not true that the capitalist class needs for workers to be educated; it is a lie. They need for us to be obedient, not to be educated. They need for us to have to work hard to make a living, not to be critical. They need for us to consume all we make each week buying their products. Above all, they need for us to lose any desire over time to broaden our scope and become citizens of the world.

But the employing class does not need for us to be disciplined. In fact, indiscipline in life puts us more in their grasp. Obedience on the job, yes; discipline in life, no. That is what the employers want from the working class.

---

33. This feature of working-class public education has its complement in the schools of the upper classes, which inculcate the idea — and did so long before Charles Murray and Richard Herrnstein wrote *The Bell Curve* — that workers will get along better over the long haul if they've internalized values accepting their station in life and "just say yes" to their "betters."

Most of you in the audience here tonight are workers. Do you have to be literate to do your job — not intelligent, but literate? Think about it. Do you have to be literate to work on the railroad? In an auto plant? Do you have to be literate to be a worker in an oil refinery? I don't think so; everything is color-coded, or number-coded. You don't need to be literate. Let alone be *educated*. Let alone have pride, self-respect, and initiative. Let alone to work together with fellow human beings to do things collectively, and to derive pleasure from it. That kind of education would be a danger for the rulers. Can you imagine people like *that* — fifteen, sixteen, seventeen, eighteen years old — coming into the workforce? They would take not only to union solidarity, but also to historical materialism and its revelatory and liberating character, like fish to water.

Only by looking at education this way can we understand the depth of the crisis. There is no meaningful education in this country under capitalism's school system, *and there won't be.* There will be some elementary reading, writing, and arithmetic. Certain people will be steered into technical specializations and a few will be drawn over time into the lower ranks of better-off social layers, in order to demonstrate to all other workers that we don't "merit" being rewarded.

A thin layer of young people — most from economically privileged backgrounds, plus a handful of lucky individuals from the working class — will even be given a chance to find their way to more creative work. That is a very thin layer, however, one that everyone would love to be a part of.

Think seriously as a worker. How many of your co-workers are functionally illiterate? How many workers weren't when they started working but became so after ten or twenty years on the job, because there was no reason for them to read anymore? My father, a worker all his life, and a capable man, became *functionally* illiterate as he aged. Do the lives working people lead — the lives of those who create all the wealth, whose labor and imagination make everything possible, without whom the world would simply stop tomorrow — do their lives and their work encourage them to learn more each year? Is whatever leisure time workers have fought for and won as a class organized to encourage them to learn?

What do workers have to know for what they do on the job? It does not make any difference, does it? But in a society that is worth a damn, it *would* make a difference. There would be *continual* education. There would be a continual connection between work and education, between work and creativity. Work would not be organized around competition to sell the labor power of our muscle and brains for eight hours a day to one of the highest bidders. And the greatest reward from work would be increased human solidarity, the pleasure and celebration that come from what we have accomplished together.

That is why the working class has such a stake in getting rid of the notion that education is a children's question instead of a *social* question. The former is a petty-bourgeois, sentimental cover-up for the true crisis of education. There will be no real education, including above all for children, in a society where working people who are supposedly being educated know that a day will come when their education simply stops. Under those conditions, young people grind away until that day comes — whether at age sixteen, seventeen, eighteen, or twenty-one. And then their "education" ends.

Work must become an activity through which a human being's desire to continually widen his or her scope — the desire to *educate* ourselves — can be realized. Professors and certain other professionals have something called a "sabbatical." It is a very good practice, even if it is often not used very well (that's another story that is not our concern). Every seven years, they take some time off — sometimes a half year at full pay, sometimes a full year at half pay. They go somewhere and study something new, broaden their experiences, improve their knowledge, meet people in other countries. That's the idea. Go to Italy, go to Japan, go to Mexico. Go to Asia, go to Nigeria, go to South Africa. It is a wonderful concept. Workers should have the same opportunity. Every worker should have a sabbatical every three years — get half the year off with pay to go to another country, or to another part of this country; to study something, to make further strides in another language, to broaden our scope. This should be a lifetime perspective.

Work should be the way Che Guevara talked and wrote about it. Read his talks to factory workers during the early years of the Cuban revolution; read "A New Attitude toward Work" and other writings and speeches in Pathfinder's collection, *Che Guevara and the Cuban Revolution*. Factories and other workplaces should be organized to promote continual requalification and ongoing education, Che said. The goal of communist workers in the factories, he wrote, is "to assure that productive labor, training, and participation in economic matters of the [production] unit become integral parts of the workers' lives, gradually becoming an irreplaceable habit."[34]

When that day comes, then there will be something that can truly be called education. When that day comes, there will be links between the very young, the teenager, the adult, the older person — and they will be *human* links, *practical* links, *revolutionary* links.

No better reason for socialist revolution

In the United States today, under capitalism, the only future we can count on is one in which education will worsen — in which education will fuel rather than retard social differentiation. There will only be "education" to squelch curiosity and creativity. There will only be "education" as regimentation. There will only be "education" as preparation to rationalize — or simply resent — class polarization.

I am not saying that everybody involved in education intends for this to happen. There are human beings in this society who

---

34. "Planning and Consciousness in the Transition to Socialism (On the Budgetary Finance System)," in *Che Guevara and the Cuban Revolution*, pp. 217–18.

are not communists and who are not workers but who genuinely, in their own way, would like to see children and other people have a better education and become more self-confident. I have had some teachers like that, as many of you have. But such individuals are not the norm, and they cannot and will not change the character of education in bourgeois society.

Instead, people are reduced under capitalism to hoping things will be different for *your* child. *Your* child *somehow* will get a decent education, *somehow* will get to college, *somehow* will not have the desire to learn beaten out of them. *Your* child *somehow* will be able to compete with everybody else and have a better life.

That is what the president of the United States did, isn't it? Clinton spent nine months campaigning about the importance of public education — and the whole working class knew what the Clintons were going to do when they had to choose a school for their daughter, Chelsea. We all knew what Clinton was going to do. And that is what he did: he sent her to an exclusive private school in Washington.

Class-conscious workers bore no resentment toward William, Hillary, or Chelsea Clinton because of this decision. Envy of the propertied classes and their spokespersons is not a revolutionary or proletarian trait; it is encouraged not by communists but by fascists. But in watching the Clintons go about selecting a school for their daughter, thinking workers recognized further confirmation of two fundamental realities of class relations under capitalism. First, there is no connection between the values and public policies sanctimoniously espoused by the ruling layers and the personal lives they and their families lead. Second, there is no such thing as classless "education" in capitalist society; schools for the working class and schools for the ruling class are qualitatively different things.

If education is not discussed this way, then revolutionaries can never be convincing. If we start where reformers and liberals throughout the capitalist world begin — with *my* children, *my* neighborhood, *my* schools, *my* problems — then we get nowhere.

And when the reformers start jabbering about defending *all* children, reach for your wallet and your watch! They are like the so-called right-to-lifers who defend children in the abstract before they are born, but oppose anything to advance a truly human life for most actual children from the moment they're born till the day they die. There *is no universal education* under capitalism; there is no such thing as education "for all." There is only "education" for the working class, and a completely different kind of "education" for the small propertied minority.

If we do not explain education under capitalism as a class question (that is, from the standpoint of the bourgeoisie, two totally separate and unrelated questions for two different classes); if we do not present working-class schooling as the social destruction of human solidarity, as the organization of a society based on class differentiation, where human beings late in their teens become units of production in the minds of personnel managers and social planners; if we do not point to the fundamental issue of truly universal, lifetime education — if we cannot explain education this way, then we cannot explain it at all.

But understood and explained correctly, there is no more important question for communists. Education as a lifetime experience — I cannot think of a better reason to make a socialist revolution. What better reason to get rid of the capitalist state, to begin transforming humanity, to begin building human solidarity?

This approach to education is what we have to explain to students, to young people, and to others. If they went to school to get a leg up in life, then they did so due to a misunderstanding — unless they are from a class background that already gives them a leg up, and attended a school that teaches them they deserve it. But youth can be convinced of this working-class perspective, especially as they become active in a few political tussles, and if they haven't yet been totally coarsened by this society. Young people want to match deeds and words. They still have vitality — they have not had it ground out of them. They can be attracted politically to the working class and communist politics, but only if we argue with them in this way.

Rightist movements, as I said, always try to play on the disappointments and resentments of youth from the lower middle classes or slightly better-off sections of the working class. That is one of the ways fascist movements are built. "You worked so hard for your education," they say. "Soon you'll be raising your children. And now *you're* going to have to pay more taxes for *their* children and *their* elderly." And the list of "thems" keeps growing.

I've been convinced for a long time that explaining the communist approach to education is part of preparing the working class for the greatest of all battles in the years ahead — the battle to throw off the self-image the rulers teach us, and to recognize that we are capable of taking power and organizing society, as we change ourselves in the process.

Washington lets Yugoslavia bleed

COMMENT: My question is about Yugoslavia. Next week, U.S. warplanes are to go on patrol as part of NATO enforcement of the "no-fly zone" over Bosnia adopted by the UN Security Council last October. There is talk that if a peace treaty is signed, there may be 50,000 troops patrolling the area, many of them from the United States. If there is no peace treaty, the war will escalate, and there will be stronger calls for imperialist military intervention. Clinton seems to have backed off from his campaign tough talk against the Serbian forces in Yugoslavia, and top U.S. military officers say they are against going into Yugoslavia, too. At the same time, there are politicians in both the Democratic and Republican parties who are calling for air strikes by Washington right now. Whatever happens in the so-called peace talks, the war just keeps going on, the death toll mounts, and bigger forces keep coming into play. I was wondering how you read all this.

RESPONSE: I do not think it is in the interests of the United States ruling class to intervene militarily in Yugoslavia right now. It is not in their interests for one and only one reason. From their standpoint, and at a political price they are willing to pay, there is no better course than what is taking place right now.

The U.S. rulers and their spokespeople have some tactical disagreements among themselves, that is true. But those are arguments among the foxes guarding the chicken coop. They are arguing about how fast the tide might turn against their interests, knowing they will likely need to go into Yugoslavia sooner or later. But there is no evidence that they are planning to go in right now. Most of the U.S. ruling class currently holds the view: "So what? So tens of thousands of people are being slaughtered and hundreds of thousands more turned into refugees. So the Serbs and Croats are killing each other and they are both killing the Muslims. So what?" The U.S. rulers don't lose sleep over "ethnic cleansing."

Some of their European rivals have vested interests in one or another of the warring gangs of the fractured bureaucratic caste in Yugoslavia. German finance capital in particular has an economic and political stake in the Croatian and Slovenian side. At the end of 1991, Bonn was the first imperialist power to recognize the governments in Croatia and Slovenia, following their public break from the Yugoslav federation a few months earlier. London, and also Paris to a degree, are trying to balance between the contending forces, each for its reasons. And the imperialist powers as a whole worry that peoples throughout the Islamic world identify with the victims of ethnic cleansing in Muslim areas of Bosnia, and that there may be pressure for Iran or other regimes in the area to get involved. Moscow maintains ties to the Serbian regime in Belgrade as a way to maintain some influence in the region, and this will be a source of conflict and tension as well.

But the current administration in Washington and the bipartisan directors of U.S. foreign policy have decided it is not in their interests to intervene directly at the moment. They hypocritically lament the horrors and ask how anyone can stand by and watch it. But they *do* stand by and they *have* been watching it. They have been doing nothing but watching it for a year. They are content to let the warring parties themselves weaken the Yugoslav workers state, and to let their European rivals spar with each other and take on the precarious policing operation in Bosnia. They are teaching a lesson on "Europe," NATO, and Washington's indispensability as a European power.

It is not some special weakness that is preventing Washington from going into Yugoslavia. To the contrary. They are simply not going to risk the price they know they will pay in this country by sending in troops until they have good reason to do so. When they are convinced the bleeding has gone on long enough, and that a change in course is now to their advantage, the U.S. rulers will weigh the costs and act accordingly. They have no strategic vision for the Balkans. Their aim is to weaken and eventually destroy the Yugoslav workers state, and gain an edge on their European rivals in the bargain. They are following a pragmatic course, as they always do.

No independent line of officer caste

I would be careful about one thing, though. Do not believe the stories you read in the newspapers attributing the fact that Washington has not yet intervened in Bosnia to some independent political position in the U.S. armed forces. Some press reports claim the most important tactical division in Washington involves the military brass, who are saying, "We don't want to use force in Yugoslavia unless we can use overwhelming force and be sure we'll win."

But the military brass is not an independent force. They will do what they are trained to do — organize the use of U.S. military might according to the needs of the ruling class, in the world as it exists today. The officer corps does not have different views from the main political currents in the ruling class; it is part of those currents.

Like every privileged bureaucratic layer in bourgeois society, the brass try to get more meat for themselves. They want a higher budget for the Pentagon. The officer caste is a wretched group, the greatest enemy of the citizen-soldier. They genuinely consider the Uniform Code of Military Justice to be higher than the U.S. Constitution and Bill of Rights, and they consider their interpretation of the Code to be higher than that of any court. But they have no independent political line on anything.

When officers of bourgeois armies lose out in the military pecking order, they often become bitter, Bonapartist demagogues and turn to the ultraright. That has been the history of those in the officer caste throughout the modern history of capitalism. If they advance in the officer caste, they sometimes become successful bourgeois politicians, maybe even president of the United States — there have been a good number of those in U.S. history, most recently Dwight Eisenhower — or chairman of the board of a big corporation or university. That is all there is to it. Losers fade away. General MacArthur faded away soon after the Korean War. General Norman Schwarzkopf faded away barely a year after the war in the Gulf.

There can be sharp conflicts with the officer corps in ruling circles around particular military questions, because the bourgeois armed forces are rigid when it comes to adjusting to social changes. That is part of their bureaucratic structure. That is a consequence of the character of bourgeois military discipline, which is an *imposed* obedience (plus "go along to get along"), not the discipline from political conviction of the cadre of a proletarian combat party or a revolutionary army.

There is a myth in bourgeois public opinion, for example, that the army is an advanced institution on race relations. That is simply a lie. The U.S. armed forces was the *last* place in the United States where a powerful social institution — the officer caste — continued to insist there were biological, psychological, genetic differences between the races. If Jim Crow segregation was not maintained in the military, they insisted, even if it was being gotten rid of in the rest of society, the armed forces would be destroyed. The armed forces were the *last* institution to finally come around.

How many years ago was it that you finally no longer had to be a Filipino under 5 foot 7 inches in order to be an officers' steward on a ship in the U.S. Navy? Not many. Watch newsreels of officers being served on Navy ships. You won't believe it. Or look at who made up the burial details during World War II — there are newsreels of that too. They were usually all Black. *That* is the United States armed forces. The Navy is still the worst, if there are slight differences among them.

At the same time, it is against the interests of the ruling class for the armed forces to get too much out of step with the concessions the rulers have had to make to social struggles. They sometimes have to shove the officer corps a little bit to get it to change course a few degrees. For example, the ban on women in a whole number of combat operations will begin being phased out this month; women will be permitted to fly combat aircraft and serve on warships for the first time, although still not in ground combat units. Adjustments such as these will be made by the brass, even if not readily or early. Others they will resist, but if they fight for very long, you can rest assured it is with the support of large layers in the ruling class. We will soon know the outcome of the dispute that has broken out with those in the officer corps and Congress who oppose Clinton's campaign promise to end the ban on gays in the armed forces.

Let me make two final points in this regard.

First, we are not seeing preparations for a military government today; that is premature in the United States. Instead, the sharpness of some of the public debates involving the officer caste reflects the growing centralization of government power in the executive branch as capitalism declines. All state structures become slightly more Bonapartist-like in the United States, as well as in other imperialist countries. The president, the executive branch, asserts more and more power over decisions on war and peace, on the use of force, on the deployment of resources, on other policy matters. The powers of the U.S. Congress and bourgeois parliaments become more limited over time.

Second, this tendency toward centralization, toward a stronger executive branch — toward what has been dubbed "the Imperial Presidency" even by some in the big-business press — does open the door at a certain stage to preparations for an attempt at a military coup. It does open the way, as crisis conditions deepen, for the establishment of a true Bonapartist regime. The veteran SWP leader Farrell Dobbs used to say that if anybody thinks we are not going to see every one of these alternatives attempted by sections of the rulers as class battles heat up in the United States, then they are dead wrong and will never build a revolutionary workers party in this country. We will see every one of those alternatives tried.

But that is not happening today. Right now, the political conflicts in which certain military officers may figure are a reflection of the more immediate danger — the growth of executive power, the power of the presidency, in the United States and other imperialist countries. We hear complaints now and again from politicians in both parties, for example, about the 1973 War Powers Act, which was adopted by Congress in the wake of Washington's defeat in Vietnam and the mass popular opposition to that war. It supposedly requires the president to inform Congress within forty-eight hours of sending U.S. troops into combat, as well as congressional approval for any deployment of U.S. forces for more than sixty days. The truth is, however, that the War Powers Act has never once been invoked by Congress — not once. Not when U.S. forces landed in Lebanon in 1982, nor in Grenada in 1983, nor in Panama in 1989, nor in the Gulf two years ago. Every administration, both Democrats and Republicans, has given the back of its hand to the act, and the bipartisan Congress has fallen in line well after the die was cast in combat.

Ten years after the fact, the press is now running exposés about U.S. government involvement in massacres in El Salvador — which everyone already knew about. But they got away with it at the time. Remember what Oliver North always says to both Democratic Party liberals and his former Reagan administration cohorts when either of them try to finger him for Washington's secret arming of Nicaraguan contras in the 1980s. Financing and equipping the contras to bring down the Sandinista government was a *bipartisan effort*, North insists. Scores of Democrats and Republicans in Congress knew what was being organized out of the White House, and they never did a thing to stop it. It was a bipartisan effort in El Salvador, too, and U.S. imperialist foreign policy continues to be bipartisan.

Whenever the rulers have to use large-scale armed forces in combat anywhere in the world, it creates a problem for them in this country. There will be resistance, and over time it will grow and become connected to other social struggles. As the conflict drags on, citizen-soldiers, the *ranks*, will begin to put their stamp on opposition to U.S. military actions. At some point, workers struggles will begin to coincide with the resistance by antiwar youth and soldiers. That is what we began to see during the Vietnam War. And we will see it again under conditions marked by depression and rising class tensions, unlike the relative capitalist prosperity and stability of the 1960s.

Opposition to capitalist austerity, to imperialist wars, and to growing rightist violence will go hand in hand in the years that lie ahead.

Capitalism destroys the environment

COMMENT: I wanted to ask a question about the environment. I attended a Militant Labor Forum in Pittsburgh last week on the fight against the opening of a toxic waste incinerator in Ohio, right across the border from Pennsylvania. Protests against the project are being organized by a coalition headed by a retired Black steelworker, who was the featured speaker at the forum. Coincidentally, I'm also working a temporary job where we are photocopying documents from the cleanup of toxic disasters. The scope of the environmental horrors I'm learning about, both from the forum and on the job, is truly incredible. Ted Turner can broadcast Captain Planet cartoons on Saturday morning and tell kids that "you're the answer," but I think it's obvious that recycling newspapers and coffee cans is not going to save the earth. I wonder if you could comment on the fight to preserve the environment and how it is related to the working-class fight against capitalist disorder.

RESPONSE: The modern communist workers movement has long had a position against capitalist degradation of the environment. Marx and Engels wrote powerfully and convincingly about capital's destruction of the soil, the water, the air, and the basis for human life and civilization. I do not think there is anything to take back from the foundation they laid.[35]

Environmental pollution is a social question, a class question. Workers must not fall into accepting the common view that the environment — any more than "education" — is a "scientific" question, a "natural" question, that somehow hovers above classes and outside the class struggle. That is how many middle-class opponents of nuclear energy, and of nuclear weapons, for example, often present those questions. Many who call themselves environmentalists say the problem is "consumerism," or industrial devel-

---

35. For example, Marx wrote in *Capital* that "Capitalist production, therefore, only develops the techniques and . . . the social process of production by simultaneously undermining the original sources of all wealth — the soil and the worker." And elsewhere in the same work: "The development of civilization and industry in general has always shown itself so active in the destruction of forests that everything that has been done for their conservation and production is completely insignificant in comparison." *Capital* vol. 1, p. 638, and vol. 2, p. 322.

opment per se. But the workers movement has to explain the true source of ecological destruction and why the answer lies along the revolutionary line of march of the working class.

It is unlikely there will ever be "an environmental movement" as such, because conflicting class interests and perspectives will point to diametrically opposed causes and irreconcilable solutions. Young people, outraged by the abuses they see all around them and looking for answers, can become involved in activities and groups that are disconnected from any line of march that points to changing the class character of the state, to changing the class structure of the government and thus the character of society. Ultimately, such activity corrodes their initial motivations and too often develops into a search for middle-class nostrums for improving their own quality of life as individuals.

Of course, there can and will be broad action coalitions to act against specific dangers to the natural environmental and human health and safety: the incinerator you mentioned, a nuclear power plant, a toxic waste dump. These fights will often involve workers, farmers, students, people from the middle class, and others. Labor must join in these battles against the horrifying breakdowns that capitalism creates and help to lead these fights. But there will never be some general, classless environmental protection movement.

The working class must also reject all forms of fake science, exaggeration, and crankism. There is a decades-long record of such frenzied prophecies — the impending exhaustion of fossil fuels and other natural resources, the "limits to growth," and so on. These originate in sections of the bourgeoisie and are then picked up and propagated by petty-bourgeois reformers. They feed into the conspiracy nostrums that are floated in the working class and labor movement, taking workers' eyes off the true source of such social ills: the capitalists and their profit system. Such views usually end up as pseudoscientific rationalizations for reactionary, and often racist, "overpopulation" propaganda and calls for belt-tightening — with "equality of sacrifice," of course — to husband the earth's disappearing riches.

In the name of protecting the environment, middle-class reformers join forces with bourgeois politicians to figure out ways
for both the state and voluntary agencies to control the benighted
masses who do not understand these questions. They call for
steeper cigarette taxes and bans on smoking anywhere; they seek
stiffer fines on individuals who do not recycle just right, while
capitalists destroy entire rivers, lakes, and forests. It is not unknown for the new First Lady herself to take this tax-and-scold
approach on a wide variety of questions. This has nothing to do
with working-class politics or protecting the interests of working
people. Instead, it has to do with the regimentation of the working class and the hysteria of middle-class social engineers.

Many things that are called environmental questions today are
not. I live in New York City and work a lot of the time in a building on the Hudson River. Virtually all of what is called the environmental movement there thought it was a stupendous victory
back in the 1980s when the renovation of the West Side Highway
was held off for years by a federal judge because of the potential
effects on the spawning of striped bass. But the whole thing was a
con. I do not know the truth about the striped bass; maybe its
spawning grounds needed to be protected. But I do know the fight
had nothing to do with protecting the striped bass, much less with
transporting working people in New York City.

Instead, it was a multibillion-dollar battle between two sections of finance capital. At issue were the conflicting interests of
current and potential bondholders, big real estate developers
with riverfront properties, and these and other capitalists weighing the likely tax credits and burdens. Billions of dollars were at
stake — massive development funds and eternal interest transfers
to coupon clippers. So, a federal judge simply put the project on
hold for a number of years until consensus was reached in the
ruling class that rebuilding the West Side Highway was not in
their best interests. And then everyone forgot about the fish.

It is important to remind ourselves of such examples, because
similar considerations are at the heart of a certain amount of what

passes for environmental questions. But if we translate everything commonly thought of as an environmental issue into how to advance the protection of the working class, and how the working class can extend that protection to all, then we can hardly ever go wrong. With that approach, we will increase the possibilities for concrete solidarity in fighting against ecological abuses and outrages.

The labor movement should expose the differential effects of pollution on the working class, including the even more devastating consequences for sections of the working class that are Black, Chicano, or foreign-born. We can point to the kinds of neighborhoods and parts of the countryside where waste dumps just happen to be located, and where incinerators just happen to be built. We can point to the impact on working farmers, and the connections with speedup and with health and safety on and off the job.

The workers movement must take the lead in actively exposing the destruction and dangers produced by capitalism and in organizing opposition to them. If labor does so, this effort can develop over time into a broad and powerful, working-class-led social movement like the CIO movement in the 1930s. It would help the working class galvanize our allies to fight for our common interests against the propertied families and their state.

True environmental horrors are accelerating under capitalism today (and the Stalinist regimes across Central and Eastern Europe and the USSR are responsible for unthinkable devastation as well). Revolutionary governments of the workers and farmers can and will reverse this deadly course.

Take a couple evenings and reread the Communist Manifesto; reread the sections in *Capital* on capitalism's destruction of the natural environment. You will be stunned at how clearly this question is placed within the historical development of capitalism, its uncontrollable tendencies, and its social consequences. You will be stunned at how uncompromising, how committed the communist workers movement was from its origins to combating capitalism's ravaging of the earth and its atmosphere.

Marx explains how human creativity is turned into its opposite under capitalism, how advances in the forces of production simultaneously increase the forces of destruction of nature itself. How the sources of all wealth — land and labor — are increasingly the victims of the domination of capital. And, most importantly, why the working-class-led struggle for a socialist revolution opens a way forward on this front as well.

The class blindness of the bourgeoisie

COMMENT: In the newspaper this morning, there was an article about store owners and wealthy businessmen in Beverly Hills, California, purchasing guns in anticipation of the verdict in the federal civil rights trial of the cops who beat Rodney King. The article quotes the cops' attorney blaming King for every blow to his head, as well as for the riots last year following the first trial. It was unbelievable! Los Angeles mayor Tom Bradley has already gone on the air saying that he has asked state officials to call up the National Guard. Could you comment on the provocative situation the capitalist politicians are building up right now around the upcoming verdict?

RESPONSE: Federal authorities initiated the second Rodney King trial because there was so much political pressure in this country and around the world to get some justice for that horrible beating. There was pressure on Washington, so they brought down the federal civil rights indictments.

If you have been following the government's case, however, you can see that they are weighing how many cops they can get away with letting off the hook. Because the rulers never like to convict cops of using force against the working class. On the other hand, they figure, "Aren't we better off convicting one or two of them? Maybe that will take the pressure off." They are trying to fine-tune it. The trial is about balancing these pressures, nothing else.[36]

As for Beverly Hills businessmen, I suspect they have been armed for a long time. For years they have been shooting down people who walk into their business establishments if they don't like your looks. Then they claim self-defense, saying they fired in the course of an attempted robbery. This is nothing new for businessmen in southern California.

After the first acquittal, when the riots began in Los Angeles, Bradley and other bourgeois figures criticized police chief Daryl Gates for responding too slowly. But the truth is that the police department Gates built for the L.A. city fathers was largely helpless when that social explosion broke over them: nothing in their training had prepared them for it. Gates's LAPD was a bargain-basement police department, organized as though bourgeois order could be maintained by a small but highly mobile force. Gates is a brutal, racist cop, just like those he commanded. His specialty was "SWAT team" operations that would swoop down on individual targets with armored personnel carriers and lots of firepower, make a splash on the evening news, and "set an example." But the minute anything big got going, the minute this kind of police force was faced with a social explosion, it was largely helpless.

So now the city fathers are trying to change the LAPD. They got rid of Gates and have brought in a replacement from Philadelphia — this time a police chief who is Black. And as you

36. Two of the four cops, Stacey Koon and Laurence Powell, were convicted on the federal civil rights charges, but the judge sentenced them to only two and one-half years in prison, below the three and one-half to seven and one-half years mandated in federal sentencing guidelines. Following their release in December 1995, a federal appeals court directed the lower court to resentence the two cops in line with federal guidelines, a ruling that would have sent them back to jail. The Supreme Court overturned the appeals court action in 1996, however, referring the matter back to the lower court, which refused to impose an additional sentence.

pointed out, Mayor Bradley and other local politicians hope that by announcing beforehand that the National Guard may be called up, people will be less likely to go into the streets if the cops are acquitted again this time. But this is all wishful thinking by bourgeois figures who do not know what to expect or what to do. The real question is: What *can* they do?

How do the capitalist rulers transform conditions in Los Angeles? How do they transform the social structure of the city, its class and national composition? How do they transform the degree of unemployment? There are no "solutions" within the framework of capitalism. The propertied families Mayor Bradley speaks for in Los Angeles have grown wealthy, in part, off interest on bonds paid out of the enormous tax base and explosive postwar capitalist development in southern California. They can or will do nothing different as the real world closes in around them.

How do the rulers transform the way they have trained the cops for decades to use brutality as a matter of course? How do they deal with racism among the cops? None of that can or will be changed either, because the purpose of the cops is to *punish*, not patrol. The purpose of the cops is to keep workers in line, to make an example of you if you come from the wrong class — and more so if you also happen to be the wrong color or the wrong nationality.

The ruling class has a "beasts in the jungle" mentality. They despise — and fear — the great mass of working people, the oppressed and exploited. They half-believe their own reactionary myths. They live in an almost comic-book world of fears of what might happen — *anytime, anywhere.* Remember the infamous comment by President Lyndon Johnson's secretary of state, Dean Rusk, during the high point of the Vietnam War and antiwar movement? He publicly voiced the great fear his class lives with. At any time of day or night, Rusk complained, two-thirds of the world's population are awake somewhere and potentially making trouble!

The only section of the ruling class with a program to respond to what they face in Los Angeles and elsewhere is the *ultraright.* Their answer is to use immediate deadly force — to shoot down hundreds. Listen to Patrick Buchanan's proposals. He explains how to stop riots: go into the first four or five areas that explode and shoot down people in the streets. The only alternative to Buchanan's answer is to transform social conditions, something the rulers cannot do and maintain capitalism.

So, the reactions you described on the part of Bradley and others in Los Angeles are not plots or plans. They are largely uncontrolled, pragmatic responses by a ruling class that has no idea what to do. How else can we explain how blind they are to so much of what is building up all around them?

In this sense, their response is reminiscent of the utter blindness of Clinton and others around him to the Zoë Baird/Kimba Wood fiascoes. It was a class blindness. They couldn't understand what the problem was. Doesn't almost everybody hire women to take care of their children? They don't know anyone who doesn't live that way. Or at least they have forgotten, if they ever did.

There is an element of rising middle-class panic in what you describe. As the social crisis deepens, we will see more of these kinds of fantasies and fears. Middle-class layers will get whipped up, and they will sometimes get out of control. Don't misunderstand me: I think the specter of armed Beverly Hills vigilantes is a wild exaggeration right now. But the underlying middle-class panic is real — and so is the lack of any political lead from the ruling class. The rulers have no proposals to deal with the social consequences of how their system works. So, the right wing's solution to how to deal with social explosions will inevitably get a broader echo among layers of the bourgeoisie.

Buchanan and his ilk give an answer. They present their own lessons from the history of riot control — shoot the rioters. But history shows that this is often the last step before a revolution, too. So, this also is part of the race with time between the political forces that will be organized by the ultraright and those that can and will be mobilized by the working-class vanguard.

THE VOTE FOR ROSS PEROT AND PATRICK BUCHANAN'S 'CULTURE WAR'

WHAT THE 1992 ELECTIONS REVEALED

The following talk was presented on November 7, 1992, four days after the presidential elections in the United States, at a Militant Labor Forum in New York City. The forum coincided with a weekend conference of the SWP National Committee, leaderships from communist leagues in other countries, and youth leaders actively involved in supporting the Socialist Workers Party's 1992 presidential ticket. It was attended by some 400 people from throughout the Northeast.

George Bush didn't lose;
he was defeated

The one thing all the commentators seem to agree on is that the central issue in the election this year was the economy. "It's the economy, stupid!" — that is the cynical sign the president-elect's strategist, James Carville, is said to have mounted on the wall of Clinton's campaign operations center in Little Rock, Arkansas. And the president-elect himself says that during his first one hundred days he will concentrate "like a laser" on the economy. That laser, he promises, will get the economy moving, change the atmosphere for enterprise, and accelerate production.

None of this is true. The election was *not* about the economy. Like all U.S. presidential elections in the late twentieth century, this one was decided on the basis of foreign policy. No one who voted could have had any idea how George Bush and William Clinton differed on "the economy." Thinking workers knew that whichever of the two main contenders won would make little difference. The capitalist class knows that no administration, Republican or Democrat, determines what the economy is going to do: the very syntax itself is nonsense. The real relationship is vice versa: the economy — or more precisely, the propertied holders of massive debt standing behind the economy — largely determines what the administration is going to do.

To the degree that domestic policy was central to the election, the real issues — that is, those that will come to dominate bourgeois and radical right-wing politics — were raised by Ross Perot and Patrick Buchanan. Perot said it was time to face the truth about the growing lack of confidence in the leading personnel of both the Democratic and Republican parties and their bipartisan policies. And Buchanan launched what he called a "culture war," a "religious war," a "battle for the soul of America." That battle *was* joined in the last six months, and it will continue and eventually dominate politics in the Congress, at the ballot box, and in the streets.

Of course, in times of capitalist crisis, economic questions increasingly are foreign policy questions. Trade wars lead toward shooting wars; collecting interest on onerous debts leads toward shooting wars. That is the central trajectory in the history of world capitalism. Lurking beneath the surface of a lot of what we hear from bourgeois opinion-makers today is the consoling notion: "We won't let that happen this time, like we did in 1914 and again in the late 1930s. We'll settle things before it goes that far." But it *will* all happen again, so long as the capitalist classes remain in power. They can compromise with regard to this or that particular crisis, but it will happen again.

The 'October surprise' that wasn't

George Bush did not lose the election. He was *defeated*. He was not defeated by the working class. The class struggle has not reached the stage in the United States where working people have a way to express themselves politically; the interests of the working class are not being registered even indirectly in elections. Nor was Bush defeated by the governor of Arkansas.

If any individual should get the credit for defeating George Bush, it is someone from Bush's own class (he would hate to admit that social fact) in another country — Saddam Hussein. That is who defeated George Bush in this election. That reality was announced by Gen. Colin Powell, chairman of the Joint Chiefs of Staff, a month before the election took place. I assume that up until roughly the Republican convention in August, many of you, like me, thought George Bush could win the election if he could pull off what the press started calling an "October surprise." If a sitting U.S. president, offering some pretext, starts a military action close enough to the November elections, he will win. That statement is not an attack on democracy; it is just a recognition of *what imperialist democracy is*, in the absence of an independent working-class voice of any weight.

There is good reason to believe that is exactly what George Bush was planning to do. But then something happened the day before the Republican convention opened in August. There was a "leak" in Washington explaining what Bush was up to. The plan had been to take out some industrial enterprises in Iraq, which Bush would claim were being used for research on nuclear weapons production. The story was splashed on the front page of every leading newspaper everywhere in the country. That, of course, took the "surprise" out of the October surprise, and scuttled the operation itself. What is important is that the "leak" came right from the top at the Pentagon itself.

Then, a month later, General Powell invited the *New York Times* to interview him. He told the *Times* that whenever he hears politicians talk about a "surgical" strike somewhere, "I head for the bunker." "As soon as they tell me it is limited [force]," he said, "it means they do not care whether you achieve a result or not." Powell said he opposed talk about "limited military intervention" in Bosnia, for example. If a U.S. administration decided to go in someplace, he told the *Times,* then it had better be planning to win.

Bravely, two days later the former senator from Tennessee — Albert Gore — gave a campaign speech about how George Bush had coddled Saddam Hussein in the late 1980s and how this had led directly to the invasion of Kuwait and the Gulf War. This was followed by a feature article in the *Wall Street Journal* headlined: "Cold War's End Shuffles Foreign-Policy Debate: Bush Urges Caution and Clinton Takes Hard Line." The article opened: "Which candidate a) criticizes his opponent for being too cozy with Communist leaders; b) has argued for using military power in the world's hottest military conflict [Yugoslavia]; c) was the first to endorse legislation expanding the embargo on Fidel Castro's Cuba? Democrat Bill Clinton has taken those stands. . . . " And the article could have added Clinton's more tough-talking rhetoric and military aid in support of Israel, as well as a raft of other examples.

General Powell was not speaking solely for himself in that interview with the *New York Times,* nor was he speaking for the military brass. We hear a lot in the big-business media about the officer corps having its own independent views, and its own debates, on U.S. military policy. That is a myth; the opinions of top officers like Powell reflect substantial currents in ruling-class circles. The truth about the election results must start with the fact that the U.S. rulers broke their teeth on the Iraq war last year. All the long-term goals they had been fighting to achieve in the Gulf for ten years — all the things tied up there with the Iran-contra deal and the so-called Iraqgate scandal — were denied them.[1]

This is connected with one final matter Bush has to clean up before leaving office: He has to decide how many pardons to give to Reagan administration officials involved in the Iran-contra deal. The news tonight reported that the White House is sending up trial balloons that Caspar Weinberger, Reagan's secretary of defense, will get the first pardon. The queen of England knighted

---

1. The U.S.-organized war against Iraq was an extension of Washington's efforts to restore U.S. imperialist dominance in the Gulf region that had been lost with the victory of the Iranian revolution in 1979. Behind a cover of official neutrality, Washington backed Baghdad's 1980–88 war against Iran, hoping that a defeat for Tehran would open the way to reimpose a more subservient regime. During the 1992 elections, Democrats played up revelations that the Reagan and Bush administrations had provided loan guarantees used by the Iraqi government in the 1980s to build up its stocks of weapons; the scandal became known as "Iraqgate" in the daily press.

In 1986 the Reagan administration had also secretly sold arms to Iran. In doing so, Washington sought to curry favor with forces in Tehran it hoped would be more pliant to U.S. demands, while at the same time securing funds to finance covert aid for armed counterrevolutionary bands in Nicaragua, the "contras." The exposure of this operation in November 1986 became know as the "Iran-contra," or "Contragate," affair.

Weinberger a few years ago to thank Washington for its indispensable help during the United Kingdom's 1982 war to steal the Malvinas Islands from Argentina a second time. Now he is facing a federal indictment for covering up what he knew about the Iran-contra deal. Of course, George Bush has a direct interest in pardoning Caspar Weinberger, since Weinberger's notes prove that Bush, too, lied all along about what he knew and was involved in as vice president. I suspect the president-elect will collaborate with others in the ruling class to prevent Weinberger's trial from even beginning.[2]

The Iran-contra affair was not just about raising secret funds to finance Washington's contra war in Nicaragua; the U.S. rulers had important goals in the Gulf too. These were the same goals they had been earlier trying to achieve in strengthening the Saddam Hussein regime; in winking at massive illegal business transactions with Baghdad by U.S. companies in competition with London, Paris, and Bonn; and in covertly backing Iraq's bloody eight-year war against Iran. Everything that led Saddam Hussein to believe he could simply get away with taking part of Kuwait is just now being "revealed" by Iraqgate. Washington's aim was to prevent the impact of the Iranian revolution from spreading in the region and to sap the strength of Iran in the Arab-Persian Gulf (and, we should add, to covertly lay the groundwork for some very profitable high-tech trade with Iraq without having to square these deals with U.S. laws, regulations, and policy stances).

2. On December 24, 1992, Bush indeed pardoned Weinberger, who had not yet gone to trial. But not Weinberger alone. He also pardoned Robert McFarlane, Reagan's national security adviser; Elliott Abrams, former assistant secretary of state for inter-American affairs; and three other Reagan administration officials. In Weinberger's case, this was the first time in U.S. history that a president had pardoned someone under indictment before a trial had even begun. The *New York Times* and other dailies with a line into top White House circles reported that Clinton administration officials had agreed beforehand not to protest the pardons. They loyally stuck to the agreement. A preview of coming attractions?

That is what Washington has been trying to do for ten years, by any means necessary. That is why Caspar Weinberger needs a pardon. And that is why Washington's allies, beginning with Bonn and Paris, are so unhappy about the matter.

But if you have been following the news coming out of the Gulf for the last year, you will know that the opposite of these goals has largely been the outcome. The relative position of the government of Iran has been strengthened vis-à-vis every one of its rivals in that part of the world, beginning with Iraq and including Saudi Arabia. And political stability has been weakened throughout the region.

The grand coalition that Washington put together in the Gulf came apart at the end. The pro-Washington, proprivatization government of Turkey, a member of NATO, was the first victim. The rebellion by the oppressed Kurdish people in southeastern Turkey gained strength, and Istanbul has not been able to get them back under control to the same degree as before. The tensions grew, and divergences between Tel Aviv and Washington widened. The German and Japanese ruling classes took advantage of the war and its outcome to each take one more step toward strategic rearmament, a rearmament that will ultimately be used to threaten the degree of Washington's supremacy in the contest over world economic and currency dominance, and to gain an edge over other momentary allies as well. The Gulf War was a genuine defeat for Washington on all these fronts.

With Bush soon to be out of office, the *New York Times* and other big-business dailies are now beginning to detail what they expect from Clinton. They expect him never again to make the error of beginning something he is politically unable to finish, as the Bush administration did in Iraq. "U.S. military leaders are understandably reluctant to see our forces used anywhere unless they can be sure of a smashing victory," writes Anthony Lewis, the most liberal among the parade of *Times* columnists who have been crusading for U.S. air strikes against Serbian forces in Bosnia. "But the world today requires the use of force in subtler ways, and we have a civilian Commander in Chief to say so." In subtler ways!

If you are going to use military power, then bring home the bacon — that was the U.S. rulers' message in the elections. That is what defeated Bush. That's also why John F. Kennedy not Richard Nixon won in 1960. Kennedy campaigned on the claim that a "missile gap" had supposedly developed under "Ike."[3] The Kennedy administration was arguably the most dangerous in post–World War II history. It carried out the unsuccessful invasion of Cuba at the Bay of Pigs in 1961, and was faced down by the revolutionary Cuban government and people when it sought to do so once again during the so-called missile crisis of October 1962. And Kennedy initiated the rapid escalation of U.S. military intervention in Vietnam that became a full-scale war during the subsequent Johnson and Nixon administrations. So, every time pliant commentators fulsomely compare the new Clinton administration to Kennedy's, we should be uneasy.

Clinton, in fact, was the point man in this election for ratcheting up hostile U.S. government moves against the Cuban revolution. Had it not been for election-year pressures, for example, there is no reason to think Bush would have signed the so-called Cuban Democracy Act tightening the economic embargo against Cuba. In fact, Bush was tactically opposed to substantial aspects of the bill, as was a substantial section of the business class in this country. But then Clinton went down to Florida and gave a speech promising full support to the bill, which was sponsored by

3. During the 1960 U.S. presidential campaign, Democratic candidate John F. Kennedy alleged that the Republican administration of president Dwight Eisenhower and vice-president Richard Nixon had allowed a "missile gap" to develop giving the USSR a military advantage over Washington. The truth was the opposite. In 1962 the U.S. government had some 5,000 nuclear warheads and 500 intercontinental missiles, while the Soviet Union had 300 or fewer nuclear warheads and only a few dozen missiles. Currently Washington has more than 7,100 nuclear warheads on intercontinental ballistic missiles, submarine launchers, and bombers; Russia has some 6,200 warheads.

a liberal Democratic House member from New Jersey, Robert Toricelli. So Bush finally signed it, not wanting to lose support from right-wing Cuban émigrés. But it was Clinton who led the charge and got the credit from the ruling class.[4]

A peaceful, more stable world?
The world in which the 1992 election campaign has taken place is marked by increased instability and growing conflicts between the major capitalist powers and ruling classes.

The one modest claim Bush makes for his administration is that for the first time since World War II our children can now go to sleep at night with the knowledge that nuclear war is not going to occur. Whatever criticisms others may have of his administration, Bush says, they cannot deny him that. When he raised this claim during the televised presidential debates, neither Clinton nor Perot would touch it. But of course Bush's assertion is false.

The likelihood is growing, not diminishing, that nuclear weapons will be used in conflicts accelerating around the world. The ones proliferating the farthest and fastest are tactical nuclear weapons, those under the control of battlefield commanders. The use of such tactical nuclear weapons, moreover, is among the actions most likely to provoke broader nuclear exchanges.

A large number of countries now deploy missiles for various military or civilian purposes that could be fitted with nuclear warheads — more than thirty countries so far, by most estimates, with others on the way to developing such missiles. And the wherewithal to produce tactical nuclear weapons is growing as well.

So, it is a lie that children should be able to sleep easier at night.

---

4. The Cuban Democracy Act of 1992 made it illegal for foreign subsidiaries of U.S. companies to trade with Cuba. It also closed U.S. ports to ships that have docked in Cuba within six months and authorized the president to apply sanctions against any country judged to be supplying aid to Cuba. In March 1996 Clinton signed into law the so-called Cuban Liberty and Democratic Solidarity (Libertad) Act, which, together with other moves over the previous three years, substantially escalated the U.S. economic assault against Cuba.

No nonproliferation agreements or anything else will stop the nuclear threat from growing. There is no economic, scientific, diplomatic, or military way under capitalism to prevent the spread of nuclear weapons and delivery systems.

Of course, there is another way to read Bush's claim — that implicitly he is only talking about children in the United States. Perhaps he is saying that children in this country do not have to worry tonight that someone will launch an intercontinental ballistic missile at them. Never forget that when the U.S. rulers talk about "our children," when they talk about "people," they are talking about *their* children, about *their* class. That grotesque class callousness is one more piece of evidence that the working class and fighting toilers around the world are the only true bearers of human solidarity.

Interimperialist conflict and the myth of a united Europe

The prospect of a breakdown in world trade is slowly but surely increasing as interimperialist conflict sharpens today. During this year's election campaign, Clinton competed with Perot and Buchanan to be the most aggressive-sounding candidate on questions of international trade. Clinton expressed doubts about signing the so-called North American Free Trade Agreement, at least before doing some arm-twisting and renegotiating with the Mexican and Canadian governments "to level the playing field." And Clinton's backers in the trade union officialdom, and among bourgeois political figures who are Black such as Jesse Jackson, were among the most vociferous in opposing what they called a "fast track" of "American jobs" to Mexico.[5]

At the same time, U.S. imperialism's protectionist assaults against its trade rivals have bipartisan support. Just this month, for example, the Bush administration threatened to levy a 200 percent import tax on white wine and other European Community products in order to force the EC, especially the capitalists in France, to back off subsidies on soybeans and other agricultural products. These are aggressive, unilateral acts by Washington. They will be repeated in one form or another over and over again. The U.S. rulers' European rivals may well back off this time, but crises like this will recur in the deflationary, depression conditions the capitalist world has entered. The stability and the patterns of world trade will be threatened. No one is in control of the pressures that erupt in these conflicts. Unilateral acts are taken in reaction to the perceived national interests of powerful capitalist classes that come into conflict with the national interests of competing capitalist classes. No one plans these clashes, and no one can ultimately prevent them.

No one plotted six months ago, for example, that a dispute over soybean oil would pose a threat to patterns of world trade that have been built up by the capitalist powers through negotiations since the end of World War II. But the conflict shaping up between Washington and Paris and other European imperialist powers is no joke. Carla Hills, the chief U.S. trade representative, is standing in front of TV cameras and saying, in essence, "Cheat us on soybeans and we'll zap your white wine!"

Why is all this happening? The big-business media offers an explanation. From reading the papers and watching TV, you would

---

5. After wresting further concessions from Ottawa and Mexico City, Clinton did put NAFTA on the "fast track" for ratification by Congress, which did so in a bipartisan vote in November 1993; the trade agreement took effect in January 1994. Opposition to NAFTA also cut across bourgeois party lines, involving forces on the far right of the Republican party such as Buchanan; much of the so-called labor-liberal-civil rights coalition in the Democratic Party; and Perot and his supporters.

think the dispute is about farmers. The problem is that farmers are being voraciously greedy — especially dirt farmers in France, who are portrayed as having more power than any social force on earth. They have supposedly pushed the entire French government to the wall. They have the European Community on the run. Working farmers in France, some of whom can barely eke out a living, are threatening to bring world trade to its knees!

But this is all demagogic camouflage. The dispute over soybeans and white wine is a direct conflict between some of the most powerful interests of rival national capitals — not a clash between debt-burdened independent commodity producers on opposite sides of the Atlantic Ocean. France is today the number-two exporter of farm products in the world, following the United States. The profits are raked in by giant French commercial trusts that monopolize trade and banking both — not by working farmers. U.S. capitalists are the world's largest traders of soybeans, accounting for close to 63 of the 86 million tons produced worldwide. So, there are big stakes for some of the largest monopolies in both countries.[6]

Moreover, the threatened tax on imported wine is less an assault on the French ruling class than it is a broadside by both Washington and London against the German ruling class, Paris's partner in the conflict. We should not forget what Bonn did a month or so ago. In September, the world's financiers, including those in Germany, decided to treat the pound sterling like a two-bit overvalued currency and crammed it down the Tory government's throat. That was after finance capital had squeezed the pound for years, helping to precipitate the deepest and most

---

6. The U.S. government withdrew its threatened import tax later in November 1992, when Washington wrested a concession from the European Community — over protests by Paris — on cuts in EC agricultural subsidies. In mid-1995 Washington threatened to impose a 100 percent import tax on thirteen models of Japanese-made automobiles until Tokyo agreed to "voluntary" quotas increasing the purchase of U.S.-made auto parts.

prolonged recession in Britain since the Great Depression of the 1930s, one it is just now beginning to come out of. The German government and banks, however, teamed up with the French rulers to prevent the same thing from happening to the French franc. So, when Wall Street and Washington take aim at Paris over trade and financial policy, they often have locked Bonn in the cross hair as well.

These conflicts between rival national capitalist classes and governments are blowing apart the myth of a "united Europe" at an accelerating pace. Since the end of the so-called Cold War, bourgeois politicians and commentators have had trouble coming up with phrases to describe the world balance of power. They talked about a New World Order for awhile, but that did not seem to fit so well in light of the outcome of the Gulf War, the permanent crises in Eastern Europe and the former USSR, and the onset of depression conditions. So some of them began talking about "the tripolar world" — the United States, Europe, and Japan were the three poles. But that description of power relationships in today's world has already bumped up against a big problem — *there is no Europe pole.*

How long ago was it that many ruling-class figures in Europe (especially in Bonn, and to a lesser degree Paris) were insisting that the European imperialist powers — whatever their problems and frictions — were on the road toward political unity? Members of the European Community would pool their funds — so the story went — and give some money to Ireland, to Portugal, to Greece, and even a little bit to Spain, so these countries could catch up and narrow the economic and social gap with the rest of capitalist Europe. They would adopt common social welfare rules, labor standards, and pollution controls. Eventually they would converge toward a common foreign and military policy. They would smooth out differences in productivity and eventually all agree to use the same tokens as a common currency. And then, this new and united Europe — with class differences slowly but surely disappearing for all practical purposes — would emerge big, powerful, and competitive with the United States and Japan.

The opposite has actually happened over the last decade, however. Despite all the talk about unity, the evolution of world capitalism has increased uneven development across Europe and made its character more explosive. And not just between the weakest capitalist powers in southern Europe and the rest. The gap has also widened, for example, between rates of capital accumulation and economic development in Britain and other, more powerful capitalist countries in Europe.[7]

Capitalism's growing world disorder is also completely intertwined with the crisis that is accelerating throughout the grotesquely deformed workers states of Central and Eastern Europe and the former Soviet Union. When the world's stock markets crashed in 1987, many apologists for capitalism sought to answer the question, "What can prevent another Great Depression?" by pointing to the prospects for opening up Russia, all of Eastern Europe, and China to massive investment. That was before the collapse of the Stalinist apparatuses in 1989 and after, following which there was an initial burst of euphoria in bourgeois circles about new prospects for the penetration of capital. The Socialist Workers Party and our sister communist leagues were nearly alone in rejecting this prognosis, both before and after the collapse of the Berlin Wall.

We said that the working classes in these countries could not be starved into submission; they would have to be beaten in combat before accepting entirely new, capitalist, social relations. They would have to be crushed before they would accept the wholesale dismemberment of the social wage, job guarantees,

---

7. According to a study reported in the May 14, 1996, issue of the London *Financial Times*, total manufacturing output in the United Kingdom between 1973 and 1992 grew by only 1.3 percent, compared to 16.5 percent in France, 32.1 percent in West Germany, and 68.6 percent in Italy. Over the same period, industrial output expanded by 68.9 percent in Japan and 55.2 percent in the United States, according to the same study.

and state-controlled prices of basic commodities they had conquered. New economic, social, and legal structures codifying bourgeois values would have to grow and become socially entrenched in these countries. And new capitalist ruling classes would have to develop and assert their domination not only over the ownership of the major means of production, banking, and commercial trade, but also over the state apparatus necessary to defend such radically transformed property relations. None of this could happen over a few short years, and without wave after wave of workers' resistance to such changes.

In saying this, we explicitly recognized that the room for development of capitalist production was substantially greater in China, given the huge reserves of exploitable labor in the countryside. But everything we are seeing in the Soviet Union is a preview of what will come in China, on an even larger scale. Turbulent economic growth, social differentiation, and class struggle will strain against the rigidities, brutalities, and uncertainties of the Beijing caste's attempt to gradually — and without losing their own privileges — graft capitalism onto a billion people and to become, in passing so to speak, a historically necessary ruling class.

None of this in and of itself, we explained, could open up a new period of self-sustaining capitalist expansion on a world scale. Instead, what the "bearers of democracy" from North America and Western Europe pointed to as opening a new period of stability and prosperity from Central Europe to the Pacific is turning out to be a capitalist sinkhole. It is part of the same crisis of the market system that is gripping not only the oppressed nations of Africa, Latin America, and Asia, but increasingly the imperialist world as well.

The collapse of the Stalinist apparatuses, we said, signaled the beginning of the end of the German rulers' goal of a Europe united under their economic and political domination. Their dream of growing ascendancy of the deutsche mark and its eventual transformation into the de facto single European currency was finished.

At the same time, conditions were improving for workers

across Europe to get together, support each other's battles against increasing social differentiation, and exchange experiences and ideas — something denied them for decades. Despite the justified hatred for Stalinism, and the confusion caused by the Stalinists speaking in the name of socialism and communism, class battles across Europe, we said, would more and more be joined over *capitalism's* betrayal of its promises. Workers both in capitalist Europe and the deformed workers states would be propelled into struggle over the bourgeoisie's incapacity to produce either economic democracy, social justice, or a stable guarantee of individual human rights anywhere in the world.

It would be in this world context, we said, that the battles over restoring the dominance of capitalist social relations would be fought in the workers states between the imperialist rulers and emerging domestic exploiting layers, on the one hand, and the working class, on the other. Advances or setbacks for the class struggle in Western Europe, North America, and elsewhere in the capitalist world weigh heavily in the outcome of these battles, which would ultimately be settled in armed conflict in the streets.

It has only taken a couple of years for the elation in top ruling-class circles at supposedly having "won the Cold War" to begin wearing thin. Among the most prominent bearers of these bad tidings have been two bourgeois politicians still bitter over their forced "retirements" — Richard Nixon and Margaret Thatcher. They are having a field day, going around preaching to others in their class: "Woe betide, you wouldn't listen, but you better listen now! Woe betide!"

Nixon made quite a sensation a few months ago, in March, when he gave a major speech in Washington, D.C., pointedly entitled "The New World," not the "New World Order." This supposedly discredited U.S. president warned his bipartisan colleagues to beware "the false premise" that "the Cold War is over and we have won it. . . . That's only half true," he said. "It is true, that as far as the Cold War is concerned, the Communists have lost it. It is not true, however, that the Free World has won it."

That question is not settled yet, Nixon said. And unless the U.S. rulers wage a successful fight to somehow transform Russia into a stable market economy, they will not be able to say they have won more than they have lost. Without that, he said, no durable regime — much less a reliable one, from the standpoint of Nixon's class — can be consolidated in Russia or anywhere else in the former Soviet Union.

Nixon's speech was front-page news, and not just here in the United States. It was televised live around the globe on CNN. It came only a few days after the publicizing of a memorandum Nixon had circulated to prominent ruling-class figures, in which he called Bush administration policy toward Russia "pathetically inadequate." That memo, entitled "How to Lose the Cold War," was also widely quoted in major newspapers in the United States and other countries.

"The hot-button issue in the 1950s was, 'Who lost China?'" Nixon said in his memo — referring to the accusation-framed-as-a-question that he and others hurled at major bourgeois politicians as part of launching the McCarthyite witch-hunt. "If Yeltsin goes down," Nixon said, "the question of 'who lost Russia' will be an infinitely more devastating issue in the 1990s." Nixon is well-qualified to make such a comparison, since he was a central instigator of the demagogic witch-hunting campaign four decades ago. The issue at that time was assessing blame for the revolutionary overturn in 1949 of the landlord-capitalist regime in China.

In his Washington, D.C., speech, Nixon said that the biggest obstacle to establishing a stable market system in Russia was what he called "the lack of a management class." The "lack of a class" is indeed the major problem the imperialists confront in the workers states — but not "a management class." The privileged bureaucratic castes in these countries include hundreds of thousands of managers. What they "lack" is a *capitalist class* — a necessary social class that has accumulated massive amounts of capital; that has established its historical dominance over production and exchange; and that has imposed the social relations necessary for that domination on the toiling majority, and to one degree or another gotten them to accept those relations as their own. But the emergence of such a class involves sharp assaults on the working class — assaults that will meet resistance and threaten social stability — as well as bloody turf wars among the rival wannabe capitalists themselves.

That is the harsh reality behind what Nixon is calling on the U.S. rulers to look at square in the face.

And you can always count on direct remarks from Margaret Thatcher warning of the specter of the Hun, especially since the reunification of Germany. Because her rivals in the Tory party are not heeding her advice, she rails, the dangers of German domination of the United Kingdom and British capital are growing — all behind idealistic-sounding prattle about "European unity." She pins the blame for the current recession in Britain on her successor John Major's policy of keeping interest rates high in line with Bonn's. And earlier this year she said that all European "convergence" means in practice is the United Kingdom and Germany giving bigger and bigger subsidies to other countries.

What neither Nixon nor Thatcher explain, however, is that they were among those in the U.S. and British bourgeois parties who helped pioneer the course the rulers have been on since the downturn in world capitalism's fortunes some two decades ago. It was Margaret Thatcher personally, for example, who approved pegging the pound to the mark at such a high rate, in order to keep British currency "strong" and squeeze the working class a bit harder at home. Now, the "Iron Lady" is seeking to wash her hands of responsibility for the devastation of the pound a few weeks ago.

Thatcher and Nixon do have a big advantage right now. No one in the ruling class in either the United Kingdom or the United States pays much attention to what they say anymore, or sets a policy course based on their assessments. They are elder statesmen — Margaret Thatcher's gender notwithstanding; they are Cassandras freer to foretell the disasters their system has in store for the epigones who followed them. So, we should enjoy it when either one of them speaks and wish them both long lives! Because the belief that the ruling class and its spokespersons are capable of intelligent, long-term, strategic policy-making — instead of pragmatic acts, focused on short-run goals and the maximization of profits — is one of the myths the labor movement must break from in charting our own independent working-class political course.

Currency crises and fetishes

International capitalism's stock, bond, and currency markets today are indeed, as widely proclaimed, becoming more and more interconnected and, partly as a result, they are also becoming more unstable. Just a little over five years ago, the world's stock markets crashed. In just one day in October 1987, the stock market in the United States plunged nearly 25 percent. The crash sent shock waves through the international bourgeoisie, and working people sensed it was the harbinger of a deepening social crisis worldwide. It was the first sharp public signal of an accelerated decline in the post–World War II curve of capitalist development — the first signal that a worldwide depression had become inevitable.

Now we have seen the Japanese stock market decline by more than half since the beginning of 1990. There is a chronic credit and banking crisis facing finance capital in Japan — a deep deflationary crisis. You may have read in the late 1980s that the value in dollar terms of a relatively small portion of real estate in Tokyo had shot up to more than that of all the real estate in the state of

"**With revolutionary leadership the international working class has the numbers, social power, culture, values, and program to defeat the reactionary forces loosed by finance capital.**"

1 COFFINS, REPRESENTING IMPERIALIST-OWNED COMPANIES EXPROPRIATED BY REVOLUTIONARY CUBAN GOVERNMENT, ARE CARRIED BY WORKERS AND YOUTH IN HAVANA TO BE THROWN IN THE SEA, AUGUST 1960.

"The fact that Cuban working people are both prepared and determined to defend their revolution is the only thing that continues to prevent Washington from launching an invasion aimed at destroying the socialist revolution in Cuba."

2 MILITIA MEMBERS IN HAVANA RESPOND TO U.S. INVASION PLANS DURING OCTOBER 1962 "MISSILE CRISIS."

3 (TOP) WORKERS FROM CIENFUEGOS, CUBA, PARTICIPATE IN NATIONAL TRADE UNION CONGRESS IN HAVANA, APRIL 1996. BANNER READS "IN CIENFUEGOS, YES WE CAN." **4** (BOTTOM) SWP CANDIDATES FOR PUBLIC OFFICE JOIN NEW YORK PICKET IN DEFENSE OF CUBAN REVOLUTION, OCTOBER 1962.

"Ever since the revolution triumphed in 1959, communists in Cuba have been on the lookout to advance revolutionary victories elsewhere."

5 (FACING PAGE) MASS RALLY IN MANAGUA, NICARAGUA, FOLLOWING OUSTER OF SOMOZA DICTATORSHIP AND ESTABLISHMENT OF WORKERS AND PEASANTS GOVERNMENT, SEPTEMBER 1979. **6** (RIGHT) CUBAN TROOPS IN ANGOLA, WHERE HUNDREDS OF THOUSANDS OF VOLUNTEERS SERVED IN INTERNATIONALIST MISSIONS BEGINNING IN MID-1970S. **7** (BELOW) PROTEST IN GRENADA CONDEMNS U.S. THREATS AGAINST REVOLUTION, MARCH 1983.

"The operation of capitalism, its unceasing drive to maximize profits, pushes the international capitalist economy into crisis, spawns savage rightist movements, and ultimately drags the toilers into worldwide slaughters."

8 (TOP) PROTEST AGAINST RIGHTIST POLITICIAN PATRICK BUCHANAN IN TUCSON, ARIZONA, FEBRUARY 1996.
9 (BOTTOM) ROAD TO BASRA, IRAQ, AFTER U.S. BOMBING AND SHELLING, IN WHAT U.S. HIGH COMMAND REFERRED TO AS A "TURKEY SHOOT," FEBRUARY 1991. MORE THAN 150,000 IRAQIS WERE KILLED DURING SIX WEEKS OF BOMBING AND SUBSEQUENT INVASION.

"In face of worsening economic and social conditions, sections of the population begin to believe that what is needed is not this or that particular solution, but a charismatic individual in high office who has the will to impose change, whatever it may be."

10 (TOP) FRENCH ULTRARIGHTIST JEAN-MARIE LE PEN. **11** (BOTTOM) REFORM PARTY LEADER ROSS PEROT PROMISED TO BREAK "GRIDLOCK," STUNNED POLLSTERS WITH 19 PERCENT OF VOTE IN 1992 U.S. PRESIDENTIAL ELECTIONS.

"Armed with the world's mightiest conventional and strategic nuclear arsenal, Washington will react to defend U.S. capitalist interests wherever, and by whomever, those interests are endangered. But it will pay the consequences."

12 (ABOVE) U.S. SECRETARY OF STATE MADELEINE ALBRIGHT AT GUARD-POST ON BORDER OF "DEMILITARIZED ZONE" IN KOREA, WHERE U.S. TROOPS HAVE BEEN STATIONED FOR MORE THAN FORTY YEARS TO MAINTAIN DIVISION OF THAT COUNTRY.
13 (RIGHT) DEMONSTRATION IN SEOUL AGAINST PRESENCE OF U.S. TROOPS, JUNE 1995.

"**A harsher and harsher bourgeois nationalism increasingly marks the language of capitalist politics throughout the imperialist world. That is why we say Clinton will be a war president.**"

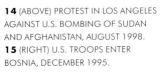

14 (ABOVE) PROTEST IN LOS ANGELES AGAINST U.S. BOMBING OF SUDAN AND AFGHANISTAN, AUGUST 1998.
15 (RIGHT) U.S. TROOPS ENTER BOSNIA, DECEMBER 1995.

"If you take London's problems in Ireland, Scotland, and Wales, and then add in the historic decline of British imperialism and the state of world capitalism, you see the strains pulling at the seams of the United Kingdom—seams that could begin to rip with a new rise in labor struggles and social mobilizations."

16 (LEFT) PROTESTERS CONFRONT BRITISH OCCUPATION FORCES IN PORTADOWN, NORTHERN IRELAND, JULY 1997. **17** (BOTTOM LEFT) ELIZABETH WINDSOR, QUEEN OF THE UNITED KINGDOM, AND HER SON CHARLES WINDSOR, PRINCE OF WALES, AT OPENING OF PARLIAMENT, OCTOBER 1996. **18** (BELOW) WORKERS PROTEST SHUTDOWN OF STEEL MILL IN SOUTH YORKSHIRE, ENGLAND, DECEMBER 1998.

"The Chinese revolution shattered racist lies and assumptions about the oppressed peoples of color that had been perpetuated for centuries by the ruling classes in Europe and North America."

19 (TOP) YOUTH IN BEIJING CELEBRATE END OF BRITISH RULE OVER HONG KONG, JULY 1997. **20** (MIDDLE) PEASANTS IN SHANGHAI BURN DEEDS OF FORMER LANDLORDS, 1951. **21** (BOTTOM) MIGRANT WORKERS CROWD ZHENGZHOU TRAIN STATION, FEBRUARY 1998.

"**Workers who are Black will comprise a much larger component of any fighting political vanguard of the working class today than ever before.**"

22 (TOP) MEMBERS OF THE BLACK FARMERS AND AGRICULTURALISTS ASSOCIATION PARTICIPATE IN MARTIN LUTHER KING DAY MARCH IN ATLANTA, GEORGIA, TO PROTEST RACIST DISCRIMINATION BY U.S. GOVERNMENT, JANUARY 1999. **23** (BOTTOM) TELEPHONE WORKERS PREPARE FOR STRIKE, NEW YORK, AUGUST 1998.

"Never in history has there been anything comparable to the position and political weight of women in the work force and labor movement today. The place of the fight for women's rights as part of the political battle to transform the workers movement compares to nothing experienced by previous generations of revolutionists."

24 (ABOVE) LOCKED-OUT MEMBERS OF THE UNITED FOOD AND COMMERCIAL WORKERS UNION PICKET MEATPACKING PLANT IN ALBERTA, CANADA, MAY 1998. **25** (RIGHT) DEFENDING ABORTION CLINIC IN DENVER, COLORADO, AUGUST 1993.

26 PROMOTING PATHFINDER BOOKS AT UNIVERSITY OF PUERTO RICO, OCTOBER 1997.

"**Above all, the outcome of coming class battles will be shaped by what worker-bolsheviks do today to utilize the space that exists to carry out communist politics.**"

27 PARTICIPANTS AT SOLIDARITY RALLY FOR WORKERS AT MEIJER FOODS IN TOLEDO, OHIO, CHECK OUT THE *MILITANT*, DURING FIGHT FOR CONTRACT BY MEMBERS OF UNITED FOOD AND COMMERCIAL WORKERS UNION LOCAL 911, NOVEMBER 1998.

"Young fighters are attracted to the social weight and potential strength of the working class, its struggles, and its organizations."

28 (LEFT) YOUNG SOCIALIST MEMBER MANUEL GONZÁLEZ SPEAKS WITH MINERS AT ENTRANCE TO KAYENTA BLACK MESA COMPLEX IN ARIZONA, JANUARY 1999. **29** (BELOW) YOUNG SOCIALIST LEADER SAMANTHA KERN ON PLATFORM WITH NEWLY ELECTED YS NATIONAL COMMITTEE AT CONCLUSION OF THIRD NATIONAL YS CONVENTION, LOS ANGELES, DECEMBER 1998. AT LEFT IS SOCIALIST WORKERS PARTY NATIONAL SECRETARY JACK BARNES.

California. What did you think when you read that? Even a person who is the most bedazzled by the fetishism of capitalism, even the most zealous worshipper at the altar of the commodity, knew that was a little much; it boded trouble. It is important to remember that private banks, not the government, create almost all the money that circulates. They do it by granting loans. And in case problems develop, banks are supposed to have assets with real value to stand behind all those checking balances they crank out. In Japan, the estimated market value of real estate makes up a big portion of those bank reserves, and the shifting ticker prices of stocks — yes, common stocks! — make up another big hunk. Land and stock prices puffed up like a giant balloon throughout the 1980s in Japan and have been plummeting just as sharply ever since, creating big problems for Japanese banks.[8]

The post–World War II capitalist land reform in Japan — imposed by U.S. occupation authorities under Gen. Douglas MacArthur — was designed from the outset to serve the interests not of working farmers, but the restoration of a stable bourgeois state. It was nothing like the Homestead Acts enacted during and after the Civil War in the United States, or the land reforms in much of Europe following the French Revolution and revolutions of 1848 — even with all their bourgeois limitations. Japan also never went through a bourgeois banking reform like that carried out in the United States in the wake of bank failures at the opening of the Great Depression of the 1930s.

Today U.S. capitalism accounts for a little over a quarter of manufactured goods worldwide, and more than 15 percent of

---

8. In January 1999, commercial land prices in Japan were more than 75 percent below their level at the opening of the decade. By the opening of 1999, Japanese banks held some $1 trillion in bad loans. And the Tokyo stock market in early 1999 was almost two-thirds off its 1989 peak. Gripped by its worst recession in half a century in 1998–99, Japan's official jobless level reached above 4 percent for the first time in decades. Hidden unemployment reached double digits, as the grinding economic crisis hit the Japanese toilers harder than at any time since the post–World War II "takeoff."

world exports. This represents a *relative* decline from what Wall Street and Washington had established in the decade or so after the close of World War II. The enormous *absolute* size of U.S. imperialism's wealth and productive capacity, however, has meant that the effects of the deepening world capitalist crisis are hitting its German and Japanese rivals substantially harder. For some time now, the relative position of German and Japanese capital has been slipping in the world imperialist system. Since the mid-1980s, U.S. capital's share of the world export market has been rising a bit once again, while Tokyo's and especially Bonn's shares have been falling. U.S. businesses have taken back markets in computer chips and hardware, machine tools, automobiles, and other industrial goods. And this trend will likely continue until the world bourgeoisie faces some cataclysmic crisis.

The U.S. rulers continue to suck in capital from all over the world, even though German long-term interest rates are several points higher than comparable U.S. rates. We should ask ourselves: Why do the biggest banks in Japan, Germany, and elsewhere transfer capital to North America to buy up pieces of paper — Treasury bonds — from the U.S. government? Why do they buy up these pieces of paper that promise to give you dollars thirty years from now, no matter what they are worth by then? It is certainly not that the U.S. capitalist economy is so rosy. Bankers around the world know what happened on Wall Street in October 1987, and they know the shape of the U.S. banking system. But they also know the much shakier condition of the banks in Japan, and what has been happening in Germany since "reunification." Bankers put their money where they anticipate it will be safer. But these enormous currency transfers increasingly turn the day-to-day business of banking into speculation, further destabilizing the world capitalist system.

Unimaginable sums of money are traded back and forth every day. With the development of computers and telecommunications, the speed and quantity of international transactions in a single twenty-four hours is mind-boggling.

In fact, the total dollar value of all the transactions on all the foreign currency markets for just seven business days equals the dollar value of world capitalist trade *for a full year.* The main function of world currency trading throughout most of the history of capitalism has been to balance out import and export deficits and surpluses between countries and repatriate the profits of superexploitation. As recently as the early 1970s, annual currency trading across borders was still only a fraction of world trade. Today, however, no government or big-business statistical agency really knows the exact scope and size of this currency trading, although most public estimates put it at more than $1 trillion each day.

As profit rates decline, capitalists look for more and more ways of using money to make money. Investing in plants and equipment does not bring them sufficiently competitive returns, so they keep inventing new kinds of paper instruments to trade and speculate with, including accelerated currency speculation. Capitalists have faced a long-run decline in profit rates at least three times before in the history of world capitalism, and each time it has led to a deep crisis before it could be turned around. But the speed of international communication today, the enormity of the monetary amounts involved, and the percentage of the world's working people brought under capitalist exploitation since the post–World War II decolonization make the potential scope and explosiveness of the coming crisis truly staggering.

Earlier I mentioned the recent run on the pound by international finance, which forced a substantial de facto devaluation in Britain. It is not that the Bank of England did too little in attempting to stop the fall; it laid out $27 billion in the effort. But the quantitative scope of the assault on the pound was beyond the bank's capacity to reverse, possibly, even if it exhausted *all* its reserves.

Governments and national banks no longer have much control over their currencies. And it is not just London — Washington, too, exercises very little control over the dollar. World currency markets are awash with dollars. Dollars are held in massive quantities by corporations all over the globe, including by many owned in full or in part by U.S. capital. In fact, some 50 percent of all private financial wealth in the world is held in dollars, as well as more than half of all exchange reserves in the vaults of foreign central banks.[9] In Russia, and even Eastern Europe to some degree, the dollar is the only real store of value today.

The conflicting national capitalist classes ultimately cannot control the results of their intensifying competition — and not because their actions are "irrational." Deep social crises result from acts that are completely rational for the profit maximization of *particular* capitalists competing with other capitalists and with other particular *national* capitals. The consequences of all these separate rational, short-term, and pragmatic decisions, however, further destabilize the *world* imperialist system.

Capitalist governments try to buffer some of these unantici-

---

9. "Dollar," in fact, is the world's most successful brand name. As recently as the mid-1970s some 80 percent of world foreign exchange reserves were held in U.S. currency. While that figure had slipped to 57.1 percent by 1997, none of the dollar's leading rivals came close to that level of dominance — neither the German deutsche mark (12.8 percent), the Japanese yen (4.9 percent), the British pound (3.4 percent), nor the French franc (1.2 percent). In addition, some 80 percent of all foreign currency transactions worldwide involve the U.S. dollar.

"Probably, not even Procter & Gamble itself could have created the global triumph that the Federal Reserve and the Bureau of Engraving and Printing (in cooperation with the Army, Navy, Air Force, Marine Corps, and Coast Guard) have achieved with the legal tender of the United States," observed U.S. financial writer James Grant in January 1999. Commenting on the launching that same month of a new currency, the euro, by eleven European governments, Grant added: "The dollar was, and remains, the top choice among the world's reserve portfolio managers. The true significance of the euro is that it offers an alternative." While the euro will gain some ground against the Yankee colossus, the dollar will remain the predominant world currency so long as Washington remains the predominant world imperialist power.

pated consequences. In a manner of speaking, they resort to a kind of socialism — the socialism of the bourgeoisie, the socialization of their losses.

The financial press wags its finger at General Motors management today, saying it would be filing for bankruptcy protection if it were a small business and that it got that way by making short-run, revenue-maximizing decisions instead of long-run investment decisions. But that is what all owners of capital do, all the more so when their profit rate is declining and their mass of profits is stagnating. When profit rates get low enough, the owners of capital consider it better to cut costs — to "downsize" — than to invest in the expansion of capacity with no foreseeable competitive returns. And it is not enough for capitalist governments to try to keep interest rates low either. Capitalists are not going to borrow to invest unless anticipated profits make that a more lucrative use of their money than some alternative — like currency speculation, for example. So the decisions by GM management in recent years are neither a plot nor a mistake — they are simply profit maximization.

Instability and sharpening conflicts will continue to mark the imperialist world. There will be more banking and credit crises in the years ahead. And along with them, confidence in the bourgeois leaderships of the imperialist countries will continue declining, too. We should note the tendency today for prime ministers, presidents, and other bourgeois officeholders to be elected with a decreasing percentage of the populace having any confidence that these political figures will be able to turn things around.

This is an important economic fact, not just a political fact. Because workers should not ever fall for the ultimate fetish of money — the notion that there is something objective that determines the worth of a currency. There is nothing objective about it. The paper currency of a national state under capitalism is only as strong as the confidence of the population, of the dominant propertied families themselves, and of international bankers in the stability and future of that ruling class and the competence of its leading figures.

Assault on the value of labor power

Workers should rid ourselves of the illusion that anything we or fellow working people have put away somewhere — in a bank, an insurance policy, a pension fund — is secure. There never has been and never will be any individual solution to weathering lay-offs, illness, or a disability, or preparing to make it through retirement. Especially during a period such as we have lived through the last fifteen years, the only sure thing is that instability will increase. Insurance companies, banks, and pension funds are not immune from collapse. And in a really deep crisis, nothing "stands behind" these institutions, no matter what we have been told about alleged government guarantees.

What if someone had told us even one year ago that some of the largest banks and insurance companies in Sweden — suppos-edly one of the most stable capitalist economies in Europe — were going to be on the verge of bankruptcy and face a forced financial reorganization before the end of 1992? That the Swedish govern-ment would raise short-term interest rates to 500 percent for sev-eral weeks in an effort to fend off devaluation in face of a massive run on the krona? And that the officialdom of the trade unions and Social Democratic Party — in order to "save Sweden" and find a way for Swedish business to compete successfully in Europe — would openly support measures that began dismantling piece by piece government-financed health care, pension benefits, and other social rights won by the working class? All that happened this year.

What is happening to the so-called welfare state in Sweden is symptomatic of the growing pressures throughout the imperialist countries on the social wage. The capitalists and their governments are stepping up attacks on the right of the working class to get back a small portion of the wealth we produce, so that we and our families can make it through a lifetime.

Since the end of World War II, workers in industrially advanced capitalist countries have, to varying degrees, come to consider as fundamental rights certain kinds of lifetime social security we have fought for and won. In a few capitalist countries, including Sweden, these social conquests by the labor movement were quite extensive. But today it is as if the film is being run backward, and we are watching the modern capitalist world regress toward its infancy. In reality, however, what we are seeing are not newsreels but previews — previews of what capitalism always reverts to as a crisis sharply accelerates. The capitalists are pushing to recreate conditions in which those of us who are young enough and well enough to work are forced to do so for as little pay as possible — and those who are too old or too sick, to hell with them!

If a worker faces desperate economic pressures, the bosses insist, such problems ought be taken care of largely by that person's family, or by charity, or by the church. Any government programs that do exist, they say, should be based purely on "need," not provided as a social right, as an entitlement, to the entire working class and population. The capitalists' goal is to deepen a division within the working class between those who earn, and those who "live off" others who earn (or are taken care of by charity). The goal is to demoralize layer after layer of the working class.

As from the earliest days of industrial capitalism, the rulers use sanctimonious religious and moral terms about charity to justify workhouses and the most heinous conditions for working people. University professors begin proposing that private orphanages be reopened across the country as the only solution to the "crisis of the single mother" and growing expenditures on Aid to Families with Dependent Children. And politicians begin echoing these reactionary proposals.[10] This is truly a battle for the soul of the working class as a class!

Moreover, beginning in the early 1970s, real wages — wages discounted for inflation, what workers can actually buy with what we bring home each week — began to slide in the United States. Last year, according to the government's own figures, average hourly wages for manufacturing workers were *lower than in 1967!* The true situation is even worse when the decline in the social wage of the working class, and of the public services we use, are included. For the first time since the Great Depression of the 1930s, the capitalists may be actually driving down the value, not just the price, of our labor power.[11]

Unemployment rates are also substantially higher today on average than they used to be. In the United States, official jobless rates of 6 percent or even more — which were sure signs of a recession prior to the mid-1970s — are today the norm during upturns in the capitalist business cycle. The average annual unemployment rate since 1974 has been just above 7 percent, compared to 4.8 percent for the quarter century prior to that. And those jobless figures — the ones Washington releases each month — do not include the growing numbers who have been forced into low-wage temporary or part-time jobs or who are not counted as "looking for work" by government agencies. That figure, which the government does not publicize very much, has averaged 10 percent since the mid-1970s, and the true situation is undoubtedly worse than that.

Unemployment is even higher across capitalist Europe. The av-

---

10. In August 1996 Clinton signed into law the "Personal Responsibility and Work Opportunity Reconciliation Act," eliminating Aid to Families with Dependent Children.

11. Six years after this talk was given, at the opening of 1999, median real earnings of workers in the United States — despite modest annual increases from 1996 through 1998 — still had not surpassed their level of the early 1970s, nor had median family income.

erage jobless figure for the countries that make up the European Community is 10 percent, and that has been the average for most of the past decade; it has not dropped below 8 percent since 1981. And the figure is substantially higher in several of the weaker imperialist countries; in Spain, for example, the official jobless rate is more than 18 percent. Contrast those figures for Europe to the average during the two decades prior to 1974 — 2.7 percent.

At the same time that unemployment is rising, overtime is stretching out the workweek the longest it has been since the end of World War II, further dividing the working class. And speedup is taking a heavier and heavier toll on health and safety on the job — and increasing the incidence of explosions, derailments, crashes, and other accidents that endanger the general public as well.

The experience of the working class over the past decade once again confirms Marx's assessment some 130 years ago that "the same circumstances which allow the capitalist in the long run to prolong the working day also allow him at first, and compel him finally, to reduce the price of labor nominally as well until the total price of the increased number of hours goes down, and therefore the daily or weekly wage falls."[12]

Radicalism, Bonapartism, and the vote for Ross Perot

The history of this century teaches us that a deepening capitalist crisis starts breeding radical attitudes before it precipitates massive class battles. Before a broad working-class radicalization be-

12. *Capital,* vol. 1 (Penguin), p. 689.

gins — with growing numbers of workers becoming more receptive to class-struggle proposals and communist ideas — radical attitudes begin getting a hearing in the middle class and among better-off layers of workers who aspire to become part of the middle class.

In a working-class radicalization, a vanguard of the labor movement begins to organize as a conscious *political* force, independent of the capitalist class and its parties. Prior to that, resistance by workers to the employers' offensive takes on a guerrilla character — a fight by a group of workers at a particular plant, a battle that explodes in a particular industry, resistance to a police attack in some city, and other partial struggles around specific abuses and demands.

But the working class currently has no class-conscious political voice, organization, or leadership of our own on any mass scale. The working class does not think and act like a class. So the political initiative today comes from currents on the right, which take advantage of their foothold within the structures of the bourgeois parties and other ruling-class institutions. Rightist forces tap into the loss of confidence in the government and suspicions about the rulers and their most prominent, established spokespeople. Nationalism, not communism; national socialism, not proletarian internationalism; not the historic line of march of a class, but the hatreds and resentment of a heterogeneous popular mass — these are the marks of this political development.

Because of the misleadership of the labor movement by the union officialdom and social democratic and Stalinist parties in the United States, the political monopoly of the capitalist Democratic and Republican parties was never really challenged by any substantial wing of the labor movement during the Great Depression and labor radicalization of the 1930s. Franklin D. Roosevelt, the preeminent war president of the capitalist class in this century, launched preparations for World War II in the late 1930s when the rate of unemployment was still only a point or so below 20 percent — and ended up with every major current in the labor movement portraying him as a prolabor reformer, except for the communist workers organized and influenced by the Socialist Workers Party. Because of the treachery of the Stalinists and social democrats, in fact, the later years of the Great Depression turned out to be a relatively stable period for the two-party system.

Behind the radicalization that is initially putting wind in the sails of the right, however, we can see fracture lines that tell us the two-party system the rulers put together before World War I is not immune to breakup. That is what this election signaled. We should never think that the only way the capitalist class can run things is through a two-party system.

The reflection of this emerging radicalism in this year's election campaign was more important than anything we saw with William Clinton and Albert Gore or with George Bush and Danforth Quayle. Everything those four said and did during the campaign could have been prerecorded on a videotape and played back on the nightly news; nobody would have known the difference. Once the October surprise had been scotched, everything else about the Bush-Clinton contest was like a choreographed dance.

But an aspect of bourgeois electoral politics this year was not choreographed — the campaigns of Ross Perot and Patrick Buchanan. The vote for Perot earlier this week — 19 percent of the ballots cast — is the most significant *electoral* phenomenon in the United States since just before World War I, when Theodore Roosevelt ran as an independent against the Democratic and Republican candidates in the 1912 elections. Roosevelt, who had been president from 1901 to 1909, had made his name as an officer in the Spanish-American War of 1898, which was the first military engagement by Washington as an emerging imperialist power. By that time, the U.S. capitalists' rivals in Britain and elsewhere in Europe already had a jump on them in colonial markets, and substantial sections of the U.S. ruling class were pressing Washington to begin acting more aggressively as a world military power. Starting with the Philippines, Hawaii, Puerto Rico, and Cuba — all either annexed or brought under Washington's heel during the Spanish-American War — growing layers of the U.S. ruling class were determined to push toward establishing their predominance in the world imperialist system that was coming into being.

It was against that background that layers of the U.S. capitalist class backed Roosevelt's candidacy as an independent in 1912, and he ended up getting around 28 percent of the vote — more than the Republican incumbent. Although Roosevelt was not elected, the goals of those who pushed his candidacy were successful. The new Democratic president Woodrow Wilson went on to win reelection four years later and led the United States into World War I in 1917. Out of that slaughter, Wall Street and Washington emerged as world imperialism's leading power, whose fortunes would determine much of the course of the twentieth century.

Theodore Roosevelt is the only "third-party" candidate in this century who polled a bigger percentage of votes than Perot. It is important to assess the Perot campaign accurately, or we will fall into the trap of accepting its portrayal by much of the bourgeois press as a bizarre anomaly. But this kind of political phenomenon — with its bizarre elements, for sure — is not abnormal for this stage of the curve of capitalist development. Thinking workers have to get used to anticipating that radical demagogues will win support from many small businessmen, farmers, and other middle-class layers, as well as sectors of the working class. These social layers are attracted to a figure who comes along and seems to offer explanations and proposals radically different from those of politicians whom growing numbers consider incurably corrupt, ineffective, and self-serving.

Every sophisticated, liberal, blow-dried newsreader on TV had written off Perot. Who, they asked, would take seriously a candidate like Perot who held a news conference to charge that a picture of his daughter was being circulated by George Bush to try to make her look immoral, and who then withdrew from the race for a while, citing that as one of the reasons? Who would take seriously a candidate who earlier during the campaign claimed to have been the target in the 1970s of an assassination plot organized by the Black Panthers and the Vietnamese government? When Perot reentered the race this fall, these pundits said he could kiss good-bye his earlier expectations of 16 or 17 percent of the vote; he would be lucky to get 4 or 5 percent now, they said.

But we should ask ourselves the question: how many millions of people in the United States believe Perot's charges? How many millions are beginning to believe that only conspiracies and plots by powerful forces who do not have the interests of "the country" at heart can explain what is happening to their lives and livelihoods, and the even bleaker future they foresee? How many millions see no explanation other than a spreading moral corruption in what they believe was once the greatest country in the world? How many "on the left" show the need to lean on conspiracy fantasies to explain the horrors of the rulers' march toward fascism and war?

When Ross Perot cried "Conspiracy!" he increased his vote. (I might add that the only actual conspiracy that was even partially documented during this election campaign was one organized earlier by Perot himself using private detectives to break up the engagement of one of his daughters because he was not going to have her marry a Jew. A number of witnesses seem to substantiate that Perot used almost exactly the same kind of blackmail scheme against his younger daughter that he charged Bush with using against her older sister.)

The vote for Perot is the prediction bourgeois pollsters were most wrong about this year. I do not usually pay much attention to opinion polls, since they rarely reveal much about what is really going on in politics and the class struggle. But the polls caught many of the trends in bourgeois politics pretty accurately this year. They were right about the shift after the Republican convention, when bourgeois public opinion swung decisively against Bush. They were right about how the Clinton-Bush race was turning out.

Why were the polls so wrong on the vote for Perot, then? I think they were wrong because a substantial number of people who intended to vote for Perot did not tell the truth when they were selected at random to be surveyed. Why? Because these people considered the pollsters — like reporters, news photographers, and most "professional politicians" — to be part of the conspiracy.

I watched the televised reports on Perot's huge rally in Long Beach, California, on Sunday night before the election. He stopped suddenly in the middle of a sentence and began shouting, "Look, look up there! There are seals! There are seals up in the rafters!" I figured, this is it — he's gone around the bend on nationwide TV. But then the camera panned the audience, and they were all cheering. Many of them knew exactly what he was talking about. He was pointing to members of the navy SEALs — the U.S. Navy's special forces, like the army's Green Berets. And then he explained to the whole audience, and to everyone watching on television, why he does not accept Secret Service protection. For his protection, Perot said, he counts on "our boys" who are trained to protect this country, to protect all of us. (Earlier this year, the New York daily *Newsday* reported that Perot has a "devoted following in the military, notably within the special-operations community.")[13] Some "community"!

Perot told the crowd in Long Beach that he had watched

13. Jesse Ventura, the Bonapartist Reform Party candidate elected governor of Minnesota in the November 1998 elections, was a member of a Navy SEAL underwater demolition team for four years during the Vietnam War. Three of the SEALs he served with stood behind him in dress blues during Ventura's January 4, 1999, inauguration ceremony in St. Paul, and he closed his speech with the SEAL greeting "Hooyah!" The opening talk in this collection, "A Sea Change in Working-Class Politics," describes the significance of Ventura's election in the deepening class polarization and mounting strains on the capitalist two-party system in the United States.

videotapes of the televised presidential debates; he called attention to how many times his eyes blinked versus how many times
Bush's and Clinton's eyes blinked. It sounds bizarre, doesn't it?
But if you are prone to believe in conspiracy theories, then isn't
eye-blinking a wonderful test of who is telling the truth? Watch
their eyes blink! Then watch mine!

These things sound irrational to us. But they get a hearing because millions are trying to find answers that can explain the ir-
rationalities of capitalism. Millions want to know what can be
done about the destabilizing consequences they fear for themselves and their families. In the absence of real explanations, the
"theories" of a Perot can seem to solve the mystery of what is
happening to the country, to the government, to the world, to
jobs — to any semblance of security in their lives.

Why capitalism appears more corrupt

Perot taps into a conviction growing among millions of people
that the established bourgeois politicians are incapable of ad-
dressing the social crisis. More and more people are open to the
suggestion that these figures are at worst plotting conspiracies; at
best they are immoral, not fit to be in office. Millions are convinced that the government is rotten; Washington and all it represents is morally degenerate; the parliamentary and democratic
institutions under capitalism are cesspools where thieves and bureaucrats and maneuverers hide. And more and more believe
that something radical must be done to break through this
spreading corruption.

The ruling class and its political spokespeople today appear to
be so much more corrupt, so scandal-ridden, because of capitalism's deepening and irresolvable problems. Actually, the propertied classes and their politicians are corrupt in all periods. They
have always cheated each other and used the government to en-
rich themselves and their friends. Why else do "public servants"
stay in government? The difference today is only that the scope of
the social crisis makes it more difficult for the exploiters to hide it

when they become what they have always become and do what they always have done.

Even when the capitalist class was on the rise historically in the eighteenth and nineteenth centuries, the executive branch of the government was always careful about what it said publicly, including in front of parliaments and congresses. Presidents, prime ministers, and their deputies lied continually. What changes in capitalism's decline, however, is the growing power of the executive branch. What changes is the executive power's need to hide more and more of what it must do to defend imperialist interests against working people at home and abroad, growing numbers of whom have won the right to be at least a part of the "political class."

The Watergate crisis surely had little to do with the episodes from which it got its name — the break-in at the Democrats' national committee office in the Watergate apartment complex, organized by the Nixon campaign committee's "offensive security" volunteers. No. Watergate registered the implications for the U.S. ruling class of Washington's defeat in Vietnam. It marked the end of the historic high point of U.S. imperialism's strength and stability. Similar problems for the U.S. rulers — revolutionary developments in Central America and the Middle East in the late 1970s and 1980s — are behind the so-called Irangate and Iraqgate scandals too.

This tendency, in the context of sharpening political polarization, increases suspicions of the rulers and their government representatives. Perot plays on this growing distrust of politicians, even as he offers a Bonapartist solution that would in fact greatly tighten the grip of the presidency. Congress is an obstacle, says Perot. Gridlock! Gridlock everywhere! Gotta cut through the gridlock! Gotta get rid of corruption to end the gridlock! Gotta watch out for conspiracies that lead to gridlock!

Perot uses insinuation effectively. Ross Perot is not a Washington insider, he boasts. There's no mystery how he made his money. Ross Perot is a self-made man — an effective businessman, "I'm spending my money, not PAC [political action committee] money, not foreign money, my money — to take this message to the people," Perot aggressively asserted during the second televised presidential debate last month.

But what about Bush and even Clinton? How did they get their wealth? How do they explain how they got where they are? Ability? Moral stature? Hardly. So what is the explanation? "Who would you give your pension fund and your savings account to, to manage?" Perot said in his closing remarks during the final presidential debate. "Who would you ask to be the trustee of your estate and take care of your children if something happened to you?" And he returned to that theme in Long Beach the other night. "If you had a small business, would you hire either one of these guys to run it?" he asked to thundering shouts of "No!" from the crowd.

But wouldn't you trust your money with Ross Perot? The guy's a billionaire, after all. He claims to be beholden to no one — no lobbyists, no bankers, no "foreign interests," nobody. He says he spent millions of dollars of his own money on the campaign. Ross puts his money where his mouth is — his own money. That's Perot's pitch.

But how, Perot insinuates, do you explain this Eastern Establishment aristocrat, George Bush — the New England Yale graduate who pretends to be from Texas? How do you explain self-controlless boy Clinton and the snooty Oxford crowd he hangs around with? How can people like that make things work? Perot asks. How can they have even a clue about what most ordinary people are facing? Why can't they break through the gridlock? Why can't they ever accomplish anything? Why do they all keep insisting there aren't any MIAs over there in Indochina?[14] We all know

14. Demagogues such as Perot agitate around the question of U.S. GIs missing in action in Vietnam, Cambodia, and Laos in order to reinforce nationalist attitudes and soften up working people for new imperialist wars. In fact, as a percentage of those killed, the number of MIAs from the Indochina war is less than 4 percent, compared to more than 19 percent from World War II and more than 15 percent from the Korean War.

there are, don't we? Perot says. Why do they lie all the time?

Perot, the self-made man, isn't afraid to explain why everybody has to accept pain, why "we all" have to sacrifice, he explains. Social Security can't be sacred, Perot says, at least not for well-off people like himself who don't need it. (That is his "populist" foot in the door, the better to open the assault against seeing Social Security as a universal social right, guaranteed for all.) A higher tax on gasoline may be necessary, too. The federal budget deficit has to be slashed at all costs. But "we" in America can do this, Perot says. *Can do!*

Perot did not win the election, but we should all watch what happens to domestic policy in this country over the next twenty-four months. Perot's economic program will come closer to what the Clinton administration and bipartisan Congress actually implement than anything either the Democratic or Republican candidates talked about during the campaign.

A warning to workers movement

Perot's radical, demagogic appeal gained a hearing from millions this year, as the election results show. I repeat: the vote for Perot is the important outcome of the 1992 elections, and it is a warning the workers movement ignores at its own peril.

All the other "third-party" candidates that have exploded onto the political scene in the United States since the entrenchment of a stable two-party system following World War I have had one thing in common: More people *said* they were going to vote for them than actually *did* vote for them. They all ended up disappointed with their vote totals. The one exception may have been George Wallace's American Independent Party in 1968, which got about 14 percent of the vote; but a lot of that was the dying gasp of the Jim Crow "Dixiecrats" in the Democratic Party in the South. The mass civil rights movement had already settled that Wallace's movement had no future.

With that one possible exception, however, this has been the pattern with every third-party movement for the past seventy years: Fewer people actually voted for these candidates than said so beforehand. The pollsters have even developed a formula for this phenomenon: only about half the "third-party" supporters vote as they say they are going to — just the hard-core, protest vote. And if the candidate goes off the rails as election day approaches, the pollsters take off several more percentage points from their projections. This is not surprising, given the hold of the bourgeois two-party system in this country. When a supporter of some third party walks into the voting booth, a substantial percentage usually say to themselves: "Well, I'm for so and so, but she'll never get elected. So why not vote for this other candidate, who at least has a chance and might be a little better?" They cast a vote for a candidate who can win, despite what they said beforehand, or even afterwards.

A vote anywhere close to the size of Perot's is rare for a third-party candidate in the United States in this century. Remember the John Anderson campaign in 1980? Anderson got less than 7 percent of the vote, running against Ronald Reagan and Jimmy Carter. In 1948 *two* third-party movements broke off from the Democrats — Strom Thurmond's segregationist States' Rights Democrats, and the Progressive Party ticket of Henry Wallace, backed by forces in and around the Stalinists and some liberal milieus. Those two parties combined, however, got less than 5 percent of the vote, and Democrat Harry Truman won the election and started consolidating the national security state for U.S. imperialism.

But Ross Perot got nearly 20 percent of the vote — 4 to 5 percent *more* than predicted on the basis of those who said beforehand they would vote for him. The Perot vote registers the growing view that no established Democratic or Republican party candidate will ever be any different. It registers the glorification of the armed forces and their special elite units that gains momentum at times of social crisis — no corruption there! It converges with the glorification of the cops. It reflects the elevation of the so-called self-made businessman (like Perot) who knows how to cut through red tape. "I'm Ross. You're the boss!" — that became Perot's demagogic, populist watchword as the campaign progressed. Together, we will cut through the pretense of democracy in Washington, the gridlock of elected institutions, and *get things done!*

To get a feel for the way similar forces evolved earlier in the century in the United States, it is useful to read a novel called *All the King's Men* by Robert Penn Warren. It is based on the life of Huey Long, the demagogue who became governor of Louisiana during the crisis-ridden years of the late 1920s and early 1930s. Warren brings to life some of the social reality behind the rise of Bonapartist-minded demagogues such as Ross Perot. This is not a new phenomenon in the United States. What is new is the acceleration of the social crisis that begins to provide a social base for such rightist developments again today. These movements all combine populist demagogy with deeply undemocratic attitudes and proposals, always built around conspiracies.

The social and political pressures reflected in the vote for Ross Perot have nothing to do with him as an individual. The vote he received has nothing to do with what may or may not happen to Perot or to his "United We Stand" movement tomorrow. What is new is that a candidate running outside the two major bourgeois parties, with the kind of radical demagogy he spouted, got close to 20 percent of the vote in the United States of America in the closing decade of the twentieth century. To drive home how new it is, we should just ask ourselves the question: "What would I have thought if I had turned on the television ten years ago, or even five, and heard a major candidate for president saying these things?"

This kind of movement, this kind of demagogy is going to be a permanent and growing aspect of the intersection of bourgeois and petty-bourgeois politics in the period we have entered. It is an inevitable product of a world capitalist order heading toward intensified trade wars, economic breakdowns, banking and currency crises, accelerated war drives, and their inevitable accompaniment — class battles.

Perot's radicalism is a manifestation of the increasingly brutal politics of capitalism in decline. It is a radicalism that pits human beings against each other and reinforces all the most savage competitiveness and dog-eat-dog values of capitalist society. It singles out scapegoats among the most oppressed and exploited layers of our class. When Perot explains what "we" can and must do, the "we" is a lie. But when he says that "we" must act quickly and decisively, because "time is not on our side," Perot is pointing to a fundamental class truth — he is just deliberately using the wrong pronoun. Time is not on *their* side — the side of the capitalists and rightist demagogues who seek to salvage their system. But time is on *our* side — the side of the working class, in the United States and around the world.

That is why it is so important for workers and revolutionary-minded youth to absorb that radicalization per se is not in the interests of the working class. In and of itself it has no class content. Radicalism has staked out a permanent place in bourgeois politics, one that will expand as the crisis deepens. Perot may or may not be among its standard-bearers next time around. But the bourgeois right will win adherents to their own radical — radically reactionary — views and proposals until the working class begins to forge a leadership with class-struggle answers out of the fighting vanguard of the toilers.

Buchanan: 'Street by street, block by block'

On the surface, it would appear that Patrick Buchanan's campaign for the presidency this year did not do as well as Perot's. In fact, I think, Buchanan did better.

Buchanan comes at many of the same fundamental questions as Perot, but from a different angle. On some questions, there seems to be a striking convergence. Many of us remember watching that moment at the Republican convention in August, when Buchanan ended his speech by painting a rather sensationalized picture of how U.S. Army and National Guard units in Los Angeles last spring — "M-16s at the ready" — had taken back the city "block by block." That is how the war "for the soul of America" will have to be won as well, Buchanan said.

While many of us recall Buchanan's convention speech, what we may not remember, or never have known, is that in 1988, Perot advocated cordoning off entire neighborhoods of the Black community in Dallas and conducting house-by-house searches for drug dealers. And at his Long Beach rally last week, Perot repeated this theme, saying that the navy SEALs are the kinds of reliable forces that can "take back" drug-infested neighborhoods in this country.

The similarity between Buchanan's and Perot's rhetoric, while striking on one level, obscures a deeper difference, however. Buchanan, like Perot, is quite ready, when the relationship of forces permits, to call in the repressive forces of the capitalist state against labor and the oppressed, of course. But that was not the main point of Buchanan's metaphor at the Republican convention: he was pointing to the need to mobilize a mass popular movement that can storm to victory in the culture war. "And as those boys took back the streets of Los Angeles, block by block, my friends," Buchanan said, "we must take back our cities and take back our culture and take back our country." Perot presented some initial elements of an unworked-out, socially reactionary program to address the insecurities of the middle class and serve the interests of capital at a time of crisis. Buchanan, on the other hand, presented his reactionary views and proposals clearly and forcefully, with the aim above all of beginning to draw together the cadres of an incipient fascist movement in this country. That is why, in my opinion, there is not much overlap between Buchanan supporters and Perot supporters right now.

One common explanation of Bush's electoral loss, if you have been following the bourgeois commentators over the past several days, is that the Republicans made a big mistake allowing Buchanan, Pat Robertson, and other ultrarightists to speak at the August convention and put their stamp on it politically. That ruined Bush's chances, these pundits say, because he needed to appear more middle-of-the-road.

But this was not a mistake. For something to be a *mistake*, there has to have been an alternative that was both correct and possible. There has to be something that could have been done differently. But the Republican Party could not have done anything about Buchanan's speech this year, because of the various components that make up the party's base. Everyone slated to speak at the convention turned over their speeches ahead of time to be vetted. There is no evidence Buchanan was pressured to change his talk or any part of it by convention organizers. They offered Buchanan eight minutes; he took twenty four. And then he stood there and took seven minutes of applause; he had been told to take no more than two. Altogether, Buchanan ended up pushing Ronald Reagan's speech out of prime time.

All Buchanan was doing was consolidating the turf he had already taken. All he was doing was playing out this aspect of the breakdown of bourgeois politics. And showing that a little bit of coarse muscling works against bourgeois politicians.

Why is Hillary Clinton a particular target of Buchanan and his people? It is important to be clear on this question, because there are reasons — good reasons — why workers do not think much of Hillary Clinton either. She is a well-off lawyer and bureaucrat for the employing class; she wants to meddle in our lives; she exudes the officious, holier-than-thou, "social-engineering" mentality that workers hate. Just like her husband and the whole class they speak for, Hillary Clinton is bad news for working people, and they don't want her messing with them. But that is not why she is a target of Patrick Buchanan, even if he takes advantage of all that in his demagogy.

Women, I think, often sense more keenly than men the hatred the Buchananites and the Robertsonites express when they spew the word "Hillary" from their mouths. When they spoke at the Republican convention, the name rolled off their tongues in a peculiarly venomous way. And when it was spoken by Marilyn Quayle at that convention, the venom seemed even more toxic. But the target is not really Hillary Clinton; the target is every woman who begins acting like a political person, like a political equal. For Buchanan and other rightists, Hillary Clinton is simply a highly visible and convenient target to drive home the reactionary idea that a woman's place is in the home. Their target is every woman who refuses to accept the second-class social status that makes them so much easier to exploit; that keeps down the value of their labor power; and that holds down the wages and conditions of every working person as a result.

Perot this year led the demagogic campaign to prepare to break gridlock in high places, pointing to the military as his model. Buchanan led the reactionary campaign to whip up emotional energy against social norms and values that are slowly changing in a historically progressive direction, a proletarian direction. He wagged his finger at excesses that coincided with these changes as evidence of personal immorality and corruption. He launched the "culture war," the "religious war," the crusade for "family values."

The question Buchanan poses will not go away, because *it is the question*. What large social group, what identifiable social class, can take the moral high ground in today's world? What layer of society can lead humanity out of the economic and social catastrophe that becomes clearer to millions each day?

This is not a side issue.

Workers can stop the march toward fascism and war

It was not possible for the working class to have stopped World War I. Looking back in history that is obvious. The relative economic and social weight of the working class at that time; its small size and lack of experience in working with toilers outside Europe and North America; the resulting geographical narrowness of the world socialist movement and relative weakness within it of proletarian revolutionary currents — all this was such that nothing could have stopped the capitalist rulers from marching our class into the terrible slaughter of World War I. We were at the dawn of the imperialist epoch, imperialism's decline was ahead of us, and our class worldwide was still marked by the character of its limitations.

The same cannot be said of the two decades that ended in World War II, however. By then our class was larger, more experienced, more diverse and representative internationally, and its weight was felt more heavily worldwide. The October 1917 revolution had brought the world's first workers state into existence, and produced a worldwide example to emulate — the Bolshevik example. Across Europe in the 1930s, workers put up courageous resistance to the conditions that were leading to the war — in France, Spain, and elsewhere. But Stalinism blocked the working class from any chance of taking power out of the hands of the capitalist rulers and preventing the horrors of fascism and war.

At the peak of an extended wave of capitalist development, automatic mechanisms come into play bringing an inevitable decline, comparable to what happens at the top of the much more frequent and more regular capitalist business cycles. But in the downswing of the long-term curve of capitalist development, such as the one that has been under way since the mid-1970s and is accelerating today, there is no automatic mechanism that sets off a new wave of expansion. The extent and duration of the slide downward are indeterminate. That is finally settled *only* by the class struggle. The capitalists are either enabled to carry out the massive destruction of value-producing wealth and reduction in the value of labor power, without which a new period of self-perpetuating capitalist growth cannot get off the ground — or they are *prevented* from doing so by the action and leadership of the working class.

Capitalism is a horrible, inhuman system. The propertied rulers' ultimate victory in a social crisis is, first, to defeat the working class in bloody, pitched battles; and, second, on the basis of those defeats to enter into destructive wars among themselves that enable the victor to reaccumulate capital and place the system on profitable foundations — until the next long-term slide. In this century, the world's toilers have already paid a staggering price for capitalism's two previous bloody efforts to resolve its crises. The price for fascism and a third world war is almost unimaginable.

As the capitalist economic and social crises that lead to such slaughters deepen worldwide, the bourgeoisie needs to use a greatly strengthened state to maintain its rule. They will come to rely on mass rightist movements to impose that repressive solution, radical petty-bourgeois movements that initially present themselves as a form of socialism — the "national socialism" proclaimed by the Nazis in Germany, and earlier by Mussolini's fascist movement in Italy.

But working-class resistance to the rulers' assaults — which we have so far seen in the forms of guerrilla skirmishes on the job, and limited fights around a range of questions — will mount and become generalized as well. Moreover, the generations that make up the vast majority of the working class worldwide today are undefeated. Nowhere in the imperialist countries has the working class been taken on in decisive battle by the rulers, defeated, and brutally repressed and atomized. There is no capitalist country today in which the current generation of workers has experienced the kinds of bloody defeats suffered by the working class in several countries in the early 1920s, let alone what began happening to working people in 1933 with the devastating spread of fascist victories in Europe. By 1939, as these defeats culminated in the triumph of fascist forces in the Spanish civil war, it had once again become impossible for the working class to prevent an impending imperialist slaughter. World War II had become inevitable. The workers vanguard above all had to prepare for the initial blows of the war — and at the same time for the struggles by workers, farmers, soldiers, and oppressed nations the war would soon set in motion.

Since the curve of capitalist development turned downward once again more than two decades ago, however, the working class has not experienced anything comparable to those shattering defeats — not in a single imperialist country.

As communists, our eyes remain fixed on the ranks, on the workers of the world. And we can point to five facts that put the working class today in a stronger position than ever before to point a way forward for humanity out of the crises and decay of capitalism.

Women in the labor force
The first fact is that never before in history have women had the weight in economic and social struggles that they occupy today. Compelled by capitalism's whip, by its need to drive down the price of labor power, an ever-declining percentage of women are simply "invisible" producers and service providers within the home, with no independent weight in the market economy. Women make up a higher and higher percentage of the wage-earning workforce, not just in the imperialist countries but in the semicolonial world as well. More and more they are individual and independent actors.

The economic, social, and political gains women have won in the last half century are one of the reasons they are among the main targets of the culture war declared by the Buchanans and their followers here in the United States. The assaults on the rights and basic humanity of women by the ultrarightists are so strident and vulgar that they sometimes seem irrational. But they are not. And despite the counterassault of reaction, women are still gaining. There have been blows to abortion rights over the past decade by courts and legislative bodies, for example, but the right wing is on the defensive, not the offensive. Women's right to abortion is nowhere close to being rolled back.

The weight women's struggles for emancipation have in society today — that is the first historic change that improves the odds of the working class.

Growth of immigrant worker populations

The second fact is the growing internationalization of the working class. It is not just that the industrial and urban working class is growing qualitatively larger and stronger in virtually every region of the world — Latin America, Asia, the Middle East, parts of Africa. That is true, and it creates prospects for a truly *world* communist workers movement in ways never before objectively attainable. In addition to that shift, however, the growing internationalization of the working class *within* the imperialist countries — as well as in a growing number of the most economically advanced semicolonial countries — is unprecedented.

More immigrants have come to the United States over the past decade than ever before in history, more even than during the decade prior to World War I. In fact, more immigrants came to the United States over the past ten years than to the rest of the countries of the imperialist world combined. And this is not because there has been little emigration to other countries; in fact, there has been a massive growth of immigrant populations throughout Western Europe in recent decades. Some two million immigrants are estimated to have come to North America or Europe in the last two years alone. Even the "white Australia" immigration policies have been broken through over the past quarter century, with hundreds of thousands of people emigrating from Asia and the Pacific in particular. The one exception, Japan, has a small immigrant worker population, but even there it is growing and the substantial Korean community is having a bigger impact on politics and the class struggle.[15]

15. In 1993 some 900,000 permanent residents of Japan were estimated to be of

Like the employment of women, this immigration is being forced by economic necessity, by the laws of motion of capital itself. It is being forced by the dispossession of rural toilers throughout Latin America and the Caribbean, Asia and the Pacific, Africa, and the Middle East. It is being accelerated by the worsening economic and social conditions of the majority of peasants and workers in these countries, by the "successes" of the "market miracle" in the semicolonial world.

The Patrick Buchanans can talk all they want about building trenches and walls along the border with Mexico. They can talk all they want about massive roundups and deportations, and even about firing on unarmed workers trying to cross into the United States. Other Republican and Democratic politicians can make their slightly more genteel-sounding proposals. But nothing will stop the swelling immigration into the United States and other imperialist countries. In fact, the anti-immigrant rhetoric in the mouths of these politicians is not even primarily intended to stop the immigration. The central aim is to keep the level of fear and intimidation high enough so that the level of wages and working conditions can be kept low.

How do class-struggle-minded workers answer the trade union bureaucrats' demagogic cry that NAFTA will result in losing "American jobs" to Mexico? There is only one answer: There is no such thing as an "American job" or a "Mexican job," only workers' jobs. Workers in the United States have to get together with workers in Mexico and with workers in other countries and organize ourselves to defend our interests as a class, as part of the vast toiling majority of humanity. We must not support policies that strengthen our common class enemy. If workers give any other answer, the bu-

---

non-Japanese origin. Of these, 80 percent are Korean, with the majority of the rest from the Philippines, Thailand, China, or other Asian countries. In face of mounting opposition to its racist, anti-immigrant practices, Tokyo in 1993 ended its long-standing policy of requiring that Koreans living in Japan be fingerprinted; they must still carry an "Alien Registration Card" at all times.

reaucrats and the liberals and the reactionaries will win the argument. If workers give any *national* answer, our exploiters will only strengthen their power over all those who work for a living.

Class-conscious workers oppose NAFTA, as we oppose all economic and military pacts entered into by the imperialist government at home with other capitalist regimes. But we do so from an internationalist standpoint, rejecting any notion of common interests with the employing class in bolstering their competitiveness against their rivals or helping them reinforce the pariah status and superexploitation of immigrant workers. The only "we" we recognize is that of working people and our allies in the United States, Canada, and Mexico — and the rest of the Americas and the world. Not "we" Americans, "we" English speakers, "we" the white race, or anything else that chains us to the class that grows wealthy off the exploitation of our labor and that of our toiling brothers and sisters the world over.

The capitalist rulers in Europe cannot turn back the tide of immigration either. The German government can put people in boxcars and send them back to Romania. (The *Militant* should print the photos of those trains!) But that is not going to reverse the growing numbers of immigrants in Germany — the workers from Turkey, from Yugoslavia, from elsewhere in Eastern and Central Europe, and from other corners of the world. The German rulers have not even begun the battle to defeat the working class, west and east, and the immigrants are a growing part of that class who bring new experiences and give new power to struggles by workers throughout Germany.

The objective possibilities today to bring the weight of an international class to bear on unfolding fights are greater than at any other time in history, and nothing will reverse this trend.

Vanguard place of workers who are Black

The third great change is the political weight and vanguard place of the oppressed Black nationality in the United States. This factor, one the communist movement has taken into account since our origins, has taken on qualitatively greater significance with the post–World War II urbanization and proletarianization of the Black population.

The greatest blow to the working class and working farmers in U.S. history was the defeat of Radical Reconstruction a little more than a decade following the U.S. Civil War. The defeat of Reconstruction by 1877 registered the crushing of efforts to forge a fighting land and labor alliance in this country, coming out of the victory of the second American revolution — the defeat of the slavocracy by the Union armies. That end of Reconstruction blocked prospects for toilers of all shades of skin color joining together to advance their common class interests against the rising industrial capitalist class. It set back the convergence in economic growth and social structure of the North and South. Blacks in the United States, overwhelmingly in the rural South at that time, emerged from this defeat as an oppressed nationality. Over the next decade, near-peonage conditions were reestablished in substantial parts of the territory of the former slavocracy, enforced by organized lynch-mob terror.

In the 1930s the majority of the Black nationality still lived and worked on the land, almost all in the South. The social and political weight of this still largely rural Black population was such, however, that the SWP already recognized at that time that workers who are Black would have disproportionate weight in the vanguard of the proletarian revolution in the United States. The Socialist Workers Party was helped in reaching this strategic conclusion by leadership discussions with Leon Trotsky. Trotsky drew on his experience as a leader of the Bolsheviks and Communist International in Lenin's time to help us understand the dynamics of struggles by toilers from oppressed nationalities in the imperialist epoch, to help us understand the revolutionary possibilities that grow as these nationalities become more and more proletarian in composition.[16]

16. See *Leon Trotsky on Black Nationalism and Self-Determination* (New York: Pathfinder, 1967, 1978).

Prior to World War II, the growing numbers of workers who were Black played an important role in tenant farmer and other rural struggles, as well as in the fighting vanguard of the battles that built the industrial unions, the CIO movement. The urbanization, proletarianization, and migration northward and westward of the Black population increased as the U.S. government prepared to enter the imperialist slaughter, and then took on historic dimensions as the United States became the great industrial powerhouse that defeated Germany and Japan. The battles against racist discrimination during the war and its aftermath — struggles that picked up again, after a pause, in the mid-1950s — were fueled by these sweeping economic and social changes. They put the race question more than ever at the center of working-class politics in the United States and, by example, lent it added weight throughout the world. The post–World War II rise of the colonial revolution gave a powerful impulse to the Black struggle in the United States, just as the struggles and victories of the U.S. civil rights movement reverberated throughout the colonial world.

The struggles in the 1950s and 1960s that brought down Jim Crow segregation opened the road to forging working-class unity against the capitalist rulers. They laid the foundations for the emergence of Malcolm X, an outstanding leader not only of the oppressed Black nationality but also of revolutionary-minded working people and youth in the United States, whatever their skin color or national origins. Armed with the historical experience and political confidence conquered by those mass civil rights fights and their results, workers who are Black will comprise a much larger component of any fighting political vanguard of the working class than during the last labor radicalization in the United States.

Universalization of proletarian leadership

The fourth fact is the emergence in recent decades of revolutionary working-class leaders from struggles by toilers in diverse parts of the world. Earlier in this century it was simply not possible for proletarian communist leadership — leadership that begins to be looked to by vanguard fighters the world over — to develop from the conditions and class relations that existed in most of the world. It took the kind of economic development imposed by imperialism throughout this century to create the necessary conditions. It took time and hard-earned experiences in struggle over decades by our class and its allies. No such leadership emerged from struggles by the oppressed in the semicolonial countries prior to World War II or even during the initial surge of anticolonial struggles afterwards.

Over the past few decades, however, such leadership developments have happened even in very small, very economically backward countries. Of course, Cuba is the most outstanding example of a world-class communist leadership being forged in the course of anti-imperialist struggles. But outstanding proletarian leaders have been forged out of a generation of fighting workers, poor farmers, and youth elsewhere, too. It happened in Burkina Faso in West Africa; it happened in Grenada in the Caribbean. The most politically conscious and self-sacrificing leaders among these fighters have sought to learn the lessons of revolutionary struggles from earlier times and other parts of the world. We have seen that happen over the past quarter century, and we will see it many more times.

An important variant of this trend in world politics is unfolding at an accelerating pace in South Africa right now. Within the African National Congress leadership, the course best exemplified by Nelson Mandela aims to press forward the democratic revolution in a determined manner that promises to open a deep-going transformation of social and political relations in that country. Progress in advancing such a transformation will depend on the development of a communist leadership of the working class and revolutionary developments outside as well as inside South Africa.

The international communist movement we are part of has helped produce books of writings and speeches by leaders of these and other revolutions that have taken place since World

War II in nations oppressed by imperialism. We have helped edit, publish, print, and distribute speeches and writings by leaders of the Cuban revolution such as Ernesto Che Guevara and Fidel Castro; by Thomas Sankara from Burkina Faso; by Maurice Bishop of Grenada; by leaders of the Sandinista National Liberation Front in Nicaragua; by Nelson Mandela. These books are an integral part of the political arsenal of the modern revolutionary movement. We can take these speeches and writings anywhere in the world and find fighters and workers who want them and feel they need them. Workers who read and study these books will be better equipped for their own struggles. Compare that to even thirty-five or forty years ago.

Weakening of Stalinism

The fifth fact is one we have already discussed at some length: that Stalinism has been qualitatively weakened over the past half decade. Given the toll paid by the working class for Stalinist betrayals across more than six decades — including shattered opportunities to conquer power in the 1920s and 1930s and turn back the onslaught of fascism and world war — the blows dealt to Stalinism since 1989 were bound to come prior to big new possibilities to extend the world revolution. The collapse of the Stalinist apparatuses was inevitable, however, and possibilities now open up for revolutionists and communists that were closed off for decades.

The battles by working people in the former Soviet Union and across Eastern Europe, working-class struggles in China — all these are coming. They will be battles against the depredations of world capitalism — against efforts by finance capital to impose on the workers of these countries the conditions the exploiters must impose on the working class the world over. These battles will be fought even more vigorously as the bitter promises by international capital, and by wannabe-bourgeois bureaucrats, of a glorious life under the market economy clash more and more sharply with social reality.

Convergence toward a clear political understanding of Stalinism is not what will draw workers from various countries together to begin with. That is a political question that will be conquered over time. What will draw workers toward each other first and foremost will be the common internationalist and working-class values that come out of struggling together, shoulder to shoulder.

❖

It is the capitalists who will initiate the big class battles that are coming. Throughout modern history, the exploiting classes have picked every fight that became a revolutionary struggle. Capitalist deflation will grind away at living standards and job conditions. There will be sharp and sudden alternations with periods of rapid and ruinous inflation. Social tensions will heighten, and political polarization will deepen. And these class tensions, despite ups and downs, and even brief pauses, will not be resolved until the fundamental economic and political forces that produce them have been resolved. If the tension is too much for someone who chooses to be a revolutionist, then he or she is in for a rough life — a "stressful" one, as they say these days. But revolutionaries look forward to the struggles and opportunities that will emerge on a world scale. That is what vanguard fighters in South Africa know they face. That is what the political leaders of the current generation of revolutionary-minded workers and youth in Cuba look forward to.

These tensions persist and will intensify because the capitalists are nowhere close to winning. These grinding tensions come right into our class and exacerbate divisions and differentiation, too. Because workers must go through enough experiences in class battles before an expanding vanguard begins to see there is no way to win unless we struggle together and unless we draw on the lessons and ideas that previous generations of revolutionary workers have conquered in blood.

But this is the world reality that was reflected, however partially, in this year's U.S. presidential election. This international picture and its political implications could not be hidden. They were present in this election campaign.

All the capitalist candidates talked about what "we" — as part of the nation, as part of the USA — must do together to solve the crises "we" face. As Ross Perot put it, "My children and your children are in this together."

But that is the biggest lie of all — whether in Perot's mouth, or that of George Bush, William Clinton, or Patrick Buchanan. Those who represent the interests of working people and workers organizations in the United States or anywhere else have nothing in common with the capitalists, their governments, their parties and spokespersons, or the demagogues who arise to help them maintain their system of class exploitation as it sinks deeper into crisis. There is no "we" that includes the workers and the capitalists of any country. There is only "we," the workers of the world, and "they," the propertied classes.

This election registered the fact that *they* have not won, that the contradictions are deepening for *them*, and that each thing *they* do opens up new possibilities for struggles by working people. And it is those battles that will finally eliminate the capitalists' inhuman system from the face of the earth.

DISCUSSION

No 'domestic issues' were joined

COMMENT: Could you say a bit more about some of the domestic issues in the election?

RESPONSE: I do not think there were any domestic issues. That is, I do not think anyone can honestly explain the difference between what the Republican administration was doing and the Democratic candidate was promising to do. You *could* explain the difference with Buchanan. You *could* explain the difference with Perot, who advocated a number of concrete actions: beginning to dismantle the Social Security system; imposing more regressive taxes on consumption goods; launching a national campaign of "sacrifice" modeled on World War II.

A lot of people interviewed in the so-called exit polls on election day said they were voting for one or another candidate because they thought the person winning would offer the best chance to "improve the economy." But I did not hear even a single voter, or a single interviewer, who concretely cited any substantial difference between the two major candidates on economic policy.

Neither the Republican nor the Democratic candidates came close to winning the confidence of a majority of people in this country, nor even a majority of those who actually voted. The *New York Times* ran a hilarious headline right after the election: "Clinton takes monumental, fragile mandate." I know what a monument is — something usually made out of marble, or perhaps granite, and frequently quite large. I also know what "fragile" means. But what is a monumental, fragile mandate? Perhaps it means that Clinton has got monumental problems, and that U.S. capitalism is much more fragile than it pretends, so he better watch out!

Let me raise another point. This was not "The Year of the Woman," though some bourgeois commentators declared it so because of the number of female candidates elected last Tuesday. Like the last four or five presidential elections, it *was* a period during which the capitalist parties had to adjust their pitch to the relationship of forces arising from the conquests of women's rights struggles over the past couple of decades. The Clinton camp has "leaked" the news that during his first hundred days, the new president will reverse the order by the Bush administration preventing federally funded health clinics from counseling women about the availability of abortion. Of course, Bush's order had already been reversed by a federal district court the morning before Clinton made his announcement.

The de facto coming together of Democratic and Republican party domestic policy deeply frustrates the ultraright wing, even though this convergence takes place in the framework of a bipartisan slide to the right. The right-wingers perpetuate the myth of some grand conspiracy behind Bush's decision to break his 1988 "read my lips" pledge not to raise taxes. They posit some rotten bargain between the members of the House, the Senate, and the White House. But the majority of representatives in both parties will do the same thing once again whenever the rulers face a similar situation.

Some commentators are saying that the Clinton administration will reverse the policy barring openly gay men and women from the armed forces. We will see. Just yesterday, a federal court for the first time reinstated a navy junior officer who had been forced out with an honorable discharge after he announced publicly he was gay. The court reinstated him with his prior rank, pay, and responsibilities until his suit against the federal government is settled.

These court decisions on the right to abortion counseling and against discrimination are not the fruits of Democratic or Republican party campaign promises. They are reflections of the class struggle, registering the rulers' incapacity to win and hold the moral high ground in politics.

So, I submit there were precious few domestic issues that clearly differentiated the two parties. Where their platforms did differ — on attitudes toward abortion rights — neither charted a course either to fight to reverse the existing Supreme Court decisions, in the case of the Republicans, or to extend those gains, in the case of the Democrats. Left to their own devices, both would preside over a slow diminishing of the possibilities of women to easily use the right to choose.

Such a convergence at this stage of social crisis is not unusual for bourgeois politics in the United States. There were no fundamental domestic differences when Franklin Roosevelt ran against Herbert Hoover in 1932, three years after the Wall Street crash of 1929. Those who supported Roosevelt that year were simply hoping that something would change and he would do something. (He campaigned insistently on the need to balance the budget and started out to do so!)

This year both the Republican and Democratic candidates ran on balancing the budget, cutting the deficit, and stabilizing the dollar. Clinton made an extremely strong point of supporting the independence of the Federal Reserve Board and insisting he would keep its current chairman, Alan Greenspan, a conservative Republican, in office. Clinton made those remarks after bond markets worldwide put pressure on the U.S. long bond in order to warn the new administration to keep in line.

The majority of people who voted for Bush and the majority of those who voted for Clinton voted for the same thing: the hope that the new administration would do something to step up the rate of economic growth in this country, improve the availability of jobs, increase profit rates for small businessmen, and avoid bankruptcy for working farmers.

Rising social tensions in former USSR

COMMENT: A few days ago in the former Soviet Union, in Lithuania, the Stalinists were competing in one of those multiparty elections the bourgeoisie is so wild about and they won. On the one hand, I want to feel good about what's happening, because they're choosing a noncapitalist alternative. But at the same time, the people being elected are scum. So, I'm a little confused about what to think about these Stalinists winning an election. What do you think?

RESPONSE: What is happening in the elections in the former Soviet republics is not much different from what you are used to here in the United States. Scum, as you call them, run against each other. Workers have no organized class alternative in the elections. So workers — if they bother to vote at all — vote for one of the scum. They vote for the one they hope will do the least harm, or perhaps make things a little better, or is endorsed by a party they believe reflects their interests better than the alternatives. The worse the problems are, the more likely it is that workers and others will vote for whoever is not in the government at the moment. Not much more is involved.

If what was happening were the reestablishment and consolidation of a Stalinist regime in Lithuania, of course, that would be a setback for the working class. But that is not what is happening at all. The new government, like the one it replaced, is made up of a collection of individuals most of whom are from the privileged caste that has grown up over the past seven decades. They will continue to try to deepen the use of capitalist formulas and methods, beg for help from the imperialist states, and take what they can get.

But there is deepening polarization in the former Soviet Union; nothing is stable. Rightist forces are also growing. Blocs are being formed between those who want to return to the good old days of the Stalinist police state and right-wing nationalists. As the privileged layers in the grotesquely degenerated workers states look to imperialism for help to become more integrated into the world capitalist system, the problems that are produced begin breaking through old ideas and opening political debate, including in the working class, on how to deal with the accelerating crisis.

Revolutionists would have been very happy, of course, if a genuine communist current had arisen in any one of these countries. On the organizational level, however, that political continuity had been broken prior to World War II, and even on the level of individual cadres it was broken not long afterwards. It has not been reknit. For a principled communist current to begin rebuilding, workers and young fighters must gain experience through a series of interconnected struggles in the workers states and elsewhere around the world. Those fights will come: we should think about ourselves, about how we came to revolutionary politics, about the challenges we face in building a communist organization here in the United States.

Why should we feel any different about an individual Stalinist being elected to some post in one of the fragments of the former Soviet Union than we do about Clinton being elected last Tuesday? What do either one of these election results have to do with the working class? Would we be surprised if a Republican won the election four years from now? No. We would just say: What Clinton was doing wasn't working, so a lot of people voted for something different. That is the way it works until the working class has its own party and a class-conscious leadership, or at least until the elections reflect a clearer stage of the organization of class currents.

Politics in the former Soviet Union remains at a very primitive level. Deeper integration into world capitalism and its market economy constantly bumps up against social relations established by the working class through one of the mightiest revolutions in the history of humanity. The Yeltsins in Russia and the other deformed workers states fear the explosive consequences of a head-on assault against gains of the Bolshevik-led revolution that have been internalized by millions of workers — guaranteed employment, a broad if inadequate social wage, the absence of the insecurities of a business cycle.

The conflicts and contradictions will be worked out concretely in politics. But that is a process that is just now beginning to unfold, and there are no shortcuts.

Political leverage and political space

One thing for sure is changing. Each six months, more workers and youth in these countries will become interested in politics. And layers of them, over time, will be interested in the same books, the same questions, the same arguments as fighters anywhere else in the world: the same discussions will occur in Vilnius, or Moscow, or Prague as in Johannesburg, or Havana, or Tokyo, or Hong Kong, or Tehran, or Los Angeles, or Montreal, or London, or Mexico City. There will be a growing demand for books by Marx and Engels, by Lenin, by Trotsky; by those who have been leaders of the Socialist Workers Party in the United States; by leaders of revolutions in Cuba, Grenada, Burkina Faso, South Africa, and elsewhere; by Malcolm X.

The collapse of the Stalinist apparatuses that had long ago driven workers out of politics through terror, demoralization, and corruption has initiated a process that cannot be reversed. The big-business media focuses all their attention on the elections, so-called privatization schemes and the trickle of imperialist investment, blocs between openly fascist currents and Stalinist outfits that claim to represent the working class, and the blows being struck to living and working conditions. At the same time, however, a slow but sure process begins to unfold — at first simply on the level of individuals seeking answers — as workers in these countries head toward coming into the world and into politics.

Never before in history has there been a bigger disproportion between the current small numerical size and negligible social weight of communist organizations in the mass labor movement, and the leverage of the political weapons we produce, translate, edit, circulate, and get around in whatever ways we can. There is nothing like it in the history of the workers movement. I do not know what better word to choose than "*leverage*" — it is an easy, physical analogy. Whether we are participating in a book fair in Tokyo or Tehran, a university conference in Cuba, or a meeting of young fighters in South Africa — we have the same experiences everywhere. Fighters want to get their hands on the Communist Manifesto, on books about the Russian revolution, on copies of *New International* magazine, on books about politics and the labor movement in the United States, on literature about the revolutions in Cuba and South Africa, on books about the Black struggle, on works that give a scientific explanation of women's oppression and the road to their liberation.

Last month many of us watched television specials marking the thirtieth anniversary of what is called the "Cuban missile crisis" in the United States. In Cuba it is called the October Crisis, since it was not really about missiles; it was about Washington's unsuccessful effort in October 1962 to destroy the socialist revolution in Cuba. I think there were five network specials on the crisis last month. The three I saw were extremely interesting. It would be useful for communist workers to get the videotapes of a couple and play them for fellow workers; many productive political discussions would result.

The interviews, documents, and other materials used in these programs confirm things that many of us have long believed to be true, things that have generally been covered up or denied by the U.S. rulers and their bipartisan political spokespersons.

Above all, they establish once and for all that an invasion to crush the socialist revolution in Cuba was being prepared by Washington, by the Kennedy administration. Previously secret government documents that have been recently released bear out what communists in Cuba and in the United States have explained for three decades — and what has been obvious to any objective observer of what the U.S. government has *done*, no matter what it has *said*. Using these records, the TV documentaries reported on the rising economic sabotage against Cuba in the early 1960s; the campaign of U.S.-organized terror and attempted assassinations carried out under the code name Operation Mongoose; and the large-scale preparations for a U.S. military assault aimed at doing what the 1961 Bay of Pigs invasion had miserably failed to accomplish — crushing the revolution.[17]

But I was struck in watching all of these documentaries by an inaccuracy that gave me a new insight into the importance of the political leverage communists have today through the use of our propaganda arsenal. Each of them portrayed what was happening in the United States at the time as universal mass hysteria. But if you lived through the missile crisis as a political person, as a revolutionist, you know that was not true.

The TV specials showed residents of the United States running into grocery stores to buy canned goods, taking them home, putting them in shelters, and carrying out air raid drills in schools

17. On April 17, 1961, 1,500 Cuban-born mercenaries invaded Cuba at the Bay of Pigs on the southern coast. The action, organized by Washington, aimed to establish a "provisional government" to appeal for direct U.S. intervention. The invaders, however, were defeated within seventy-two hours by Cuba's militia and its Revolutionary Armed Forces. On April 19 the last invaders surrendered at Playa Girón (Girón Beach), which is the name Cubans use to designate the battle. The day before the abortive invasion, at a mass rally called to honor those killed or wounded in U.S.-organized attacks on airfields in Havana, Santiago de Cuba, and San Antonio de los Baños, Fidel Castro had proclaimed the socialist character of the revolution in Cuba and called the people of Cuba to arms in its defense.

and workplaces. The idea that everybody in the United States in 1962 joined together as "we Americans" and just waited in a patriotic panic for the Kennedys to incinerate the world is utterly inaccurate.

I lived through those days as a young person and as a relatively new member of the Young Socialist Alliance and Socialist Workers Party. I know from my own experience that there were thousands of people in the United States who worked round the clock to stop Washington from invading Cuba. We did not stock up on canned goods. In fact, we did not buy much of anything. We were too busy — we hardly had time to eat. We were organizing people to come down to the picket lines. I remember marching in downtown Chicago across the street from a Woolworth store, for example, where we had picketed earlier in support of civil rights sit-in fighters. Some people who worked at the store came out and supported the picket line.

This single-minded effort was the response of the overwhelming majority of Socialist Workers Party and Young Socialist Alliance members of all generations. They responded to Washington's heightened war threats against Cuba with the immediacy of a revolutionary fighting instinct. This political course was discussed and decided by the party's Political Committee and the Young Socialist Alliance National Executive Committee and was carried in the news coverage, analysis, and editorial line in the pages of the *Militant.*

Pressures originating in bourgeois public opinion get translated into petty-bourgeois hysteria at such times, however, and these pressures are never without an echo inside the communist movement. The organizer of the Berkeley YSA, for example, literally jumped on his Kawasaki motorbike and rode off into the hills for several days in October 1962. The rest of the cadres noticed he was gone, but they didn't miss a beat. In the tense days following the assassination of U.S. President John Kennedy a year later, as the media was playing up reports that Lee Harvey Oswald was a member of the Fair Play for Cuba Committee, the same comrade went jelly-bellied again. Late one night he knocked on the apartment door of two other members of the chapter's executive committee and in a panicky voice informed them that, "as the new, young secondary leadership," they should be prepared to take charge.

But by then the Berkeley YSA was qualitatively stronger than a year before. The self-styled "primary leadership" was soon removed by decisive vote of the chapter's members and the "secondary leadership" became the new executive committee. The former organizer and the rest of the first string rapidly decided they had joined the wrong movement and went on their way.

The party went through a similar experience — and registered similar accomplishments — at the time of the near meltdown of the Three Mile Island nuclear reactor in 1979.

A bolshevik party is not and does not try to be monolithic. It does, however, strive for political homogeneity and common struggle experience to prepare for our inevitable responsibilities. In the crunch, it has had a helluva batting average.

One of the most difficult things for capitalism's propagandists to understand and portray accurately is how a political vanguard of the working class reaches out to others to use and defend *political space* — as we did during the October missile crisis. Communists have no schemas or timetables. But we do know that the tensions inevitably rising from world capitalism's depression conditions and its inexorable march toward fascism and war keep leading not only to unanticipated crises, but also to resistance out of which vanguard workers can build a movement. Right now, we can anticipate that growing interest among working people and youth in radical ideas ignored by them in the past — or rejected without serious study — will keep ahead of the pace of mass popular struggles.

But these political realities cannot even be seen, much less understood, unless we recognize the space that exists inside the working class and the unions — space that can be used by revolutionary-minded workers to practice politics. This space is not seen or registered by anything in bourgeois public opinion. It can only be seen from inside the working class and the unions. It can best be seen by workers who are communists who are *using* that space to talk politics with other workers, to promote revolutionary literature, to bring co-workers and their unions into fights around social and political issues, and to participate in guerrilla skirmishes around conditions on the job. Without using this political space, the tensions just seem like tensions, the openings are missed, and the space will be diminished over time.

As I was watching those television specials last month, I realized that as a young revolutionist during the missile crisis I had learned a little bit about using political space. I was not fully conscious at the time of everything I was learning, but it turned out to be very useful. That is why I was so struck by the inaccuracy of that aspect of the documentaries. There are people at this meeting tonight — not a whole lot, but not just two or three either — who became different people during those ten days in October 1962, and not because they went out and bought canned goods. They developed a deeper political relationship with others in the YSA and SWP who were working together unflinchingly along the same lines.

During the crisis, I never thought there was going to be a nuclear war. I am not misremembering — I genuinely never thought so. I did know that the U.S. rulers were driving to start a war to crush the socialist revolution in Cuba, and I knew that they would put the future of the world in stupendous danger if they did so. So, like thousands of others, I spent day and night trying to stop that from happening. We saw there was space to do this, and we used it. What is more, as we did so we won some new, young fighters to the communist movement who were strengthened and given greater staying power by the test of fire.

Today there are opportunities to win a new generation of revolutionists to the Socialist Workers Party. Many of them right now will not initially come out of a revitalized labor movement. Through the proletarian party, however, they can be won to join in building a leadership that can organize the working class to make a popular revolution and prevent the fascist devastation and world war that capitalism is dragging humanity toward. Fighters from this generation will reach out to find parties of revolutionists who are workers, revolutionists who have some experience in the class struggle. They will want to emulate communist workers who have learned to defend and use space within the organizations of the working class, and who can show them how to do politics — how to do *working-class politics*, a differentiation most of these fighters will not have thought about beforehand.

This is the kind of working-class experience that nobody will ever get through election campaigns. This is the kind of politics that for bourgeois public opinion does not exist.

Defending ballot rights

COMMENT: I have a question about the ballot rights fights the Socialist Workers campaign carried out in a number of states. There seemed to be more of them this year. Do you see some pattern to these attacks that socialists must take into account in getting ready for future election campaigns and in defending other democratic rights?

RESPONSE: There are other people in this room who were more directly involved in the party's election campaign and are more qualified to answer your questions. I hope you can take advantage of campaigners being present here from a dozen cities and share experiences with them this evening after the meeting adjourns. I will make two observations.

First, we announced plans last spring to get on the ballot in too many states. We have made that mistake before in recent years. The communist movement in the United States is not as large as we were a decade ago, and we sometimes still make the mistake of misjudging what we can do and what our priorities should be.

We sometimes base our projections on organizational energy, political commitment, and objective possibilities for meeting petitioning requirements in each given state or city — and conclude on that basis that we should be able to get on the ballot in "x" number of states. But then other opportunities come up unexpectedly. Political priorities can shift and sometimes oblige us to cut back. We need to build in some flexibility in advance, so we can judge our forces accurately as time passes and make necessary adjustments.

Whenever we consider a campaign to get on the ballot, of course, we recognize all the things we can accomplish politically if we carry it out successfully. But if we leave it at that, then we end up projecting more than we can do. We have to take account of the unexpected and weigh the gains to be made through the petitioning effort in relationship to other political priorities. Members and supporters of the communist movement display enormous energy when they know what they are doing has been given careful thought and preparation. But even revolutionists get tired if they sense that the goals and objectives have not been carefully selected and may in their totality be unrealizable. So we have to judge more accurately how to sustain a rhythm of political life around projected petitioning efforts.

Secondly, I do not think there are big new problems in getting on the ballot. To draw that conclusion would be a political misjudgment. The majority of the ruling class recognizes that they do not need to try to close down democratic space of that kind in this country right now, nor do the conditions exist for them to do so.

As a general rule, the capitalists and their twin parties have not had much success in rolling back democratic rights won by working people and the oppressed earlier in this century. Take abortion rights, which we touched on earlier, for example. There has been no serious attempt by the rulers to reverse women's democratic right to abortion. The workings of capitalism, especially in these times of economic crisis, perpetuate and deepen class inequalities in women's access to abortions. Well over half of the counties in the United States do not have a medical facility that carries out abortion procedures, and the number of such counties is slowly growing. There have been setbacks in some states — parental and husband notification restrictions, twenty-four-hour waiting periods, and so on — and these exacerbate both class inequities and the gap between city and country.

But the capitalists would have to launch an altogether different kind of assault to try to reestablish as a social norm that a woman must break the law in order to get an abortion. The rulers could only accomplish this as the product of a much bigger round of blows dealt to the working class. The same considerations hold, of course, for any successful assault on the gains won through the mass Black rights struggles of the 1950s and 1960s.

The ballot fights you alluded to in your question were important ones. Supporters of the Socialist Workers campaign took them seriously, organized to fight back to the degree our resources allowed, and publicized these fights through the pages of the *Militant* and more broadly.[18] But those attacks do not register

18. The Socialist Workers 1992 presidential ticket of James Warren and Estelle DeBates was on the ballot in thirteen states and the District of Columbia, and had official write-in status in four states. In addition, the SWP fielded 113 candidates for state and local office in twenty-one states and the District of Columbia, some on the ballot and others as write-ins.

Supporters of the 1992 Socialist Workers campaign waged fights against the undemocratic exclusion of socialist candidates from the ballot in five states. In two of those states, Delaware and Massachusetts, Socialist Workers campaign committees filed lawsuits that were struck down by state courts; the following year the SWP won a legal battle with the Delaware state government, which agreed in an out-of-court settlement to drop its undemocratic requirement that individuals who sign nominating petitions for parties without permanent ballot status must include their Social Security numbers. In

any shift in the relationship of forces against the working class.

The evidence is that socialists still have a lot of political space in this country today to fight for ballot rights — far more space than we have the resources to take full advantage of. We know this not just from our experience with petitioning drives per se, but more generally by continually testing the space we have to practice politics, above all in the working class and labor movement. We test it by engaging in struggles — both on the job and in social protests. We test it by gauging whether or not being known as a socialist, as a communist, diminishes our ability to do political work on the job. The evidence is that we have growing political space if we organize to use it.

Capitalism and fascism

COMMENT: In a talk you gave earlier this year on the fight against Buchananism you made the point that fascism is not a form of capitalist rule.[19] I wonder if you could explain that, because I've always thought of fascism as being precisely a form of capitalist rule.

RESPONSE: The communist movement has written a great deal

the first half of 1992 the SWP had also filed a friend of the court brief in a lawsuit challenging Hawaii's ban on write-in votes; the U.S. Supreme Court upheld the state's undemocratic law later that same year.

19. The March 28, 1992, talk by Jack Barnes, entitled "Buchananism: What It Is and How to Fight It," was reported on in an article by Steve Clark in the *International Socialist Review* supplement to the April 10, 1992, issue of the *Militant*. Reprints of the supplement, including biographies of the SWP's 1992 presidential and vice-presidential candidates, were widely distributed over the next several months by supporters of the SWP campaign.

about "fascism, what it is and how to fight," to use the name of a very valuable pamphlet by Leon Trotsky that is published by Pathfinder. But the person from whom I learned the most about fascism concretely was Farrell Dobbs. Farrell was the national secretary of the Socialist Workers Party from 1953 until 1972, and in the 1930s was a central leader of the strikes and over-the-road organizing campaigns that built the Teamsters in the upper Midwest into a fighting industrial union movement. I learned from Farrell both directly, in the course of our work together for nearly a quarter century until his death in 1983, and from his four-volume series on the Teamsters struggles published by Pathfinder.

In the third volume, *Teamster Politics*, Farrell explains how small fascist outfits began to grow in this country in response to the deep economic and social crisis and the rise of workers' struggles in the 1930s. "Clashes between capital and labor in times of social crisis tend to stimulate activity among political demagogues with a fascist mentality," he wrote. "They anticipate that intensification of the class struggle will cause sections of the ruling class to turn away from parliamentary democracy and its methods of rule, and resort to fascism as the way to hold on to state power and protect special privilege."[20]

Farrell understood that if workers are misled into believing there is some choice between capitalism as they know it and some qualitatively worse form of capitalism called fascism, then the argument to choose capitalism as it is — and even to fight to defend it under certain conditions — can appear strong. For decades, that is the way the Stalinists have miseducated working people, convincing them to subordinate their own class interests and organizations to various bourgeois parties and governments — to prevent something worse from happening. There are the "democratic capitalists" and the fascists, the Stalinists say, so workers must sup-

20. *Teamster Politics* (New York: Pathfinder, 1975), pp. 139–48.

port the democratic capitalists in order to stop the fascists.

But fascism is precisely a movement set in motion and financed by sections of the ruling class in desperate circumstances in order to maintain capitalist rule. It is not an alternative to "democratic capitalism"; it is *bred* by "democratic capitalism." When workers understand what fascism really is, then the enormity of the responsibility to get rid of capitalism — a task only the working class can organize and lead — becomes that much clearer.

When we say that fascism is not a *form* of capitalist rule, but a way of *maintaining* capitalist rule, we do so in order to stress that fascism is not a way of organizing capitalism. Instead, it is a radical petty-bourgeois movement in the streets — the most horrible, malignant such movement in history. Banal, mediocre, figures — but ones adept at radical demagogy, nationalism, phrase-mongering, and organization — rise to leadership in these movements. Thugs rise among the cadres. The fascists ape much of the language of currents in the workers movement. "Nazi" was short for National Socialist German Workers Party.

These movements never begin with broad ruling-class support. At first, the rulers in their majority alternately scorn and fear this rowdy "rabble"; only handfuls of capitalists back them at the outset. But as the bourgeoisie become convinced they confront an irresolvable social crisis, and as the working class puts up an increasingly serious challenge to capitalist rule itself, growing layers of the exploiters start supporting, or tolerating, the fascists in order to try to smash the workers and their organizations. That is the job the fascists are finally enlisted to do by the bourgeoisie when the threat to capitalist rule reaches a certain threshold.

The fascists' stock of "ideas," encrusted with historical mystification, are borrowed from the sewers of the bourgeoisie's own views, values, and attitudes. The things the capitalist rulers say privately among themselves, the subtle and not-so-subtle bigotry they promote, are taken up as the banners of a radical mass movement. The demagogues use these banners to mobilize and

channel the energies of radicalized layers of the frightened, resentful, and ruined middle classes in bourgeois society.

The fascists initially rail against "high finance" and the bankers, lacing their nationalist demagogy with anticapitalist rhetoric.
When they come to power with support from weighty sectors of
finance capital, however, the anticapitalist rhetoric slacks off
quickly. That is what happened in Italy under Benito Mussolini
in the early 1920s after *il duce* also became premier. That is what
happened in Germany under Adolf Hitler a decade later after the
führer also became chancellor. Once these new regimes set about
reviving industry, building roads, and preparing for war, radical
diatribes against capital went into rapid decline.

SWP leader Joseph Hansen wrote quite a bit about the experience of the working class with fascist movements in this century. He
pointed out that when a fascist movement conquers, its character
rapidly changes. The new government demobilizes many of the
most radical sectors on which the movement rose to power, bloodily suppressing some of its own cadres if need be, and begins functioning basically as a military-police dictatorship. In mid-1934, a
year after he was appointed chancellor, for example, Hitler dis-
banded the Storm Troopers — the "Brownshirts" — that he had
mobilized for more than a decade as the party's radical, street-
fighting squads against the workers movement. He summarily executed their chief, Ernst Röhm, and murdered dozens of other leaders of the Nazis' longtime cadre.

The regimes that come to power on the back of fascist movements are capitalist governments. It is misleading to talk about "a
fascist regime" for that reason. It is not something historically
different in class terms from a capitalist regime. Once fascist
movements come to power, they use the state and forms of capitalist economic planning to bolster the strongest components of
the bourgeoisie against smaller rival capitalists and against the
toilers. Historically, these governments are short-lived. They become more and more bureaucratized, corrupt, and brittle. But a
horrible logic is played out — a drive toward war, a monstrously

brutal crushing and atomization of the labor movement, a drastic reduction in the value of labor power, crimes such as the scapegoating and extermination of the Jews in Germany and others that challenge language to describe. This is how a declining capitalism, in an unplanned and pragmatic manner, attempts to restabilize itself.

Without understanding what fascism is, workers are disarmed in figuring out how to fight it. It is an inevitable product of the crisis of *capitalism*. Regardless of anyone's individual intentions, fascism is bred by the workings of the capitalist system. That is what happened in the 1920s and 1930s, and that is what we see the initial seeds of today.

A rising fascist movement will divide the bourgeoisie. Some capitalists and bourgeois politicians will be slower than others to throw their backing behind fascist movements; some never will. Revolutionary-minded workers will fight alongside anyone, including bourgeois forces, in concrete actions to resist particular fascist assaults on democratic rights and to defend workers' space to organize and practice politics. But anybody who tells workers we can stop fascism by giving political support to one or another wing of the capitalists is setting our class up for the slaughter — that is the lesson from the class struggle in this century. Crisis-ridden capitalism will generate victorious fascist movements if the working class does not organize to stop it by advancing along a line of march aimed uncompromisingly at making a socialist revolution and overturning capitalist rule.

That is why the workers movement must offer a fighting perspective, present clear political answers that radically break with the capitalist status quo, and set a courageous example for farmers and others outside the working class who become radicalized by the capitalist crisis. We will compete with the fascists for the allegiance of millions of toilers and people of modest means in the middle layers who are being crushed under the pressures of capitalism in decay.

The workers vanguard must chart a course to mobilize and

lead the working class and our allies to take power. Along the way, the labor movement will have to defend our organizations and those of other oppressed layers against fascist thuggery and murderous violence.

Back in the early 1970s, at the height of the youth radicalization engendered by the Vietnamese resistance to U.S. imperialism, some petty-bourgeois ultraleft groups, in Europe especially, adopted a stance of "crushing fascism in the egg." But a small group of socialists cannot organize to physically smash equally tiny groups of fascists and think they have contributed to stopping fascism. In fact, they will have actually done the opposite by disorienting potentially valuable cadres within the communist youth movement, miseducating them to believe fascist movements can be defeated by small armed groups *outside* the main battalions of the workers movement. As we argued against ultraleft currents in our own movement at the time, "Our egg can't crush their egg."

Fascist movements will be bred and rebred by capitalism in crisis, and workers cannot defeat them by going "egg on egg." Nor — and this is the other side of the same coin — can fascist forces be defeated by calling on the bourgeois state to ban their speech and writings, or curtail their right to organize. At various times opportunist, centrist, and other petty-bourgeois currents in the workers movement all combine ultraleft adventures with a dependence on the cops, courts, and parties of the capitalist rulers in the name of the fight against fascism.

Communist workers defend our meetings, our meeting halls, our demonstrations and picket lines, as well as those of other workers and farmers who come under attack. But the workers movement will begin to deal devastating blows to the fascists only as experience is gained in real class combat, as picket squads are transformed into defense organizations, as we take the moral high ground in defense of all workers' rights, and as a mass communist party is forged in revolutionary struggle.

Fascism is nowhere close to conquering anywhere in the world right now. What we are seeing today — and this is new — is the development of nuclei of incipient fascist movements in more and more countries, including here in the United States. They are finding ways of legitimizing themselves in bourgeois politics. In parts of Europe, some of these fascist outfits have carried out violent mobilizations in the streets, especially against immigrants. Because of the nationalist, class-collaborationist character of the labor misleadership throughout the imperialist world, the workers movement has been blunted from effectively explaining the dangerous logic of these incipient fascist currents or responding in a timely and vigorous way to their reactionary acts. All this is part of the battle ahead of class-conscious workers.

Before fascism triumphs anywhere, however, the capitalist economic and social crisis must first have accelerated to the point that intolerable pressures and tensions are hammering broad sections of the middle classes in particular. And before fascist organizations begin enlisting enraged petty-bourgeois cadres by the tens and then hundreds of thousands, the labor movement itself must be engaged in a sustained fightback against assaults by the exploiters. The revolutionary workers movement will already be rallying masses of toilers and impoverished middle-class layers to our banner and actually beginning to threaten capitalist rule. Only then does the ruling class increasingly turn to the fascist movement for help.

Under these conditions, the working class will have the opportunity once again — as on numerous occasions during the two decades between the first and second world wars — to stop the march toward fascism and war by taking power out of the hands of the capitalists. If proletarian combat parties have not been built that are capable of leading the workers and farmers in making a socialist revolution, however, then the effort will fail, horrible disappointment in the potential of the working-class movement will set in, and the fascists can and will make their own bid for power. Never in this century has a fascist movement conquered and taken the reins of government except under these conditions — *after* the working-class movement has first had a chance at victory and been *defeated.*

We are not currently at that stage in the class struggle anywhere in the world. But that is what communist workers must be preparing for right now, as we carry out our political work and develop the habits and discipline of proletarian functioning. Otherwise, labor will have no tested and competent revolutionary leadership as mass working-class combat begins to unfold — as it will, with explosive rhythms and a pace that neither we nor the exploiters can foresee.

Stalinism versus communism

COMMENT: I don't like to sound a pessimistic note, because I largely agree that revolutionists have openings today that have not existed before. But thirty years ago young people in my generation, radicalized by the Cuban revolution, were convinced that revolution was going to sweep through a good many countries in Latin America. Despite Cuba's survival and the example it has set, however, and despite even more miserable conditions for millions of peasants and workers, there has not been another successful revolution in Latin America that has survived and developed along socialist lines. The most vociferously radical group operating now in Peru reminds me a good deal of Pol Pot's Khmer Rouge in Kampuchea. So, I'm wondering, is Stalinism responsible for this reality too, or were there other factors that essentially choked off revolutionary opportunities?

RESPONSE: The Shining Path movement in Peru is very similar to the Pol Pot movement. It is a Stalinist formation that has metastasized into a particularly virulent anti-working-class movement. Without lending any credence to the Peruvian bourgeoisie's rationalizations for its permanent campaign of terror and repression against the toilers, the international working-class movement has no interest in giving any political support whatsoever to Shining Path and its reactionary course.

Thirty years ago, young fighters won to communism by the Cuban revolution — you and me among them — did think revolution was going to sweep Latin America, and we were right. It did. The simple, single answer to why revolutionary movements and proletarian uprisings in one country after another failed to establish workers and farmers governments is Stalinism. The weight of the Stalinist movement worldwide, not just in Latin America, has taken its toll on revolutionary forces in the Americas as elsewhere.

Stalinism posed tremendous difficulties for the revolutionary leadership in Cuba both before and after the 1959 victory. Knitting together the most courageous, principled, and uncompromising organization of toilers to battle for power and then begin the transition to socialism had to be accomplished *despite* the role of the Popular Socialist Party, the Stalinist party there, not in collaboration with it. As Fidel Castro put it a couple of years ago, "Had we been willing to follow the schemas, we would not be gathered here today. We would not have had a July 26, we would not have had a socialist revolution in this hemisphere — perhaps there would not have been any yet. Had we been willing to follow the schemas, theory had it that no revolution could be made here; that's . . . what the manuals used to say."[21]

The manuals referred to were not just plucked off the shelf of some library. They were the guidelines on "communist theory" actively promoted by Stalinist parties throughout Latin America, and they were internalized by the cadres of these parties, including those in the PSP in Cuba. Both from a careful study of the Cuban revolution itself, and from Che Guevara's later experi-

21. Fidel Castro, *Cuba Will Never Adopt Capitalist Methods* (New York: Pathfinder, 1988), p. 13.

ences recounted in the *Bolivian Diary*, we can get a clear political understanding of the consequences revolutionists faced if they relied on Stalinist parties to carry out tasks decisive to the success or failure of the struggle.

There are, in addition, various objective factors that must be taken into account in assessing the outcome of the class struggle in Latin America over the past three decades. The debt crisis weighs heavily on the toilers. But the entire history of the workers movement rebuts any fatalistic view that worsening economic and social conditions preclude revolution. There has been differential class development and the growth of substantially larger middle classes across Latin America. But that too in no way accounts for the setbacks to revolutionary struggles in these countries over the past quarter century. Stalinism is the most important factor by far.

That is unquestionably the weightiest reason, for example, for the incapacity of the Sandinista leadership in Nicaragua to build on the enormous revolutionary capacities they demonstrated in the opening years of the revolution. Serious revolutionary-minded workers need to answer the question: Why was a tested leadership of the caliber of those in the FSLN — a leadership that organized the toilers to overturn the Somoza dictatorship and then defeat the bloody U.S.-organized counterrevolution — unable to lead working people in defending and advancing the workers and peasants government? Go back and read the speeches by central Sandinista leaders from the first three years after the July 19, 1979, victory — they are available in a Pathfinder book — and compare the revolutionary trajectory of the leadership then to the course that culminated in the defeat of the workers and peasants government during the latter half of the 1980s.[22] The social democracy also increasingly influenced certain individuals and layers in the Sandinista leader-

---

22. See Tomás Borge, Carlos Fonseca, Daniel Ortega, and others, *Sandinistas Speak* (New York: Pathfinder, 1982). See also issue no. 9 of *New International* on "The Rise and Fall of the Nicaraguan Revolution."

ship, but the political survival of that class-collaborationist current over the past seventy years has been dependent above all on the weight of Stalinism in the international workers movement.

Stalinism was directly responsible for the overthrow of the workers and farmers government in Grenada too. In this case, I would urge you go back and read Fidel Castro's speech in late 1983 about the murder of Maurice Bishop, the outstanding central leader of the Grenada revolution. Pathfinder reprinted it as an appendix to the best available collection of speeches by Bishop from the four years of that revolution. In terms the bitterness of which is difficult to overstate, Castro expressed a deep class hatred for those in Grenada who destroyed the chance to continue doing elsewhere in the Caribbean what Cuban revolutionists had set out to do a quarter century earlier. Castro denounced what he called the "Pol Potism" of Bernard Coard and others who murdered Bishop and scores of Grenadan working people and youth in October 1983. The Cuban leader's words were so biting because this was a crime that came from *inside* a revolution, destroying the capacity of workers and farmers to defend what they had fought for and conquered.[23]

The weight of Moscow and its followers worldwide for so many decades had a subtly corrupting effect even on many revolutionary-minded forces with whom the Stalinists maintained relations. The Stalinists hindered rather than helped these forces in fighting for power, regardless of the revolutionary orientation, capacities, and commitment of many cadres and leaders

23. Castro's speech is reprinted as an appendix to *Maurice Bishop Speaks: The Grenada Revolution and Its Overthrow, 1979–83*, published by Pathfinder. Bishop was murdered along with other revolutionary leaders and dozens of working people during a counterrevolutionary coup organized in October 1983 by a Stalinist faction led by Bernard Coard in the governing New Jewel Movement. The coup destroyed the workers and farmers government that had been established in Grenada in March 1979 and opened the way for a U.S. invasion of the island later in October. See "The Second Assassination of Maurice Bishop" by Steve Clark, in *New International* no. 6.

in such organizations. If these revolutionists triumphed nonetheless, as in Nicaragua and Grenada, Stalinism remained an obstacle in using that power to advance the workers and peasants along their historic line of march. The working-class movement throughout the Americas has paid a horrible price for the political miseducation and training of many generations of revolutionary-minded workers, peasants, and youth.

Stalinism was largely responsible for the death of Che Guevara and his comrades in Bolivia in 1967 and the defeat of the revolutionary movement he was fighting to build together with Bolivian, Peruvian, and other Latin American revolutionists in the Southern Cone. It was not a question of direct collusion between the Bolivian Communist Party leadership and the military regime. Once Che had rejected the demands of the Bolivian CP's central leadership that military command of the revolutionary front be turned over to them, however, Bolivian CP leaders sabotaged essential support work and called on Bolivian CP members who were fighting together with Guevara to desert. They cut their relations with members of the youth who joined the guerrilla front and worked to convince young fighters returning from training in Cuba not to join the guerrilla forces in the mountains.

Che had no illusions that the Bolivian CP was a revolutionary organization, any more than the PSP had been in Cuba. But he thought that while many would waver and defect, others, including in its leadership, could be won to support a struggle led by a determined communist vanguard. He underestimated what would be necessary to bypass the Stalinist obstacle in Bolivia. They went into the mountains relying on the Bolivian CP to provide a link between the guerrillas and workers in the cities and peasants outside their base of operations. Ultimately, this proved fatal.

Joseph Hansen wrote an excellent article in 1969 explaining both our fundamental areas of agreement with Che's course in working to advance the socialist revolution in Latin America and at the same time pointing to political errors in the Bolivian campaign.[24] This campaign, undertaken with the backing of Fidel Castro and the top leadership of the Cuban revolution, was not some crazy adventure. To the contrary, the conditions for revolutionary struggle were growing rapidly exactly in the Southern Cone of Latin America, as shown by the developments in Argentina, Chile, and Bolivia itself over the years just following the defeat of Che's guerrilla column.[25] The outcome was not predetermined. If communist leadership had had greater weight in the workers movement in the 1960s and early 1970s, the Cuban socialist revolution would have been joined by others in Latin America.

Revolutionary prospects

There are going to be other revolutionary upsurges in Latin America, as elsewhere in the world, and the size and the social weight of the proletariat will continue to grow. The biggest difference today is that the relative political influence of Stalinism will be less. There is less likelihood than at any time since the years just following the Russian revolution that fighters and revolutionists will turn to the Stalinists for leadership and be betrayed or corrupted. That is no guarantee of victory. The chances of victory will be determined by what human beings do under revolutionary conditions. Prospects for victory will be the product above all of success by new generations of workers in building a communist leadership in struggle. The blows that have been dealt to Stalinism make a historic difference in bettering the odds to build revolutionary leaderships worthy of the name.

It is worth mentioning that the comrade who asked this ques-

24. Hansen's views on this question appear under the title "The Seven Errors Made by Che Guevara" in his *Dynamics of the Cuban Revolution,* pp. 235–41, as well as in *The Leninist Strategy of Party Building,* pp. 63–69. Both are published by Pathfinder.

25. See the discussion of these revolutionary developments in Argentina and the Southern Cone in chapter 2 of this book.

tion and I were part of a group of young people from the United States who visited Cuba in the summer of 1960 to find out the truth about the revolution for ourselves. We marched down the Malecón — the oceanfront drive in Havana — with hundreds of thousands of Cuban workers and young people that summer, helping them carry symbolic coffins bearing the names of one imperialist company after another that had been expropriated by the workers led by their revolutionary government. Then we tossed those coffins over the seawall into the waves below.

The social and political atmosphere in Cuba in those first years of the revolution was wide open. It was electric. We talked about everything with workers and young people. Even diehard Stalinists from the PSP felt under pressure to engage in civil debate.

Over the next several decades, communists in Cuba were always on the lookout for opportunities to advance revolutionary victories elsewhere in the Americas and to find allies who would stand up to Washington's unceasing efforts to destroy the Cuban revolution. The Cubans sought to work with groups of revolutionary-minded fighters wherever they could find them. They put together various forums where revolutionists from the Americas and elsewhere could meet together and collaborate. They confronted all the problems of working with small groups of revolutionists under difficult conditions all across Latin America. They put great hope and effort in guerrilla warfare as a revolutionary strategy and then tried to learn the lessons from failures in the late 1960s and early 1970s. They maintained a revolutionary perspective in face of these setbacks, without falling into adventurism out of frustration. They selflessly embraced and did what they could — anything and everything they were asked — to aid successful revolutions in Grenada and Nicaragua, as well as revolutionists fighting against capitalist tyranny in southern Africa and elsewhere.

Revolutionists in Cuba faced all these very real problems and challenges and stood up courageously to enormous imperialist pressures. But the biggest problem they faced was none of these.

The biggest problem was the objective obstacle of the Stalinist forces on a world scale.

So the revolutionary perspectives we are discussing at this meeting tonight are not a matter of "optimism" versus "pessimism." Stalinism has been the greatest block to the world revolution since the closing years of the 1920s, and that obstacle has now been weakened in ways that are irreversible. Imperialism is the big loser from this development.

Fascism and Stalinism

COMMENT: There have been television news reports and articles in the paper recently about racist gangs and fascist groups in Russia and in Central and Eastern Europe, especially in what used to be the German Democratic Republic. You said that fascism is a way of maintaining capitalism when it's having big difficulties. Do you think fascism is likely to appear in the countries of Eastern Europe and the former Soviet Union, as imperialism and new ruling groups try to reimpose capitalism?

RESPONSE: First, we should not identify, as one and the same thing, sympathy among layers of the population with certain racist or reactionary attitudes and the growth of an actual fascist movement. But for all the reasons we have been discussing tonight, ultrarightist and fascist currents will certainly arise in the workers states formerly dominated by the Stalinists — from Russia to eastern Germany. As elsewhere, such reactionary petty-bourgeois movements will be an inevitable product of deep social crisis. The political miseducation and bourgeois values and attitudes inculcated by the Stalinists themselves will fertilize the soil in which roots will be sunk.

Fascist currents will demagogically exploit popular disappointment with the failure of world capitalism's false promises about the wonders of the "free market." They will fan the flames of nationalist resentment against "Western" imperialist greed, arrogance, and blackmail. Fascist cadres will emerge from the so-called mafiosi in Russia and elsewhere, through whom the imperialist bourgeoisie work to foster capital accumulation even as they rail against the gangsterism of those who get crosswise with the management of capitalist companies or institutions.

You mentioned the former German Democratic Republic in your question. What is going to happen in Germany for sure, east and west, are big class battles. The imperialist rulers in Bonn are determined to put the lid on any rapid motion toward equalization of wages, other than continuing to press wages in the west down toward those in the east. They will continue to liquidate antiquated industrial and other enterprises in east Germany, resulting in more unemployment and social dislocation. They will keep trying to divide the labor movement and to divide "German" workers from the growing numbers of immigrant workers in Germany. They will try to protect the deutsche mark, which both registers and helps reinforce the dominance of German finance capital in capitalist Europe.

As the social peace and political stability in Germany is shaken, a broad range of political questions are emerging. A fight over women's right to abortion hangs over the capitalist rulers in Bonn, for example. Just as workers are demanding that wage levels in the east be raised and equalized with the west, supporters of abortion rights in Germany are demanding that instead of applying the Federal Republic's restrictive anti-abortion legislation in the east, that this fundamental right — guaranteed by law in the German Democratic Republic during the first three months of pregnancy — be extended to women throughout the country.[26]

Only in the course of big class battles will the question be decided whether or not the German bourgeoisie can transform the workers state in the east into a stable bourgeois state based on capitalist relations of production and organization of labor. With the collapse of the Berlin Wall, workers from both the eastern and western parts of the country have the opportunity for the first time in decades to combine forces to advance their common class interests and begin forging a communist leadership of the working class. As class combat develops, fascist organizations will gain momentum too, and they will win support not only from growing layers of the bourgeoisie but forces from within the old Stalinist apparatus in the GDR.

In the 1930s, Bolshevik leader Leon Trotsky pointed to the similarities between fascist movements and the Stalinist movement — on an ideological plane, in their political structure, and other ways. "Stalinism and fascism, in spite of a deep difference in social foundations, are symmetrical phenomena," he wrote in *The Revolution Betrayed.* "In many of their features they show a deadly similarity."[27] Both fascism and Stalinism are radical, nationalist, petty-bourgeois, anti-working-class movements. So we

26. In 1995 the German parliament adopted legislation that kept abortion formally illegal but made the operation permissible during the first three months of pregnancy, following consultation with a physician and counselors. Prior to reunification, government-funded abortions were legal in the German Democratic Republic during the first three months, but not in the Federal Republic of Germany.

27. *The Revolution Betrayed* (New York: Pathfinder, 1972, 1998), p. 251. In the programmatic document Trotsky drafted in 1938 for discussion and adoption by the SWP and the world communist movement it was helping to lead, he wrote: "As in fascist countries, the chief strength of the bureaucracy lies not in itself but in the disillusionment of the masses, in the lack of a new perspective. As in fascist countries, from which Stalin's political apparatus does not differ save in more unbridled savagery, only preparatory propagandistic work is possible today in the USSR." *The Transitional Program for Socialist Revolution* (New York: Pathfinder, 1977), p. 145.

should not be surprised, under the pressures of deepening polarization, to find individuals and political currents originating in the Stalinist movement heading in a fascist direction. That happened in the buildup to World War II, and it will happen again in years to come.

Fascism per se, of course, can arise only in a country with a substantial degree of industrial capitalist development and a working class that is strong enough to potentially challenge the capitalist ruling class. But even in much more economically backward countries, movements can arise in the modern world that have many of the characteristics of fascism. Emulation also has weight here, conscious and semiconscious. That is what happened in Cambodia, for example. There were substantial fascist-like elements to the middle-class mobilizations the bourgeoisie in Chile used to help set the stage for the right-wing military coup headed by Gen. Augusto Pinochet in 1973.

As the decay of capitalism accelerates, fascist movements in diverse parts of the world will draw on energies from many different political directions. They will come from growing anti-immigrant currents that act on the deep racism and nationalist prejudices in ruling-class circles in Germany, France, Austria, Sweden, Switzerland, and elsewhere. They will come from currents in many countries that share Patrick Buchanan's view on the place of women in society. Rightist thugs will honeycomb the cops, where we already see the reactionary, racist, anti-working-class brutality bursting out into the streets as social pressures mount.

The fascists will rail against the deteriorating social conditions under capitalism and then place the blame on those among the toilers who are the greatest victims of these conditions. In lurid, almost pornographic terms, they will harp on the decadence of the leading personalities of the capitalist ruling classes. They will excoriate capitalism itself. In all these ways and more, the wellspring of fascist agitation draws from the reactionary attitudes and values that already exist and are continually bred by the bourgeoisie itself, values aped by the privileged layers in the Stalinist castes.

Bondholders and 'the national debt'

COMMENT: I was wondering if you could say something about the deficit and the national debt? Perot especially talked a lot about that during the election campaign. How significant are the deficit and the debt to the capitalist crisis? Is it really something that the ruling class is worried about? Or is it just another way that they try to justify attacking the working class?

RESPONSE: Yes, the U.S. rulers are worried about the budget deficit. When a government deficit remains very large as a percentage of overall production, one of two things (or some combination of the two) has to happen: either taxation will increase, or the national currency is devalued. The capitalist class does not like either one to happen.

The propertied families do not like to raise taxes — especially income or wealth-related taxes — because taxation is a deduction from surplus value, so that puts further downward pressure on their profit rates. To most workers, it seems strange to say that taxes come out of surplus value. When we look at our paystubs, it seems like a lot of taxes come out of our wages. And that perception reflects the social reality of regressive taxation under capitalism, whereby the *form* of all sorts of levies is a very real burden on workers. Socialists are for lifting all taxes from the shoulders of working people. From the origins of the modern communist workers movement, we have advocated a steeply graduated income tax that falls only on the capitalists and better-off professional and middle classes.

Scientifically, however, most of what are usually called taxes ultimately comes out of the capitalists' surplus value. Under a given relationship of class forces between capital and labor, if the government squeezes too much from our paychecks in the form of taxes, then the capitalists simply end up over time having to raise wages in order to compensate. So, the rulers do not like to see taxation go up more than absolutely necessary to maintain a government that can act to defend the interests of their class.

The capitalists do not like to devalue the currency either. That makes it much more difficult and expensive for them to attract funds into the country that they can use as capital to make more profits for themselves and compete with their rivals.

The great bulk of the wealth of the imperialist ruling classes today is held in debt. It is hard for workers to get comfortable with this idea, since it is so far-removed from our own experience with debt. Workers associate debt with economic pressure, not wealth. We say to ourselves: "I've got some debts. I owe MasterCard a couple of thousand dollars and my brother-in-law a few hundred bucks. What does that have to do with being wealthy?"

But alas! That is the difference between classes. That is the difference between those who live off surplus value and those whose labor produces it.

Interest-bearing bonds is the form in which the capitalists hold most of this debt. And what the bondholders fear above all is that the value of their bonds will be driven down by currency devaluation. At about the same time Abraham Lincoln was getting ready to announce the Emancipation Proclamation some 130 years ago, he started pumping out "greenbacks" — the first nationwide paper currency in U.S. history — to finance the Northern war effort. At that time, Lincoln won the agreement of northern capitalists to do so by agreeing that government bonds would be paid off in gold specie, not in devalued slips of paper. For most of the time since, then, however, the coupon-clippers have had to tally their capital gains or losses in dollars, so they view currency devaluation as a theft of wealth just short of outright expropriation!

That is why farmers and small businessmen — always deep in debt — support inflationary policies and fall for the populist demagogy of those who rail against "the cross of gold" and offer "cheap money" as the solution to the ills of the common man. Because there are two ways to get rid of debt: either pay it back, or inflate it away. If the currency is debased enough, the value of the debt dwindles to little or nothing.

The stories many of us have heard about people having to fill up a wheelbarrow with German marks in the early 1920s just to buy a loaf of bread are not fairy tales. The value of German currency in 1923 was one-million-millionth of its 1913 value! That is one way the capitalist market destroys debt when it becomes too enormous to pay off. We might ask: Haven't the imperialists learned they can never again squeeze countries like the victors in World War I sought to extort wealth from Germany in the form of "reparations"? The answer is no. The barons of finance capital will do it again; they *are* doing it again. They will always make their decisions short-term, pragmatically, on the basis of maximizing their own profits in competition with other capitalists.

Much of what Clinton said during the final two and a half months of the election campaign was carefully designed to satisfy the bondholders about his determination to decrease the deficit. Because a collapse of the bond market in response to his election would have driven up interest rates like crazy, getting the new administration off on a very bad foot with the powers-that-be on Wall Street. And short of a working-class movement that threatens him, or at least threatens his reelection, there is no reason to believe he will shift from this course.

So, the capitalist rulers are worried about the deficit and the national debt. What is of interest to the working class, however, is how they try to solve it. One of the biggest causes of the growing deficit, of course, is interest payments to the holders of U.S. Treasury bonds. The big capitalists in this country and abroad who hold that government debt are paid some $200 billion each

year, some 15 percent of the federal budget — more than all government spending on education, transportation, food stamps,
housing, and aid to families with dependent children combined.
But those payments will not be touched.

Instead, the capitalist parties clamp down harder and harder
on the working class and increase exploitation. Above all, they
are taking aim today at the social rights working people have
won. As a by-product of the mass social movement that built the
industrial unions in the 1930s, and then of the civil rights battles
of the 1950s and 1960s, working people in the United States won
the right to a minimum level of lifetime income security.

What became known as the Social Security system in the
United States was the opposite of any kind of charity, which is all
that most workers previously had to rely on once meager family
resources were spent. It was the opposite of what is called
"welfare" today — paltry sums doled out to working people on
the basis of degrading means tests and invasion of privacy by so-
called social workers. Social Security was something different. It
was a social wage paid out over a worker's entire lifetime in the
form of jobless benefits, disability pay, and a pension. Workers
and other toilers who produce society's wealth began to look at
such things as social rights.

This is what Ross Perot openly takes aim at. As usual, he does
it demagogically. "I'm a multimillionaire," he says. "Why should
I and others in my situation get Social Security free and clear?
Shouldn't I at least have to pay taxes on it?" But workers need to
think carefully about where Perot's populist-sounding argument
actually leads. It heads back toward charity, toward means-tested
welfare, toward the workhouse, the poorhouse, the flophouse,
and the orphanage. It is only the *universal* character of social security programs — their quality as social *rights* enjoyed by all,
like public education — that stamps them as lasting social conquests of the working class and other toilers. That is true whether
we are talking about the United States, Europe, Australia, New
Zealand, or elsewhere.

Now that the curve of capitalist development has been heading down for more than a decade and a half, this social wage is among the capitalists' central targets. But the rulers find it politically difficult to attack these gains head-on, since tens of millions of working people, and many in the middle classes, now consider these gains to be universal social rights.

Perot is actually a stalking horse for politicians in both the Democratic and Republican parties. The Clinton administration and bipartisan Congress will do more to begin carrying out Perot's program in this regard than anything they themselves advocated during the election campaign. The bond markets will periodically remind them to keep working at it. And they will.

5

YOUTH AND THE COMMUNIST MOVEMENT

The communist movement in the United Kingdom held a special congress in Sheffield over the June 27–28 weekend in 1992. It had been called to discuss and decide on a proposed fusion of the Communist League and three groups of Young Socialists in London, Manchester, and Sheffield. The proposal was part of a course that leaders of the communist movement in several countries, including in the United States, had discussed and begun implementing earlier in the year.

The weekend before the congress, the leaderships of the Communist League and Young Socialists groups met in London to discuss and adopt proposals to place before the delegates. An international leadership delegation participated in the London meeting, including Socialist Workers Party national secretary Jack Barnes, who was asked to present the world political report to the upcoming congress and initiate discussion on the proposed fusion and the political basis for it.

The following is Barnes's report, the summary of discussion on it, and closing conference summary. The congress adopted the proposals and the general line of the presentations.

Tasks of the fusion congress

What the Communist League and the Young Socialists are engaged in here today is a political maneuver. It is the most important one the Communist League has engaged in since its founding in January 1988. This course is important not only to the fortunes of advancing communism here in the United Kingdom. It is an integral part of an international maneuver as well.

In several other countries where organized nuclei of communist workers exist, the same maneuver is being carried out. Those who have built the communist movement for some time are combining forces with new levies from a younger generation, many of whom came into politics as part of the resistance to imperialism's war against Iraq last year. Fighters from this new generation have a better chance today to be won to communism, not to a *counterfeit* of communism, than at any time in decades.

I use the term "maneuver" in the military sense — the movement of forces to place them in relationship to each other so that their organized strength, for carrying out a common goal, is greater in their new deployment than it was before the maneuver. It is not a tactic in the narrow sense. It is not an attempt to rally our forces. It does not depend on any IOUs or promises of rapid growth. It simply aims to put the communist movement in a stronger position to confront the possibilities and opportunities for political activity that are before us. It should be done for purely objective reasons.

The proposal that this special congress was called to discuss and vote on is similar to the fusion carried out by the Communist League and Young Socialists in Canada several weeks ago. It is similar to the course decided on in March by a joint leadership meeting of the Socialist Workers Party and Young Socialist Alliance in the United States. At that meeting and over the few months since then, the SWP has taken into membership former YSA members and other young socialists who had not previously joined the party.

This maneuver — this redeployment of the forces already gathered in the organizations of our movement — also puts us in a better position to seize any opportunities to fuse with clumps of young fighters who will come forward in the course of political struggles in the months and years ahead and can be won to communism. As this happens, these young fighters will grab the chance to build an international communist youth organization on a new footing, and with a favorable relationship of forces vis-à-vis the Stalinist movement that could not have been realistically conceived of for more than half a century.

Fusion will strengthen turn party

In order to vote for the proposal before this congress in good conscience, delegates have to be convinced that it will strengthen the parties our world movement together set out to build some years ago.

We must be convinced, first of all, that the party that ensues from this step will be more proletarian than the formations that preceded it. Above all, we must be better equipped to function on the basis of the norms of a proletarian party. We should be better able to engage in politics on the basis of the values and habits of discipline we have studied in *The Struggle for a Proletarian Party* by James P. Cannon and *In Defense of Marxism* by Leon Trotsky;

norms codified in *The Organizational Character of the Socialist Workers Party* and explained by Farrell Dobbs and other veteran leaders of the communist movement. We should be more prepared to sustain a rhythm of political activity on the basis of these norms. We must be convinced that our propaganda institutions — the weekly Militant Labor Forums, sales of the *Militant* and *Perspectiva Mundial,* all the ways of utilizing Pathfinder books and pamphlets, socialist election campaigns — will be more effective vehicles for our participation in the working-class movement. The goal is for the character of our movement as a *campaign* party to be strengthened.

Second, delegates must be convinced that carrying out the proposals before you here will increase the effectiveness of the work of our industrial union fractions on the job and in the labor movement. That it will make our parties more attractive to workers who are fighting and who are looking for an alternative course to prepare the labor movement to respond to the crisis the capitalists are imposing on our class. It will help make us look more like, and act more like, the worker-bolsheviks somebody would expect to see after he or she had just finished reading *The Changing Face of U.S. Politics.*

Third, this fusion, if it is the correct next step, will give us the opportunity to deepen and extend the braiding together of generations of revolutionists in the communist movement. Our capacity to do so is, and always will be, the only road to maintaining — which includes revitalizing — the proletarian political continuity of a revolutionary workers organization.

Fourth, the fusion should give us new opportunities over time to regroup communist forces. We should be in a better position to attract political forces — both in the countries where we already function and elsewhere — in ways that would not be possible if we were not being strengthened by the integration of a new generation into our ranks and leaderships.

Finally, this maneuver should bring closer the launching of an independent communist youth organization, on an international and national level, that will draw in forces substantially larger and from different backgrounds than those of our movement today, and will fight alongside revolutionary communist youth organizations worldwide.

Building on our strengths

The steps being proposed here, like those decided by communist organizations in Canada and the United States, are possible because we can build on the strengths of what we have already accomplished. We must also have a clear recognition of our limits, of course. We must not pretend to be larger than we are, richer than we are, stronger than we are, or geographically spread out more than we are. We need to recognize our limitations, including those that result from the retreat of our class for much of the 1980s in face of the capitalists' escalating offensive, the labor officialdom's default in organizing resistance, and the defeats of popular revolutions in Grenada and Nicaragua.

So long as we do not ignore these limits, we can be confident there are substantial strengths in both the Communist League and young socialists that make the proposed fusion a registration and codification of *a victory you have won*. It is something you have worked for and earned. It is something that was not possible six months ago and could not have been planned one year ago.

Our world movement passed the test of the Gulf War; we proved ourselves as proletarian internationalist organizations. We have described this experience in some detail in "The Opening Guns of World War III" in *New International* no. 7, including some of the mistakes we made along the way. The Communist League here in the United Kingdom, like other components of our movement, responded as worker-bolsheviks as the shooting began. You refused to bend your knees before British imperialism, and you went deeper into your class. The three socialist youth groups here in Britain largely had their origins among fighters attracted to your campaign against imperialism and war and joined together with young members of the league in order to fight more effectively. So this test is one of the strengths we are building on in proposing a fusion of our forces at this congress.

That experience was not unique to the United Kingdom. In the United States, for example, a layer of youth was won to the Young Socialist Alliance during the Gulf War. The SWP collaborated with the youth leadership in carrying out a fusion of younger party members with the Young Socialist Alliance at the YSA convention in August 1991. This resulted in a somewhat larger youth organization with a slightly more experienced National Committee. That maneuver, in turn, prepared the leaderships of both organizations for the subsequent decision to dissolve the YSA and temporarily combine our forces in the party.[1]

1. In March 1992 the National Committees of the Socialist Workers Party and Young Socialist Alliance held a joint meeting in New York to discuss how best to take advantage of opportunities for youth recruitment. Over the previous decade, as the labor movement both in the United States and worldwide suffered blows, the YSA had declined in size, while the median age of its membership and leadership had risen above the norm for a communist youth organization. The joint leadership meeting decided that the next step in winning a new generation to proletarian politics, while maintaining the communist continuity of the revolutionary youth movement embodied in the Young Socialist Alliance, was to dissolve the YSA "into a movement of young people who are actively organizing support for the socialist alternative in 1992 to the bipartisan candidates of war, racism, and depression and who are engaged in actions of social protest and other political activity along with members of the Socialist Workers Party." Such a course would create the best conditions for young revolutionists to begin rebuilding a communist youth organization.

Less than two years later, in early 1994, groups of revolutionary-minded young people from several cities in the United States and other countries began collaborating to launch an international socialist youth organization. At meetings in Chicago, Illinois, in April 1994 and Oberlin, Ohio, in August of that year, they initially took the name Socialist Youth Organizing Committee and later the Young Socialists. On the basis of further common political activity and experience, the Young Socialists held their founding convention in Minneapolis, Minnesota, in April 1996. Delegates from YS chapters across

Our world movement as a whole has gone through experiences similar to these over the past year and a half. Responding to these opportunities and challenges has prepared us to take new steps in a timely way along the road to relaunching strengthened communist youth organizations as opportunities arise, and renewing the cadres and leaderships of turn parties.

This congress in the United Kingdom is part of that process. We will begin by discussing, debating, and exchanging ideas to achieve political clarification and to judge whether what we are proposing to do is objectively justified and the best option among those open to us.

This congress will then elect an authoritative leadership of a special kind. I say "of a special kind," because the leadership elected by a fusion congress must be different from one that comes out of an ordinary congress, where the makeup of the organization itself is not changed by the delegates' decisions. The leadership you elect this weekend will reflect the strengths of all four of the organizations that are coming into the fusion — the Communist League, and the Young Socialists groups in London, Manchester, and here in Sheffield — and it will be chosen on the basis of what these organizations have collectively accomplished. The job of that leadership will be to fuse the forces of the new organization in practice, so they become a more organic whole. The task will be to lead them, through activity in the class struggle, toward fuller participation in the international communist movement.

On that basis, the next congress of the Communist League will be of a different kind and character from this one. It will be a

the United States, joined by fraternal delegates from other countries, discussed and adopted a statement of political and organizational principles, voted to campaign for the Socialist Workers Party ticket in the 1996 U.S. presidential elections, elected a National Committee, and reaffirmed the international character of their movement. The second national convention of the Young Socialists was held in Atlanta, Georgia, March 28–30, 1997, and its third convention in Los Angeles, California, December 4–6, 1998.

gathering of an organization slightly stronger than the sum of the four in the room today.

Drive toward war, depression, and reaction

What is the assessment of the world political situation today that our international movement holds in common? Does it justify the maneuver we are discussing here? That is where we should begin.

First, we stand on the analysis and prognoses in "The Opening Guns of World War III." Washington's war against Iraq put a spotlight on the inevitable character of the drive toward conflict bred by sharpening interimperialist competition and the accelerated disintegration of the stability of the capitalist world order. It confirmed that the imperialist rulers are on a course toward stepped-up militarization, war drives, and military interventions whose logic — unless the working class is successful in its revolutionary struggle to take power from their hands — marches inexorably toward a world conflagration.

From the slaughter in Yugoslavia to heightened tensions in Asia; from U.S. imperialism's continuing threats against the Cuban revolution to the instability and expanding conflicts in the former Soviet Union — these are all evidence of the accuracy of the assessment presented in "The Opening Guns." We share a common understanding of the consequences of Washington's political defeat coming out of the Gulf War. The leaderships of our organizations worked together in hammering out this analysis, and the cadres in each of our organizations have discussed and adopted it at previous national gatherings.

Second, we stand on the analysis of "What the 1987 Stock Market Crash Foretold," the political resolution adopted in 1988 at an international conference held in the United States.[2] At the time we adopted that resolution, of course, nobody could have predicted the concrete timing of events that would further complicate the shape of the capitalists' crisis: the rapid collapse of the Stalinist apparatuses in Central and Eastern Europe and the former Soviet Union; the price the German imperialist rulers would pay for formal reunification of the country and its impact on capitalist Europe and the world; the Iraq war and its consequences; and the results of the worst destabilization of the international monetary system since the 1930s.

We now recognize that by the opening years of this decade, the capitalist world had already entered depression conditions. International finance capital cannot and will not escape from this deflation of growth rates, despite ups and downs in the business cycle, short of big class battles in which it is able to defeat the working class. But the capitalist rulers cannot and will not inflict such defeats without the working class first having the chance to fight, to win, and to establish workers and farmers governments that can open a new chapter in human history.

What is precluded today is a massive, self-propelling expansion of capital that makes possible substantial concessions to a broad layer of the working class, heading off such class battles in coming years. To the contrary, the capitalists are taking, not giving. Somewhere along this road — which they have come to hope is eternal — they will be surprised, and then panicked, when the labor movement stiffens its resistance. We cannot predict the timing, evolution, and character of the crises that will give rise to such battles, or their initial outcome. That those bat-

---

2. That resolution appears in issue no. 10 of *New International,* along with "Imperialism's March toward Fascism and War," the resolution adopted by the Socialist Workers Party at a convention and international conference in August 1994.

tles are coming, however, and that the working class will have a chance to fight them and win, is a fact.

Third, we stand on our assessment of the importance of the growing manifestations of Bonapartism — and its most radical and virulent form, fascism — that are developing once again in the imperialist countries. In the United States we are seeing the heat lightning of the Patrick Buchanan campaign in the Republican primaries this year. Then came the sudden appearance, for the first time in half a century, of a true Bonapartist figure in U.S. presidential politics — H. Ross Perot. This is the beginning of the breakdown of long-established patterns of bourgeois politics that we see to varying degrees in all imperialist countries. It is ultimately a thrust toward other forms of Bonapartism — all partaking of the "popular" radical demagogy of the far right, appealing to growing layers of demoralized and panicked members of the middle class, and to layers of youth, women, and working people as well.

This sharpening political polarization and these rising class tensions — in face of the growing economic crisis of the capitalist system, interimperialist conflicts, and war threats we have analyzed — will mark our political lives and the lives of all communist organizations in the years ahead. That is the world this congress and our entire international movement must understand, explain clearly to co-workers and fighting youth, and on that basis prepare for deepening involvement in politics and class battles.

World politics in the 1990s

If we look at the unfolding slaughter in Yugoslavia, we will see many elements of the world we are describing. The most difficult things to come to grips with in discussing Yugoslavia are not the theoretical questions; we have adopted reports on those questions and written about them well.[3] The most difficult thing is to acknowledge the reality of a murderous war, the scope and horror of which has not been seen in continental Europe for decades. Even more difficult to accept is the fact this war is not an aberration, but instead a foreshadowing of the direction of world politics today.

Most bourgeois commentators would have us believe that the slaughter in Yugoslavia signifies a new rise of nationalism — or as they often prefer saying, a new rise of "tribalism." Outside a few white enclaves in "the West," they imply, world civilization is threatening to break down along lines of "age-old ethnic hatreds." The truth is the opposite. The slaughter in Yugoslavia is the product of the breakdown of the capitalist world order; it is the product of intensifying conflicts among rival capitalist classes in the imperialist countries and would-be capitalists in the deformed workers states. These conflicts, in which exploiting layers demagogically don national garb to defend their narrow class interests, will increasingly mark world politics.

What is happening in Yugoslavia also bloodily demonstrates the fact that Stalinist leaderships cannot unite toilers from different national origins on a lasting basis to open up a broadening federation of soviet republics working together to build socialism. Several years after the October 1917 revolution in Russia, the Bolsheviks under the leadership of Lenin formed the Union of Soviet Socialist Republics as a voluntary federation of workers and peasants republics. The Bolsheviks in Lenin's time were a revolutionary workers vanguard that fought uncompromisingly for the right of oppressed nations to self-determination, for the complete equality of nations and nationalities, and against every vestige of national privilege, arrogance, and chauvinism. They took the lead in placing that internationalist perspec-

---

3. See *The Truth about Yugoslavia: Why Working People Should Oppose Intervention* by George Fyson, Argiris Malapanis, and Jonathan Silberman (New York: Pathfinder, 1993).

tive at the heart of the program and practice of the Communist International. As part of the political counterrevolution carried out by the petty-bourgeois social caste whose spokesman was Joseph Stalin, however, this proletarian internationalist course gave way to the return of Great Russian chauvinism, now dressed up as the "new Soviet nation" and "Soviet man."[4]

The federated Yugoslav workers state that the imperialists and rival Stalinist gangs are now trying to tear apart was a gigantic accomplishment of the Yugoslav revolution of 1942–46. Workers and peasants who were Serbian, Croatian, Bosnian, and from other nationalities forged unity to oust the Nazi occupation forces and their local collaborators, carry out a radical land reform, and expropriate the capitalist exploiters. It was truly one of the great revolutions of this century, a proletarian socialist revolution.

The Stalinist leadership of the Yugoslav Communist Party, headed by Josip Broz (known by his *nom de guerre* Tito), however, blocked the toilers of different nationalities from building on their conquests and solidly cementing the federation together. The socialist revolution in Yugoslavia was deformed from birth. Nonetheless, substantial layers of toilers in Yugoslavia — whether Bosnian, Serb, or Croat, whether Christian or Muslim in their current beliefs or family origins — have continued even today to demonstrate their will to resist the horrors thrust on them by the rival bureaucratic

---

4. The historic communist position on these questions is explained in *The Right of Nations to Self-Determination* and *Questions of National Policy and Proletarian Internationalism*, both by V.I. Lenin (Moscow: Progress Publishers); and *Workers of the World and Oppressed Peoples, Unite!*, the proceedings of the Second Congress of the Communist International (Pathfinder, 1991). Lenin's battle against the first efforts to reverse this communist course are traced in *Lenin's Final Fight: Speeches and Writings, 1922–23* (Pathfinder, 1995). Leon Trotsky, the most prominent Bolshevik active in the leadership of the October revolution who fought to continue Lenin's course, recounted the social and political factors that made possible the Stalinist counterrevolution, including on the national question, in his classic 1936 work, *The Revolution Betrayed: What Is the Soviet Union and Where Is It Going?* All these titles are available from Pathfinder.

gangs that emerged from the crumbling Stalinist apparatus.

The consequences of the bloodbath in Yugoslavia also provide further confirmation that refugees are increasingly becoming actors in world politics today. Every time we hear the word "refugee," in any language, we should always translate it in our minds as "fellow worker." It is not enough for class-conscious workers to reject the chauvinist portrayal of refugees as pariahs. Above all, we must resist turning refugees simply into victims, rather than potential soldiers in the battalions of the international working class. We take communist politics to these fellow workers, and we fight alongside them for their rights, their dignity, and the common interests of working people the world over.

The slaughter in Yugoslavia shows every sign of deepening and drawing in other countries. There is already a United Nations intervention force there — so-called "peace-keeping" troops — for the first time ever in Europe. We cannot predict whether the war will expand, or foresee the forms an escalation might take. Nor do we know how long the current imperialist "peacekeeping" will take; we do know the longer it takes, the more likely it is to turn into "peacebreaking." Our job as communist workers is to demand a halt to the imperialist intervention and fight every attempt to deepen it. We need to keep speaking the truth about the stake workers have in this struggle, and to support the toilers throughout the Yugoslav workers state who are trying to defend their social conquests and bring the butchery to an end.

Sharpening interimperialist rivalry

The war in Yugoslavia sharpens interimperialist conflicts. It sharpens the divisions between the United States and Europe, as well as divisions within Europe itself.

Margaret Thatcher — "retired" against her will as prime minister of the United Kingdom, but also freed from some of the diplomatic niceties required while serving at that post — is wagging a finger at her successor John Major, warning that the dream of a stable, prosperous, reunified, and peaceful Germany at the heart of Europe is a lie. Major's signing of the Maastricht treaty last year, outlining plans for greater European economic and political integration, including a common currency, endangers Britain's capitalist rulers, Thatcher scolds. "A reunited Germany cannot and won't subordinate its national interests in economic or in foreign policy to those of the [European] community indefinitely," she warned in a widely publicized speech in the Netherlands last month. "Germany's power is a problem — as much for the Germans as for the rest of Europe."

Major's cabinet ministers reacted furiously to Thatcher's thinly veiled accusation that the current Tory government is leading the United Kingdom down the primrose path. Thatcher is "a spent force," one minister told reporters, and another disdained her speech as "the cry of the unemployed."

Trying to maintain a "special relationship" with Washington is becoming more necessary than ever for the British bourgeoisie, and not just for them alone. The capitalist rulers in Scandinavia and elsewhere are also sidling up to the Yankees, hoping somehow to protect their relative positions and profits in face of Bonn's economic strength in Europe. At the very same time, however, U.S. capitalism itself shows declining capacity for self-sustaining economic expansion and is becoming more and more dependent on its massive military might to offset its own mounting weaknesses.

The ruling families of Germany and Japan are confronting the need to be able to use their armed forces once again to intervene abroad to defend their class interests against those of their rivals. As they take steps forward in doing so, however, they are meeting opposition both at home and abroad. As Japanese troops were dispatched to Cambodia this year under UN auspices, the specter of the imperial army of Japan once again acting as "peacekeepers" in Asia has sparked debate throughout the region. In fact, that controversy has so far made the debate in Europe over the use of German troops abroad — with the dispatch of a ship and three planes as part of the UN operation in Yugoslavia — seem mild by comparison.

For Bonn and Tokyo to try to justify rebuilding their armies for deployment abroad, the rulers will have to wage a political fight at home as well. Workers and youth will resist these plans, as they press on other fronts to turn back assaults on the economic and social needs of the working class. A few days ago, for example, a leading public opinion pollster in Germany reported to a military seminar in Berlin that 42 percent of those questioned recently could not think of any good reason Germany should have an army at all — 42 percent! And an additional 11 percent were undecided.

Whether in North America, Europe, or Asia and the Pacific, working people over time will move into action against the devastating consequences of capitalist militarism and the rulers' drive toward World War III. In order to succeed, these struggles cannot be "we in Britain" against "them in Germany" or "we in the United States" against "them in Japan." There is a *we* and a *they* — but it is a *we* of the working class and a *they* of the capitalist class. This *we* and *they*, moreover, have irreconcilable class interests. Either the workers of the world will unite to fight against the oppressive social and political conditions that will increasingly bear down on all of us, or the working class in each country will be torn apart and defeated by our respective capitalist rulers one by one.

It is the outcome of this struggle that will decide whether or not the march toward a third world war and its unthinkable consequences will become inevitable once again — as it had earlier in this century, by 1939 — or will be stopped this time by the advance of the world socialist revolution.

Operation Desert Sham

Each month that passes since the end of the Iraq war in late February 1991, the more the myth of unqualified military success of high-tech U.S. weaponry continues to erode. The U.S. rulers have a harder and harder time suppressing the truth. Not only was the outcome of the war a political fiasco for U.S. imperialism, for the reasons we explained in "The Opening Guns of World War III." It was also far from being the astounding display of unbeatable modern military prowess the U.S. rulers pretended. "Operation

Desert Sham" is no longer an underground term, even among bourgeois journalists in the United States.

The communist movement explained the sham right in the midst of the war. The *Militant* was the first newspaper to insist, as facts began to emerge from nooks and crannies in the bourgeois press, that the Patriot missile success story was a scam to build up support for ballistic missile defense. The *Militant's* only competition on this score was Israeli armed forces intelligence, and they could not say it out loud until after the war was over! Later last year, however, an Israeli Air Force report concluded that — contrary to initial Pentagon claims that the Patriot had destroyed 41 of 42 Iraqi Scud missiles aimed at Israel — "there is no evidence of even a single successful intercept." Generously, the report added there was "circumstantial evidence" for one possible intercept.[5]

We now know that U.S. General Norman Schwarzkopf's claim that U.S. weapons destroyed all of Iraq's Scud launchers was also a lie. A recent report by the United Nations task force in charge of supervising the destruction of Iraqi weapons revealed that *not a single mobile launcher was destroyed*, and only twelve of the twenty-eight fixed launchers were put out of commission. The U.S. government simply lied, and the press reported the lies. U.S. generals ordered their forces to bomb trucks, take pictures of the demolished chassis, and claim they had destroyed Scud launchers.[6]

---

5. In a November 1993 television documentary, Moshe Arens, Israeli defense minister during the Gulf War, said the number of successful Patriot interceptions was "minuscule and is in fact meaningless." While U.S. Department of Defense officials reduced their initial claims to perhaps a 40 percent success rate against Scuds aimed at Israel, congressional investigators and an MIT study agreed with the conclusion of Israeli officials that the Patriot may not have scored more than one clean hit.

6. In 1996, a study by the U.S. government's General Accounting Office (GAO) concluded that the Pentagon and military contractors made claims for the pinpoint precision of Stealth fighter jets, Tomahawk land-attack missiles, and laser-guided "smart bombs" during the Gulf War that "were overstated, misleading, inconsistent with the best available data, or unverifiable." The GAO found that Washington's vaunted "smart bombs" did not necessarily

Why are these facts so important to explain? Not only because they show how the U.S. rulers and their government lie, and how the big-business press covers up for them. That is true, and something that cannot be explained too often. But there is a more important reason as well.

According to the U.S. rulers, the war against Iraq proved that no government or people can stand up against U.S. military power today and win. That may have been possible as recently as the Vietnam War, so the story goes, but not now — not in the days of "smart bombs" and other high-tech weapons. But the outcome of the Gulf War was not determined by U.S. technology or firepower. The war ended with the refusal by the bourgeois regime of Saddam Hussein to organize a fight, leaving Iraqi soldiers and the civilian population alike defenseless for several weeks in face of murderous and indiscriminate U.S. bombing raids, rocket attacks, and the final horrendous slaughter on the road to Basra.

Such refusal to organize resistance will *not* be the norm in the battles imperialism will have to fight, however. The U.S. rulers know that. There is only one thing, for example, that continues to prevent Washington from launching an invasion aimed at destroying the socialist revolution in Cuba. Cuban working people

---

perform better than those with no electronic guidance systems. In an April 28, 1996, letter to the GAO, the Department of Defense did not dispute the findings and said it "acknowledges the shortcomings" of these weapons, adding, however, that it was making improvements.

The most sustained bombing campaign against the Iraqi people since the 1991 Gulf War was launched by the Clinton administration with four days of air strikes in mid-December 1998. Over the next two months, as the editorial work on this book was being completed, Washington, assisted by the Labour Party government in London, carried out regular, often daily, air and missile assaults against Iraqi planes, antiaircraft batteries, and other targets, devastating neighborhoods in Basra and other parts of the country. This was the fourth round of air assaults against Iraq since the beginning of the Clinton administration. Attacks already under way during his inauguration in January 1992, ordered by the Bush White House, were hailed by Clinton. The Democratic administration renewed the aggression in July 1993 and September 1996.

are both prepared and determined to defend their revolution, and the U.S. rulers fear the destabilizing political ramifications at home of the enormous casualties they know U.S. invading troops would rapidly and inevitably sustain.

All of us, both in the United Kingdom and the United States, also have a much better idea after the Gulf War of what "friendly fire" really means, even if we were acquainted with the term before.7 There was an important moment during the Vietnam War when a young U.S. soldier from a farm family in Iowa was killed and his family simply tried to get his body back and find out how he died. After months of fighting their way through deliberately evasive and misleading information from the Pentagon, they were told their son had been killed by "friendly fire." It was the strangest term his family, and millions of others in the United States, had ever heard — how could the GI have died by friendly fire? This incident was a turning point, one that brought new forces, wider layers of the people in the United States, into the fight against the U.S. war in Vietnam.

There will be many more families of workers and farmers in uniform in the United States who will learn what the imperialists mean by "friendly fire." They will also learn about the class character of the officer corps and why the communist movement says that working people are used as "cannon fodder" by the imperialists in their wars.

Asia, Hong Kong, and China

The consequences of slowing capital accumulation and sharpening interimperialist conflict are also at work throughout Asia and the Pacific — from Japan, to Australia and New Zealand, to Korea,

---

7. Of the 24 British soldiers killed in combat, 9 — more than one-third — died as a result of "friendly fire" from U.S. aircraft. Washington rejected requests by the families of these soldiers that the U.S. pilots involved in this incident testify at a May 1992 inquest into the deaths in Oxford in the United Kingdom. According to Pentagon figures, 35 of the 146 U.S. soldiers killed in action during the Gulf War — nearly one-quarter — were victims of "friendly fire."

Southeast Asia, and the Indian subcontinent. And there, too, capitalism is expanding the size of the working class, whose prospects are ever more tightly linked to those of workers around the world.

We should never underestimate how attractive the Chinese revolution remains to hundreds of millions of toilers, especially to peoples of color long oppressed and exploited by imperialism. Despite the crimes of its Stalinist misleadership, China stands as an example of a people — more than a billion strong, abused by both European and Asian imperialist powers for more than a century — who carried out a powerful revolution, swept aside the landlord and capitalist exploiters, and restored their national sovereignty and dignity.

Today, more and more toilers in China are being drawn out of the countryside and into factories, mines, and mills owned by the state and increasingly also by foreign and domestic capital. As this process unfolds, the breakdown of Stalinist apparatuses that we have seen in Europe and the former USSR will inevitably shake the deformed Chinese workers state as well. It will take time, but class tensions and conflicts are already growing in China's cities and workplaces, as well as in the countryside. And when the day comes that a young and rapidly growing working class enters into combat in larger battalions, the Stalinists will find that their bloody suppression of the Tiananmen Square youth rebellion in 1989 cannot be endlessly repeated. The struggles that are coming, whatever their tempo and exact forms, will be larger and more explosive than anything in China since the revolution itself.

Hong Kong should be of special interest to us, as we meet here in the home base of the declining British Empire. With London's impending return of that territory to China in 1997, the Tories are coming under hypocritical criticism from other imperialist powers for denying the people of Hong Kong the opportunity for "democracy."[8] But democracy had nothing to do with the scramble by

8. At midnight, July 1, 1997, Hong Kong returned to Chinese sovereignty, un-

European, U.S., and Japanese capitalists for more than a century to establish their domination over the enormous Chinese market and source of cheap labor and raw materials. The Crown simply held on a little longer than its rivals to the little hunk of sovereign Chinese territory it stole more than 150 years ago. (Wall Street is happy to get a little more elbow room vis-à-vis its British rivals in Hong Kong, too. After all, the Yankees figure, for the past nine years the Hong Kong dollar has been pegged to Uncle Sam's currency, not sterling, so why not grab all they can?)

What is really going on is not simply that the People's Republic of China is about to gobble up Hong Kong. What is happening instead is the "Hong Kong-ization" of southern China. What is developing in China today is an accelerated expansion of capitalist methods and penetration by international finance capital — the growing sway of the law of value in southern China especially, as well as Shanghai and other coastal areas.

Many of you have probably read newspaper reports about the so-called Special Economic Zones in southern China, where much of the imperialist investment is concentrated. These zones are located in huge, and growing, population centers. The Shenzen and other Special Economic Zones in Guangdong [Canton] Province and the Pearl River Delta, around Hong Kong, are in an area with about 80 million people. Companies based in Hong Kong are estimated already to employ as many as 3 million factory workers in this region.

---

der terms of a 1984 agreement between the governments of China and the United Kingdom. Hundreds of thousands in Hong Kong, the Chinese mainland, and immigrant Chinese communities in New York City and elsewhere took to the streets that week to celebrate the end of more than 150 years of British colonial rule. The representatives of the British and U.S. governments to the July 1 turnover ceremonies boycotted the installation of Hong Kong's new Provisional Legislature, claiming they could not in good conscience seem to approve a body appointed by the Chinese government. London ruled Hong Kong with no elected legislature of any kind until 1985. The first full direct elections to the Crown-imposed Legislative Council were held in 1995.

Among Deng Xiaoping's pithy sayings of late was one this past January, during a visit to Guangdong. In another twenty years, Deng said, the province would become the "Fifth Small Dragon" of Asia, joining Singapore, Taiwan, South Korea, and Hong Kong itself. Think of the depth of the political bankruptcy! The main spokesperson of a supposedly socialist country says the goal they are pursuing — and are well along the road to achieving — is to become more like Singapore, Taiwan, South Korea, and Hong Kong.

But that is the goal of the dominant wing of the bourgeois-minded bureaucratic caste in China. Desperately poor peasants are being drawn from the countryside and into the cities, where to survive they are forced to work long hours, under extreme speedup, for minimal wages in both state- and capitalist-owned factories. In the medium term, these conditions will permit a relatively rapid economic expansion.

The Tories did not send Chris Patten, the former party chairman, to be the new governor of Hong Kong as a throwaway. The imperialists are already fighting over which of them will get the biggest shares of investment in China — and British capital is already losing out to its rivals in Tokyo and on Wall Street, and even to capitalists in Taiwan and Singapore. Hong Kong capital itself accounts for well over half of all foreign investment in China.[9] The southern and central coastal areas of China are further advanced in the introduction of capitalist methods and foreign capital than some Stalinist regimes in Eastern Europe or the Soviet Union were by the end of the 1980s.

In 1991 there was nearly $5 billion of new foreign investment in China, for example. This year, at the rate of the first three months, it will be in the range of $10 billion. China is becoming a much bigger market for foreign capitalist investment than the Soviet Union and

9. In 1996 Hong Kong still accounted for nearly 40 percent of all foreign capital investment in China. The next largest amounts of capital came from the United States and Singapore (around 9 percent each); Taiwan and Japan (around 7 percent each); and south Korea (nearly 6 percent).

all of Eastern Europe combined.[10] Just last month Beijing announced that still another Special Economic Zone, the sixth, will be opened. This one will not be in southern China, but in the north in Manchuria, the border region between Russia and North Korea, widening the area opened to imperialism.

The Japanese, U.S., and other capitalists investing in China think they have died and gone to heaven. They have most of the rights of capitalists, but the state "handles" the workers for them. The state, including the Communist Party and its functionaries, makes sure the workers do not get out of line on the job, do not strike — do not do much except work very hard, for very long hours, for very little pay. It seems like a dream!

Of course, the dream will not last. As capitalist exploitation increases throughout China, so do strikes, peasant protests, and attacks on bosses. A few weeks ago, for example, the *New York Times* ran an article headlined, "Capitalist-Style Layoffs Ignite Sabotage and Strikes in China." The home of a Chinese bank director, a "reformer," had been firebombed after he had fired numerous workers. In another case, a factory boss known for "Western-style management" had been run over by a truck, and workers at the plant rejected the government's proposal to honor him as a "martyr" for reform. The article cited spreading wildcat strikes, sabotage, and smashing of machinery across China. The *Times* reporter noted that these "incidents suggest that opposition to fundamental changes is increasingly coming not only from octogenarian Communist hard-

---

10. In 1996 China was the recipient of $45.3 billion of foreign direct investment. That accounted for some 40 percent of all investment in plant and equipment that year in the Third World combined, and was a billion dollars more than the total foreign direct investment in Eastern Europe and the former USSR as a whole for 1990–96. In face of the currency crisis that swept across Asia beginning in 1997, the propertied classes slowed their export of capital to China, which had rapidly accelerated up to that point in the 1990s. In both 1997 and 1998 the inflow of foreign direct investment into China stagnated at roughly $45 billion each year.

liners but also from many ordinary blue-collar workers."[11]

Ignore the correspondent's imaginary bloc between angry workers and senile Stalinists. The resistance reported in the article is real, however. Workers in China will conduct more fights like these, and they will eventually link up with dissatisfied peasants and also win support from young people attracted to the working class as the force that can revitalize society. *That will be the real bloc.* It will be forged through enormous class battles, and as that happens growing numbers of fighters will be open to the ideas of the communist movement.

In preparing for what is coming in Asia, we should remember that there is a big difference between the position of United States imperialism in that part of the world and its position in Europe. In the wake of the U.S. victory in World War II, U.S. imperialism engineered the NATO alliance as the codification of its permanent European presence. Ever since the war, Washington has been the dominant "European" power. As interimperialist conflict and class struggles intensify across capitalist Europe, as well as in Central and Eastern Europe, those battles take place with the reality of the U.S.-dominated NATO existing cheek and jowl with the European Community and various military alliances among the European ruling classes themselves. According to the interests of each national ruling class, there will be both shifting alliances with Washington and growing conflicts with it, as the U.S. rulers tenaciously hold on to their military foothold in Europe as part of maintaining their dominance in the world imperialist system.

In Asia, on the other hand, Washington still has to bring its power to bear under conditions more comparable to the 1920s and 1930s.

---

11. In July 1997 the *China Market Economic News,* a Chinese government publication, reported that labor disputes were up 59 percent in the first half of 1997 compared to the same period in 1996, continuing an upward trend. "Our nation is now in a period of numerous labor disputes and they are ever more complicated and varied, with new situations emerging in an endless stream," the newspaper said.

U.S. forces intervene militarily in the region, of course, and some 100,000 U.S. troops are stationed in Japan, Korea, and aboard warships afloat in the Pacific. But U.S. imperialism is not integrated as the dominant force in any Asian military alliance with other powers. That makes U.S. armed intervention in Asia less "legitimate" and thus more explosive, and the reactions to such aggression across the region will be explosive as well.[12]

The United States ruling class is armed to the teeth and will not back off being the world's top cop — with the world's mightiest conventional and strategic nuclear arsenal in its holster. Washington is and will remain both an Atlantic and a Pacific power, and it will react to defend U.S. capitalist interests wherever, and by whomever, those interests are endangered. But it will pay the consequences.

Myth of nuclear disarmament

I do not know how the big-business press here in Britain played up Russian president Boris Yeltsin's visit to Washington earlier this month. But in the United States, and I suspect elsewhere around

---

12. An article in the July 13, 1996, issue of the London financial weekly the *Economist* pointed out: "The Americans have said they will keep about 100,000 fighting men in the Asia-Pacific area, the same number as they propose to keep in Europe. But the 100,000 in Asia are much less securely dug in than their comrades in Europe. For a start, the 20,000 American marines stationed on the Japanese island of Okinawa [are] not well loved by the locals these days.... The Americans have already given up their bases in the Philippines. And after next year their warships will no longer find a welcome in Hong Kong. If and when Korea waves the boys good-bye, that promised 100,000-man presence in the Asian-Pacific region will look pretty hazy. The real American front line may one day be no farther west than Hawaii."

This scenario glosses over the Pentagon's determination to maintain a strong U.S. military presence in Asia, as well as that of some of Washington's more vulnerable allied capitalist regimes in the region. The *Economist*, however, does highlight some of Washington's strategic weaknesses in the Pacific, as seen from the vantage point of its junior European ally and rival, British imperialism.

the world, headlines proclaimed that Yeltsin and Bush had announced plans to destroy a far greater number of nuclear warheads than had previously been anticipated. As a result, the world is supposed to be less threatened by the use of nuclear weapons.

What is actually happening, however, is the opposite of what the headlines imply.

Here in the United Kingdom, and in France as well, the imperialist governments are strengthening their nuclear arsenals, for example. Prime Minister John Major tips his hat to nuclear cutbacks, announcing plans to remove tactical nuclear warheads from aboard ships and aircraft — tactical weapons that British armed forces never had a realistic way of using. At the same time, however, London is expanding undersea nuclear weapons by installing more accurate, multiwarhead Trident II missiles on British submarines. Paris, for its part, is building five new submarines, armed with new multiwarhead missiles that will double the size of its nuclear force.

What Bush is really pushing Yeltsin to concede, in exchange for promised economic aid, is Moscow's agreement to set aside the 1972 Anti-Ballistic Missile treaty, allowing Washington the option to deploy a ground-based antiballistic missile system. The U.S. rulers intend to place themselves in a stronger position against all those powers that are continuing to build up their nuclear arsenals, and against all those that will acquire them in the coming decades. That is what the talks with Yeltsin are all about, not the destruction of nuclear weapons on the road to a more peaceful world.[13]

13. In January 1999 the Clinton administration announced plans to spend nearly $7 billion over six years to build a long-range antiballistic missile (ABM) system, similar to the "Star Wars" program pressed by the Reagan White House in the 1980s. Implementation of Clinton's plan would mark a substantial escalation of strategic weaponry, placing Washington in a position to launch a nuclear first strike for the first time since the development by the Soviet Union of a hydrogen bomb and intercontinental missiles. Constructing the planned U.S. antiballistic missile system would abrogate

There will be more armed conflict and spreading wars in coming years. More governments in every part of the world will get their hands not only on nuclear weapons but also on ballistic missile delivery systems. At the same time, however, the working class and other toilers who have to fight and die on behalf of the interests of the exploiters will be a powerful source of resistance to such wars and preparations for war. We will have the opportunity to take power out of the hands of the capitalist rulers who are responsible for war, and for the nuclear threat that continues to hang over humanity.

During the war drive and bloody onslaught against Iraq, communist workers learned in practice how we can fight to defend space in the working class and labor movement to campaign against imperialism and war. We did so even during the stage when the capitalist rulers are always most successful in mounting patriotic backing for their war efforts — when U.S. forces go into combat,

---

the 1972 ABM agreement signed by Washington and Moscow, under which both governments are currently bound not to develop such a system.

While the U.S. government claims this move is designed solely as "defense" against "threats" from "rogue nations" such as North Korea and Iraq, its first strategic target is in reality the workers state in China — which has a substantially less developed nuclear arsenal and missile system than the workers state in Russia. Beijing immediately protested Washington's announcement. "It will have a comprehensive and far-reaching impact on the strategic balance and stability of the region and world at large in the 21st century," said a Chinese foreign ministry spokesperson. The statement warned of the added danger of joint development of an antimissile system between the U.S. and other countries, clearly referring above all to the often-mentioned potential U.S. partners near China's borders, such as Taiwan, Japan, and south Korea, as well as Russia.

Already confronted with Washington's decision to expand NATO membership to several former Warsaw Pact countries close to Russia's borders, Moscow has so far refused to ratify the START II treaty on nuclear warheads reduction, which was the topic of the 1992 talks between Bush and Yeltsin referred to above. Clinton's ABM plans diminish still further the chances of any START II ratification, and bring the danger for Russia of a U.S. first-strike capacity that much closer.

but before body bags begin returning home in unexpectedly large numbers. During the Gulf War, we saw just the beginnings of how antiwar resistance can develop among workers and youth. And we will see a similar process — similar debates, similar pressures, similar opportunities — as the capitalists mount more war drives and launch new wars.

Bonapartism and the working class

The United States today is gripped by what bourgeois commentators consider a most peculiar phenomenon. Newspaper columnists, TV talk-show pundits, and academic "experts" talk about it more and more these days. They do not know what words to use to describe it — "a peculiar unease," "a mini-panic." Why, they ask, is unrest and insecurity mounting unevenly but seemingly inexorably among so many millions of people?

But there is no mystery. For some fifteen years even before U.S. capitalism entered its current depression conditions, the experience of a growing majority of working people, and increasingly of certain middle-class layers as well, has been that economic and social conditions keep getting worse and worse. The conviction is deepening among millions that no one knows where it is all heading. Under these circumstances, small but significant sections of the population do feel panic. Many of them for the first time start looking for radical answers to the problems they face, problems they are convinced the two big-business parties have neither the will nor the capacity to resolve.

The most perceptive comment on the Perot candidacy in the major U.S. press was in the *Wall Street Journal* about ten days ago.

You did not even need to read the article; the headline said it all. "Ross's Army: Meet Perot's Fans: They Crave Change, Not Specific Proposals." That was the main headline. The subhead continued: "They Span Political Spectrum, Shrug Off His Positions." That is, before Perot's backers began supporting him, they may have called themselves either a Democrat or a Republican, a liberal or a conservative or a moderate. But now they simply crave change, and they glory in his lack of specific proposals.

This is a mass psychology most of us have not seen in our political lifetimes — a widespread belief among layers of people that what is needed is not this or that particular solution, but a charismatic individual in high office who also has *the will to impose change*, whatever it may be. The conflicting class interests that underlie the rising social crisis get covered up in capitalist society; the fact that the mounting economic and social problems faced by millions are class questions is kept hidden. Nothing that happens in U.S. politics today openly takes the form of class politics.

Politically, fighting workers are the last remaining liberals in the United States today. As the bipartisan axis of social policy has kept shifting to the right over the past twenty years, most self-proclaimed liberals have become less and less liberals of the New Deal/Fair Deal variety. But fighting workers still *talk like* liberals, because it is the only politics they know. There is no politics except bourgeois politics in the United States on any mass level, and there has not been for decades.

We should never be fooled by this political reality into concluding that workers in the United States are somehow committed to bourgeois liberalism, however; they are not. Any more than we should be fooled into thinking that the working class here in Britain has moved to the right because many workers vote Conservative when the Tories promise lower taxes. No, it is just that as the Labour Party acts more and more openly as a bourgeois party, workers — if they go to the polls at all — vote under normal conditions for what they hope may at least improve their immediate situation. Both examples underline the absence of any genuinely independent political voice of the working class, either in the United States or the United Kingdom.

Nowhere in the world today, in fact, does the working class have a political voice powerful enough to be heard on any mass scale (with the exception of revolutionary Cuba, that is). Many organizations speak in the *name* of the working class — social democratic and Stalinist parties, centrist formations, union officialdoms. But none of them speaks for the *interests* of the working class. These voices *pretending* to speak for labor, pretending to speak for the traditions of socialism, actually speak as lieutenants of the capitalist rulers in decline, who are squeezing the working class.

This political misleadership, this lack of any clear working-class political alternative or program, tosses layers of workers into the same pot with hundreds of thousands, and eventually millions, from the middle classes who find the radical solutions they are looking for among demagogic voices on the far right of bourgeois politics.

Space for politics in working class

Although workers place no independent class stamp on the initial manifestations of this radicalization, opportunities do start growing under these conditions for the working class to begin to act in its own interests. These changes are virtually invisible to those outside the working class, however. Only from within the factories and the unions are these changing opportunities evident. But this increasing space to practice politics in the working class and labor movement is the most important single political fact for the communist movement today.

In the United States, this lesson was driven home to us once again recently by the explosion in the streets of Los Angeles after the acquittal of the cops who beat Rodney King. What was most striking, especially in the Los Angeles area itself, was that among workers on the job, there were no physical confrontations. The rulers were not able to whip up those kinds of divisions. Instead, in workplace after workplace, working people talked about these events, argued about them, and sometimes had heated disagreements. But workers with different viewpoints could say what they thought. This is the last thing anyone could have learned about from reading the race-baiting big-business press, however.

Communist workers had similar experiences during the Gulf War, as I mentioned earlier. But it is not just under these kinds of pressure-cooker conditions that we find space for politics in the working class. That is simply one of the payoffs for the work we do, day in and day out, talking socialism on the job with fellow workers and seeking to draw them into political discussions and activity.

This space to do politics in the working class explains why no previous presidential campaign of the Socialist Workers Party has had the kinds of opportunities open to the ticket of James Warren and Estelle DeBates this year to bring the socialist alternative — to bring real class politics — to workers in factories and at plant gates across the country. We did not even have such opportunities in 1948 when Farrell Dobbs, the SWP presidential candidate that year, was still known by fighting workers for the role he played in leading the CIO industrial union movement in the Midwest.

The communist workers movement today has only one way to test whether our assessment of the political situation and what we are doing is right or wrong. It is not by polls or election results. The test for us is whether or not the space on the job and in the unions to discuss politics, to take initiatives, and to gain a hearing for the communist point of view stays open or begins to narrow in face of today's rising class tensions and polarization. If we are right, then that space will not close down, but will instead open up, with whatever ebbs and flows.

As workers begin finding ways to fight back against the capitalist offensive, as waves of strikes and other struggles begin to accelerate, this political space will expand. The bourgeoisie cannot simply take back this space, nor can the liberals, the Stalinists, the social democrats, or the union officialdom. This space within the working class and unions can only be taken back by the bosses and their labor lieutenants through class battles in which big defeats are inflicted on the working class. Each advance and victory by workers in these battles, on the other hand, will expand that space and strengthen the prospects for independent working-class political action and organization.

Cop brutality, racist assaults, frame-ups, attacks on workers' social wage and conditions on and off the job — these attacks go on here in the United Kingdom, in the United States, and across the capitalist world. But the resistance against these attacks and the politicization of working people through our collective efforts to push them back — this too grows. But anybody trying to follow politics just by reading the bourgeois press, or to engage in politics outside the branch and union fraction structures of a proletarian party, will never know what is happening in the working class.

Reaction cannot succeed without a fight

Given the shape world capitalism is in, the ruling propertied families no longer have the option of postponing the deepening conflicts engendered by their system with social policies and concessions to broad layers of the working class. They cannot adopt new legislation that significantly expands the social wage and buffers class tensions for an extended period of time. Their declining profit rates and intensifying competition drive them in exactly the opposite direction. There is only one way the rulers can try to resolve the crisis of their social system — by taking on the working class and labor movement in battle and defeating us.

In periods of a great expansion of the world capitalist economy, such as the quarter century from the late 1940s through the early 1970s, the rulers promote a particular kind of social differentiation in the working class, economically and socially. On the basis of a real, even if modest, rise in the living standards of tens of millions of workers, the rulers maintain their domination short of a decisive fight. Wide disparities continue to exist in the working class, but the class-collaborationist labor officialdom is able to keep resistance in check by appealing to a broad enough layer whose conditions are slowly improving. That alternative is not open to the capitalists today, however, so the labor officialdom is less able than at any time in several decades to beg crumbs from the bosses' table.

Last week, I had the opportunity to be an invited guest at a joint leadership meeting in London of the Central Committee of the Communist League and the three young socialists groups that discussed and adopted the proposals before this congress. One of the young socialists at that leadership meeting asked the question: Can fascism conquer rapidly in the deformed workers states where Stalinist apparatuses have crumbled? Is that possible in Yugoslavia, for example? Is it possible in Russia or Ukraine? It was a useful question.

The answer, I believe, is no. Fascism cannot conquer there, any more than it can conquer here in the United Kingdom or any other imperialist country, until massive class battles have been fought, in the course of which the working class will have the chance to put its stamp on the outcome. Fascist reaction has never conquered on the basis of its own strength — not once in history. In every case where fascism has conquered, it has only done so following a betrayal of ascending workers struggles and mass working-class movements that were capable, with revolutionary leadership, of resolving the capitalist crisis in the interests of the toiling majority. Fascism has only triumphed in the wake of demoralization from such betrayals, which have driven the hard-pressed middle layers in society against the working class and into the arms of reaction. Such betrayals always deepen divisions within the working class and labor movement, as well.

Under those conditions, following class battles in which the workers are misled into defeats, the fascists then conquer with little effort. That is what happened in Italy at the opening of the 1920s, following the social democrats' betrayal of a wave of strikes and factory occupations. That is what happened in Germany in the early

1930s, as the Stalinists' factionalism and ultraleftism combined with the social democrats' ongoing treachery to block a powerfully organized working class from mobilizing united resistance to the Nazis' rise to power. That is what happened in Spain in the latter 1930s, when the Stalinists murdered revolutionary-minded workers and poor farmers and — aided once again by social democrats and various centrist forces, including the anarchists — destroyed any prospects for a victorious proletarian revolution. Fascism conquered in Europe on the corpses of these defeated revolutions.

Whether fascism will once again conquer in the future depends on one thing and one thing alone: whether a proletarian combat party — with a leadership that is genuinely revolutionary, genuinely communist, and genuinely working-class — can be built in time.

Better prospects for communism today

When I brought greetings from the Socialist Workers Party to the fusion congress in Canada last month, I made a remark that, to my surprise, has sparked some controversy since it was reported in the *Militant* newspaper. The article, I thought, paraphrased what I recall saying quite accurately. "Barnes stressed the fact that individuals in all parts of the world," the article reported, "are more open to being reached by the ideas of communist politics now than at any time since the opening years of the Russian revolution" — and, I would add, the first five years of the Communist International, up to sometime in the mid-1920s.

There is a sense in which this assessment has to be true if other things we are saying are true — and if there is a realistic possibility of successfully advancing along the course we are discussing here. Perhaps a good rewrite person on the city desk could have made the sentence less open to misunderstanding by phrasing it, "Barnes stressed that individuals in all parts of the world face *fewer obstacles within the working-class movement* to being reached by the ideas of communist politics" and so on. But this assessment is true, in my opinion. It's true even if the Marxist movement in the late twenties, in the mid- and late thirties, and in the forties just after World War II was capable for brief periods of mobilizing larger forces than we are currently capable of doing. The difference between those periods and today are marginal historically, since in each of the earlier cases the overwhelming majority of revolutionary-minded workers and youth who reached out for communist ideas actually ended up grasping a *counterfeit* that politically destroyed them as fighters and revolutionists.

Since the latter half of the 1920s, Stalinism has been the biggest obstacle to building a communist movement in the course of large class battles. Once the privileged bureaucratic caste was consolidated — once the Stalinists laid claim to the mantle of the Russian revolution on the basis of holding state power in the Soviet Union and dominating the Communist International — there was no way to build a mass revolutionary vanguard that could lead the working class to challenge for power *until that obstacle began to be broken up.*

Ever since then, the biggest problem confronting revolutionists within the working-class movement has not been that weak people, political cowards, or corrupt individuals have been attracted to Stalinist organizations. The problem has been that revolutionary-minded workers, peasants, and youth looking for communist answers — the best and most self-sacrificing representatives of their generations — ended up joining Stalinist organizations. They ended up internalizing ways of carrying out politics that are the counterrevolutionary opposite of communism. That was what happened to the overwhelming majority of such fighters; only small numbers somehow found their way to the communist movement.

But today that obstacle has crumbled. The Stalinists still exist and have political influence, of course. But they are no longer a force with state power in the Soviet Union and Eastern Europe, with the attendant massive resources. They find it more difficult to misrepresent themselves as the continuity of the Bolshevik-led Russian revolution and mislead fighters on the basis of that spurious political authority. As a result, the Stalinist lie that there is a way of building *national socialism* has also begun to crumble. The lie that socialism can be built by bureaucrats, social engineers, and a massive police apparatus has been weakened. And the lie of both the Stalinists and social democrats that socialism can be advanced in alliance with one or another wing of the bourgeoisie has been undermined.

As the apparatuses whose very existence depended on perpetuating such lies have begun to crack, the possibilities have opened up as never before in the past seven decades for workers and fighting youth to find their way to genuine communist ideas. That is the political conclusion our movement draws in preparing for the class battles that lie ahead for labor and our allies.

Youth and the workers movement

Recoiling from this world we have been describing, growing numbers of young people have begun radicalizing to a degree we have not seen for some years. They cannot and will not simply accept the horrors capitalism is multiplying in its decline, and they are looking for answers. Our world movement is bending every fiber and nerve to respond and attract these young fighters toward the working class.

Experience teaches us that as youth begin to politicize, they do not begin by demanding a winning strategy, or a guarantee of victories. The politicization of youth begins with their unwillingness to accept what is presented to them as the way the world has to be. "That's just the way things are." Young people simply reject that answer so often heard at home, in school, and all around them in bourgeois society — and so often acquiesced in by elders who are just plumb tuckered out. Young rebels want to say no to injustice, to racism, to antiwoman bigotry, to immigrant scapegoating, to cops, to reaction in all its forms. They want to say no to all brutality and corruption, in the deepest sense of those words.

Growing numbers of young people sense the devastating social consequences of a protracted world depression. They sense that racism and chauvinism are somehow inseparably connected with the workings of the system itself. They awake to the reality that those with wealth and power cannot be counted on to stop short of resorting to fascist terror to suppress resistance to injustice. They feel the social forces dominating the existing order marching toward broader and more horrible wars.

Even if young fighters are not yet politically equipped to think it out to the end, they sense that there have been important changes in the Black population, in the immigrant population, and among women compared to what they have heard about and read about from the past. They sense that these oppressed layers and allies of the working class have greater social weight than the last time there was a broad social and political radicalization in the industrially advanced countries in which the weight of the working class was decisive — during the Great Depression of the 1930s. Young people identify with the struggles against racist discrimination, anti-immigrant chauvinism, and women's second-class status. They are attracted to political fights, whether in the countries where they live or elsewhere, and want to understand what these struggles are really about. They want to learn about and discuss the most basic ideas about how capitalist society operates — to discover the underlying social forces and most basic class dynamics.

Some of you have read the four-volume series by Farrell Dobbs on the fight to build the Teamsters union and a class-struggle leadership of the labor movement in the United States in the 1930s, as well as his two books on the forging of a communist movement in the United States, *Revolutionary Continuity*.[14] If so,

---

14. The four volumes in the Teamster series are *Teamster Rebellion, Teamster*

you will remember that at the opening of the first book in both series, Farrell describes his own political evolution as a young person. Only a year or so before Farrell was leading more workers in combat in a revolutionary manner than any other strike leader of the decade, he was a young worker who did not know whether to vote Democrat or Republican in the 1932 elections and ended up casting his ballot for Herbert Hoover. Just a year earlier, Farrell recounts, he had run across H.G. Wells's *History of the World* in the Omaha public library and read it line by line, hoping to find some ideas on what the world of the Great Depression was all about and where it had come from. Farrell says he read it twice before giving up on discovering anything in it that helped. If he had found the Communist Manifesto, not H.G. Wells, at the library instead, then he might have picked it up first and gotten some answers that began making sense.

We should not be surprised when young people and other fighters pick up the Communist Manifesto off a literature table, or select it from the shelf at a Pathfinder bookstore, or borrow it from a co-worker or a friend. We should not be surprised when prisoners or individuals fighting frame-up charges get interested in reading *Socialism on Trial* by James P. Cannon — part of the trial record of revolutionists framed up at the beginning of World War II for organizing working-class opposition to the coming slaughter — in order to get an initial understanding of what the entire capitalist system is all about.

Many young people dislike who they are becoming in this world. The entire system is set up to corrupt us, to make "I," "me," "mine" all we care about. I do not believe any young person becomes a revolutionist without part of the decision involving a rejection of this me-centered approach to life. Young people aspire to some higher

---

Power, Teamster Politics, and *Teamster Bureaucracy.* The two volumes of *Revolutionary Continuity: Marxist Leadership in the United States* are subtitled, "The Early Years: 1848–1917" and "Birth of the Communist Movement, 1918–1922." All six books are published by Pathfinder.

values than cutthroat competition to "look out for number one." They cannot stand the person they are going to become if they do not do something different, if they do not change themselves as they work with others to change the world.

The revolutionary workers movement does not promise anything to young people except the chance to do just that. We make that one promise. We say we are convinced that the communist movement is the most effective way to organize together to fight to remake the world — by building a revolutionary working-class movement and, in the process, transforming ourselves and each other.

Ideas, a class, and a tradition

Young fighters are ultimately attracted to a class. Whether they know it or not initially, they are attracted to the social weight and potential strength of the working class, its struggles, and its organizations.

Youth must also be offered a tradition. Without a political tradition, there is no chance whatsoever of building a working-class movement. Moreover, young people have to find living carriers of that tradition, fighters whose experience draws from more than one generation of working-class struggle. Youth have to find others like themselves from previous generations whom they can join with in building a common movement.

Just being a radical, just being against the bourgeoisie, just negating bourgeois values is no more likely to lead somebody to communism than to fascism. We should think about the political implications of this fact. It is only finding the working-class movement, and finding the human beings who carry its tradition, that leads rebel youth in the direction of communism.

Communists sometimes underestimate, or even disparage, the importance of tradition. But we should never do so. Proletarian tradition is the opposite of maudlin sentimentality. We should never forget that revolutionists only have a tradition today because workers who came before us fought so hard, for so many decades to maintain it.

The Stalinists severed that tradition in the *mass* workers movement more than sixty years ago. The continuity of organized, living forces whose traditions in the workers movement went back over interlinked generations to Marx and Engels and to the Bolsheviks and Communist International in Lenin's time — that revolutionary continuity was maintained only by a force that had marginal weight in the labor movement through most of those decades. Not long after World War II, that political continuity was completely severed in the Soviet Union, even on the level of tiny groups or individual cadres; nobody was left to carry on the fight, and no new generation of communists has yet come forward. Without such traditions, without a braiding of revolutionary generations, there is no communism and cannot be.

The largest and most established parties around the world that had historic links to the Soviet Union and called themselves communist ceased well over half a century ago to be communist in any way. Given this reality, the prospect over time that the Marxist tradition — and *any* living bearers of it — would also be obliterated was the greatest historic threat facing the working class.

This is why communists explain that if all the libraries in the world were suddenly to burn down tomorrow, the class rule of the bourgeoisie would not be shaken — it wouldn't even be felt, except for the loss of some technical and scientific manuals, perhaps. Social ideas are not a necessity for the bourgeoisie. The exploiting classes have no ideas, need no ideas, and use no ideas. Until they are overthrown, the law of value serves them and saves them. The rulers have state power, and they use it ruthlessly to maintain the capitalist property relations upon which their wealth and prerogatives depend. They have a monopoly over land and the means of production. What they call ideas are just the rationalizations of that monopoly against any challenges by thinking workers and youth — their class ideology. Without a single library, the capitalists would keep on exploiting workers and farmers, producing profits, using the armed power of the state against working people at home and abroad — and generating "ideas," and professors and writers and preachers to package those "ideas."

To the workers movement, on the other hand, the ideas of a living class tradition are a matter of life or death. They are the political generalizations of the efforts of the workers movement to learn from our experience in the battle to eliminate capitalism, so we can make fewer mistakes in the battles to come. It is to these ideas, to the working class, and to a living communist tradition carried by generations of fighters from that class that revolutionary youth can be and will be won. This is the only road along which science and the forces of production can be kept from becoming hellish forces of destruction.

Students, youth, and a turn party

As we attract young forces to us, some will be students. Being a student is not an occupation; it is a temporary condition. Students are not a class. The length of time someone is a student is very brief.

In winning students to the communist movement, it is important for us to remember that when they end their formal studies, or whether they graduate from whatever school they are enrolled in, is their decision to make. One way or another, the decision to get a job will be upon them very quickly: the need for food, shelter, transportation — that takes care of the whole thing. It's not a party decision; it's an individual decision, one which the party takes no position on. A party of industrial workers that openly says what kind of organization we are out to build will only gain by the recruitment of student youth.

Since the dissolution of the Young Socialist Alliance in the United States, several of the students who have joined the SWP said they had previously been uncomfortable in doing so, because they weren't sure what the party's attitude was toward recruiting students. Since they had picked up conflicting attitudes from different party members, these comrades just stayed in the YSA in sort of a holding pattern. So it's important to get this clarified. The SWP, of course, wants to recruit revolutionary-minded students. We want to recruit young people whose experience in our movement convinces both them and the party that they agree with our political goals. That's the way we will win them to the perspective of getting into an industrial union fraction once they — and they alone — decide to stop going to school. By explicit decision, this is the one exception the party makes to our norm that individuals being considered for membership by a branch agree to join the jobs committee and get into a union fraction. By confidently asking these former YSA members to join the party, and explaining why we thought they would strengthen a turn party, we were able to recruit them.

Today is not the first time the communist movement has addressed the question of winning students, and we have done so under widely varying conditions. It was Lenin who explained this the best, recognizing it also as a serious theoretical question of importance in building a communist movement. Lenin, moreover, was operating in a time and place in which virtually all university students, unlike today, were from families in the propertied or middle classes; only the tiniest handfuls were from working-class or modest peasant backgrounds. But Lenin was outraged by those in the Marxist movement in Russia who sought to rationalize abstention from political activity among students by portraying them as a homogenous social class with interests hostile to the toilers. Students are in a period of transition in their lives, he explained. They "are not cut off from the rest of society and therefore always and inevitably reflect the political groupings of society as a whole."[15]

Without the renewal and braiding together of generations, through which the tradition of the communist workers movement can be maintained and applied in living class politics, no proletarian party can survive. A shrinking organization, with an aging membership, might formally retain a communist program, but without the recruitment and political integration of youth its

15. "The Tasks of the Revolutionary Youth" in Lenin's *Collected Works*, vol. 7 (Moscow: Progress Publishers, 1965), p. 49.

character as a disciplined workers party will wither away. A communist organization must have a spread of generations linked together as a living revolutionary movement.

"We need young forces," Lenin insistently wrote from exile to party leaders in Russia during the opening days of the 1905 revolution. "The youth — the students, and still more so the young workers — will decide the issue of the whole struggle. Get rid of all the old habits of immobility, of respect for rank, and so on. . . . Do not fear their lack of training, do not tremble at their inexperience and lack of development. . . . Either you create *new*, young, fresh, energetic, battle organizations everywhere for revolutionary . . . work of all varieties among all strata, or you will go under wearing the halo of 'committee' bureaucrats."[16]

Coming out of the retreat in working-class political activity of the 1950s, the Socialist Workers Party in the United States confronted the problem of a "missing generation." Relatively few students or young workers had been recruited since the late 1940s. The party remained proletarian in outlook, in our organizational norms and habits of political conduct, and in our social composition — the majority of party members in most branches were still industrial workers. But we had been forced to retreat from our structure of national union fractions.

By the early 1960s youth were beginning to be recruited to the newly formed Young Socialist Alliance, and — largely through the YSA — to the SWP as well. We won young fighters from civil rights struggles, then from activity in defense of the Cuban revolution, and then at an accelerating pace from the anti–Vietnam War movement and battles for Black rights, Chicano rights, and women's equality. As we did so, however, the SWP was initially not yet strong enough to rebuild itself as a party structured around industrial union fractions. That required some further changes in the objective situation, combined with step-by-step leadership preparations for the turn to

16. "Letter to Bogdanov and Gusev," in *Collected Works*, vol. 8, p. 146.

industry beginning in the late 1960s. This is all described in some detail in *The Changing Face of U.S. Politics*.

Today, the SWP and other organizations in our world movement are more fortunate in this regard. If we are right about the world we are discussing at this congress, then we will have a structure of both party branches and union fractions in place as opportunities increase to win students and young workers to the communist movement. As we act on the proposals before us here, and continue building parties along the lines presented in *The Changing Face of U.S. Politics*, drawing young forces toward us, including students, will strengthen the proletarian character of our parties, the turn, and our industrial union fractions.

Auxiliary organizations

The maneuver our entire world movement is confronting is a necessary step along the road to relaunching communist youth organizations. This has been an important aspect of building the international Marxist movement throughout this century.

Youth organizations are among the political formations that Lenin referred to as "auxiliary organizations" of the communist party. I have always liked that term, because it is precise and political — and not sentimental. A communist workers party, once it reaches a certain size, begins to build women's organizations, peasants' and rural toilers' associations, organizations of trade unionists, writers' groups, and youth organizations. Without these auxiliary organizations — that is what they were called by the Communist International in Lenin's day — a communist party would never be able to lead the workers and their oppressed and toiling allies to take power, hold it, and use it.

Auxiliary groups organize independently of the communist party, but they are programmatically subordinated to it. They take their political lead from the communist party. They are different in this way from various united front or other mass organizations that communists also participate in. Auxiliary organizations help the communist movement transform its institutions into stronger ones that reach more deeply into our class and its allies.

Within this broader context, Lenin called attention to the particular character and tasks of communist youth organizations. "Necessarily, the youth must come to socialism *in a different way, by other paths, in other forms, under other circumstances* than their fathers," Lenin wrote in 1916. "Incidentally, this is why we must be decidedly in favor of the *organizational independence* of the Youth League, not only because the opportunists fear this independence, but because of the very nature of the case; for unless they have complete independence the youth *will be unable* either to train good Socialists from their midst, or to prepare themselves to lead socialism *forward.*

"We stand for complete independence of the Youth Leagues, but also," Lenin added, "for complete freedom for comradely criticism of their errors. We must not flatter the youth."[17]

Communist youth organizations are historically the first auxiliary organization that a communist party becomes strong enough to help build and sustain politically. This does not happen along a straight line, however. Over the more than sixty-year history of the Socialist Workers Party, for example, there have been periods when we have had no youth organizations of any kind; periods when particular branches have launched youth committees; and periods when we have had national youth organizations such as the YSA. There is no smooth history. There are no rules that can be applied by rote.

If building independent communist youth organizations is our goal, then why are we now proposing a fusion of the Communist League and socialist youth groups here in the United

---

17. "The Youth International," in *Collected Works,* vol. 23, p. 164. This article, and others cited in this article, are also available in *Lenin on Youth* (Moscow: Progress Publishers, 1967). See also the "Theses on the Youth Movement," adopted by the Executive Committee of the Communist International in August 1920, printed in *Workers of the World and Oppressed Peoples Unite!* pp. 999–1001, part of Pathfinder's series The Communist International in Lenin's Time.

Kingdom? Why was the Young Socialist Alliance dissolved earlier this year in the United States, and the Young Socialists groups in Canada a few weeks ago? That is a question anyone with common sense would ask, and we have to be able to answer it.

The answer is that the combined forces of our parties and youth, considered as a common movement, are simply not strong enough today to organize as separate entities that can advance together in a sustainable way. We cannot do it because of the blows our class took in the 1980s, and their registration in the declining size and rising average age of our parties. And if our parties are not strong enough to help sustain politically viable youth organizations right now, then for certain the youth groups themselves are not strong enough to do so. Instead, the road to putting both our parties and the youth into the best position to rebuild youth organizations is a fusion of our forces. That is the conclusion both party and youth leaderships have come to in North America this year, and I believe it is true here in the United Kingdom too. Anyway, that is the decision this congress has been called to discuss and vote on.

The question before us is not whether our parties and the youth groups, taken separately, can be reformed and strengthened. Is there something else we could do, some preferable alternative? Can our parties somehow, on our own steam, achieve the modest renewal and reinforcement that is the goal of this fusion? Can the youth organization? That is a political judgment of organizations — not a judgment of individual cadres. Our movement is made up of capable, intelligent, hard-working, and self-sacrificing revolutionaries. If that were not the case, then fusing our forces would not accomplish anything.

Our problem is not one of political capacity, understanding, or will. It is a matter of making an objective assessment of the strength of our organizations *today* — not a few years ago, and we hope not a few years from now. At present, however, we cannot do what our parties need without the fusion, nor can we help the young fighters in and around our movement take the next steps toward a viable communist youth organization.

First, we need to draw on our common forces, including our younger members, to give some new life to all the institutions of the communist movement. These institutions are built by the party, not by a youth organization. But they are the political property of the movement as a whole to be used in winning fighters to communism, and they are open to other fighters who want to use them as well.

To the degree the fusion is a success, we will reinvigorate our weekly sales of the *Militant*, *Perspectiva Mundial*, and *New International*, and of Pathfinder books and pamphlets through our bookstores, street tables, and sales on the job. More workers and youth will start coming to the weekly Militant Labor Forums and dropping by Pathfinder bookstores to browse, talk politics, and pick up another title or two. Our socialist election campaigns will become more timely and politically focused, and we will involve more young people in our weekly plant-gate sales teams. This is the road along which our combined forces can take the next steps in strengthening these proletarian institutions, enabling us more effectively to carry out revolutionary propaganda and educational work according to the rhythms of a turn party, and to recruit.

The fusion gives us the best chance to renew the party's character as a campaigning party. It puts us on a better footing to be more timely in our response to political developments, to take initiatives, to reach out to work with others around common goals, and to take our communist arsenal to fighters on the streets and picket lines who are looking for and need these political ideas. When young workers watch us go into action, we want them to see others like themselves. They need to see a party in tune with what they are experiencing, feeling, and trying to figure out.

That is the kind of party that can recruit and can collaborate with and help build a communist youth organization when the time comes. This is the road both to stronger, more proletarian parties and to an international communist youth movement. And this road is open to us because of the strengths of each of the organizations represented here today — the Communist League and the three young socialists groups. It is open to us because the leaderships of these organizations have demonstrated the capacity to see this opportunity and act on it.

With this common perspective, moreover, we will be able to collaborate more effectively as a common international movement. We will be stronger than simply the sum of our parts. We will be a bigger help politically to other revolutionists around the world who want to work with us, discuss politics, and mount a better organized and more powerful challenge to imperialist oppression and capitalist exploitation in all its forms. So, the international stakes of the fusion are bigger than the fortunes of revolutionists here in the United Kingdom or in other countries where our world movement currently has organizations. Other political forces, other young fighters have a direct stake in what we do as well.

If this course is the correct one, then in addition to attracting individual young people to the communist movement, our strengthened organizations should also be better able to converge politically with some "clumps" of young fighters. We should be able to fight alongside them, to share experiences and ideas with them. We are no longer blocked off from reaching young fighters today by the sheer weight of some massive bureaucratic force, such as the Stalinists. Our capacity to attract even one or two small groups of young revolutionists to the communist movement over the next year or so will enhance possibilities for further gains and broader convergence.

If we do not see all these dimensions of the fusion perspective, then the importance of the decision you are discussing here at this congress is diluted. Above all, we would miss how important *you* and *your deeds* are in making possible this next step forward.

The election of leadership
At the conclusion of this congress, delegates will elect a leadership. The formalities will be very important. The motion placed before you by the joint meeting of the Communist League and Young So-

cialists leaderships last weekend is that the congress elect a twelve-person Central Committee, five of whom must have been members of the young socialists organizations taking part in this fusion.

Electing a Central Committee is ordinarily quite a simple task. The criteria are straightforward. First, we consider which comrades, as part of a disciplined cadre that functions collectively, have taken the lead most consistently since the last congress in advancing the work of the turn party in the United Kingdom. Second, we work to ensure that the leadership reflects the generations that make up the party in order to move forward together on the basis of a shared communist tradition. We take many other concrete factors into account, but all of them relate in one way or another to these two criteria. Here, too, *The Changing Face of U.S. Politics* is our best guide.

If delegates adopt the proposals that are before this congress, however, you will have to weigh an additional factor. You will have to decide which five members of the Young Socialists demonstrated the greatest leadership capacities in building *those three organizations*, so we could all reach this stage in strengthening the communist movement in Britain. That, and that alone, must be the criterion for choosing those five; otherwise this is not a fusion.

I repeat, a fusion is a very formal affair. We can allow ourselves to be informal about many things; we are small and know each other quite well. But in electing a leadership at this congress, too much informality would lead to damaging mistakes. In doing so, we do not have to exaggerate anything. We know that the three Young Socialists groups are small, and that many of their members are also members of the Communist League. But if the fusion is possible because of the strengths of the organizations coming into it, then we have to add the criterion of leadership in the Young Socialists to those we would ordinarily consider in electing a Central Committee.

Farrell Dobbs often said that if a communist organization gets down to just two generations in its cadre, it is within a couple years of extinction. If it spans three generations, it still has a chance. If it has four, then it can start cookin'.

The communist movement in the United Kingdom is lucky in this regard. In your active cadre you have individuals from the generation that became communists during World War II and the great labor upsurge that followed it, and also from the time of the Korean War a few years later, in the early 1950s. You have a few comrades of the generation that became communists and built our movement in the 1960s and early 1970s, the years of the Cuban revolution, the international movement against the war in Vietnam, and new struggles for equality by women and Blacks. You have a substantially larger number who came to our movement in the late 1970s and the 1980s, under the impact of the Nicaraguan and Grenadan revolutions, with the new impulse that gave to Cuba, and to the rising struggle in South Africa; those were also the years when we began the steady course of rebuilding our industrial union fractions and transforming the work of the party in that process. In a very real way, the Communist League was forged out of the political struggle to respond to those challenges as a proletarian internationalist party.

And now the communist movement in Britain has another generation, the one that has brought us to this special congress, these opportunities, and this set of decisions. It is the political generation that has built the Young Socialists groups. We are taking another step here in braiding the initial forces of this newest generation with the rest.

Two conflicting world views

There are only two conflicting views of the world today that are of basic interest or importance.

According to one view, there is no question that since the events of 1989–90, the "West" is well along the way to conquering the "East." Recognizing that there will inevitably be some difficulties, the proponents of this view believe that capitalism will triumph in all the workers states where the Stalinist regimes have crumbled; capital will prevail worldwide. American "restructuring" and "cost-cutting" will sweep the world. Some go as far as saying that this triumph of what they call "democratic capitalism," or "liberal democracy," represents "the end of history." Much will change in centuries to come, they say, and there may even still be wars, but humanity has at last settled on the global social system that will prevail through the ages.

To this communists counterpose our world view. What capitalism has in store is not a long wave of economic expansion and political democracy, but worldwide depression, deepening social crisis and the rise of Bonapartism, increasing interimperialist conflicts, and the march toward fascism and World War III. Moreover, what disintegrated in Central and Eastern Europe and the former Soviet Union was not socialism; these Stalinist regimes were the transmission belts within the workers movement of capitalist values and pressures against the toilers in those horribly deformed workers states and worldwide. What the future holds is growing resistance by working people to the pressures and conflicts generated by capitalism. That struggle will bring the workers of the world together to fight for their interests, which are the interests of the great majority of humankind.

According to the first view, there is a new rise of nationalism worldwide that has begun to dominate politics and will continue to do so in the decades ahead. Ethnic and religious conflicts, including the specter of "Islamic fundamentalism" in the "East," will tear peoples apart and lead to new horrors around the globe.

To that communists counterpose our view: the soviet alternative, *soviet power* — such as the world witnessed during the opening years of the Russian revolution. The historic line of march of our class is to build a socialist world, in which people of all national origins, languages, and skin colors work together — as free men and women — in a world without borders, nationalities, or "eth-nic" identities.

According to the first view, the working class is finished as a factor for revolutionary change in the world. Socialism is finished; communism is finished. The rulers do not even have to worry about them anymore, and the toiling majority should now place this chapter behind them.

To that communists counterpose our conviction that the workers' fight for socialism is nowhere close to having been re-solved. Although we are still in the very early stages, the working class is moving toward big class battles in the decades ahead, in the course of which workers will have the best chance in history to conquer power and establish workers and farmers govern-ments. There is no guarantee that the working class will succeed in this round, but we will have our chance on a world scale to overturn capitalist social relations once and for all and open a socialist future.

Above all, the outcome will be shaped by what worker-bolsheviks do *today* to utilize the space that exists to carry out communist poli-tics. That will determine whether we have the kind of disciplined workers parties, whose cadres have internalized the necessary prole-tarian norms and values, that can respond and grow rapidly in face of explosive political developments.

Surely, this was the glory of the Bolshevik Party under Lenin's leadership long before 1917. Almost no one in the international bourgeoisie, or in the increasingly bankrupt leadership of the world Socialist movement of that time, thought that this small political current in Russia would ever amount to anything. But it never occurred to the Bolsheviks that they were doing anything else but preparing to lead the workers and peasants to storm heaven, as Marx said of the Paris Communards of 1871, and to emerge victorious. The Bolsheviks did not rely on any apparatus anywhere in the world for assistance; they based themselves on political and financial support from factory workers and other toilers in Russia.

After the October 1917 revolution, the Bolsheviks were looked at around the world as if they were men and women from nowhere. But the Bolsheviks themselves knew that this was far from the truth. Because they knew something that no one in the bourgeoisie in Russia or anywhere else knew or was interested in. The Bolsheviks knew what was happening in the working class in Russia. They knew that nothing had been settled — not by tsarist repression, not by the defeat of the 1905 revolution, not by the capitalist profits that were accompanying the industrial transformation of Russia. They were solidly based among worker-bolsheviks in the factories — politically trained cadres who used the space they had in the working class. They knew their class would have its chance.

So when the revolutionary crisis broke out in early 1917 under the devastating strains of the imperialist slaughter, the Bolsheviks were able within months to take the leadership of millions of workers and peasants in struggle and lead them to the conquest of power.

There was no guarantee for the Bolsheviks then, and there is none for us now. But it can be done. It was done in Russia, and the way the Bolsheviks did it is what we seek to emulate.

REPORT SUMMARY

The following is the summary presentation on the congress discussion of the world political report.

Greater openings for the communist movement

The issues before our world movement have been joined in the discussion at this congress on two levels: our political analysis, and the fusion maneuver itself and its political and organizational implications. I will try to respond on both levels, so the questions and decisions before the delegates are as clear as possible.

One comrade disagreed with the statement in the report, reaffirming what I said at the fusion convention in Canada last month, that "individuals in all parts of the world are more open to being reached by the ideas of communist politics now than at any time since the opening years of the Russian revolution." This question is important, because it has practical implications for the work of our movement. In particular, it has direct consequences for the amount of resources and leadership effort we put into the production of Pathfinder books and pamphlets and the other propaganda weapons our world movement produces — *New International*, the *Militant*, *Perspectiva Mundial*.

Using the leverage of Pathfinder books

In assessing what the Pathfinder arsenal helps open up for the communist movement worldwide, I find the mechanical concept of *leverage* to be a useful one. That is, when we apply our weight to that lever, it gives us the ability to exert greater force than our size and strength alone would allow. Through Pathfinder books and pamphlets and the *New International* magazine, we reach more fighters, young people, and workers around the world who can be attracted to Marxist ideas than communists have been able to do for many decades.

Properly understood, propaganda work is what the communist movement does, almost exclusively, at this stage in the class struggle. That is how we advance our goal of building combat parties that are proletarian in composition and in their organizational norms and structure. We distribute our books, pamphlets, magazines, and newspapers as widely as possible, and we try to attract fighters toward us through our bookstores, weekly forums, election campaigns, and other institutions. The protest actions we participate in together with others are propaganda too. That is all they can be at this stage in the class struggle. That is the character of the actions we helped build during the Gulf War. That is what we are doing when we organize demonstrations against cop brutality, or in defense of abortion clinics, or to oppose U.S. policy toward Cuba, or even an action in solidarity with a strike in most cases.

Communist organizations do not yet have any social weight in the unions or mass movement anywhere in the world, and we have not had for decades. Opportunities for experience in class combat and mass working-class action are still very limited, not just for communists but for other fighters and revolutionists in most parts of the world. In years ahead, moreover, when worker-bolsheviks will be in the thick of leading millions in disciplined mass class combat, communist parties will continue campaigning and propagandizing, only on a much larger scale.

In the report, I said our ability to reach fighters with communist ideas was greater today than at any time "since the opening years of the Russian revolution," not "since 1917." The latter would not be correct, since there were great revolutionary openings for communists in countries around the world during the first decade following the revolution. But this was already beginning to change by the mid-1920s, and there was a qualitative shift by at least the end of 1928.

What happened during the subsequent sixty-four years is certainly no revelation to the communist movement. We know that history very well. After the first levies of revolutionists who came to our movement in 1928 and 1929 out of the Communist parties in the United States and other countries as they were becoming Stalinized, we never once broke off a significant current, even a small one, from the Stalinist movement.

Our movement can point with pride to many accomplishments over these years, including our leadership role in class combat in the Teamsters struggles of the mid- and late 1930s. Despite those achievements, however, for every fighter our movement won to the communist tradition, the Stalinists attracted a hundred, five hundred, a thousand to block that tradition and undermine it. They did so in the most damaging way — from inside the workers movement, using the power of the existing fact in Russia and its red glow to politically corrupt fighters. And all this was done in the name of communism.

Not only was a massive murder machine consolidated in the Soviet Union based on a broad, petty-bourgeois social layer, but it also laid claim to the legacy of Marxism, its literature, history, and traditions. This Stalinist apparatus turned the overwhelming majority of potential communists in the working-class and national liberation movements into *pseudo*communists who believed they *were* communists, and who believed one of their duties to be the physical marginalization, if not the murder, of apostate communists. Moscow and the leaderships subservient to it convinced fighters and revolutionists that their biggest enemy was the small minority who fought to continue a communist course. And the Stalinists organized their cadres to support — and participate in — the persecution and prosecution of communists and other revolutionists for decades.

During the discussion, a comrade described what it is like to have a Stalinist for a shop steward. While I am sure that is true, we should also keep it in perspective. In the old days, if a Stalinist shop steward saw a worker in an auto plant talking to one of us, that worker would be punished for stepping out of line. Something would happen the very next day, and that co-worker would not talk to us again. That was common; every communist who lived through that period had to confront it. The Stalinists — in the United States, in Britain, all over the world — broke up meetings, beat up workers selling communist literature, assaulted picket lines, and organized assassinations of revolutionists and other fighters.

The strength of Stalinism gave social democracy a new lease on life as well. The Stalinists and social democrats always claim to hate each other. On one level, they do; they ultimately served different masters — the parasitic regime in Moscow, on the one hand, and the imperialist ruling classes, on the other. For a few years in the late 1920s and early 1930s the Stalinists called the social democrats "social fascists." The social democrats decried "totalitarian communism." Notwithstanding, the Stalinists and social democrats have come together many times in "popular fronts" to make sure the working class stays under the thumb of the capitalist state and does not threaten the international status quo. They compete for union posts, but are also quick to make common cause against the ranks whenever necessary. Together, Stalinism and social democracy reinforce the scope of class collaborationism in the labor movement and the officialdom's charade as socialists.

Under these conditions, which dominated international working-class politics for the better part of a century, our movement was never able to win any substantial group of fighters away from Stalinism to communism. Whether they remained in those parties or simply dropped away from the workers movement over time, they were destroyed as principled working-class fighters and revolutionists. The impossibility of winning significant forces away from the Stalinist parties was not something our founding cadres had initially anticipated, and it was the biggest disappointment in the history of our movement. The Stalinist murder machine had hijacked the Soviet government and Communist Party, and Stalinism came to be seen as the ideology upholding the banner of communism. That was the great obstacle that communists faced. That is what it took us the longest to understand and come to grips with objectively after 1928–29.

It reminds me of what Malcolm X confronted after he broke with the Nation of Islam in early 1964, taking a small layer of his closest associates with him. What was Malcolm's biggest disappointment after that? It was discovering that he could not carve anything further out of the cadres of the Nation of Islam, even a month after he left it. As that became clear, he began looking in other directions.

The qualitative enormity of the Stalinist obstacle to the influence of the communist movement and our ideas is now behind us, however. *That is what has changed.* Yes, the Stalinists are still around in large numbers, and will continue to be. But shorn of any linkage to state power falsely endowed with historical authority, the material basis of Stalinist organizations, the trough from which they fed, has now substantially dried up. They have been irreversibly weakened. And this decline of Stalinism weakens social democracy and a number of ultraleft and centrist currents in the workers movement as well.

We are seeing a differentiation and transformation of various Stalinist formations. The Communist parties in France, Greece, and Portugal, for example, remain relatively traditional Stalinist parties, although with declining memberships and peripheries to varying degrees. Their leaders are still the same thugs they always were, but they cannot get away with nearly as much today because of the sharply changed relationship of class forces. Other Stalinist formations, like the majority of the former Communist Party in Italy, have become virtually indistinguishable from other class-collaborationist political forces.

You know about this differentiation firsthand, from the evolution of the much smaller Stalinist outfits here in Britain. There used to be a magazine called *Marxism Today*, whose editors a year or so ago decided to declare "Marxism Never!" and go out of business. It had already become little more than a pink-Thatcherite monthly, and last year the organization associated with it changed its name from the Communist Party of Great Britain to the Democratic Left. Then you have the Stalinists here who continue to put out the *Morning Star* newspaper and whose hopes were dashed by the failure of the abortive coup in Moscow last August. These currents may be at loggerheads with each other, but both become more indistinguishable from other centrist forces that practice class collaborationism here in the United Kingdom.

In the United States, the Communist Party USA remains the same slavish Stalinist, class-collaborationist organization it has been since the late 1920s. At the end of last year, shaken by the collapse of the Stalinist apparatus in the Soviet Union, it underwent a split. A current including such prominent CPUSA figures as Kendra Alexander, Herbert Aptheker, Charlene Mitchell, and Angela Davis is now outside the party, and has recently announced the formation of a "network" called the Committees of Correspondence. Yes, a "network," not even a party-in-becoming. They honestly disclaim any such effort. They have retained most of the CPUSA's politics, but none of its weight as an organization. They bring with them their political tutelage in corruption, but not any firepower. The prognosis for the organization is shaky.

A historic shift

In recent years, our movement has gained some initial experience in taking political advantage of these new openings. We have participated in conferences and book fairs around the world, including some that communists would have been excluded from only a few years ago. A leadership delegation from our movement in the United States, for example, is participating this month in an Americas regional conference of the World Federation of Democratic Youth (WFDY), held in Colombia. Young Socialists from here in Britain, from Sweden, and from the United States will be going to Greece next month to participate in a conference of youth from throughout the Balkans, also organized by WFDY.

Only a few years ago, it would have been inconceivable that Young Socialists from our movement would be accepted into membership in the World Federation of Democratic Youth by majority vote, as they were earlier this year. Because although not every WFDY affiliate was a Stalinist organization, WFDY itself, from its founding in 1945, was part of the world Stalinist apparatus, as were the big majority of its member organizations. What has happened in WFDY over the past year or so is the product of the paroxysm that Stalinism has experienced.

This is only one example, and not the most important, of the new opportunities communists face in today's world. We have greater openings to approach fighters of all kinds with communist ideas — from activists defending abortion clinics in Buffalo, New York, to workers and rebel youth in northern Ireland. Each of the two WFDY-related trips I just mentioned are combined with other opportunities. The leadership delegation to Latin America also participated in a conference on Che Guevara in Argentina, involving representatives of political organizations from throughout the region. The youth delegation to Greece will go from there to Yugoslavia, where they will talk to young people, workers, and soldiers; sell *The Changing Face of U.S. Politics* and other revolutionary literature; write articles for the *Militant*; and help equip youth and others to oppose imperialist intervention there more effectively.

What the communist movement can accomplish, even at our current size and strength, cannot be predetermined in some absolute terms. What we can accomplish is always relative to our leverage within the vanguard of the working class, and the size and activity of that vanguard. It is always relative to the strength or weakness of historic obstacles that make it difficult to get communist ideas to the working class. Being right on all the fundamental questions of world politics is not enough, in and of itself; we have been right since 1928 and before. Nor is there any guarantee of success for communists just because the working class and its allies are in a fighting mood. Stalinism has dealt many of its biggest blows during big class battles and in the midst of historic revolutionary developments.

Stalinism has deep historical roots in the most important working-class struggles of this century. It has affected broad social and political forces. We are not asking delegates to vote on historical assessments here. What we are insisting on, however, is that revolutionary politicians need to recognize that, because of the weakening of Stalinism's weight, our propaganda weapons give communists the greatest relative political leverage and widest potential audience we have had in some six decades.

Revolutionary-minded workers and youth, who even five years ago would have been attracted in much larger numbers to the Stalinists, are today more open to communist ideas. More of them have a chance to at least consider these ideas before they are either convinced of a counterfeit, or end up rejecting communism because of what has been done in its name. We can now get books like *The Changing Face of U.S. Politics*, issues of *New International* magazine, and other Marxist literature published and distributed by Pathfinder into the hands of a broad range of fighters and revolutionists we meet and are working with around the world.

If the world communist movement does not recognize the enormity of that historic change — *and act accordingly* — then we cannot make the right decisions on our party-building priorities and allocation of leadership time and resources.

Strengthening proletarian parties through the fusion

One delegate suggested that in carrying out this fusion, the Communist League needs "to recover the turn." While I agree with what I took to be the point, I do not think "recover" is the right word. Better, it seems to me, is to say that the fusion will put the League on a firmer footing to reverse the slippage that has occurred in the turn, and in the structures of the turn. It will put the League on a firmer footing to function as a party of worker-bolsheviks building both branches and industrial union fractions that, through their interconnected activity, reinforce each other and advance communist propaganda work in ways that would otherwise not be possible.

That certainly is our goal in the United States. By combining the forces of the Socialist Workers Party and Young Socialist Alliance this spring, we are now in position to take on the task of strengthening the leadership structures and political functioning of our national industrial union fractions as well as our branches.

I suspect that each of the communist leagues can make progress along these lines, so long as we recognize that nothing we are doing makes it possible right now to *deepen* the turn. Deepening the turn will take changes in the objective situation — changes that enable us to build a different kind of union fractions, ones that are more directly engaged in class combat, that are a growing part of a broader, developing rank-and-file vanguard of the labor movement. That is not possible now anywhere there are communist leagues.

But *strengthening* the turn is an essential part of what we are doing in making the fusion. That is one of the central tasks this congress must discuss and that the Central Committee you elect must begin leading.

Leadership is taken, not given

Another delegate disagreed with the proposal before the congress that five of the twelve members elected to the Central Committee be members of the three youth organizations taking part in the fusion. This comrade said the proposal seemed contrary to our movement's norm that leadership is not given, it must be taken.

In electing the Central Committee, of course, the congress will have to decide whether there are at least five comrades among the members of the Young Socialists who have taken leadership. Did their leadership help advance the progress that will be measured at this congress in strengthening the forces of the communist movement here in Britain?

"Yes" was the answer given by comrades at the leadership gathering last week that adopted the proposals before you; now it is the job of the delegates to decide. But if your answer is also "yes," then you are not *giving* anybody a place on the Central Committee; you are *recognizing* the leadership that five cadres have *taken* in building the Young Socialists. You are not putting some young people on the Central Committee to gain experience; communists never elect anybody to the leadership just because they are young. Instead, you are recognizing the political leadership that made a new, strengthened organization possible, and electing a Central Committee that reflects it.

The Young Socialists are a formation that has had an organized political life and activity. They elected leadership committees. They went through political experiences, made some mistakes, registered some achievements. Together, the party and youth leaderships came to the conclusion that the communist movement here in the United Kingdom is not strong enough to sustain an independent communist youth organization right now. Leaders of the Young Socialists helped take the initiative in these discussions.

So, the congress has to decide how to weigh these factors. If delegates conclude that electing a Central Committee in the normal way would yield a stronger leadership, then that in itself is evidence that the fusion is at least premature. But if you are truly bringing together the experiences of independent organizations — with each bringing its strengths into a common organization — then the fusion is justified and the proposed formalities for the leadership election are necessary.

The same delegate who raised this objection to the leadership proposal also was concerned that for the first time we seem to be introducing quotas on the Central Committee. The comrade is right, of course, that the communist movement has never had quotas in electing the leadership — except in one case, *when there is a fusion.* Then the communist movement has *always* had quotas. Because if you do not have quotas in that case, then you do not have a fusion!

During the discussion a comrade referred to the Bolsheviks' fusion in 1917 with Leon Trotsky's organization, the Mezhrayontsi. That is a good example. That fusion, like others in the history of the communist movement, was accompanied by a quota in the newly elected Bolshevik Central Committee.[18] Following that fusion, Lenin was confident that at the next party congress, there would be an undifferentiated cadre of political equals, and the quotas would be over and done with. It never occurred to him that a former Mezhrayontsi member would receive any different treatment or consideration than a long-time Bolshevik. They would be treated on the merits of their record.

In that sense, the formalities of the election of the Central Committee at this congress will be the best test of the fusion. At the next Communist League convention, there will be no quotas. The party, strengthened by the fusion, will elect a Central Committee as you have done before, and you will do so from a cadre of political equals.

Youth work after the fusion

Communism is a movement, not just an organization, not just a party. As a result of the fusion, the communist movement here in the United Kingdom will take the form of the party alone for a while. But from day one, the movement will be better situated to

18. The Mezhrayontsi (Russian for "Inter-District Committee") was a revolutionary organization in Petrograd of some 4,000 members, whose most prominent leader was Leon Trotsky. Formed in 1913, it fused with the Bolsheviks at the July-August 1917 party congress. The congress suspended party rules on the membership duration of candidates for the Central Committee and placed Trotsky and two other Mezhrayontsi leader directly onto the body.

carry out effective youth work than we have been for years.

This maneuver does not imply a long-term strategic perspective. We are making a judgment about what is timely *now*. We are making a judgment about what our movement can and should do *next*. Yes, we could improve this or that aspect of our work if we continued pretending we were strong enough to lead separate party and youth organizations. We would do so, however, at the cost of setting ourselves back politically. But if we carry out the proposals before this congress, as part of a course our whole world movement is tackling together, then we will be slightly stronger for it. That is all we claim for these proposals, but that's enough!

Communists always do youth work, and always with an eye to making possible the formation of an independent socialist youth organization. Our fused organizations — here in the United Kingdom, in Canada, in the United States — will reach out into politics through our branches and union fractions to collaborate with young fighters and win them to the communist movement by the ones and twos. In addition, all of us must be alert to meeting clumps of young fighters, both in the countries where we currently have communist leagues and elsewhere. We must be alert to potential opportunities in youth formations that, while well short of being a communist youth organization, are at the same time substantially larger than any current communist youth organization.

Being alert to such opportunities — and at the same time on guard against mirages promising false opportunities — is not just a task of communist youth work. In all likelihood, for example, communists here in Britain at some time in the future are going to function to some extent inside the Labour Party. It is not foreordained that a broad rank-and-file vanguard emerging from an upsurge in class battles will flow through the channel of the Labour Party, of course. It would certainly be better if a mass revolutionary workers party were to develop directly, in opposition to the class-collaborationist perspectives of the Labour officialdom.

Due to the structure, history, and realities of the labor movement in the United Kingdom, however, it is at least very likely that communists will be doing substantial political work inside the Labour Party for a period of time as part of a broader vanguard of fighting workers.

Anyway, if we are always practicing politics as part of the ranks, we will figure out what to do tactically as a real upsurge develops. We will be fighting alongside them in class battles, going with them through whatever forms and experiences those struggles take. We will function with fellow fighters like pros, not amateurs, in working-class politics.

None of us can say right now what openings we will find to work with larger numbers of young forces around the world. We have no way of anticipating the forms, and it is worse than useless to speculate or always be looking. If we just keep our eyes out for the fights and the fighters, then we will not miss the opportunities. We are the only international communist current in today's world. If we work with other revolutionists as equals, and if we never make a fetish of forms, then we can be confident that our movement will be of special interest to workers and youth heading toward communism from other directions and other traditions.

CONFERENCE SUMMARY

The following is the summary presentation at the fusion congress of the Communist League and Young Socialist groups.

The working-class line of march

After participating in the discussion at this congress, I am convinced our world movement is right to begin thinking about the next steps in party building with the communist movement as a whole, not with the party alone.

The fusion proposal before the delegates is not an organizational correction. The problem is not that the Communist League here in the United Kingdom made a mistake a year or so ago in helping to initiate the young socialists groups, and now you are rectifying that error. No, most of us are convinced, I think, that the experience of the young socialists groups and their recruitment to our movement have been an irreplaceable help in getting us to where we are today. A number of younger comrades have taken leadership in the communist movement through their work in the young socialists — as well as in the political discussion at this congress — and that advance will be registered in the Central Committee the delegates will elect later today.

As we have discussed here this weekend, the proposals you will be voting on soon are similar to those other communist leagues are carrying out. The concrete forms are different, and are the most complex in the Socialist Workers Party because it is the largest organization in our world movement. Fundamentally, however, what each of our organizations is doing stems from similar opportunities and weaknesses and has the same political goals.

The form the fusion has taken in the SWP will have gone through some initial tests by the beginning of next year. We will know by then how well we have done in involving some young people, and some groupings of young people, in campaigning with us for the SWP presidential ticket and other socialist candidates. We will have some more experience in working with youth in activities in defense of the Cuban revolution and in various social protest actions. We will be able to gauge our initial success in recruiting some new members, and, in the process, drawing more young people into the party leadership. As I reported earlier this weekend, a number of former Young Socialist Alliance members have already joined the party over the past month or so — a fact that, taken alone, is sufficient justification for this course.

The communist leagues here in the United Kingdom and in Canada will have similar openings and face similar tests in the months ahead. And comrades in New Zealand, in Sweden, in Australia, and in Iceland and France are also all discussing how to organize themselves most effectively to draw youth into the movement and continue strengthening the proletarian character of their organizations. Guests at this congress from all these organizations will take back experiences from it that will help them decide their next steps.

Each component of our world movement faces concrete challenges, and the decisions each of us makes will be specific to that particular situation. Our success in each case, however, depends on precisely the same criteria: to what degree we can fuse the experience and political continuity of the communist movement with a new generation, in order to braid together a stronger proletarian cadre and leadership.

A historic change in world politics

During the discussion earlier today, a delegate raised what he considered to be a contradiction — at least in the *Militant* coverage — between the analysis presented in the political report adopted by the fusion convention in Canada last month and the report I presented there, which we have already had quite a bit of discussion about this weekend.

At the Toronto gathering, Communist League leader Steve Penner explained why both the party and youth were too weak at this time to maintain separate organizations. In doing so, he reviewed some of the factors in world politics since the mid-1980s that have resulted in a further retreat by the labor movement and taken a toll on small communist organizations as well. That report was briefly summarized in an article on the convention in the July 26 issue of the *Militant*, which is on sale here.

Isn't that assessment, a delegate asked earlier today, at odds with the statement that our movement now has openings to reach more people with communist ideas than at any time since the mid-1920s? I do not think so, and it seems useful in summarizing the congress to explain why.

The *Militant* article on the convention in Canada quoted the political report's reference to "the refusal of the union officialdom to lead workers in struggle," and the consequent weakening of union power to defend the class interests of working people as the employers have stiffened their offensive over the past decade. This seems like an accurate assessment to me, and I expect to many of you at this congress as well. The default, if not treachery, by the labor officialdom and its consequences for the working class are not a peculiarity of politics in Canada, but a fact of the class struggle throughout the imperialist world.

Don't we and other workers *feel* the impact of the growing weakness of strikes as a weapon in recent years? Don't we *feel* the results of the officialdom's refusal to organize effective labor solidarity when other workers go into a fight. Doesn't a strike today need to be substantially stronger than would have been necessary just seven or eight years ago to accomplish the same ends?

The report to the convention in Canada also cited "the absence of new revolutionary victories" anywhere in the world. That, too, is accurate. In fact, the two most recent victories — the workers and farmers governments in Grenada and Nicaragua — both had gone down to defeat by the end of the 1980s. Our movement understood the reasons for those defeats and drew the clearest political lessons from them. But those important political conquests did not soften the blow from these grave political setbacks.

Communists and other revolutionary-minded workers and youth, of course, still look to, learn from, and draw political inspiration from the socialist revolution in Cuba and its proletarian internationalist leadership. As irreplaceable as that living example remains, however, it is not the same (including for revolutionists in Cuba) as experiencing *the rise of a new socialist revolution* today. It is not the same as being able to follow — week by week, day by day — the titanic forces of the working class and other toilers carrying out a radical land reform, challenging all forms of discrimination, oppression, and exploitation, and, in the case of Cuba, overturning capitalist property relations.

That is how the Cuban revolution affected the generation that came to the communist movement at the end of the 1950s and early 1960s. That is how the Grenada and Nicaragua revolution brought a generation to the communist movement in the late 1970s and early 1980s. That is how the Russian revolution affected workers and youth for a decade after 1917. That is how even the Yugoslav and Chinese revolutions, with all the limitations of their Stalinist misleaderships, affected workers and toilers in the years after World War II.

The political report adopted by the comrades in Canada was correct in pointing to the objective factors we have been describing here and how they have weighed on the fighting vanguard of the working class, including on its communist component. They do not, however, negate the political implications for communists of the two factors we have been concentrating on this weekend: the depression conditions of world capitalism today and its destabilizing logic; and the disintegration of the main transmission belt within the workers movement of imperialism's pressures and dog-eat-dog values, the Stalinist world machine.

For nearly sixty years, the communist movement has been

determined to support in any way possible, participate in, and help lead a political revolution by the workers in the Soviet Union (and, following World War II, in the deformed workers states of Central and Eastern Europe). What do we mean by a "political revolution"? In his 1936 work *The Revolution Betrayed: What Is the Soviet Union and Where Is It Going?*, Bolshevik leader Leon Trotsky explained that the revolution to overturn the bureaucratic caste "will not be social, like the October Revolution of 1917. It is not a question this time of changing the economic foundations of society, or of replacing certain forms of property with other forms. History has known elsewhere not only social revolutions which substituted the bourgeois for the feudal regime, but also political revolutions which, without destroying the economic foundations of society, swept out the old ruling upper crust (1830 and 1848 in France, February 1917 in Russia, etc.). The overthrow of the Bonapartist caste will, of course, have deep social consequences, but in itself it will be confined within the limits of political revolution."[19]

That is still what is needed in the deformed workers states in Russia and throughout Eastern Europe today, as well as in China. It took the events of the last several years, however, for our movement to fully absorb the consequences of the fact that communist continuity in the working class of these workers states had been completely broken at least by the 1960s if not earlier. The communist vanguard had been physically liquidated in the purge trials, labor camps, and post–World War II witch-hunts. The working class in these countries had been pushed out of independent political life for decades, and blocked off from struggles by workers in other parts of the world.

Given this vacuum of proletarian leadership, the breakup of the political apparatus of these Stalinist regimes necessarily had to come before the possibility of political revolution would again be on the agenda. That, in turn, meant the objective opening up

19. *The Revolution Betrayed,* p. 259.

of these workers states to greater dangers of capitalist restoration. But the belatedness of the political revolution because of the limits of the extension of the world revolution determined that this was the only way the working class in these countries could begin going through the kinds of experiences once again that can and will give rise to revolutionary currents and a new openness to communist ideas.

Imperialism's incapacity to resolve its deepening, late-twentieth-century crisis through economic and social concessions, as well as the breakup of the Stalinist apparatuses — both have become fact *before* large fighting currents of the working class have begun to be forged in battle. Before the vanguard of the workers movement has gone through the kind of class combat that makes it possible to begin growing in significant numbers, the consequences of both these historical realities are already having expanding political repercussions worldwide. Most important, however, remains the fact that communists can act in face of this new international capitalist disorder *before* the working class and labor movement have suffered a defeat by the exploiting classes anywhere in the world.

This is our appreciation of the relationship of forces in the world class struggle, as it has developed since the international stock market crash of 1987. The test of events since then convinces us that this world view is correct. Moreover, as a delegate pointed out here, big political shocks such as the Gulf War bring into sharper focus for working people and youth the much slower, cumulative effects of capitalism's depression conditions.

What is changing today is not that youth we work with are more capable, more courageous, or have more integrity than young people who were won to the Stalinist movement over the last sixty years. What has changed is the *world*.

As a result, fighters who go into action against the oppression and exploitation bred by capitalism can once again begin to converge with the historic line of march of the working class, rather than being diverted from that course by a counterfeit of Marxism.

Fighters all over the world, coming from different backgrounds and experiences, can discuss ideas on how to move forward with other revolutionists with no a priori exclusions; there is no longer an "Index" of books, magazines, and newspapers anyone is proscribed from buying and studying. All this means communists do not have the odds stacked against us from the outset, as during the radicalization of the 1930s and again in the 1960s.

Consider, for example, the political obstacles that faced the Black Panthers and many other fighters for Black rights in the sixties. Many young people with experience in civil rights struggles became convinced of the need to look for something beyond their initial aims. The victories registered in those battles accelerated the search by young militants for generalizing, universalizing strategies that addressed the roots of the oppression they were fighting and offered an effective way to fight and win. They reached for Marxism, they reached for communism — and most found Stalinism instead. And that is what happened to millions of workers, peasants, and youth all over the world.

Building a proletarian party in time

New advances in the class struggle, no matter how large or tumultuous, cannot transform centrist organizations — let alone Stalinist or social democratic currents — into disciplined communist parties capable of leading the working class and our allies to victory. If proletarian organizations — based in the industrial working class and unions, and part of a world communist movement — have not been built beforehand, then there will be no leadership capable of winning the fighting vanguard of the toilers and forging a mass revolutionary party in the heat of rising class battles. And there will be horribly costly defeats.

That has been the experience of the working class for at least a century, and it provides further reason to move forward along the course we are on. We can be more confident today than any time since the late 1920s that workers in battle can and will be won to the historic line of march of their class. We can collaborate as equals with fighters and revolutionists coming from many political origins.

Most protest actions communists participate in today are not called by us or by other revolutionary forces. We participate in these actions, fight alongside others for common goals, and exchange experiences and ideas with those attracted to these fights. We do so, moreover, without adapting to the political framework of the forces that initiate and lead these actions.

For worker-bolsheviks, the starting point is the working class, the labor movement, and the space that exists there for revolutionary political work — *if we use it*. If communists use the space open to us in the working class, and move out into politics *on that basis*, then every aspect of our party-building work will be strengthened.

Workers involved in fights on the job get attracted to young forces organizing protest actions against imperialist war, in defense of abortion rights, and against racist abuse. It makes workers more interested in communist ideas, more interested in getting their hands on Pathfinder books, the *New International*, the *Militant*, and *Perspectiva Mundial*.

Students and other youth moving into political life, regardless of their class background, are attracted to workers' struggles and to the potential social and political power of the working-class and labor movement. That is the last thing communists need to worry about. Young fighters are attracted to a political party of workers with organized fractions in the trade unions. That has never been a problem in the modern revolutionary workers movement — not for the 150 years since the young Karl Marx and Frederick Engels were recruited to the world's first modern proletarian party, the Communist League, by a cadre of seasoned revolutionary workers from Germany and elsewhere in Europe.

Toward the end of his life, Engels recounted how, as a young radical democrat being won to communism, he had been profoundly affected by three of these workers' leaders whom he got to know and began collaborating with. "They were the first revolutionary proletarians whom I met," Engels recounted in 1885, "and however far apart our views were at that time in de-tails — for I still owned, as against their narrow-minded egalitar-ian communism, a goodly dose of just as narrow-minded philo-sophical arrogance — I shall never forget the deep impression that these three real men made upon me, who was then still only wanting to become a man."[20]

Communists have no way of foreseeing the timing or accumu-lation of events that will initiate a sustained labor upsurge com-parable to the fights by the Teamsters in 1934 in the United States and the broader industrial union movement of which they were part, or the sit-down strikes in France and Spanish revolu-tion of the latter 1930s. We know that class battles of that scope and larger are closer in today's world than at any time since World War II, but we have no control over the tempo of the class struggle.

What communists do have control over right now, however, is our preparation for those battles. That is why the proposals this congress will vote on in a few minutes, and the leadership you will elect later today, are important. These are the next steps that can be taken here in the United Kingdom, as part of a course being followed throughout our world movement, to lay the basis to rebuild communist youth organizations, strengthen our nuclei of proletarian parties, and strengthen their "turn" character.

We recognize that our small size and current lack of weight in the labor movement make it unlikely that our organizations will grow in some linear fashion into the leadership of mass struggles of the working class. These class battles will develop, in some cases much more rapidly than we can anticipate. Communists must be ready for all sorts of tactical maneuvers that no one can imagine today.

What can we do to prepare? On a tactical level, absolutely

20. "On the History of the Communist League" (1885), in Marx and Engels, *Collected Works*, vol. 26 (New York: International Publishers, 1990), p. 314.

nothing. But we can and must prepare by being political, being proletarian, being internationalist to the core, and always being objective in our working relations with other fighters and revolutionists. We prepare by organizing communist parties along the lines described in *The Changing Face of U.S. Politics, The Struggle for a Proletarian Party,* the Communist Manifesto, and other documents that make up the political continuity of the modern revolutionary workers movement.

INDEX

JACK BARNES
THE CHANGING FACE OF U.S. POLITICS
Working-class politics and the unions

The Changing Face of U.S. Politics
Working-Class Politics and the Trade Unions
JACK BARNES A handbook for workers coming into the factories, mines, and mills, as they react to the uncertain life, ceaseless turmoil, and brutality of capitalism today. It shows how millions of workers, as political resistance grows, will revolutionize themselves, their unions, and all of society. $19.95 Also available in Spanish and French.

Background to "The Changing Face of U.S. Politics" and "U.S. Imperialism Has Lost the Cold War"
JACK BARNES, JOEL BRITTON, AND MARY-ALICE WATERS Reports and resolutions of the Socialist Workers Party on trade union policy, proletarian leadership versus clique functioning, the poison of race baiting in the workers movement, and the membership norms of the revolutionary party. A companion to *The Changing Face of U.S. Politics* and the 1990 SWP resolution "U.S. Imperialism Has Lost the Cold War," published in issue no. 11 of *New International*. $7.00

The Struggle for a Proletarian Party
JAMES P. CANNON A founding leader of the Socialist Workers Party defends the centrality of proletarianization within the political and organizational principles of Marxism in a polemic against a petty-bougeois current in the party. The debate unfolded as Washington prepared to drag U.S. working people into the slaughter of World War II. $19.95

Background to "The Struggle for a Proletarian Party"
JAMES P. CANNON AND LEON TROTSKY The challenges faced by the Socialist Workers Party in deepening its involvement in the organizations and struggles of the industrial working class in the late 1930s. The SWP must "orient in practice the whole organization toward the factories, the strikes, the unions," writes Leon Trotsky in a 1937 letter to party leader James P. Cannon. $6.00

The state

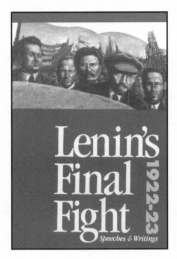

Lenin's Final Fight
Speeches and Writings, 1922–23
V.I. LENIN
In the early 1920s Lenin waged a political battle in the leadership of the Communist Party of
the USSR to maintain the course that had
enabled workers and peasants to overthrow the
tsarist empire, carry out the first socialist revolution, and begin building a world communist
movement. The issues posed in his political fight
remain central to world politics today. $19.95
Also available in Spanish.

The Revolution Betrayed
What Is the Soviet Union and Where Is It Going?
LEON TROTSKY
In 1917 the toilers of Russia carried out one of the most
profound revolutions in history. Yet within ten years a political counterrevolution by a privileged social layer whose chief
spokesperson was Joseph Stalin was being consolidated. This
classic study of the Soviet workers state and its degeneration illuminates the roots of the crisis unfolding in the former Soviet Union today. $19.95
Also available in Russian and Spanish.

The Truth about Yugoslavia
Why Working People Should Oppose Intervention
GEORGE FYSON, ARGIRIS MALAPANIS, AND JONATHAN SILBERMAN
Examines the roots of the carnage in Yugoslavia, where
Washington and its imperialist rivals in Europe are interven-
ing militarily in an attempt to defeat the working class and
reimpose capitalism. $8.95

and revolution

The Origin of the Family, Private Property, and the State
FREDERICK ENGELS

How the emergence of class-divided society gave rise to repressive state bodies and family structures that protect the property of ruling layers, enabling them to pass along wealth and privilege. Engels discusses the consequences for working people of these class institutions—from their original forms to their modern versions. $16.95

State and Revolution
V.I. LENIN

On the eve of the October 1917 Russian revolution, Lenin reaffirms the views of Marx and Engels—and lessons from the 1905 and February 1917 revolutions—on the need for workers to overthrow the state of their oppressor and establish their own government and state. Progress Publishers $4.95

For a Workers and Farmers Government in the United States
JACK BARNES

Explains why the workers and farmers government is "the most powerful instrument the working class can wield" as it moves toward expropriating the capitalists and landlords and opening the road to socialism. $7.00

The Workers and Farmers Government
JOSEPH HANSEN

How experiences in revolutions following World War II in Yugoslavia, China, Algeria, and Cuba enriched communists' theoretical understanding of revolutionary governments of the toilers. $7.00

From Pathfinder. Write for a free catalog.

New International

A MAGAZINE OF MARXIST POLITICS AND THEORY

New International no. 11

U.S. Imperialism Has Lost the Cold War *by Jack Barnes* • The Communist Strategy of Party Building Today *by Mary-Alice Waters* • Socialism: A Viable Option *by José Ramón Balaguer* • Young Socialists Manifesto • Ours Is the Epoch of World Revolution *by Jack Barnes and Mary-Alice Waters* $14.00

New International no. 10

Imperialism's March toward Fascism and War *by Jack Barnes* • What the 1987 Stock Market Crash Foretold • Defending Cuba, Defending Cuba's Socialist Revolution *by Mary-Alice Waters* • The Curve of Capitalist Development *by Leon Trotsky* $14.00

New International no. 9

The Triumph of the Nicaraguan Revolution • Washington's Contra War and the Challenge of Forging Proletarian Leadership • The Political Degeneration of the FSLN and the Demise of the Workers and Farmers Government. Documents and resolutions of the Socialist Workers Party by *Jack Barnes, Steve Clark,* and *Larry Seigle.* $14.00

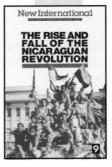

New International no. 8

The Politics of Economics: Che Guevara
and Marxist Continuity *by Steve Clark and
Jack Barnes* • Che's Contribution to the
Cuban Economy *by Carlos Rafael Rodríguez*
• On the Concept of Value *and* The
Meaning of Socialist Planning, two articles *by
Ernesto Che Guevara* $10.00

New International no. 7

Opening Guns of World War III: Washington's Assault on Iraq
by Jack Barnes • Communist Policy in Wartime as well as in
Peacetime *by Mary-Alice Waters* • Lessons from the Iran-Iraq
War *by Samad Sharif* $12.00

New International no. 6

The Second Assassination of Maurice Bishop
by Steve Clark • Washington's 50-year
Domestic Contra Operation *by Larry Seigle*
• Land, Labor, and the Canadian
Revolution *by Michel Dugré* • Renewal or
Death: Cuba's Rectification Process, two
speeches *by Fidel Castro* $10.00

New International no. 5

The Coming Revolution in South Africa *by
Jack Barnes* • The Future Belongs to the
Majority *by Oliver Tambo* • Why Cuban
Volunteers Are in Angola, two speeches *by
Fidel Castro* $9.00

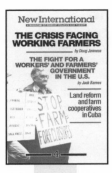

New International no. 4

The Fight for a Workers and Farmers Government in the United States *by Jack Barnes* • The Crisis Facing Working Farmers *by Doug Jenness* • Land Reform and Farm Cooperatives in Cuba, two speeches *by Fidel Castro* $9.00

New International no. 3

Communism and the Fight for a Popular Revolutionary Government: 1848 to Today *by Mary-Alice Waters* • 'A Nose for Power': Preparing the Nicaraguan Revolution *by Tomás Borge* • National Liberation and Socialism in the Americas *by Manuel Piñeiro* $8.00

New International no. 2

The Aristocracy of Labor: Development of the Marxist Position *by Steve Clark* • The Working-Class Fight for Peace *by Brian Grogan* • The Social Roots of Opportunism *by Gregory Zinoviev* $8.00

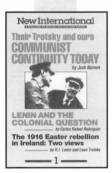

New International no. 1

Their Trotsky and Ours: Communist Continuity Today *by Jack Barnes* • Lenin and the Colonial Question *by Carlos Rafael Rodríguez* • The 1916 Easter Rebellion in Ireland: Two Views *by V.I. Lenin and Leon Trotsky* $8.00

Distributed by Pathfinder

Many of the articles that appear in *New International* are also available in Spanish in *Nueva Internacional,* in French in *Nouvelle Internationale,* and in Swedish in *Ny International.*

Unions Their past, present, and future

The Eastern Airlines Strike

ACCOMPLISHMENTS OF THE
RANK-AND-FILE MACHINISTS

Ernie Mailhot, Judy Stranahan, and Jack Barnes
The story of the 686-day strike in which a
rank-and-file resistance by Machinists
prevented Eastern's union-busting onslaught
from becoming the road toward a profitable
nonunion airline. $9.95

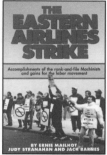

The 1985–86 Hormel Meat-Packers Strike in Austin, Minnesota

Fred Halstead
The hard-fought strike against Hormel opened a round of battles
by packinghouse workers that—together with strikes by paper
workers, cannery workers, and western coal miners—marked a
break in the rout of U.S. unions that began during the 1981–82
recession. $3.50

Trade Unions in the Epoch of Imperialist Decay

Leon Trotsky
FEATURING "TRADE UNIONS: THEIR PAST, PRESENT,
AND FUTURE" BY KARL MARX

The trade unions must "learn to act deliberately as organizing centers of the working class [and] convince the world at large that
their efforts, far from being narrow and selfish, aim at the emancipation of the downtrodden millions." —*Karl Marx, 1866.*
In this book, two central leaders of the modern communist
workers movement outline the fight for this revolutionary
perspective. $14.95

Labor's Giant Step

THE FIRST TWENTY YEARS OF THE CIO: 1936–55
Art Preis
The story of the explosive labor struggles and political battles in
the 1930s and 1940s that built the industrial unions. And how
those unions became the vanguard of a mass social movement
that began transforming U.S. society. $26.95

From Pathfinder

The Cuban revolution

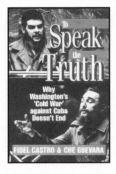

To Speak the Truth
WHY WASHINGTON'S 'COLD WAR' AGAINST
CUBA DOESN'T END
Fidel Castro and Che Guevara
In historic speeches before the United Nations
and UN bodies, Guevara and Castro address
the workers of the world, explaining why the
U.S. government so hates the example set by
the socialist revolution in Cuba and why
Washington's effort to destroy it will fail. $16.95

Episodes of the Cuban Revolutionary War, 1956–58
Ernesto Che Guevara
A firsthand account of the military campaigns
and political events that culminated in the
January 1959 popular insurrection that over-
threw the U.S.-backed dictatorship in Cuba.
With clarity and humor, Guevara describes
his own political education. He explains how
the struggle transformed the men and
women of the Rebel Army and July 26
Movement led by Fidel Castro. And how these combatants
forged a political leadership capable of guiding millions of
workers and peasants to open the socialist revolution in the
Americas. $23.95

U.S. Hands off the Mideast!
CUBA SPEAKS OUT AT THE UNITED NATIONS
Fidel Castro, Ricardo Alarcón
The case against Washington's 1990–91 war
against Iraq, as presented by the Cuban gov-
ernment at the United Nations. $10.95

and world politics ▬▬▬

How Far We Slaves Have Come!
SOUTH AFRICA AND CUBA IN TODAY'S WORLD
Nelson Mandela, Fidel Castro
Speaking together in Cuba in 1991, Mandela and Castro discuss the unique relationship and example of the struggles of the South African and Cuban peoples. $8.95 Also available in Spanish.

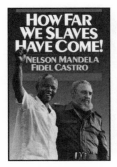

Che Guevara: Economics and Politics in the Transition to Socialism
Carlos Tablada
Quoting extensively from Guevara's writings and speeches, this book presents the interrelationship of the market, economic planning, material incentives, and voluntary work in the transition to socialism. $17.95 Also available in Spanish and French.

The Second Declaration of Havana
In February 1962, as the example of Cuba's socialist revolution spread throughout the Americas, the workers and farmers of Cuba issued their uncompromising call for a continent-wide revolutionary struggle. $4.50 Also available in Spanish, French, and Greek.

Dynamics of the Cuban Revolution
Joseph Hansen
How did the Cuban revolution come about? Why does it represent, as Joseph Hansen puts it, an "unbearable challenge" to U.S. imperialism? What political challenges has it confronted? $20.95

Write for a free catalog. See front of book for addresses.

Also from Pathfinder

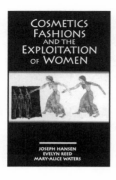

Cosmetics, Fashions, and the Exploitation of Women

JOSEPH HANSEN, EVELYN REED, AND MARY-ALICE WATERS

How big business promotes cosmetics to generate profits and perpetuate the inferior status of women. In her introduction, Mary-Alice Waters explains how the entry of millions of women into the workforce during and after World War II irreversibly changed U.S. society and laid the basis for the advances women have won through struggle over the last three decades. $12.95.

Malcolm X Talks to Young People

"I for one will join in with anyone, I don't care what color you are, as long as you want to change this miserable condition that exists on this earth"— Malcolm X, Britain, December 1964. Also includes his 1965 interview with the *Young Socialist* magazine. $10.95

The Politics of Chicano Liberation

OLGA RODRÍGUEZ AND OTHERS

Lessons from the rise of the Chicano movement in the United States in the 1960s and 1970s, which dealt lasting blows against the oppression of the Chicano people. Presents a fighting program for those determined to combat divisions within the working class based on language and national origin. $15.95

The History of American Trotskyism

Report of a Participant, 1928–38

JAMES P. CANNON

"Trotskyism is not a new movement, a new doctrine," Cannon says, "but the restoration, the revival of genuine Marxism as it was expounded and practiced in the Russian revolution and in the early days of the Communist International." In this series of twelve talks given in 1942, James P. Cannon recounts an important chapter in the efforts to build a proletarian party in the United States. $18.95

The History of the Russian Revolution

LEON TROTSKY

The social, economic, and political dynamics of the first socialist revolution. The story is told by one of the principal leaders of this victorious struggle, led by the Bolshevik Party, that changed the course of history in the twentieth century. Also available in Russian. Unabridged edition, 3 vols. in one. $35.95

Puerto Rico: Independence Is a Necessity

RAFAEL CANCEL MIRANDA

"Our people are becoming aware of their own strength, which is what the colonial powers fear," explains Puerto Rican independence leader Rafael Cancel Miranda. In two interviews, Cancel Miranda speaks out on the brutal reality of U.S. colonial domination, the campaign needed to free 16 Puerto Rican political prisoners, the example of Cuba's socialist revolution, and the resurgence of the independence movement today. In English and Spanish. $3.00

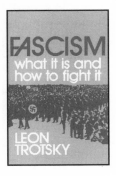

Fascism: What It Is and How to Fight It

LEON TROTSKY

Writing in the heat of struggle against the rising fascist movement in Europe in the 1930s, Russian communist leader Leon Trotsky examines the origins and nature of fascism and advances, for the first time, a working-class strategy to combat and defeat it. $3.00

Democracy and Revolution

GEORGE NOVACK

The limitations and advances of various forms of democracy in class society, from its roots in ancient Greece, through its rise and decline under capitalism. Discusses the emergence of Bonapartism, military dictatorship, and fascism, and how democracy will be advanced under a workers and farmers regime. $18.95

See front of book for addresses

Revolutionary Continuity

Marxist Leadership in the United States
FARRELL DOBBS

How successive generations of fighters took part in
the struggles of the U.S. labor movement, seeking
to build a leadership that could advance the class
interests of workers and small farmers and link up
with fellow toilers around the world.
Vol. 1: *The Early Years, 1848–1917,* $16.95.
Vol. 2: *Birth of the Communist Movement,*
1918–1922, $16.95

John Coltrane and the Jazz Revolution of the 1960s

FRANK KOFSKY

An account of John Coltrane's role in spearheading
innovations in jazz that were an expression of the
new cultural and political ferment that marked the
rise of the mass struggle for Black rights. $23.95

Thomas Sankara Speaks

The Burkina Faso Revolution, 1983–87
Peasants and workers in the West African country
of Burkina Faso established a popular revolutionary
government and began to combat the hunger,
illiteracy, and economic backwardness imposed by
imperialist domination. Thomas Sankara, who led
that struggle, explains the example set for all of
Africa. $18.95

Pathfinder Was Born with the October Revolution

Three Reports by Mary-Alice Waters
In reports presented in Canada, Cuba, and the United States, the president of Pathfinder Press explains why its publishing program seeks "to
strengthen the fighting vanguard of the working class so it is better armed
to understand the world in which we live; to understand the history of the
modern workers movement; to become more conscious of its strength and
historic responsibilities; and to chart a line of march toward taking power
and opening the road to the construction of socialism."
An *Education for Socialists* booklet. $8.00

BASIC WORKS OF MARXISM

The Communist Manifesto
KARL MARX, FREDERICK ENGELS

Founding document of the modern working-class movement, published in 1848. Explains why communism is derived not from precon-ceived principles but from facts and proletarian movements springing from the actual class struggle. $3.95 Also in Spanish.

Imperialism: The Highest Stage of Capitalism
V.I. LENIN

"The income of the bondholders is five times greater than the income obtained from the foreign trade of the greatest 'trading' country in the world [Great Britain]," wrote Lenin in this 1916 booklet. "This is the essence of imperialism and imperialist parasitism." $3.95

Collected Works of Karl Marx and Frederick Engels

The writings of the founders of the modern revolutionary working-class movement. Vols. 1–47 of 50-volume set are now available. Each vol-ume contains notes and index. Progress Publishers, cloth only. Set (47 vols.), $1,185. Write or call for prices of individual volumes.

Collected Works of V.I. Lenin

The writings of the central leader of the Bolshevik Party, the October 1917 Russian revolution, the young Soviet workers and peasants repub-lic, and the early Communist International. 45-volume set, plus 2-vol-ume index. $500

WRITE FOR A CATALOG.